AF371628

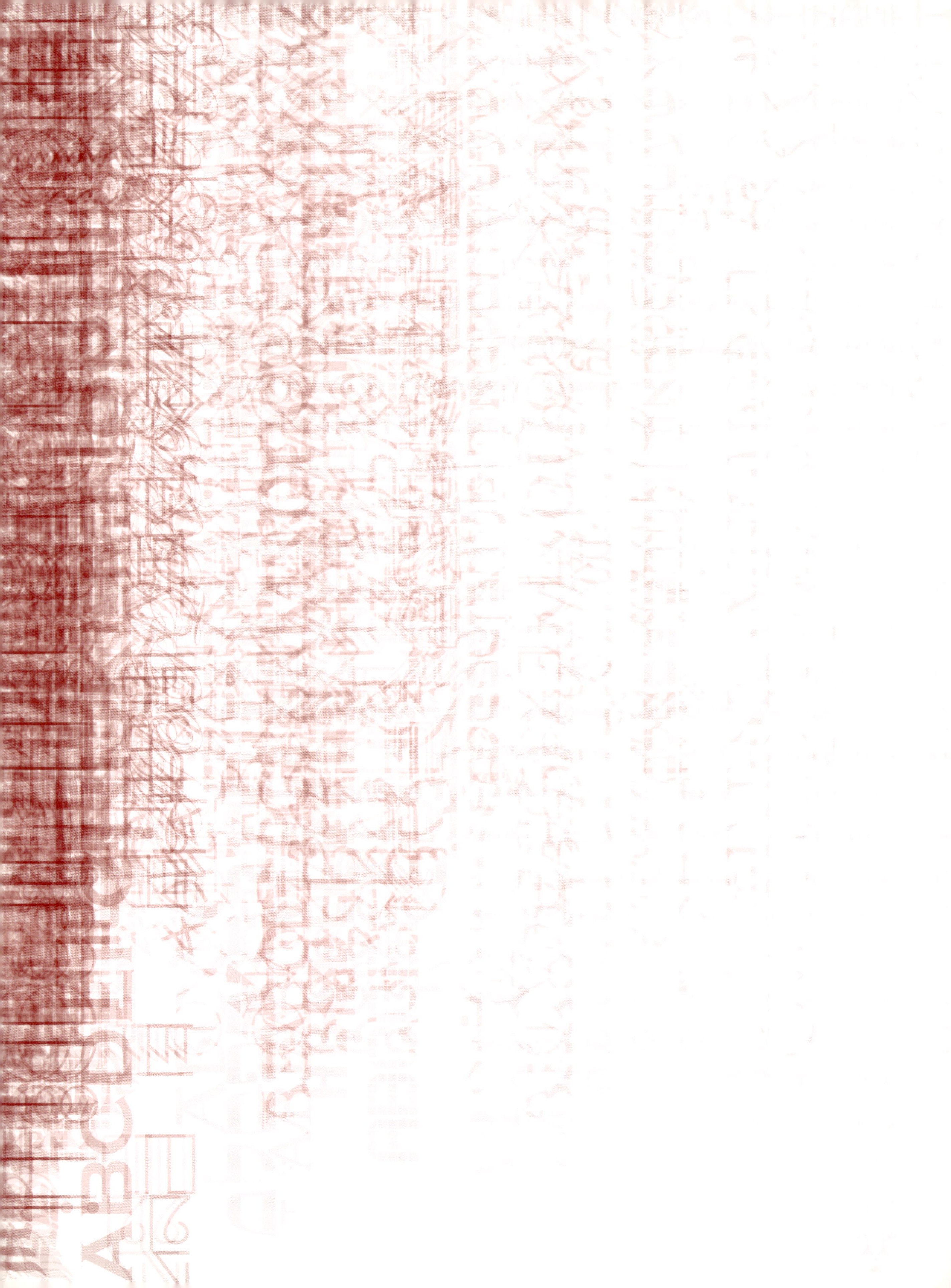

Boris Groys, Peter Weibel, eds.

MEDIUM RELIGION

Faith. Geopolitics. Art.

Verlag der Buchhandlung Walther König

Artists in the Exhibition

Documentary Installations in the Exhibition

Contents

Boris Groys, Peter Weibel

.......Religion.......
.......as.Medium.......

In our post-Enlightenment culture, religion has been generally understood to mean a collection of certain opinions. Accordingly, religion is usually discussed in connection with a demand for a freedom of opinion guaranteed by law. Religion is tolerated as an opinion so long as it remains tolerant and does not question the freedom of other opinions – that is to say, so long as it makes no exclusive, fundamentalist claim to its own truth. Thus, religion seems to be in a fairly comfortable situation. No longer, as in the dark era of the radical Enlightenment, is it criticized, ironized, or even combated in the name of scientific truth. Rather, scientific truth itself has since come to acquire the status of mere opinion. Since Friedrich Nietzsche at the latest and more especially thanks to Michel Foucault, we now know that the claim to scientific truth is dictated primarily by the will to power, and must therefore be deconstructed and deterred. Scientific opinion circulates in the same media and in the same way as does religious opinion. In both cases, opinion comes to us in the form of news disseminated by mass media. Sometimes we read about a new apparition of the Mother of God; sometimes we read that the earth is getting warmer. Neither piece of information can be tested directly by those who receive it. Experts always disagree in such cases. Hence, either piece of news may or may not be believed.

As a consequence, our culture today knows no truths, whether of a religious or scientific nature, but only opinions whose standing however is inviolable because protected by law. The various opinions are either shared or rejected by autonomous citizens. Thus, the value of an opinion can be measured precisely by determining how many people share it. The market of opinion is constantly being studied, and the results of this research tell us which opinion belongs to the mainstream and which is marginal. This data offers a reliable basis for each individual's decision with respect to how he or she wishes to draw up the budget of his or her opinion. Those who wish to be compatible withthe mainstream will adopt opinions that are either already part of the mainstream or have a chance to become so in the near future. Those who prefer to be thought of as representatives of a minority can seek out a suitable minority. If we understand truth as a private, subjective opinion, then the so-called objective truth becomes dependent on political majorities or minorities. Truth becomes a question of public agreement or acceptance. Which truth is acceptable to the majority and which is not is the pivotal question of politics today.

Truth claims are seen in many cases as advertising gimmicks, as a pushy and hence disagreeable sales strategy, as deceptive packaging par excellence. Or worse: as totalitarian coercion, as the injunction to adopt an opinion even against one's will, as an insidious attack on freedom and the dignity of the consumer. Under such conditions religion is clearly better placed to succeed on the market of opinions than is philosophy or science. There are two reasons for this. First, the historical religions are established "brands." For this reason alone they are more effective in reaching people than are philosophical or scientific doctrines. Whatever else people might say, Christ, Muhammad, and the Buddha are genuine superstars the likes of which not even Plato or René Descartes can compare, to say nothing of today's philosophers. Should your plan be to succeed on the market of opinion, you are thus well advised to appeal to the founders of religions. The universities still bristle at this, but it is only a matter of time before they abandon their resistance.

However, there is a further – if you will, deeper and weightier – reason to turn to religion. Religion can indeed be seen as a certain set of opinions insofar as it refers to the role of religion in profane space. Here, religion is associated with opinions about whether contraception should be permitted or women should wear headscarves. All religions, though, have another space: a sacred space. And religions have a different attitude toward this space – namely, the view that it represents the space of a lack of opinion, of opinionlessness. For the will of the gods or of God is ultimately concealed from the opinion of mortals. What this means is that while people in our culture are first and foremost holders of certain opinions, religion is a place where this task, this mediality of human beings, is reflected on – and precisely because religion marks and describes the state of opinionlessness: the zero level of freedom of opinion. In the same way that Kazimir Malevich's *Black Square* (1913) symbolized this for the medium of painting, because it caused all figuration to disappear, so the sacred places of religions are the places where the mediality of the human being can be thematized, precisely because they are places where people lose all their opinions and find themselves once again in a state without opinion. As men without opinion, people practice repetition tout court, that is, the kind of repetition which is no longer repetition of a certain opinion, but rather a ritual of opinionlessness. This is what the hero does in Andrei Tarkovsky's film *Nostalghia* (1983) when finding himself subject to a state of total lack of opinion; he begins by walking back and forth along the same path. This path does not by any means bring the hero forward – in whatever way the term "forward" might be meant here. Rather, by walking thus the hero connects to the movement back and forth whose very radically solitary and inescapable repetitiveness marks him as a medium of this lack of opinion.

The experience of a lack of opinion, which is a genuinely religious experience, is not necessarily tied to certain places, however. This state of a lack of opinion is a much more common and more ordinary experience than is usually assumed. Such an experience occurs, for example, when people are confronted with a situation in which all existing opinions fail. However, the same situation may also arise when people no longer desire to have opinions, when they have definitely had their fill of opinion as such, along with the market, the creation, and dissemination of opinions – when suddenly noticing that all existing opinions cancel one another out. They then once again find themselves at the zero level of freedom of opinion – and so become conscious of their own mediality. The freedom of opinion becomes the abandonment of opinion: People are equally free of all opinion, all opinion is abandoned equally. What are they to do then? How are they to react to this state of the complete abandonment of opinion? Religion and philosophy offer different answers to this question, or so it would initially appear. Philosophy believes that in such cases people have to invent a new opinion, a new truth, to lead them out of the state of opinionlessness. Religion, by contrast, considers such a reaction too superficial and optimistic, because a person who thinks in religious terms anticipates from the outset the next step in which the new truth is absorbed by the market of opinion. Instead, religion offers another solution: insisting on this lack of opinion, connecting to the long history of the absence of opinion, which, ultimately, amounts to the history of religion. Religious people are not people of opinion, representatives, or producers of opinion; rather, they are media people, people as media.

Thus, to the extent that religion is the site of a revelation of the mediality of humanity, religion can be understood as the avant-garde of our present world, determined as it is by the mass media, just as the artistic avant-garde functioned as the revelation of the mediality of art. Yet, the interest of the mass media in religion is not simply a theoretical one, for the revelation of the mediality of human beings is also an event, a piece of news that can and should be communicated. Without the mass media this news would be suppressed; the revelation would remain secret. Sites of the sacred are by definition closed, hidden, dark places. And there are still such places in our globalized world. First, they include the still well-protected sites of traditional religions. Second, ever more new sites are emerging: of secret conspiracies, violent separations from the general public, places of dark individual and collective ecstasies.

Such places incessantly draw the attention of the media, because it is precisely the hidden, the closed, the dark, and the marginal that interests today's media. Quite naturally, the media strive to bring the hidden and marginal to the light of the general audience. That is why the media are repeatedly fascinated and provoked by the inaccessibility of sacred rituals. For decades there have been novels written and films made about the secret love affairs of priests. Today it seems the da Vinci code has been cracked once and for all, finally making Christ himself a star, a celebrity, who of course cannot be thought of as such without a disclosure. The mass media are constantly seeking to outdo revelation by disclosure – and in doing so they demonstrate their essential repetitiveness. The greatest opportunity open to the mass media is a new good message, a new piece of good news, which is that things are announced to the mainstream that were once marginal and hidden. It is constantly writing a new Gospel that may, perhaps, contradict the old Gospel at the level of opinion, but nonetheless repeats the familiar ritual of revelation. The machinery of disclosure in the mass media today is merely the technical reproduction of the religious ritual of revelation. Religion is an *ur*-medium always celebrating its return when news is disseminated and believed.

Today's religious movements operate predominantly with images that can be spread across the entire world in a flash by means of contemporary mass media. The electronic image media of video and television have become the chosen media for religious propaganda as they are capable of being produced and distributed especially fast. The "return of religions" that people are currently talking about does not necessarily mean that nowadays more people have become religious. Instead, religions have moved from the private sphere of personal belief out into the public sphere of visual communication. In this, religions function, for one, as machines for the repetition and mass media distribution of mechanically produced images. For another, the role model for this repetition is found in the repeatability of religious rituals, which is the foundation for the emergence of all subsequent media-based reproduction technologies. The original media used by religions were scriptures and books, assigned with the same task of distributing belief. In addition, the text served to canonize belief. Without writing, there would be no church; without scrolls, no belief. Thus, right from the start, through the demand for repeatability embodied by the ritual, religion was not only bound to media, but was itself a medium: religion as medium complements media as religion.

The exhibition *Medium Religion* aimed at demonstrating this medial aspect of religion using current examples of religious video propaganda and the work of contemporary artists. The horizons of religious propaganda have expanded enormously through the development of electronic media. The uncomplicated recording of the message (e.g., the video message), the rapid distribution, and huge, almost global scope (e.g., television, Internet) offered a technological base for religions' reentry into public awareness. Since the mass media constitute public awareness and religion makes use of mass media (e.g., the broadcast of the Papal mass from Rome), it is only logical that it, too, will shift more into public awareness.

The result is the reevaluation of minority faiths and their messages. Among other things, also on show were the suicide confessions of religiously inspired terrorists, religious propaganda TV series, and documentaries on new religious sects and faith communities. The artistic works that were shown along with this documentary material came mainly from the same cultural circles as the corresponding religious movements. The relationship of most of the artists to religious rituals, images, and texts from their own culture is neither affirmative nor critical, but rather blasphemous. They place religious symbolism in an unconventional context in order to provoke a different mode of perception. This enables a critical analysis of the respective religious iconography as well as its transfer to a cultural modernity.

Death was one of the central themes in the exhibition as religion's most primal and basic topic – and, especially death as the result of political, artistic, or private martyrdom, much in the way it plays a central role in the political awareness of secular modernity. Through examples, the exhibition showed how the iconography of these civil religions is ritualized and artistically represented and how it works.

The exhibition *Medium Religion* thus provided comprehensive insight into the medial reproduction and significance of religion, and in particular, its manifestations in geopolitical hotspots, such as the Middle East, Asia, Russia, the U.S., and South America. Many exhibits were being shown for the first time in Europe and have been specially researched or newly produced for the exhibition. The book resumes the thematic approach of the exhibition, presenting all the works that were exhibited, and underpins the arguments with contributions by well-known theoreticians, philosophers, journalists, and artists, such as Slavoj Žižek, Peter Sloterdjik, Hent de Vries, Joshua Simon, Rabih Mroué, and others. We are grateful to have found in Seamus Kealy a partner ready to assume responsibility for the organization of an additional venue in Ireland.

We would once again like to express our thanks to the contributing artists and writers for their willingness to take the risk of communicating their views on such a controversial topic as contemporary religion.

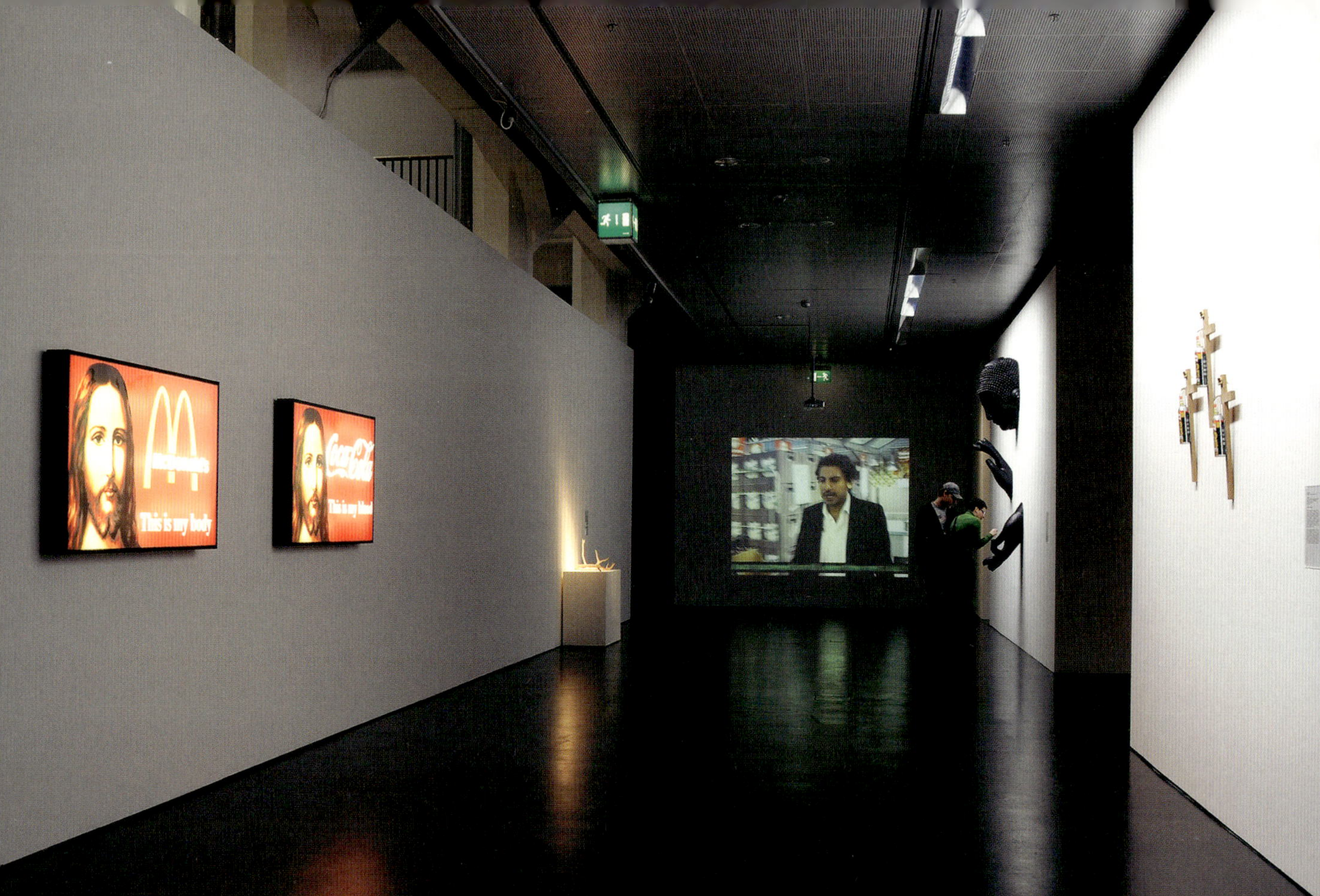

Above
From left to right

Alexander Kosolapov
This is my body, 2002,
This is my blood, 2002,
light boxes,
82 × 150 cm each

Konrad Balder Schäuffelen,
Abwurfstange, 1990, deer antler,
gold, 80 × 40 × 40 cm

Wael Shawky
The Cave, 2006, video, color,
sound, 12:45 min

Sang-Kyoon Noh
For the Worshipers, 2008, sequins
on polyester resin and fiberglass,
dimensions variable, head:
84.5 × 69 × 46.5 cm,
hand 1: 75 × 44 × 51 cm,
hand 2: 77 × 40 × 46 cm

Michael Schuster
Golgatha, 2008, oak crosses with
aluminum spray cans,
3 multiples, 56 × 25 × 8 cm each

Installation view
ZKM | Karlsruhe, 2009

Right page

In the front
Huang Yong Ping
*Loups et chèvres regardent la vidéo
de Aïd-el-Kebir*, 2006, mixed-
media installation,
mounted animals, carpets,
video, dimensions variable

In the back
Osvaldo Romberg
Mikve at Masada, 2008,
mixed-media installation, stacked
newspapers

Installation view
ZKM | Karlsruhe, 2009

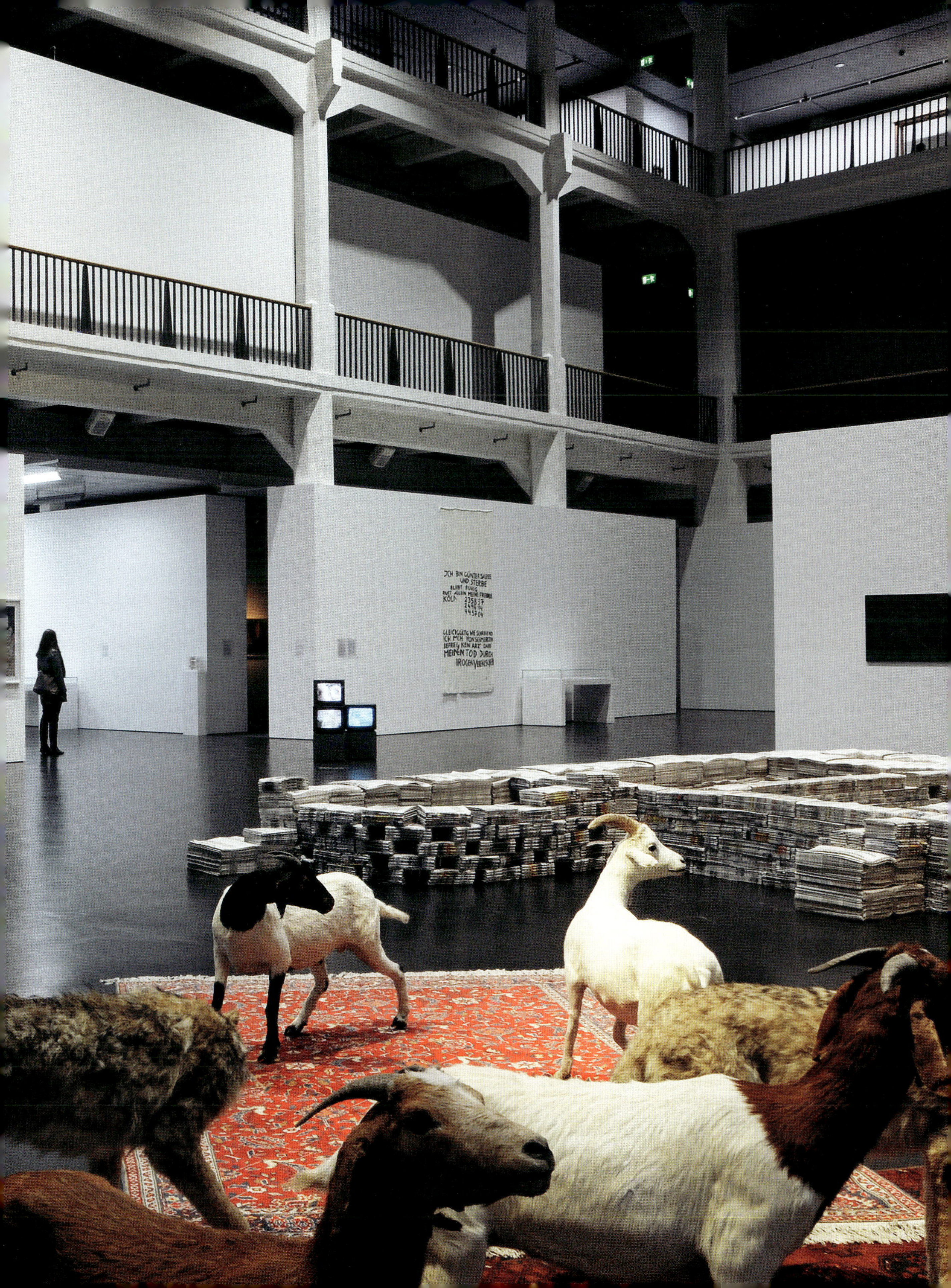

ICH BIN GÜNTER SAREE
UND STERBE
BLEIBT RUHIG
AUCH WENN MEINE FREUNDE
KÖLN   235837
               244814
               445704

GLEICHZEITIG WIE SCHREIEND
ICH MICH VON SCHMERZEN
BEFREY KEIN ARZT DARF
MEINEN TOD DURCH
DROGENVERBRAUCH

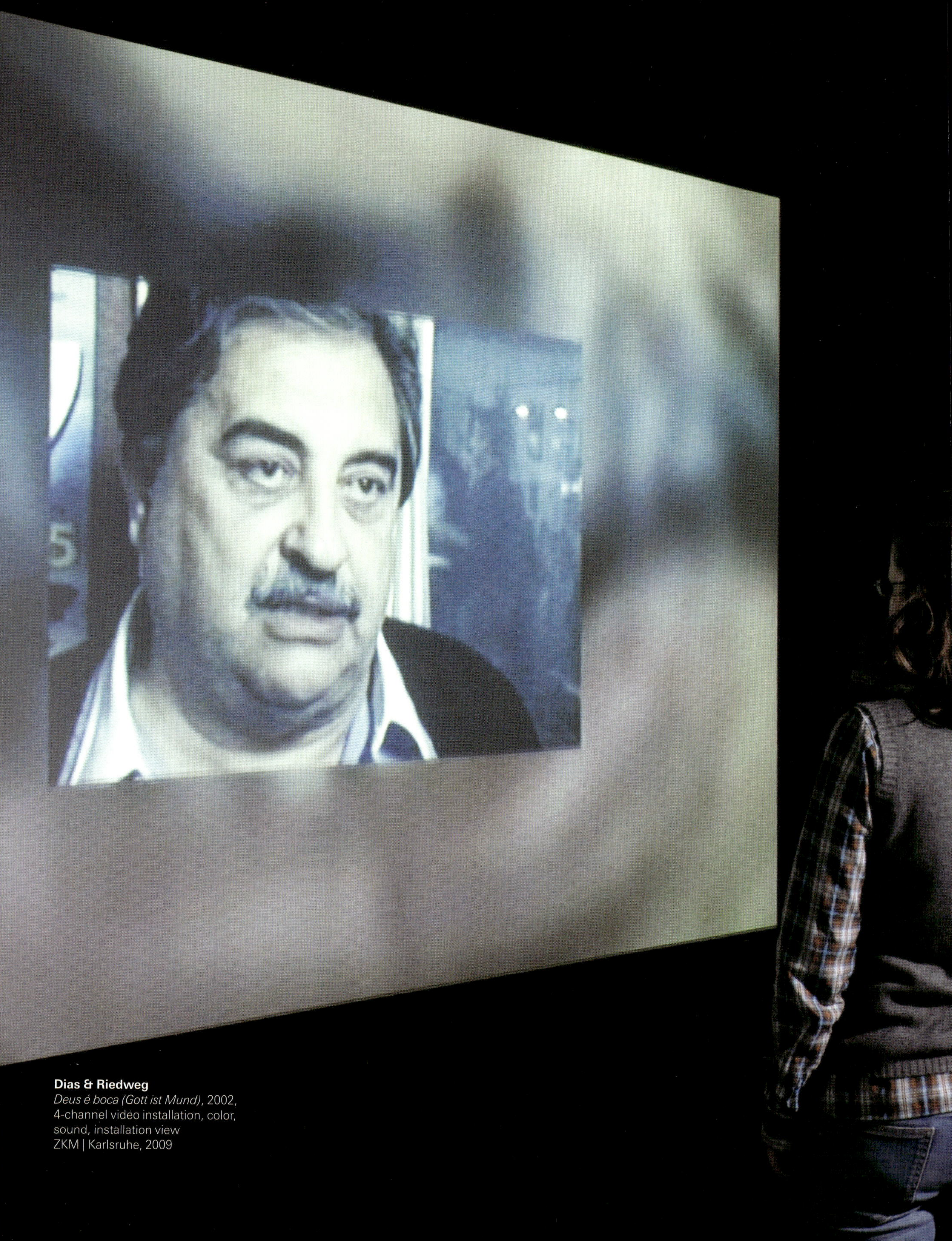

Dias & Riedweg
Deus é boca (Gott ist Mund), 2002,
4-channel video installation, color,
sound, installation view
ZKM | Karlsruhe, 2009

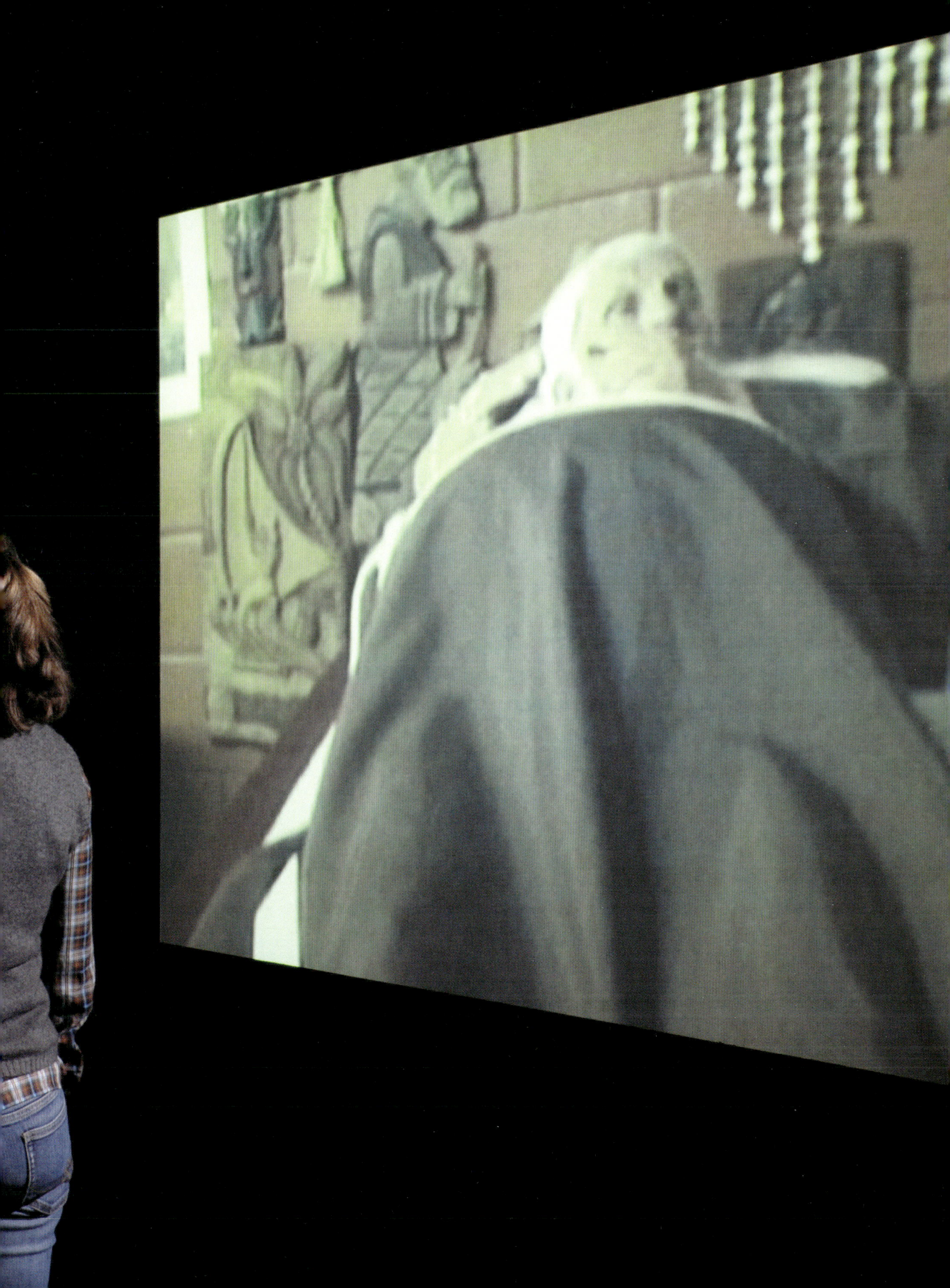

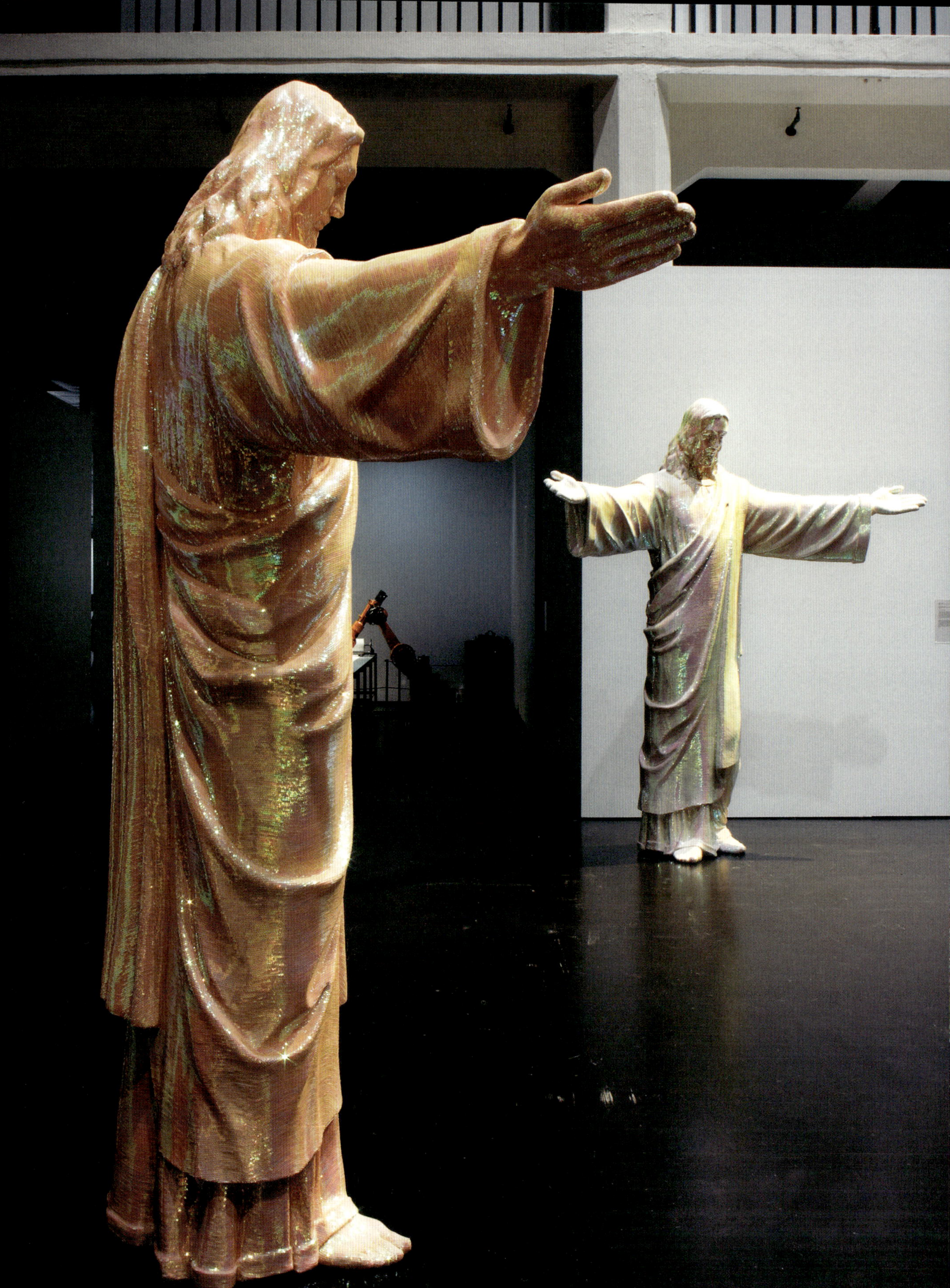

Left page
Sang-Kyoon Noh
Twin Jesus Christs, 2001,
sequins on polyester resin and
fiberglass, 267 × 265 × 78 cm each

Below
Gospel Aerobics with
Paul Eugene, ca. 2005–2008,
video, color, sound,
19:30 min, 21:50 min,
32 min, 24:30 min, 24 min,
www.pauleugene.com

Installation views
ZKM | Karlsruhe, 2009

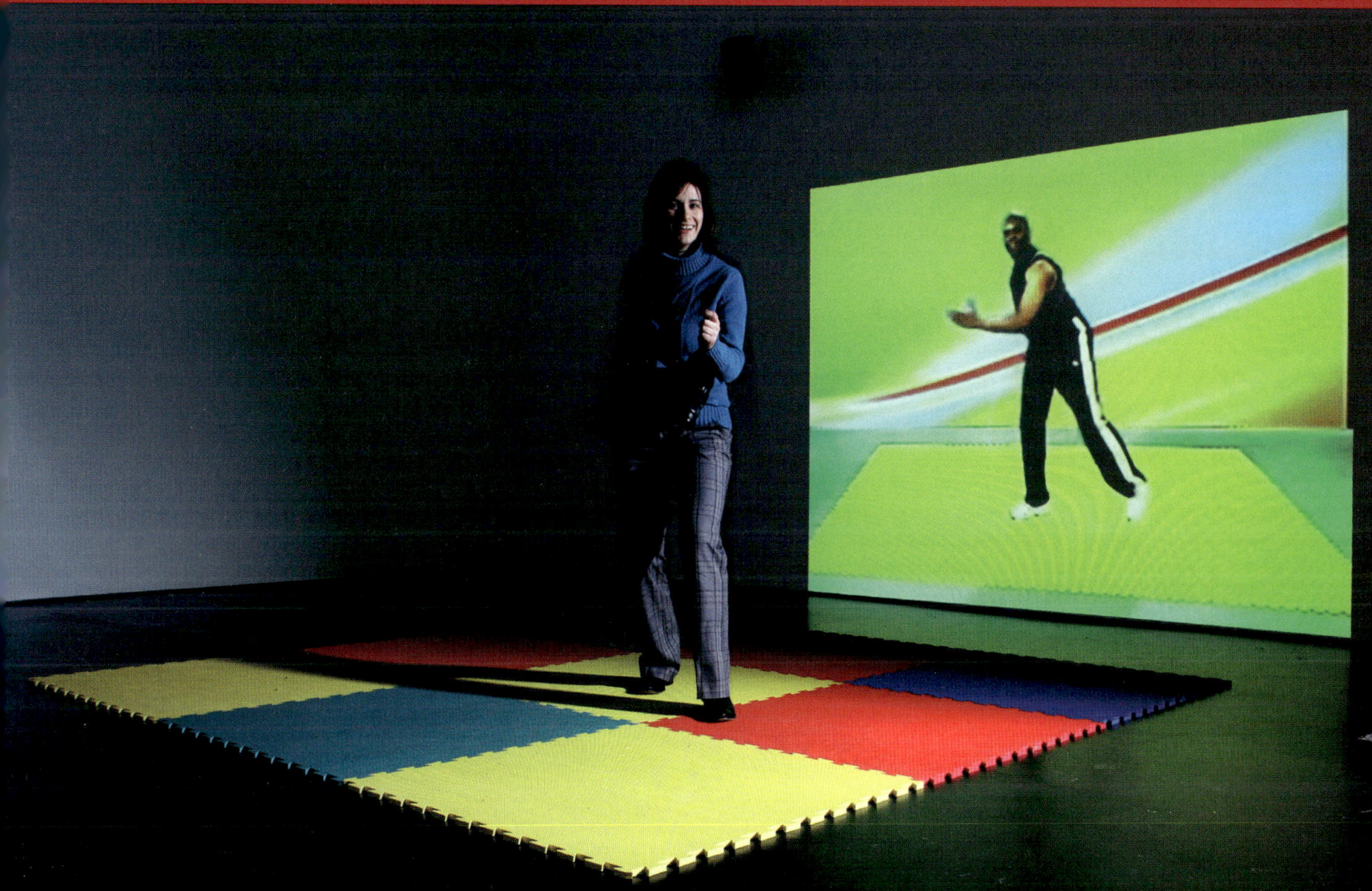

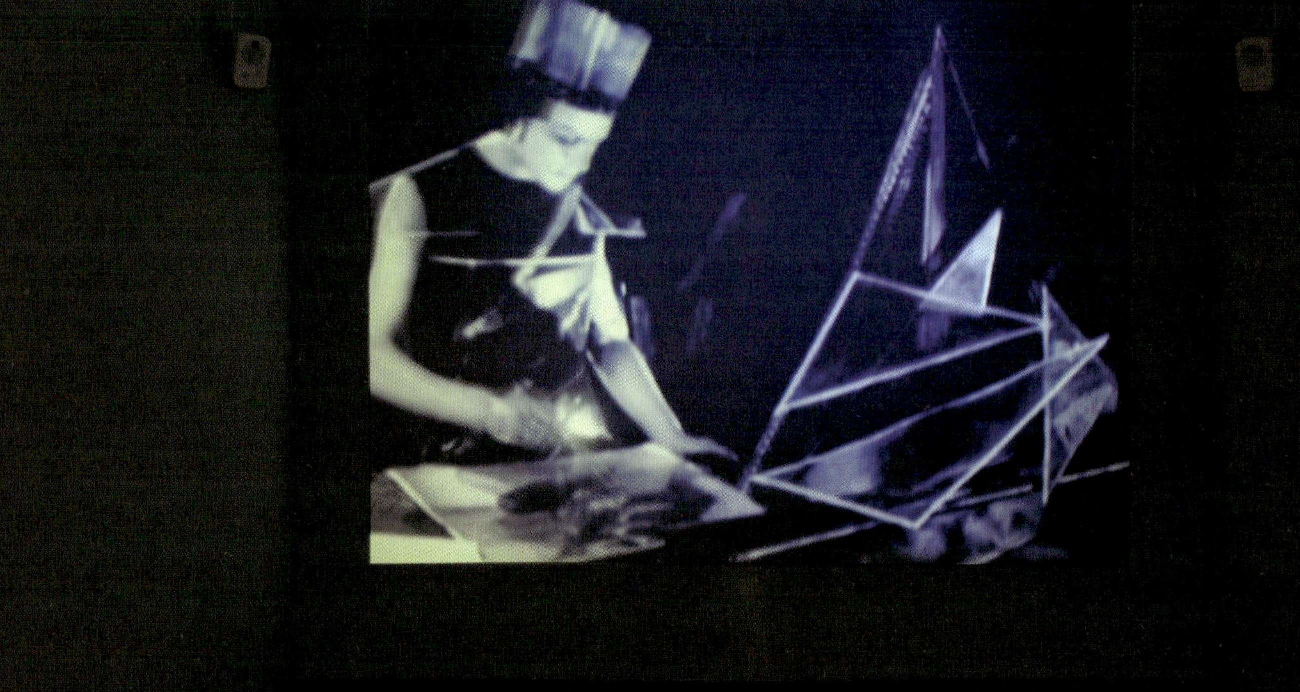

Above
Boris Groys
Unsterbliche Körper, 2007,
video lecture on DVD, color,
sound, 29 min

Right page top
Paul Chan
1st Light, 2005,
digital video projection, color,
silent, 14 min

Right page bottom
robotlab
bios [bible], 2007, robot
installation, dimensions variable,

Installation views
ZKM | Karlsruhe, 2009

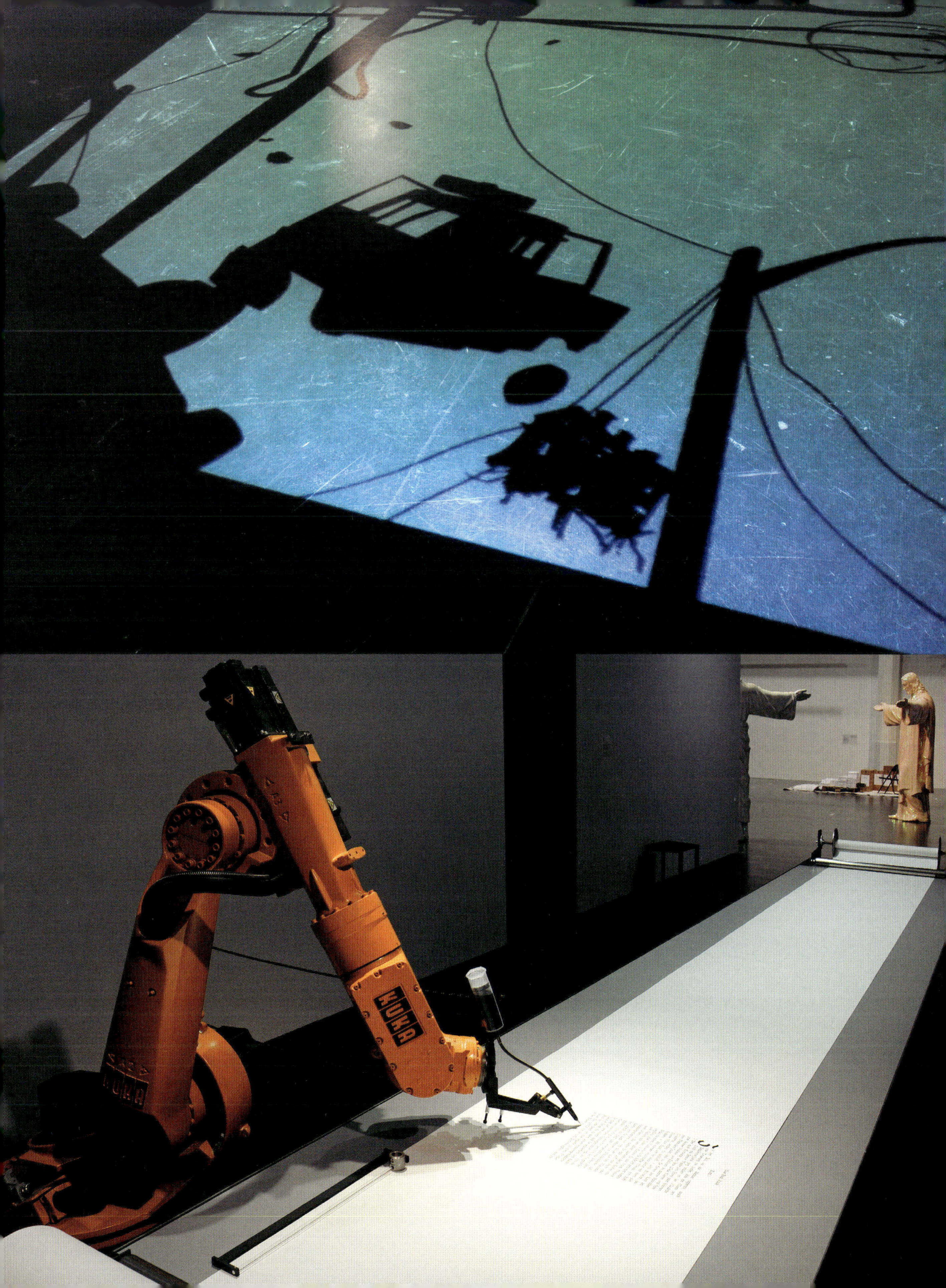

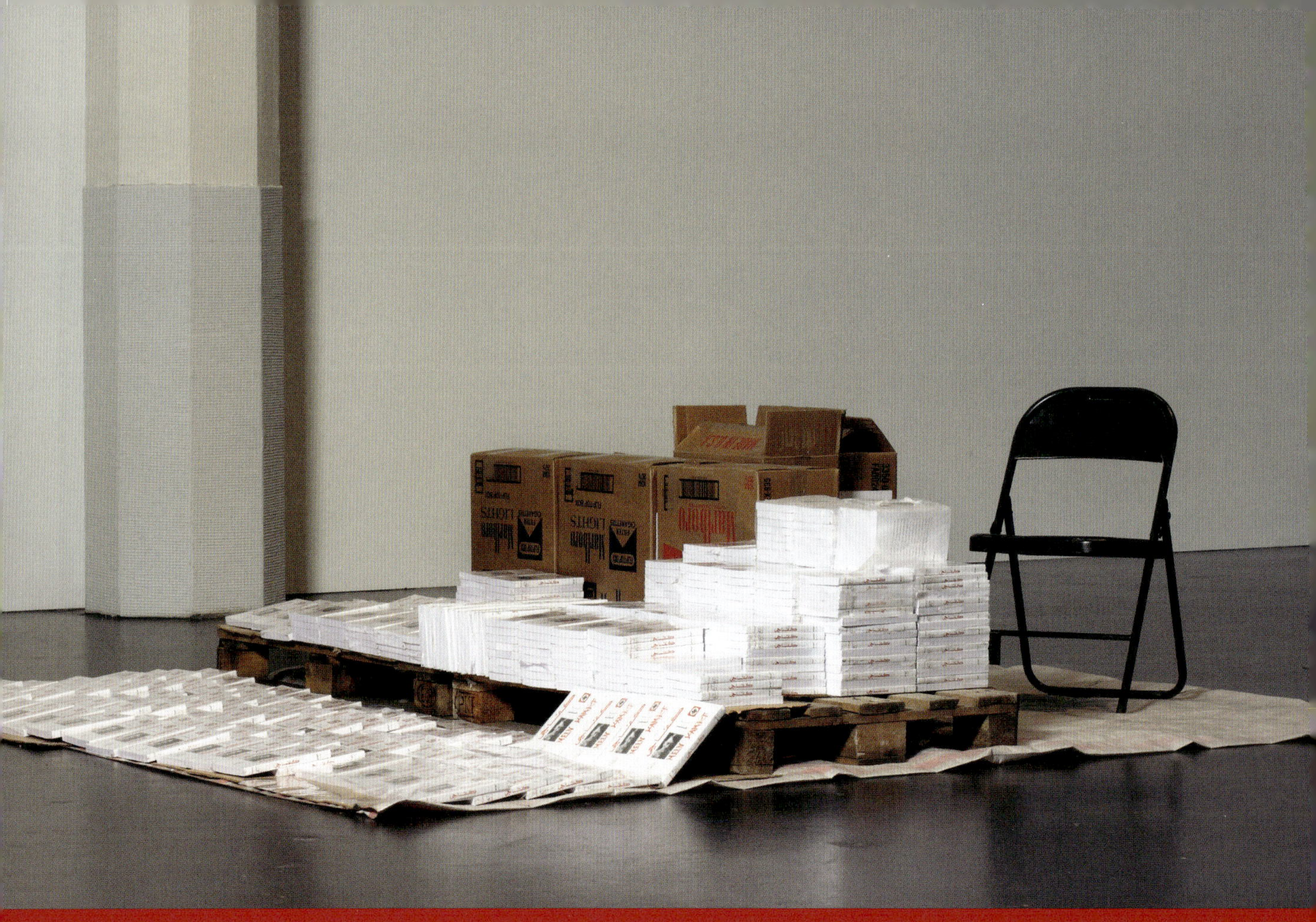

Above
Christoph Büchel
كفاحي [My Struggle], 2006,
1,000 copies of
Adolf Hitler's *Mein Kampf*
(Arabic translation), tarp, cashier
box, chair, palletts, boxes

Right page top
Alexander Kosolapov
This is my body, 2002,
This is my blood, 2002,
light boxes, 82 × 150 cm each

Right page bottom
Christoph Schlingensief
Der König wohnt in Mir, 2008,
mixed-media installation,
dimensions variable, space:
6.6 x 7.3 m, chimneys
112 × 150 × 40 cm each

Installation views
ZKM | Karlsruhe, 2009

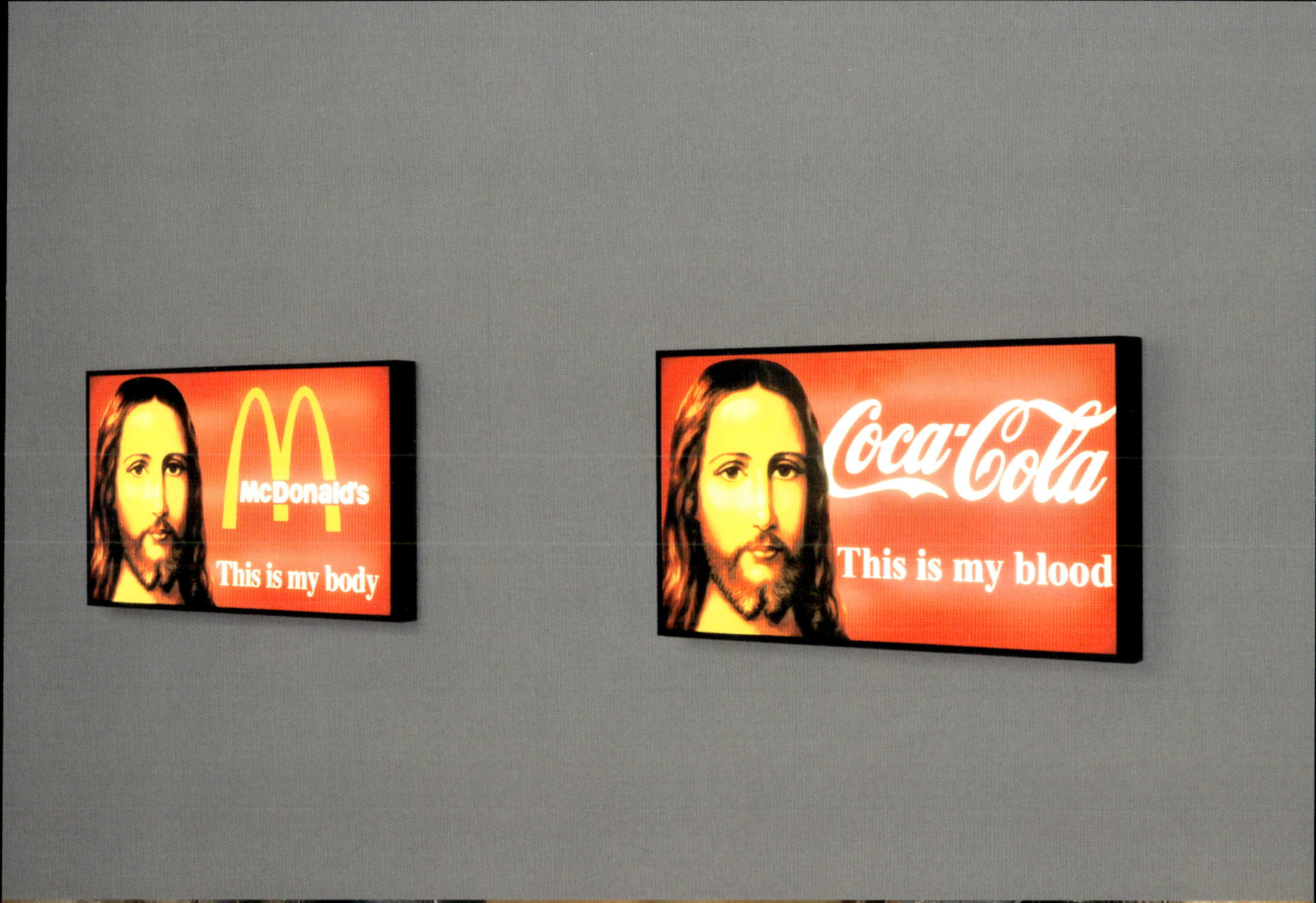

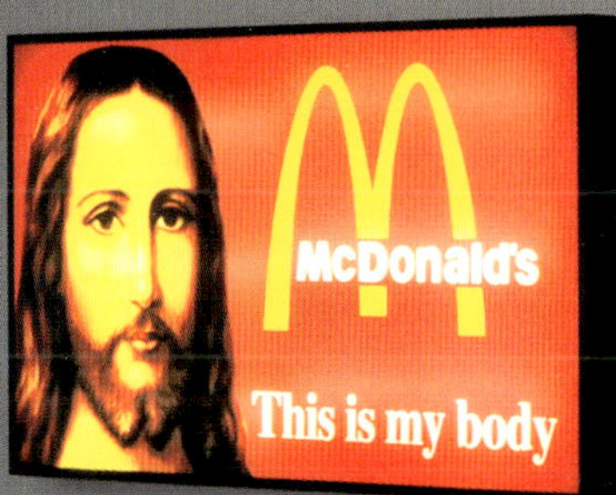

McDonald's
This is my body

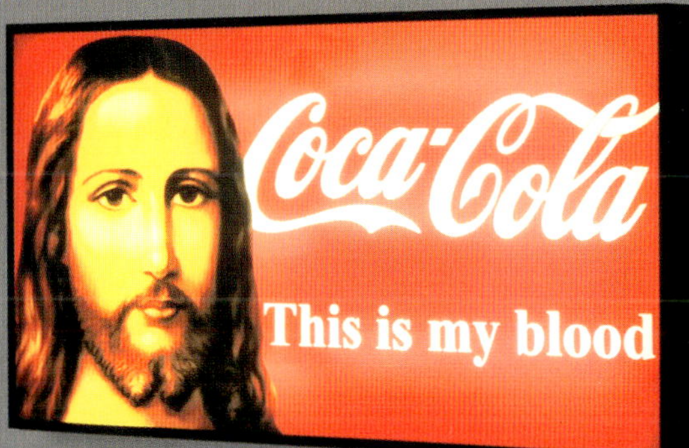

Coca-Cola
This is my blood

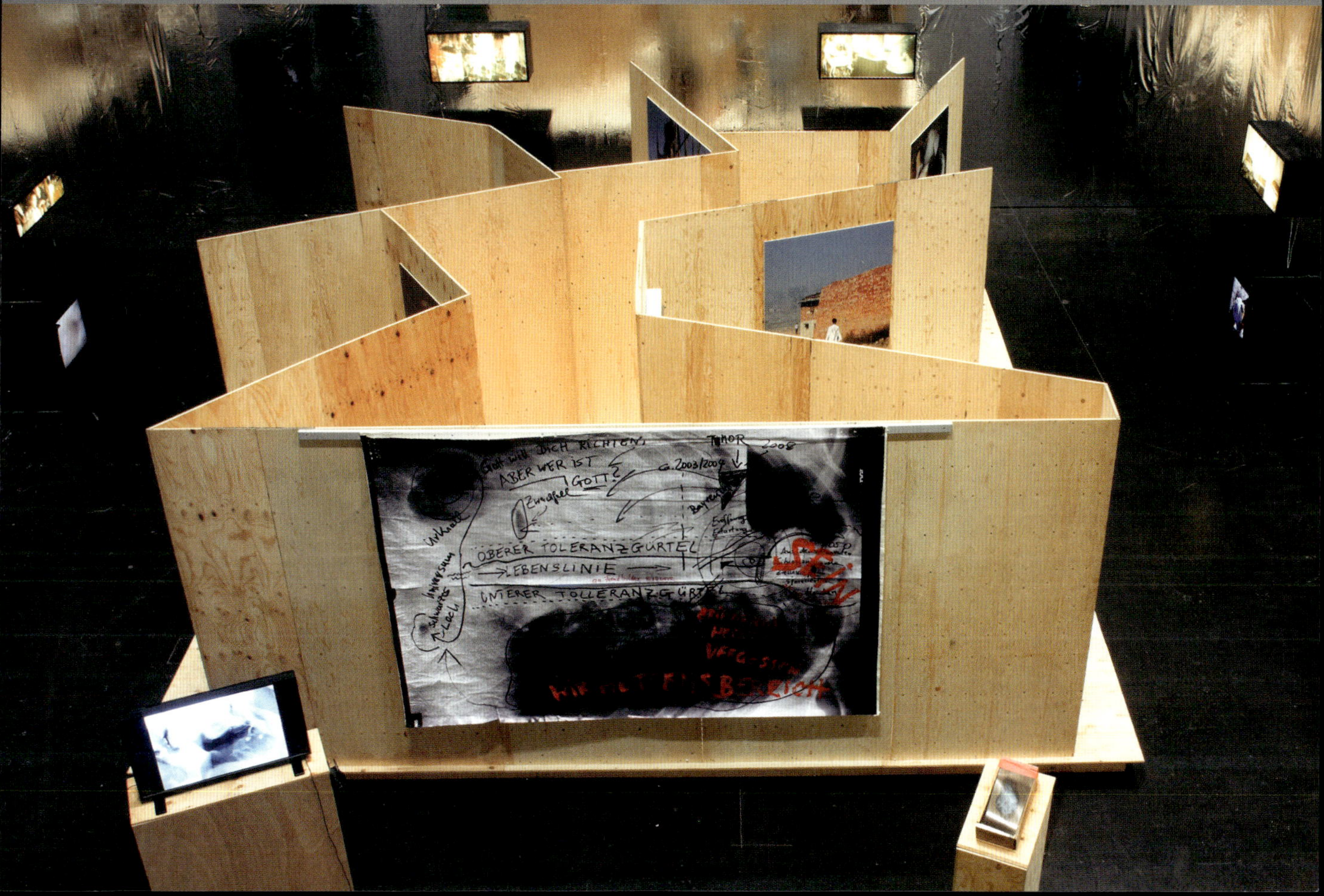

Boris Groys

...Religion.in.the...
...Age.of.Digital...
....Reproduction....

The general consensus in contemporary mass media is that the return of religion has emerged as currently the most important factor in global politics and culture. Now, those who today refer to a revival of religion clearly do not mean anything like the second coming of the Messiah or the appearance of new gods and prophets. What they are referring to is rather that religious attitudes have shifted from culturally marginal zones into the mainstream. If this is the case, and statistics would seem to corroborate the claim, the question arises as to what then may have caused religious attitudes to become mainstream.

The survival and dissemination of opinions on the global information market is regulated by a law formulated by Charles Darwin, namely, the survival of the fittest. Those opinions best adapted to the conditions under which they are disseminated will, as a matter of course, have the best odds of becoming mainstream. Today's opinions market, however, is clearly characterized by reproduction, repetition, and tautology. The widespread understanding of contemporary civilization holds that over the course of the modern age theology was replaced by philosophy, an orientation toward the past by an orientation toward the future, traditional teachings by subjective evidence, fidelity to origins by innovation, and so on. In fact, however, the modern age has not been the age in which the sacred has been abolished but rather the age of its dissemination in profane space, its democratization, its globalization. Ritual, repetition, and reproduction were hitherto matters of religion; they were practiced in isolated, sacred places. In the modern age ritual, repetition, and reproduction have become the fate of the entire world, of entire cultures. Everything reproduces itself – capital, commodities, technology, and art. Ultimately, even progress is reproductive; it consists in a constantly repeated destruction of everything that cannot be reproduced quickly and effectively. Under such conditions it should come as no surprise that religion – in all its various manifestations – has become increasingly successful. Religion operates through media channels that are from the outset products of the extension and secularization of traditional religious practices. Let us now turn to an investigation of some of the aspects of this extension and secularization that seem especially relevant for the survival and success of religions in the contemporary world.

1. The Internet and Freedom of Faith

The regime under which religion – any religion – functions in contemporary Western secular democratic societies is freedom of faith. Freedom of faith means that each individual is free to believe what he or she chooses to believe and that all are free to organize their personal and private lives according to these beliefs. At the same time this also means that the imposition of one's own faith in public life and state institutions, including atheism as a form of faith, cannot be tolerated. The significance of the Enlightenment was not so much that it resulted in the complete disappearance of religion, but that religion became a matter of private choice, which then resulted in the withdrawal of religion into the private sphere. In the contemporary world, religion became a matter of private taste, functioning in much the same way as do art and design. Naturally, this is not to suggest that religion is precluded from public discussion. However, the place of religion in relationship to public discussion is reminiscent of the place of art as outlined by Immanuel Kant in *The Critique of Judgment* (1790): Religion may be publicly discussed, but such a discussion cannot result in any conclusion that would become obligatory, neither for the participants of this discussion nor for society as a whole. Commitment to one or the other religious faith is a matter of sovereign, private choice that cannot be dictated by any public authority – including any democratically legitimized authority: even more importantly, such a decision – as in the case of art – need not be publicly argued and legitimized, rather, publicly accepted without further discussion. The legitimacy of personal faith is not based on the degree of its power of persuasion, but on the sovereign right of the individual to be committed to this faith.

In this respect, freedom of faith is fundamentally different from, let's say, the kind of freedom represented in scientific research. In the context of a scientific discussion every opinion must be argued for and against, but each opinion must also be substantiated by certain facts and verified according to fixed rules. Every participant of such a discussion is undoubtedly free – at least theoretically – to formulate his or her position and to argue in its favor. However, one may not insist on a certain scientific opinion that is not, at the same time, subject to justification, and that would contravene all proof and evidence to the contrary, without introducing any argument that would otherwise make one's position plausible and persuasive to others. Such unyielding resistance to the obvious, such blindness toward the facts, to logic and common sense, would be regarded as bordering on the insane. If someone referred to his sovereign right to insist on a certain scientific opinion without being able to legitimize this insistence by rational argument, he would be excluded from the scientific community.

This means that our contemporary, Western notion of freedom is deeply ambiguous. In fact, discourse on freedom always pivots on two radical types of freedom: an unconditional freedom of faith, that sovereign freedom permitting us to make personal choices beyond all public explanation and justification, and the conditional, institutional freedom of scientific opinion, which depends on the subject's ability to justify and legitimize this opinion in accordance with predetermined, publicly established rules. Thus, it is easy to show that our notion of democratic, free society is also ambiguous. The contemporary notion of political freedom allows us to interpret this freedom, in part, as a sovereign, in part as an institutional freedom, in part as the sovereign freedom of political commitment, and in part as the institutional free-

dom of political discussion. But whatever may be said about the contemporary global political field in general, one thing remains certain: This field is becoming increasingly influenced, or even defined by the Internet as the primary medium of global communication. The Internet favors private, unconditional, sovereign freedom vis-à-vis scientific, conditional, institutional freedom.

In an earlier age of mass media – newspapers, radio or TV – the only possible assurance of freedom of opinion was an institutionally guaranteed free access to this media. Any discussion about the freedom of opinion, therefore, centered on the politics of representation, on the question as to who and what should be included, and who and what excluded from standard news coverage and public political discussion. Today, all are free to open their own websites without the need of discussion and legitimization. Freedom of opinion, as practiced on the Internet, functions as the sovereign freedom of private commitment: neither as the institutional freedom of rational discussion nor as the politics of representation, inclusion, and exclusion. What we experience today is the immense privatization of public media space through the Internet: a private conversation between my MySpace (www.myspace.com) and YouTube (www.youtube.com) today substitutes the public discussion of the previous age. The slogan of the previous age used to be "The private is political," whereas the true slogan of the Internet is "political is private."

Obviously, this new configuration of the media field favors religion over science and sovereign religious politics over institutionalized secular politics. The Internet is the space in which it is possible for contemporary, aggressive religious movements to install their propaganda material and to act globally – without recourse to any institution for representation or application to any authority for their recognition. The Internet provides these movements with the means to operate beyond any discursively obtained legitimacy and with full sovereignty. In this sense, the contemporary return of religion can be seen as the return of sovereign freedom after many decades or even centuries of dominance of institutional freedom. Accordingly, the surge in religion may also be directly connected to the growing sovereign freedom of private consumption and capital investment on a global scale. Both are dependent on the Internet and other digital communications media that transgress the borders of national democratic institutions. In any case, both practices – religious and economic – presuppose the functioning of the media universe as an arena for private, sovereign acts and decisions. There is, moreover, one further significant similarity between capital investment and religious commitment: Both operate through language, though at the same time beyond language – where language is understood as the means of (self-)explanation, justification, and legitimization.

2. Religious Ritual and Mechanical Reproduction

Religion is often understood to be a certain set of opinions. Here, religion is associated with opinions about whether contraception should be permitted or women should wear headscarves. I would argue, however, that religion – any religion – is not a set of opinions but primarily a set of rituals, and that the religious ritual refers to a state in which there is a lack of opinions, a state of opinionlessness – a-doxia –, for it refers to the will of the gods or of God ultimately concealed from the opinions of mortals. Religious language is the language of repetition, not because its subjects insist on any specific truth they wish to repeatedly assert and communicate. Here language is embedded in ritual. And ritual is a re-enactment of the revelation of a truth ultimately impossible to communicate. Repetition of a certain religious ritual celebrates the event of the encounter with such an uncommunicable truth, of the acceptance of this truth, of being answerable to God's love and maintaining devotion to the mystery of revelation. Religious discourse praises God, and praises God such as it is supposed to please God. Religious

discourse does not operate in the opposition between truth and error, as does scientific discourse, but in the opposition between devotion and blasphemy.

The ritual, as such, is neither true nor false. In this sense, it marks the zero point of freedom of opinion, e.g. freedom from any kind of opinion, from the obligation to have an opinion. Religious ritual can be repeated, abandoned, or modified – but not legitimized, criticized, or refuted. Accordingly, the fundamentalist is a person who insists not so much on a certain set of opinions than on certain rituals not being abandoned or modified, and being faithfully and correctly reproduced. The true fundamentalist does not care about fidelity to the truth, but about the correctness of a ritual, not about the theoretical or rather theological interpretations of the faith, but about the material form of religion.

Now, if we consider those religious movements, especially those active today, we observes, that they are predominantly fundamentalist movements. Traditionally, we tend to distinguish between two kinds of repetition: (1) repetition of the spirit and in spirit, e.g. repetition of the true, inner essence of a religious message, and (2) repetition of the external form of a religious ritual. The opposition between these two types of repetition – between living spirit and dead letter – informs all Western discourse on religion. The first kind of repetition is almost always regarded as true repetition, as authentic, "inner" continuation of a religious tradition – the continuation that presupposes the possibility of a rupture with the merely external, conventional, historically accidental form of this tradition, or even requires such a rupture. According to this spiritualist interpretation of the religious tradition, the inner, spiritual fidelity to the essence of a religious message gives to a believer the right to adapt the external, material form of this message to the changing historical milieus and contexts without betraying the inner truth of this message. A religious tradition capable of transforming and adapting itself to changing circumstances without losing its inner, essential identity is usually praised as a living, spiritually powerful tradition that maintains its vitality and historical relevance. On the other hand, "superficial" adherence to the mere letter, to the external form of religion, to the "empty" ritual is, as a rule, regarded as symptomatic of the fact that the religion in question lacks vitality – and even as a betrayal of the inner truth of this tradition by the purely mechanical reproduction of its external, dead form. Now, this is precisely what fundamentalism is, namely, the insistence on the letter as opposed to the spirit.

It is for this reason that religious fundamentalism has always possessed a revolutionary dimension: while breaking with the politics of spirit, e.g. with the politics of reform, flexibility, and adaptation to the zeitgeist, it goes on to substitute these politics of spirit by advocating violent politics of the letter. Thus, contemporary religious fundamentalism may be regarded as the most radical product of the European Enlightenment and the materialist view of the world. Religious fundamentalism is religion after the death of the spirit, after the loss of spirituality. Should the spirit perish – all that remains is the letter – the material form, the ritual as event in the material world. In other words, difference in the material form of religion can no longer be compensated by identity in spirit. A rupture with the external form of the ritual cannot be compensated by the inner, spiritual fidelity to the religious truth. A material difference is now just a difference – there is no essence, no being, and no meaning underlying such a formal difference at a deeper level. In this sense, fundamentalist religious movements are religions after deconstruction. If meaning, sense, and intention cannot be stabilized, the only possibility for authentic repetition is literal repetition, mechanical reproduction – beyond any opinion, meaning, sense, and intention. Islam would be an especially good case in point. While notoriously forbidding the production of images, it does not forbid the re-production and the use of already existing images – especially in the case of so-called "mechanically pro-

duced" images, such as photography or film. While it has meanwhile become banal to say that Islam is not modern, it is obviously postmodern.

In his book *Difference and Repetition* (1968) Gilles Deleuze speaks of literal repetition as being radically artificial and, in this sense, as being in conflict with everything natural, living, changing, developing, including natural law and moral law. Hence, practicing literal repetition can be seen as initiating a rupture in the continuity of life. In his remarks on the philosophy of history, Walter Benjamin also describes the genuine revolution as a break with the continuity of historical evolution, as a literal repetition of the past in the present. He also refers to capitalism as a new kind of religion reduced to ritual and so devoid of any theology. Literal repetition however is not only a revolution effectuated by capital or against it, in other words it is not only an act of violence against the flow of historical change, and even against life as such. Literal repetition may also be seen as a way toward personal self-sacralization and immortality – immortality of the subject ready to submit him- or herself to such a repetition. It is no mere accident that the working class has performed the repetitive, alienated, one might say, ritual work in the context of modern industrial civilization, sacralized, in certain ways, by the socialist movements of the nineteenth and twentieth centuries: by contrast, an intellectual or an artist – as embodiments of the creative spirit of change – remained profane precisely because of their inability to repeat and to reproduce. Friedrich Nietzsche had already made reference to literal repetition – the eternal return of the same – as being the only possible way to think immortality after the death of spirit, of God. Here, the difference between the repetitiveness of religious ritual and the literal reproduction of the world of appearances disappears. One might say that religious ritual is the *Urform* of the mechanical reproduction that dominated the Western culture during the modern period, and which, to a certain degree, continues to dominate the contemporary world. What this suggests is that mechanical reproduction might, in its turn, be understood as a religious ritual. It is for this reason that fundamentalist religious movements have become so successful in our time, for they combine religious ritual with mechanical reproduction.

For Benjamin, of course, mechanical reproduction connotes the loss of aura, the loss of religious experience which he understands as the experience of uniqueness. He describes the religious experience as, one might say, a unique spiritual experience – in this respect his evocation of the experience of being enchanted by an Italian landscape as an example of an authentic experience, which is lost in the reproduction process is particularly characteristic. (It is the experience of happiness, of fullness, and the intensity of life.) But, one might argue, true religious experience is actually the experience of death rather than the experience of life – the experience of death in the midst of life. Hence, precisely because mechanical reproduction may be understood as the lifeless repetition of the dead image it can be also interpreted as a source of the truly religious experience. In fact, it is precisely the loss of aura that represents the most radical religious experience under the conditions of modernity, since it is in this way that a human being discovers the mechanical, machine-like, repetitive, and reproductive, one might even say, dead aspect of its own existence.

3. The Digitized Religion

However, as already mentioned in the above, the new religious movements operate primarily through the Internet by means of digital and not mechanical reproduction. During the last decades, video has become the chosen medium of contemporary religious propaganda and is distributed through different TV channels, the Internet, commercial video stores, etc. This is especially so in the case of the most recent, most active, and even aggressive religious movements. The phenomenon of confession videos of suicide bombers and many other kinds of video production reflecting the mentality of radical Islam have meanwhile become familiar to us. On the other hand, the new evangelical movements also operate with the same medium of video. If one asks those responsible for the public relations in these movements to provide information, one is initially sent videos. This use of the video as the major medium of self-presentation among different religious movements is a relatively new phenomenon. The standard traditional media rather used to be a script, a book, a painted image, or a sculpture. The question then arises as to what constitutes the difference between mechanical and digital reproduction and how this difference affects the fate of religion in our age.

At this point, I would argue that the use of video as the principle medium by contemporary religious movements is intrinsic to the message of these movements. Neither is it external to the understanding of the religious, as such, that it underlies this use. This is not to suggest, following Marshall McLuhan, that here the medium is the message but rather, as I would argue, that the message has become the medium – a certain religious message has become the digital code.

Digital images have the propensity to generate, to multiply, and to distribute themselves almost anonymously through open fields of the contemporary means of communication. The origin of these messages is difficult, or even impossible to locate, much like the origin of divine, religious messages. At the same time, digitalization seems to guarantee a literal reproduction of a text or an image more effectively than any other known technique. Naturally, it is not so much the digital image itself as the image file, the digital data which remains identical through the process of its reproduction and distribution. However, the image file is not an image – the image file is invisible. The digital image is an effect of the visualization of the invisible image file, of the invisible digital data. Only the protagonists of the movie *Matrix* (1999) were able to see the image files, the digital code as such. The average spectator however does not have the magic pill that would allow him or her, like the protagonists of *Matrix*, to enter the invisible space otherwise concealed behind the digital image for the purposes of directly confronting the digital data itself. And such a spectator is not in command of the technique that would enable him to transfer the digital data directly into the brain and to experience it in the mode of pure, non-visualizable suffering as depicted by the protagonist of another movie – *Johnny Mnemonic* (1995). (Actually, pure suffering is, as we know, the most adequate experience of the invisible.) Digital data should be visualized, should become an image which can be seen. Here we have a situation whereby the perennial spirit/matter dichotomy is reinterpreted as a dichotomy between digital file and its visualization, or "immaterial information" and "material" image, including visible text. In more theological terms: The digital file functions as an angel – as an invisible messenger transmitting a divine command. But a human being remains external to this message, to this command, so condemned to contemplate only its visual effects. We are confronted here with a transposition of a dichotomy between the divine and the human, from a metaphysical to a technical level – a transposition that, as Martin Heidegger would argue, is only possible by virtue of this dichotomy being implicitly technical from the outset.

And, by extension, a digital image that can be seen cannot be merely exhibited or copied (as an analogue image) but always only staged or performed. Here, the image begins to function as a piece of music, whose score, as is generally known, is not identical to the music piece – the score being not audible, but silent. For the music to resound, it has to be performed. One could argue that digitization turns visual arts into performing arts. To perform something, however, means interpreting it, betraying it, distorting it. Every performance is an interpretation and every interpretation is a misuse. The situation is especially difficult in the case of the invisible original: If the original is visible it can be com-

pared to a copy – so the copy can be corrected and the feeling of distortion reduced. But if the original is invisible no such comparison is possible – any visualization remains uncertain in its relationship to the original; or one could even say that every such performance itself becomes an original.

Moreover, today information technology is in a state of perpetual change – hardware, software, simply everything. For this reason alone, the image is transformed with each act of visualization that uses a different and new technology. Today's technology conceives in terms of generations – we speak of computer generations, of generations of photographic and video equipment. But where generations are involved, so also are generational conflicts, oedipal struggles. Anyone attempting to transfer his or her old text or image files to new software experiences the power of the Oedipus complex over current technology – many data are destroyed, evaporate in the void. The biological metaphor says it all: it is not only life which is notorious in this respect, but technology as well, which, supposedly opposing nature, has now become the medium of non-identical reproduction. Benjamin's central assumption in his famous essay "The Work of Art in the Age of Mechanical Reproduction" (1935/1936) – namely, that an advanced technology can guarantee the material identity between original and copy – was not born out by the later technological developments. The real technological development went in the opposite direction – towards a diversification of the conditions under which a copy is produced and distributed and, accordingly, the diversification of the resulting visual images. And even were technology to guarantee the visual identity between the different visualizations of the same data, they would still remain non-identical due to the changing social contexts of their appearances.

The act of visualizing invisible digital data is thus analogous to the appearance of the invisible inside the topography of the visible world (biblically speaking, signs and wonders) that generate the religious rituals. In this respect, the digital image functions as a Byzantine icon – as a visible representation of invisible digital data. The digital code seems to guarantee the identity of different images that function as visualizations of this code. The identity is established here not at the level of spirit, essence, or meaning but on the material and technical level. Thus, it is in this way that the promise of literal repetition seems to acquire a solid foundation – the digital file is, after all, supposed to be something more material and tangible than invisible God. However, the digital file does remain invisible, hidden. What this signifies is that its self-identity remains a matter of belief. Indeed, we are compelled to believe that each act of visualization of a certain digital data amounts to a revelation of the same data, much as we obliged to believe that every performance of a certain religious ritual refers to the same invisible God. And this means that opinion about what is identical and what is different, or what is original and what is a copy, is an act of belief, an effect of a sovereign decision that cannot be fully justified empirically or logically.

Digital video substitutes the spiritual guarantees of immortality allegedly waiting for us beyond this world by the technical guarantees of potentially eternal repetition inside this word – a repetition that becomes a form of immortality because of its ability to interrupt the flow of historical time. It is this new prospect of materialist, technically guaranteed immortality that the new religious movements de facto offer their adepts – beyond the metaphysical uncertainties of their theological past. Placing human actions in loop, both practices – ritual and video – realize the Nietzschean promise of a new immortality: The eternal return of the same. However, this new technical guarantee remains a matter of belief and sovereign decision. To recognize two different images as copies of the same image or as visualizations of the same digital file means to value the immortality over originality. To recognize them as different means to prefer originality in time to the prospect of immortality. Both decisions are necessarily sovereign – and both acts of faith.

Peter Weibel

.......Religion........
......as.a.Medium.–....
......the.Media........
....of.Religion.......

[…] solam scripturam regnare […].

Martin Luther*

The Source of Belief Is Already a Question of Belief

Everything that God created succeeds in telling its own story: for example, the mountains write their geological strata, and the trees write with the rings in their trunks and the lines on their leaves. The universe is a book of memories, and the earth is a diary.[1] God himself does not write, however. God has, as well known, not included the Bible in his bibliography. He does not even have a bibliography. There are, however, authors of texts and books who emphasize that God dictated the content to them, be it directly or via a divine messenger. These holy scriptures are at the heart of the belief of countless religions. The holiness of these writings is a matter of faith, as the nature of the sources is unclear, confused, or even contradictory. Not until 50 to 150 years after Christianity was founded, did people start writing down the story of its genesis and the content thereof. One is tempted to say that the holy scriptures are a form of public relations a posteriori or rather post mortem.

Be they Christianity, Islamism, Zoroastrianism, Hinduism, Buddhism, Sikhism, Taoism, Confucianism, or whatever, all religions rely on scriptures. These text documents not only convey the content of the belief, such as an explanation of Creation and prescriptions on how the right life must be led, but by claiming to be a communication by God himself, and thus to be of divine origin, they are a tautological means of creating a religious system. God exists because he is considered the author of a text present to humans. The text is credible because God is the author.

The status of the texts is not certain, but the belief cannot be shattered by proof as "belief" does not stand for an assumed probability here. The matter at hand is not only deemed hypothetically to be true and its possible falsification accepted. Rather, belief signifies a basic stance as regards trust in the origin. The word "believe" stems from the Old English *gliefan*, and in German *glauben* stems from the Old High German *gilouben* – to be loved – and thus both come from the stem for love in the broadest sense.[2]

In other words, it does not denote doubt or an antipode of knowledge, but attests to the will to believe and obey, even if there is no proof for this.[3] This stance can clearly not be challenged by facts, as is already evidenced by studies on profane opinion making. In directed perception, a person only tolerates facts that already support an existing opinion.

This essay seeks to point to the problematic status of the sources of various systems of belief, to the structure of religious narrative and the ways it is handed down. The focus is on the relationship between systems of belief and the written word, or, more generally, between belief systems and the media of information storage and information transmission.

From Word and Ritual to Script

The so-called "holy scriptures" were preceded by periods of oral transmission extending over differing time spans. To put it simply, we could say that down through the millennia, peoples who did not know the written word devised myths and rites in attempts to create a picture of the world which they would adjure as a means to survive within it. With their myths and narratives handed down orally they attempted to explain the world and its events, natural disasters and epidemics, birth and death, sunrise and sunset, the changing seasons and the stars in the skies, the growth of plants and the life of animals. They even asked themselves what it all meant, why they were living in this world in the first place. Man was purportedly subject to the will of the spirits and the gods. This was the first explanation and narrative that formed the basis for the emergence of religions. In order to optimize the conditions of man's survival and to influence the course of events, man communicated with spirits and gods which he would both serve and offer sacrifices. Thus there came into being over the millennia the various spiritual and divine systems along with their respective rules and rituals – programs for living and

***** Martin Luther, *Assertio omnium articulorum M. Lutheri per bullam Leonis X. novissimam damnatorum*, WA 7, 98,40, 1521.

1 "In fact, all that I have created dreams of telling its own story and in one way or another manages to do so. The mountains write with their geological strata, the trees with rings in their trunks and lines in their leaves, the animals through the traces they carry of their ancestors before. Even a blade of grass writes and rewrites its biography. The universe is a book of recollections, the earth is a journal." Franco Ferrucci, *The Life of God (as Told by Himself)*, University of Chicago Press, Chicago, 1996, p. 100.

2 See: *Duden. Das Herkunftswörterbuch*, Dudenverlag, Mannheim, 2007.

3 See: Leo Festinger, *A Theory of Cognitive Dissonance*, Stanford University Press, Stanford, CA, 1957.

4 See: Karl Jaspers, *Vom Ursprung und Ziel der Geschichte*, Piper, Munich, 1949.

5 See: Karen Armstrong, *Die Achsenzeit. Vom Ursprung der Weltreligionen*, Siedler, Munich, 2006. See: Shmuel N. Eisenstadt (ed.), *Kulturen der Achsenzeit. Ihre Ursprünge und ihre Vielfalt*, Suhrkamp, Frankfurt am Main, 1987. Some scholars include the birth of Islam, which actually falls outside this model, in the "Axial Age"; see: Shmuel N. Eisenstadt, "Die Achsenzeit der Weltgeschichte," in: Hans Joas and Klaus Wiegandt (eds.), *Die kulturellen Werte Europas*, Fischer, Frankfurt am Main, 2005, pp. 60ff.

6 See: Wilhelm Nestle, *Vom Mythos zum Logos. Die Selbstentfaltung des griechischen Denkens von Homer bis auf die Sophistik und Sokrates*, Kröner, Stuttgart, 1940.

7 See: Bruno Snell, *Die Entdeckung des Geistes. Studien zur Entstehung des europäischen Denkens bei den Griechen*, Claassen & Goverts, Hamburg, 1946.

8 See the concept of "recording systems" used by Friedrich Kittler, in his work *Aufschreibesysteme 1800/1900*, Fink, Munich, 1985, p. 519.

surviving. Many of the rituals of the systems of spirits among primitive peoples, such as the sacrifice, were then retained by subsequent religious systems, the advanced systems of the gods.

Over millennia, these myths traveled across the globe along with the peoples from whom they derived, the dissemination of a given myth thus following the dispersion of a given people. In the process, they were interpreted afresh, varied, supplemented by new commentaries, elaborated, and expanded upon. The further evolution of what had originally been source of local and common experience took place over a period of millennia and across vast geographic expanses. Religious communities would repeatedly break away to form new religious communities and bring with them the old myths and narratives before subjecting these to further transformation. Over tens of thousands of years this ongoing reinterpretation and reworking of these myths took place orally. It was with the onset of encoding myths in written form that a new epoch of signification began.

The pivotal event occurred around 3,500 years B.C. with the invention of writing by the Sumerians and Egyptians. However, in his work *The Origin and Goal of History* (German original 1949, English translation 1953), Karl Jaspers drew attention to a second period that was decisive for civilization and religion, namely, the era spanning from 800 down to 200 B.C., which he termed the "Axial Age."[4] In this period, in four independent areas of culture, the philosophical and technological progress that still forms the intellectual basis of human civilization today and that represents the source of world religions was made simultaneously.[5] In China, it was Taoism and Confucianism that came into being; in India, Hinduism and Buddhism; in the Orient, Judaism and Zoroastrianism. The West was marked by Greek rationalism, by the transformation "from myth to logos"[6] and "the discovery of the intellect."[7] And it was only thanks to a radical innovation that this transformation was possible in the first place: around 700 B.C. vowel alphabetical writing first gained sway. The abstract written alphabet of the Greeks, which constituted an advance on the Phoenician script, enabled the spoken word to be reproduced without abbreviation. Writing became the decisive medium of the logos, the medium of the materialization of the spirit. Sequencing the infinite and continuous stream of sounds into a finite, limited repertoire of visual symbols is perhaps the most amazing achievement in the history of mankind. Written script is the invention of sequencing and thus as a method marks the beginning of other acts of sequencing, such as the sequencing of the genes.

The Written Word as Medium of Transcendence and Absence

As a result of sequencing, writing is the first technical carrying medium and storage system.[8] With writing, be it hieroglyphs and cuneiform, alphabetic scripts, syllabic scripts, or ideographical characters, tools emerged that humans could use to abstract from actual situations. Legends, myths, and rites were stored thanks to written characters on bone, clay, papyrus, stone, wood, bark, leather, parchment, and, finally, on paper. By writing, people were able to connect with other ages, with the past and the future, and with other places. People were able to tie experiences and knowledge of the past into the present through narrative, store knowledge of the present for the future, and transmit it to different places.

It was the advent of writing that first allowed communication to extend beyond location and the present time. Time and present form a unity in speech. With written characters that represent the spoken word, in a systematic and reproducible order, communication was free from the prison house of immanence, the *hic et nunc*. Spoken words could only be communicated from face to face. It implied the immediacy of bodily presence. Writing enabled the spoken word to leave the body, to be temporarily stored in a medium, and then to be incorporated into another body, translated there into nerve impulses and the metabolism, and interpreted as a message. The written word is a system of navigation, analogous to the stars which gave travelers orientation in the world over centuries. The written word is our first tool with which to navigate space and time, and indeed one which takes us beyond the borders of immediate sensory perception. If speech is the medium of immanence, then writing is the medium of transcendence, as it allows one to transgress the iron grid of space and time as scientifically defined by the four axes x, y, z, and t and determined by the body's natural sensory organs. In other words, transcendence is a technical property of the medium of writing. For this reason, writing is the ideal medium for practicing transcendence and yearning for it. If religion is a technique of transcendence, then writing, as a medium of transcendence, is the ideal medium for it. Like all cultural techniques, writing is not a neutral medium in this regard. As a technique it co-constitutes the content that it both generates and mediates.

Religion also needs writing and its power to cross space and time if it is to win out against rival religions. And writing was thus advanced and spread by priests – alongside the actors in commerce and the administration, for the first written records made by the Sumerians were not a matter of myths or verses, but were primarily agricultural tables and lists.

Prior to the preeminence of the written word, knowledge of all kinds was transmitted by word of mouth, but also by rituals, which stored and conveyed it by way of repetition and mimicry. Techniques, most especially those of knowledge transfer, do not necessarily replace one another, but can exist in parallel and then assume different tasks in the course of differentiation. The ritual of repetition was strongly reanimated in the twentieth century by the emergence of the technical media and sedimented as a technology. Thus, the invention of writing seemed to pave the way for religious knowledge in the longterm to free itself from the person who embodied the rituals and thus rendered them valid, liberating it from a structure in which through rituals one class monopolized knowledge. Shamanist rituals among the so-called primitive peoples promised healing, salvation, and protection. Priests and shamans (the term "shaman" derives from the Tungusish *šaman*, "the knowledgeable one") formed the class who laid claim to this monopoly. Writing essentially broke the monopoly because it is a medium of distribution, but did not in the process erase the desire for shamans. The success of artists such as Joseph Beuys, who claimed to be a modern shaman, not to mention the large number of followers of the priests and leaders of sects of all kinds in the twentieth century, goes to show that these needs persist. Tele-evangelists, like artists, are the shamans of the media age, and with their performances, recitals, and theatrical orchestrations they lay claim once again to the monopoly on knowledge and redemption. The electronic audiovisual media (radio, TV, video, computer) respond to this eternal desire. They permit the "physical" presence of religious leaders and priests across all spatial and temporal limits. These technologies are tele-media, i.e., media relating to distance (*tele*, Greek for far away, remote): television, telephone, telex/facsimile. As tele-technologies, or, to be more precise, technologies to overcome distance, the tele-media are obviously the technologies of transcendence. They are therefore the new and ideal support media for the religions and the transcendence they promise. The technical media continue the work of writing as the medium of transcendence. The media age multiplies the options for transcendence and thus opens the door to the return of religions. This may be a reason for the new impact of the religious in the public and political domain, whereby the holy scriptures serve now only as the legitimating basis to which indirect reference is made.

The sentence "In the beginning was the Word and the Word was with God, and the Word was God" at the beginning of the Gospel according to John (1:1–2) is the decisive statement in the Bible for the exhibition *Medium Religion*. We have no facts on the life of Jesus. We only have words, written down several decades after the death of the fictitious or real man from Bethlehem. Jesus is a being who exists qua words. God's medium, the medium of the life of Jesus, and indeed the medium of religion is that of the written word. This is the function of the Bible, as John the Apostle himself wrote, "Therefore many other signs Jesus also performed in the presence of the disciples, which are not written in this book; but these have been written so that you may believe that Jesus is the Christ, the Son of God; and that believing you may have life in His name." (John 20:30–31) The written word is the sole guarantee for the existence of Christ and that he is the Son of God. The written word is the medium of belief.

The texts collected together under the general term "Bible" were written with the intention of convincing readers of three truths. First, that Jesus existed; second, that he was the long-awaited Messiah; and, third, that he was the Son of God. These assertions were expressed through the medium of the written word. Jacques Derrida is thus correct in this respect when he writes that *"then it is without doubt a matter of language, or, to be more precise, of the idiom, literalness, the written word, as writing forms an irreducible and untranslatable element of each* revelation *and* each belief."[9]

However, the sentence beginning with the words "In the beginning was the word" contains a metaphysical problem, which is solved by the concrete poets with the pun, "In the beginning was the word *in*," as Timm Ulrichs put it. This assertion of a beginning represents the quintessential metaphysical proposition: one assumes that existence *has* a beginning.

If we follow Martin Heidegger's doctrine of ontological or ontic-ontological difference (the differentiation between being and essence),[10] then existence cannot have arisen from nothing, but must rather have always existed. If it has always existed, then existence cannot have had a beginning. What *can* have happened, however, is the transformation of the essent, that is, the beginning and end of the essent, and the transcriptions of this process. Thus, through this metaphysical proposition it becomes clear that religion offers neither ontology nor the embodiment of being. Instead it exists purely through the medium of the written word.

In *Civilization and its Discontents* (1930), Sigmund Freud writes that "[w]riting was in its origin the voice of an absent person."[11] Writing is per se the medium of absence, it was for centuries the most important of all the cultural techniques that serve the externalization, storage, and dissemination of thought. If writing is a medium of absence, then religion is itself a medium of absence, too. Since religion can only refer to the medium of the written word, to a certain extent, religion becomes one with the object of its description: the absent or hidden God, *deus absconditus* (Isiah 45:15). A fact can never convey anything about the hidden God, only written references can. The medium of absence answers to *absconditus*, and this absent God is reflected in the writings.

The contemporary dissemination of religious images through the electronic media of television, video, and the Internet represents nothing less than the continuation of the work conducted by the written word as a "language of absence": The Internet and television, which is now almost a thing of the past and is fast in the process of dissolving into new convergent technologies, assume the functions that the book possessed for millennia as the primary medium for religion – partly in the form of writing, but increasingly in the form of audio and video recordings and transmissions.

Evidently there are religions without a written tradition, and which rely on lore and ritual for dissemination and transfer, but it is those religions which are based on holy scriptures that have for thousands of years been vying for world supremacy. Therefore, religions have a technical basis: the written word and its continuation through technical media. With the changes in media the religions also changed, and they continue to change.

9 Jacques Derrida, "Glaube und Wissen. Die beiden Quellen der 'Religion' an den Grenzen der bloßen Vernunft," in: Jacques Derrida and Gianni Vattimo (eds.), *Die Religion*, Suhrkamp, Frankfurt am Main, 2001, p. 13; translated from the German by Jeremy Gaines.
10 See: Martin Heidegger, *Gesamtausgabe Bd. 24. Abt. 2, Vorlesungen 1923–1944. Die Grundprobleme der Phänomenologie*, Klostermann, Frankfurt am Main, 1975 [1927], p. 22.
11 Sigmund Freud, *Civilization and its Discontents*, Norton, New York, 1961, p. 38.

12 Gerardus van der Leeuw, *Phänomenologie der Religion*, Mohr, Tübingen, 1977 [1965], p. 498; translated from the German by Jeremy Gaines.

13 See: Carsten Colpe, "Sakralisierung von Texten und Filiationen von Kanons," in: Aleida Assmann and Jan Assmann (eds.), *Kanon und Zensur. Beiträge zur Archäologie der literarischen Kommunikation*, Fink, Munich, 1987, pp. 80–92.

14 Popular history – and here history proves to be the "true novel," as French historian of antiquity Paul Veyne put it aptly (see: Paul Veyne, *Comment on écrit l'histoire. Essai d'épistémologie*, Seuil, Paris, 1971, p. 10) – tells us that in the year 312 A.D. Constantine had a vision at Saxa Rubra, the battle for Rome. Indeed, a monogram of Christ supposedly appeared to him in a dream, proclaiming that this was a sign he would win the battle *(in hoc signo vinces)*. Out of gratitude for his consequent victory in the realm of reality, he is said to have converted to Christianity and made it the state religion. In actual fact, in a treaty of 313 A.D. which lent itself far less to being captured in paint, Constantine, the Emperor of the West, agreed the so-called "Milan Agreement" with Licinius, Emperor of the East, granting not just Christians but all citizens the right to belong to the religion of their choice. It may not have been until the year 380, some 68 years later under the reign of Emperor Theodosius I, that Christianity was officially declared the state religion, but in the Milan Agreement it had already won a privileged position. The Milan Agreement can be seen as a supplement and extension of the "Tolerance Edict" published by Emperor Galerius in early 311 A.D. This edict halted the persecution of Christians as well as making Christianity a *religio licita* (permitted religion). In other words, it was the first legal recognition of any kind granted to Christians.

The Problem of the Origin

Were we to enquire into the process how writings become "holy scriptures" from a literary critical standpoint, the answer would be: by means of canonization, origin, and restriction. "The writings become the holy book. The power of the holy word has been banished into this book. The boundaries have been drawn tightest in Islam, Judaism, and Christianity. Other religions also have their more or less cohesive holy books: the Vadas, the Avesta, the Buddhist Tripitaka, etc."[12] Only canonized religious writings are holy and possess religious authority. Carsten Colpe is of the opinion that in the history of religion only two independent canons emerged, namely, the Hebrew Bible and the Buddhist Tripitaka. All the other holy scriptures, the Koran, the Jaina canon, and the Confucian and Taoist scriptures are, he suggests, derived from these two.[13] It bears emphasizing that the objects summarized under the common heading of "holy scriptures" exhibit literary differences and their status differs from one religion to the next.

Despite the existence of extensive collections of scriptures, the process of establishing a religion can only be reconstructed to a limited extent. In the case of most religions, as stated, the written sources available were only penned decades after the death of the religion's founder and, for the most part, not even by eyewitnesses. The events, the foundation of the belief, and the content thereof had been passed down by oral tradition until they were written down. Even at this point, we must assume that in this oral tradition the contents were constantly related in a new way, interpreted, complemented and enriched with fragments of other narratives. An analysis of religious texts shows that they are the product of a continual process of rewriting; indeed over the millennia, research into the actual meaning of the religious scriptures, the exegesis of the text sources, has produced millions of books and thousands of competing religious communities. The study of the sources of religious texts has itself produced religions and the process of copy and paste has generated a variety of religious formats.

An exemplary instance of the problem of the origin and also of the power of legitimacy that arises at the same time from the medium of the written word is to be found in the *Historia ecclesiastica* or *Historia ecclesiae* which Emperor Constantine commissioned. Constantine, with whose person the historically erroneous story of the *in hoc signo vinces* at the Battle of Saxa Rubra is inextricably bound up,[14] commissioned Eusebius, Bishop of Caesarea (born 260/264; died 339/340) to write a history of the Church. Eusebius produced a history in ten volumes, stretching from the very beginnings of the Church the historical present, i.e., the year 324 A.D. It was the first time that a piece of critical, historical writing on Christian beliefs had been undertaken. A normative, simplified legal text, equipped with the gesture of legitimizing religion and a secular claim to power. This history delivered the benchmark against which all future histories of the Church would be judged, and anyone who diverged from the official line was branded a heretic. With the power of writing, Eusebius, as commissioned by Constantinople, devised a history of the Church and world which tallied with his and Constantine's view. In short, to put it bluntly, we are talking about a propaganda text.

This history of the Church, written at a distance of approximately 300 years after the emergence of Christianity, was written in Greek but survived over the centuries in Latin, Syrian, and Armenian manuscripts. Eusebius used numerous ecclesiastical monuments and documents, acts of martyrdom, letters, as well as extracts of old Christian writings and integrated them into his text as detailed quotations. His interpretation of sources was not impartial, but it served to legitimize the Christian religion and safeguard Emperor Constantine's rule. After the latter's death, Eusebius dedicated the openly partisan panegyric *Vita Constantini* [The Life of Constantine], a work which is comprised of four books and was designed to serve the incoming rulers as instructions on how to face the looming internal conflicts that existed within the Church.

It should be emphasized that Greek, the language in which Constantine had the *Historia ecclesiastica* written, was not in actual fact the language of the first Christians, or early Christians. They spoke Aramaic, a genetic subcategory of the Semitic languages. The early Christian texts, like the texts of Eusebius' history of the Church, are various links in a chain of transcriptions devoid of a palpable origin. For the reports go far beyond the life time of Christ: in the Christian narrative, pre-religious myths resurface that were passed on by word of mouth down through the millennia and in the course of which they were changed, until finally, in about 3,000 years, they were gradually written down, mixed further, and then differentiated. Thus, if Eusebius was writing a history of the Church, this was a history without an origin, indeed a history without original sources. The individual sources were texts from other languages which had, in turn, already been transcribed from other languages. In other words, Eusebius built his history of the Church on the foundations of a cascade of transcriptions, aimed at providing Constantine's rule with foundation and legitimization.

Through the transcriptions from language to language, from language to scripture, and from scripture to scripture the content of the texts, the legends, myths, rites, and memories were transcribed according to specific interests. Pre-religious myths and religious narratives and metaphors were transcribed as social facts; events were invented to back up fictions; old fictions were replaced by new ones which better fitted the contemporary *episteme*, which define the thought structures, insights, and knowledge of the respective epoch.

Morphology of Religions

Despite great differentiation and a wide range of narratives, the various religious reports resemble one another. The structure of the stories concerning the founders of the religions and their message is similar. The affinity between the rules for their structure and the similarity between the characters in the narratives and the functions of the actions in all religions, both classical and modern, is striking. The structural morphology of the folk tale, in other words, the phenomenon that the fairy tales with their changing content exhibit a shared immutable deep structure of action, as discovered by Vladimir Propp (1895–1970) back in 1928, could also be transferred to the systems of religion.[15] What we would need, therefore, is a work with the title "Morphology of the Religions," to follow on from the work of Vladimir Propp. Using a body of hundred folk tales, he was able to demonstrate that in Russian fairy tales there is a total of only seven characters and that the action can be reduced to (a maximum of) 31 functions. Of course, this analysis always revolves around a compositional core, which means that individual functions or characters may be left out. Like folk tales, the religious narratives also demonstrate many similar or joint features and structures. The systems of belief also consist of only a few basic elements – birth, calling, message, exile, death – and of variations on these.

The concordant morphological structure of the Gospels is less of an indication of their factuality than it is of their literary fictionality. It is clear to see that the four Gospels display the same structure, of course with the variations, omissions, and addenda that Propp discovered for the morphology of the fairy tale. The characters are: Jesus the hero, the Pharisees as villains, the false hero or the betrayer, the disciples as helpers, God as the dispatcher, and the miracles as donors. The action functions are the birth, the struggle against the Pharisees, the hero's deeds and miracles, the suffering, the death, and the resurrection of Christ.

Accordingly, if, in our search for rules of structure for the design of a morphology of religion, we restrict ourselves to modern religions, this is because in this case the source situation is clearer than it is with the establishment of ancient religions. Let us take three very well-known religious communi-

15 See: Vladimir Propp, *Morfologija skazki*, Academia, Leningrad, 1928. See: Vladimir Propp, *Morphology of the Folktale*, Indiana University, Bloomington, IN, 1958. See: Vladimir Propp, *Morphologie des Märchens*, Hanser, Munich, 1972.

ties of the modern era or the present day as examples so as to be able to define the structural elements that can be combined: Mormonism, the Jehovah's Witnesses, and the Church of Scientology.

In the Christian-Western cultural region there are a series of new religious formations that shape the content of Christianity in a clearly new form and legitimize themselves with new Christian sources (in addition to the Holy Scripture of the Old and New Testament). Like most religious communities, the Mormons, who, according to their religious self-understanding, belong to the family of the Christian churches, invoke the authority of their founder and the latter's spiritual awakening that entails God directly dictating the contents of belief to this founder. The founder of the Mormon movement, the Church of Jesus Christ of Latter-day Saints, was Joseph Smith, Jr. (1805–1844), who, whilst in pretrial custody, was murdered in a prison by an angry mob in 1844. In "Joseph Smith – History" ("JS-H"), his autobiographical text written in 1838, which forms a major part of *The Pearl of Great Price* that was to become one of the canonical holy texts of the Mormon Church, Smith reports that he had his "first vision" in 1820, followed, he claims, by 133 more revelations. Furthermore, he reports in one such vision in 1823, that the heavenly being Moroni appeared before him and showed him a hill in which ancient gold plates had been buried, but which he was allowed to take for himself only in 1828. A divine text had been engraved on these plates. With God's assistance, Smith translated this text into English before having to give the plates back. The source was, so to speak, deleted. In 1830, *The Book of Mormon. An Account Written by the Hand of Mormon upon Plates Taken from the Plates of Nephi* was published and the Church of Jesus Christ of Latter-day Saints was founded.

It is interesting to note that even within the Mormon Church it is not completely clear whether Joseph Smith, Jr. even had recourse to the physical plates for the trans-

lation. Smith is said to have possessed a "seer stone." The three witnesses of the Book of Mormon and his wife Emma report that Smith threw a magical seer stone into a hat, buried his face in it, and commenced translating and dictating.

The syncretic character of this new religion is clearly visible. The Mormons see themselves as early Christians. According to the Book of Mormon, the lost tribes of Israel divide up into the Nephites, who were believers, and the Lamanites, who committed apostasy. In the fifth century the Nephites were destroyed by the Lamanites. The prophet Moroni was said to be the last surviving Nephite and he apparently passed on the original contents of the Christian belief to Joseph Smith, Jr. in a revelation.

In Mormonism and many other religious communities, we find common structural elements; for example, the revelation or the handover of canonic texts: God gave Moses the Ten Commandments on stone slabs, Smith received the sacred texts on golden plates. The meaning of these texts was only made accessible to Smith with God's assistance. He is therefore the chosen one, the one appointed by God. The source upon which the religion is based was thus a text that was handed over or supplied directly by God.

Alongside the Presbyterians (as of 1553), the Congregationalists (as of 1580), the Methodists (as of 1738), and the Adventists (as of 1863), the Jehovah's Witnesses are a Christian religious community that, like the Mormons, derive their faith from a strong belief in the Bible, that is, from the interpretation of the Holy Scripture. For this reason, the religious community established in 1876 by Charles Taze Russell originally called itself the "Bible Student Movement" and started out as a Bible reading group. Russell was originally a member of the Congregational Church. It was only as of 1931 that the Bible Students started calling themselves "Jehovah's Witnesses."

Russell propagated Christ's second coming, most likely in the year 1874, and the "earthly phase of the Kingdom of God" as of 1914. From 1879 he started publishing a magazine, *Zion's Watch Tower and Herald of Christ's Presence* (today *The Watchtower Announcing Jehova's Kingdom*), that has a circulation of tens of millions today. For the Jehovah's Witnesses, the basis of their faith is the Bible which contains the religious truth revealed by God. However, in their interpretation of the Bible, they differ from other religious communities on many scores. They deny the Trinity, for example. God himself is a benevolent, loving God and an invisible spirit. The resurrection of Christ should not be understood physically. Jehovah's Witnesses believe in the restoration of paradise on earth. When Armageddon comes, the Jehovah's Witnesses are the only ones who will be under Jehovah's special protection. Russell did not assert that he received Christ's message directly from God, but referred exclusively to the Bible. However, for him the aspect of exegesis, of correct interpretation, is of vital importance. From this viewpoint, he too is a chosen one, or "the leading body," "anointed and guided by God's holy spirit." *The Watchtower* always demonstrates the current state of exegesis, which is binding. Like the Jews, the Jehovah's Witnesses are chosen as a community; accordingly, they will be the only organization that Jehovah will offer especial protection and whose survival he will guarantee when the lost paradise is restored. The community's extreme missionary character is based on this promise. People have to become Jehovah's Witnesses now in order to be able to be saved later.

The Church of Scientology works with a similar dramatization of fantasies relating to the end of time. In his work published in 1950, *Dianetics*, science fiction author L. Ron Hubbard defined his Church of Scientology as "an applied religious philosophy," as he himself called it. In his book *Du mußt dein Leben ändern*[16] [You Must Change Your Life] (2009), Peter Sloterdijk investigated Hubbard's formal religious strategies and his reconstruction of the phenomenon church

as a "valuable elucidation of the general conditions for the establishment of religions" in an exemplary fashion. Incidentally, this chapter goes by the telling title of "There are no religions." Taking Hubbard as his example, Sloterdijk is able to demonstrate what it means "when a company selling old familiar autosuggestion methods can be expanded to create a globally operative psychagogic business with claims on religion."[17] Hubbard developed psychotechnics or rather gave instructions for the psychotechnics with which "to survive in the jungle warfare of egotism."[18] The syncretic character of Hubbard's religion is typical in its imitation of "original religions," shedding light on "the fabrication and constitution of 'religion' in general."[19] "The fates of Olympism and the way that the Church of Scientology is operated allow us to see that religion in the sense that the exploiters of the terms understand it does not exist – and never has existed. […] What we are actually dealing with […] are more or less misinterpreted anthropo-technological exercise systems and sets of rules and regulations on self-realization through one's inner and outer deportment."[20] With the Church of Scientology it is possible to recognize the self-congratulatory system behind this church and "the founder cult without boundaries": "The celebration of the master as the one who has aroused mankind runs through the entire scientological media sphere."[21] The psychotherapeutic dimension and the fictionality of every religion are particularly noticeable in the Church of Scientology.

The strict controls and hierarchy, the persecution of dissenters, two things for which the Scientologists are reproached, are also the brainchildren of the early Christian church and its deadly inquisition. The missionary zeal of the Scientologists is a mild version of the militant missionary journeys made by Paul of Tarsus.

The history of Paul again highlights the parallel structures of narratives on religious founders: born in Cilicia to Jewish parents, Paul of Tarsus, an educated scholar of Greek,

16 Peter Sloterdijk, *Du mußt dein Leben ändern. Über Anthropotechnik*, Suhrkamp, Frankfurt am Main, 2001
17 Ibid., p. 134 ; translated from the German by Jeremy Gaines.
18 Ibid., p. 168.
19 Ibid., p. 134.
20 Ibid.
21 Ibid., p. 161.

originally followed the disciples of Jesus of Nazareth, whom he had never met. In 32 or 33 A.D., apparently on his way to Damascus, he had his famous calling or conversion experience. Saul did not change his name to Paul as the popular, but incorrect saying goes. His change of religion did not imply a change of name; instead, Paul always did have two given names as was quite customary in the Greco-Roman-Hellenic world: "Saul, who was also called Paul." (Acts 13:9) In his letters, the apostle always used his name Paul, while the second name Saul, or in Hebrew שָׁאוּל [Sha'ul], was used in the familiar setting of his home.[22]

Paul's call as the "Apostle of the Gospel for the People" ("Letter to the Galatians," 1:15f) belongs to a series of less recent appearances of Christ which he had probably heard reports about the first time he visited Jerusalem. The versions in the story of the Apostles contradict one another. In one, Paul only saw a light, while his companions only heard a voice. In another version, his companions saw the light but did not hear the voice. Basically, the report is formulaic: God revealed himself to Paul and addressed a message to him directly. The kind of revelation, conversion, and vocation that cannot be verified directly form the beginning of his mission.

Called by God approximately two or three years after the death of Jesus of Nazareth, Paul composed his famous epistles around 50 to 60 years A.D., roughly seventeen to eighteen years after the crucifixion. His epistles – of which today only seven are attributed to Paul – are older than the four Gospels and yet were written without any personal knowledge of Jesus.

As with the modern sects, so for Paul, his transmissionary teachings formed the basis of his theology of the imminent approach of the end of the world. Paul preached that only belief could save, that all, even the heathens, could be saved in this way. This is why Paul had to evangelize, in order to inform the whole world. The letters serve as a medium of belief and as a means of spreading the belief. The connection between belief and writing, between the expectation of redemption and a message of redemption cannot be portrayed more clearly.

Performativity of the Written Word

"And the Word became flesh, and dwelt among us […]." (John 1:14) With this statement from the Gospel according to St. John, the process of the transition from the immaterial sphere of the mind to the material sphere of the body is described. The written word transforms itself into a body. This transformation is one of the most astonishing of Christianity's claims, but in truth it is in the tradition of ghost stories. In all of the latter, invisible ghosts suddenly appear as visible beings, that is, as if nebulous then at least as slightly material apparitions.

The power of this quotation stems not just from God becoming flesh, but from the belief in the power of the word. If the word and/or writing is the only source of legitimacy, then the power of religion derives from the power of the word, the power of the Holy Scripture, as this stems from God. Belief in the power of the word thus invests belief itself with power.

Freedom is an effect of the written word. In the case of the Phoenician alphabet, which knows no vowels, a teacher was required to instruct the reader and to help him place the absent vowels in the right place in order to construct the meaning of the word. Not until the introduction of an alphabet including vowels by the Greeks around 900 B.C. did an autonomous reader come into being. Because now no expert in the script was required who inserted the vowels on the reader's behalf. This autonomous, emancipated reader fulfilled the conditions for Immanuel Kant's notion of Enlightenment perfectly, namely, "to make use of one's own understanding without direction from another."[23]

Judaism and Christianity constitute a kind of regression compared with the worlds peopled by many gods. The scholars of the scriptures did not wish to hand over their power and monopoly on the interpretation of the word to "laymen" or "amateurs."

22 See: Reinhold Then, *Mit Paulus unterwegs*, Verlag Katholisches Bibelwerk, Stuttgart, 2003, pp. 17–23.

23 Immanuel Kant, "What Is Enlightenment?," in: idem, *Critical Philosophy*, Cambridge University Press, Cambridge, MA, 1999, p. 17.

Jesus of Nazareth was thus, as a reformer of Judaism, in conflict with the scholars of the scriptures. He embodied the revolt of the amateur against the expert. Jesus referred to the readers' freedom, as was granted by writing per se and its essence. He knew that the script itself made him free. Not until later did the Church of Christianity legitimize the results of his reform of Judaism, his way of reading the scriptures as approved by God because he was God's son. He himself did not need his own arguments as he knew that an alphabet, which included vowels, in any case empowered him as an autonomous reader. His autonomy does not require the support of an absolute master such as God. This argument and recourse to God is contradicted by writing itself, as the freedom of interpretation is part and parcel of the written word. Any limitation of the freedom of the word, such as mystifying it as Holy Scripture, is a form of repression that leads to intolerance and inquisition.

While in former times it was the priests and shamans as the monopoly holders on ritual who had the power in their hands, it was later the scholars of the scriptures who possessed the monopoly of belief/knowledge, and thus the power. Today, it is lawyers and politicians who with their words take decisions that decisively change the life of the addresses in a material manner, too. A judge's sentence can place a person in prison, a politician's view can force citizens to pay higher taxes. In today's terminology, this power of language to effect real changes may be considered the essence of performativity. The quote from the Gospel according to St. John may thus be regarded as a reference to the performativity of writing and thus the power of writing over the life of the believers. Church orders, monastic orders, orders of monks, the plethora of church organizations and operations, from prayer through to the Inquisition, all rest on the power of languages. The essence of religion stems from the essence of the written word and its performativity.

From the philosophy of language we know that language is not just a system of rules but also a system of commands, a system of signs which effectuates tangible change. In the twentieth-century philosophy of language we refer to this relationship between representation and reality as "performative turn," principally formulated by John Langshaw Austin in his 1962 work *How to Do Things with Words*[24]. Not only is language descriptive of facts, it is also constitutive of them. In this way, holy scriptures have led peoples into war. Had the opponents restricted themselves to wars of words, there would have been no developments beyond the level of theological dispute. But when these words were converted into action and the medium of absence transformed into the flesh of physical reality, war was the result. This performative act was played out in no clearer form than the original scene of the Judeo-Christian religion, namely, in the original scene of the Christian religion as the crucifixion of Christ. At the moment when the Romans saw that the words of Christ could change reality, they thought they had to crucify him. As performative act, the word of religion becomes the violence of one man enacted upon another. The written word is recognized as sacred: its authors and exegesists even purport to speak in the name of God. At that moment, the written word has the ability to transform into the medium of action, or into the medium of the sword. That the word became flesh means: "The word becomes the sword. In the name of the word I unsheathe my sword." The fact that the holy scriptures can also be a medium of charity, offering instruction of respecting others, a medium of devoted love and of non-egotistical intention, is something one might forget when casting a glance at the bloody history of humanity.

The aspect of performativity also emerges clearly in the function of religious texts as instructions for ritually repeated acts. In his book *Du mußt dein Leben ändern* Peter Sloterdijk describes religions as systems of "zones for exercises." Religious texts can also be a medium of part spiritual and part physical exercises, latched onto the text of the book. Blaise Pascal captured this

24 See: John Langshaw Austin, *How to Do Things with Words. The William James Lectures Delivered at Harvard University in 1955*, Harvard University Press, Cambridge, MA, 1962.

context in a famous formulation, which Louis Althusser has passed down to us as follows: "Kneel down, move your lips in prayer and you will believe!"[25]

Religion Is the Medium, the Media Are Religion

Religion was from the outset not only tied to media, but was and is itself a medium. As stated, all communications technologies are tele-technologies (telephone, television, facsimile, etc.). In this function of bridging spatial and temporal distances such as we are aware of owing to the natural sensory organs, and thus use technology to overcome the four prison bars or coordinates of space-time by technical means, that is, free man from the prison house of time and space, technology comes close to some of the promises made by theology. The notion of the "angel" is an early derivation of the Greek word for messenger, *ággelos*. The word *Engel* entered into the German language through the Arianic missionaries (Middle High German *engel*, Old High German *engil*, Gothic *aggilus*, Dutch *engel*, Old English *engel*, Swedish *ängel*) and denotes God's messenger, the intermediary between God and man. The angels were thus those who brought God's messages, they originally had a function in terms of news transmission. What the technical media promise is comparable to what religion has always held in prospect: the overcoming of time and space and the promise of eternal life. After drawing and writing, media such as photography, the telegraph, the telephone, film, radio, TV, video, computer, and the Internet, as well as all the other inventions of the last 150 years, are essentially the technical redemption of the religious promise, the proof of its feasibility in terms of the apparatus.

With my concept of "theo-technology" I seek to summarize this proposition: tele-technology is essentially always theo-technology. Religion is continued by the apparatuses of the tele-media and supplemented in the process. This makes it clear that religion itself is a proto-medium. Precisely as a medium of absence, religion is the medium per se, because it seems to render present something that is absent. It is the task and objective of every medium to render that which is absent in time and place present. Religion is the proto-medium, the first medium, the original medium of all media.

Religion has promised the immortality of our soul; the hard drives of our computers save traces of our individuality. Religion has promised us levitational phenomena, to float freely; airplanes assist us in our endeavor to overcome gravity. Religion has shown us how prophets walk across water; hovercraft vessels glide with us across the sea. Religion has promised us the transformation of water into wine; chemistry has fulfilled the dream of converting substances. Religion offered us events of the sort which are now broadcast directly into our houses each night on the evening news. In his book *Angels: A Modern Myth* Michel Serres described in 1993 how many concepts and phenomena that now occur in informatics and the new technologies correspond to concepts that philosophers formulated in Medieval times in angelology, in the study of angels.[26]

Theo-technology does not get us closer to God, but makes us more similar to God, even if only in the form of prosthetic gods. Thus, Sigmund Freud wrote in his essay *On Civilization and Its Discontents* that science and technology "are an actual fulfilment of every – or of almost every – fairy-tale wish. [...] Long ago he formed an ideal conception of omnipotence and omniscience which he embodied in his gods. To these gods he attributed everything that seemed unattainable to his wishes, or that was forbidden to him. One may say, therefore, that these gods were cultural ideals. Today he has come very close to the attainment of this ideal [...]. [...] Man has, as it were, become a kind of prosthetic God. When he puts on all his auxiliary organs he is truly magnificent; but those organs have not grown on to him and they still give him much trouble at times."[27]

The religions reveal their medial character and the media reveal their religious traits specifically in the phenomenon of repetition, namely, in the ritual. In all religions, ideally

25 Louis Althusser, *Ideologie und ideologische Staatsapparate. Aufsätze zur marxistischen Theorie*, VSA, Hamburg, 1977, p. 138; translated from the German by Jeremy Gaines.
26 See: Michel Serres, *Angels: A Modern Myth*, Flammarion, Paris, 1995 (original French edition 1993).
27 Freud 1961, pp. 38f.

28 See: Sloterdijk 2009, p. 16.

29 Ibid., p. 12; translated from the German by Jeremy Gaines.

30 See: Hans Gerald Hödl, "Alternative Formen des Religiösen," in: Johann Figl (ed.), *Handbuch Religionswissenschaft. Religionen und ihre zentralen Themen*, Tyrolia, Innsbruck, Vandenhoeck & Ruprecht, Göttingen, 2003, pp. 507f.

31 See: Hubert Knoblauch, *Religionssoziologie*, de Gruyter, Berlin, New York, 1999, p. 204.

32 Back at the end of the 1970s, commentators already pointed to the linkage of TV and religion. See: George Gerbner and Kathleen Connolly, "Television as New Religion," in: *New Catholic World*, vol. 221, no. 1322, March/April 1978, pp. 52–56. See: Hans-Jürgen Benedict, "Fernsehen als Sinnsystem?," in: Wolfram Fischer and Wolfgang Marhold (eds.), *Religionssoziologie als Wissenssoziologie*, Kohlhammer, Stuttgart et al., 1978, pp. 117–135. See also: Horst Albrecht, *Die Religion der Massenmedien*, Kohlhammer, Stuttgart et al., 1993.

33 See: Knoblauch 1999, p. 205.

34 See: http://en.wikipedia.org/wiki/Televangelism, November 10, 2010.

prayers are spoken daily. Specific transmission formats are followed each day on TV or at the computer or repeatedly played on video or a PC. On the buttons that define our perception of the world, our culture, and our view of ourselves stands "repeat" and "replay." Among other things, the cultic rituals had the role of storing knowledge by repetition and passing it on. This function was then assumed by the technology of writing. The holy scriptures, be they chiseled in stone or written on papyrus, strengthened and enhanced this function of ritual by giving this knowledge an absolute status and presenting it as God's knowledge. Technology assumed this function of rituals, but rendered it democratic by ending the monopoly on knowledge and making it universally accessible – with the invention of movable type by Johannes Gutenberg. Electronic technology is thus the profane form given to the record and repeat functions of ritual and writing.

The possibility of repetition is a characteristic par excellence of every technical medium that shapes our present. Repetition is also a central tenet of religious exercises.[28] Peter Sloterdijk has even gone so far to show in his work *Du mußt dein Leben ändern* that there is no religion or religions, but there are merely "misunderstood systems of exercise, regardless of whether these are practiced collectively (traditionally in church, ordo, umma, or sangha, for example) or in personal interaction with their own 'God' with whom modern citizens take out their insurance."[29]

The process of secularization, the extraction of various areas of life from their definition by the Christian faith, did not lead to the slow and complete demise of religion, but to a loss of traditional religiousness, while at the same time new forms of religion arose that accord with the increased individualization of society.[30]

"Media religiousness"[31] as is shaped by ritual repetitions, occurs above all in the mass medium of TV and in the medium of the Internet, which is detached from time: While the former once brought together entire nations before the TV screen in ritual, it is now the epidemically disseminated videos that are viewed again and again on millions of computers.[32] It remains to be seen just how the change from TV as the house altar with a fixed program over to handheld devices that are constantly connected to data from the Internet impacts on media religiousness. Seen superficially, this seems to correspond to a difference between Sunday churchgoing, coupled with clear systems of order and symbols, on the one hand, and private syncretistic religious practices as are socially anchored through the visible "like it" statements by Facebook friends, YouTube users, etc., on the other. The users compile the content of different religions, sects, and cult groups, and they respond to a medium, in which the Old Testament is only a click away from the channeled messages of Aleister Crowley. This is reminiscent of the fact that for all the structural consideration of the media as a religion, many religious groupings (the USA is a prime example here) use electronic media to communicate religious content. As early as the 1950s, the large religious associations worked together with U.S. TV channels and established decidedly successful TV formats.[33] In 2006, there were 1,600 radio stations and 240 TV stations in the United States spreading religious content around the clock. Televangelists[34] hope for a sudden revelation among their viewers. In Europe, TV stations such as bibel.tv, k-TV, or ERF (Evangeliums-Rundfunk Fernsehen) [Gospel-broadcasting Television] only reach a five-digit or at most a six-digit audience each day.

Civilizing Religion, Art, and the Media

If we consider the mass-media character of religion and at the same time the religious character of media, it is obvious – and this contradicts the Hegelian conception of the relationship between the two – how little they have diverged from one another. It is precisely this obsession with immortality and death, areas of intrinsic importance for religion, which shows art to be a rival of religion. Circulation in the mass media promises an ever greater sense of immortality than religion ever could. Andy Warhol, for example, linked the star cult with the religious heritage of the arts. Anyone who sat for a Warhol portrait hoped to mask their own mortality, as from the very outset Warhol photographed and decorated so many immortals. Indeed, Albrecht Dürer's self-portraits are also exemplary for how the artist has been pressing (in the image of Christ) for art to be seen as religion and for the artist to be seen as a savior. This sacred side of art is naturally thoroughly contradictory when seen in the same context as the demands of Modernity, which has ever since G. W. F. Hegel seen itself as freeing itself of religion. Art's distinctly non-modern character can be seen in its stagings of death, its fantasies of immortality, and its image of the artist as some sort of God of creation or long-suffering hero. It is not the art which appears in churches commissioned by religion which is a nuisance, no: it is so-called "free" art which acts as if it were a religion, or at least a replacement for religion in all the formal and medial spheres within which it operates.

Just as there can be no civil religion nowadays, there is also no real civil art. I am deriving the concept of the "civil" here from "civilization," the totality of all living conditions improved by advances in science and technology, which are inseparably linked to an ideal of equality and liberty, to a structure in which every individual, without having to wait for the promised afterlife or to bow down to a genius artist or a religious prophet, has the same opportunities to realize his/her own self and projected world. The precondition for a civil religion *(religion civile)*[35] is the separation of state and church. This would mean that a civil art, and likewise the civil media, would have to shed all their religious aspects.

With the Enlightenment, or to be more precise, the ideals of the French Enlightenment, the task was set to civilize religions by consciously rendering their media-based character explicit – a call that the ZKM's exhibition *Medium Religion* has followed. It would likewise be necessary in a civil society to reduce the religious character of the media, i.e., to not simply believe all the media content and ignore what our reason tells us, just as we do with regard to religious contents. Sigmund Freud hoped that reason could be strengthened such that it would emerge victorious over the passions and the feeling of powerlessness and helplessness, and that humans would then no longer succumb to the illusion that religion afforded protection. As he noted with optimism: "[…] the voice of the intellect is a soft one, but it does not rest till it has gained a hearing. This is one of the few things about which one may be optimistic respecting mankind's future – something, moreover, of no mere trivial significance."[36] The way towards such an optimistic enlightened future lies in the recognition of religion as medium.

35 See: Jean-Jacques Rousseau, *Du contrat social ou Principes du droit politique*, Marc-Michel Rey, Amsterdam, 1762.
36 Sigmund Freud, "The Future of an Illusion," in: Freud 1991, p. 238.

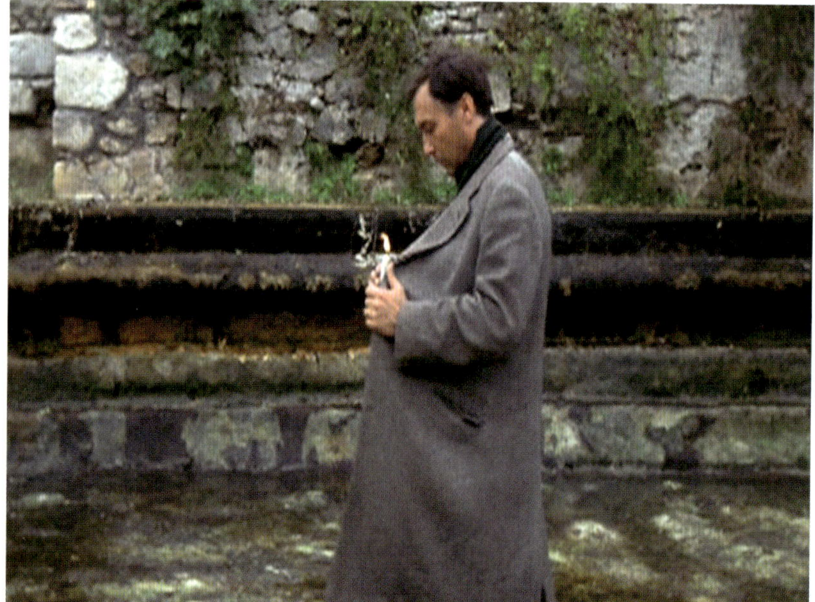

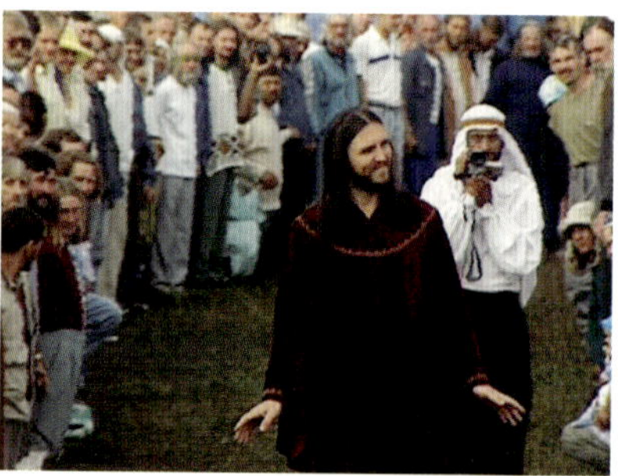

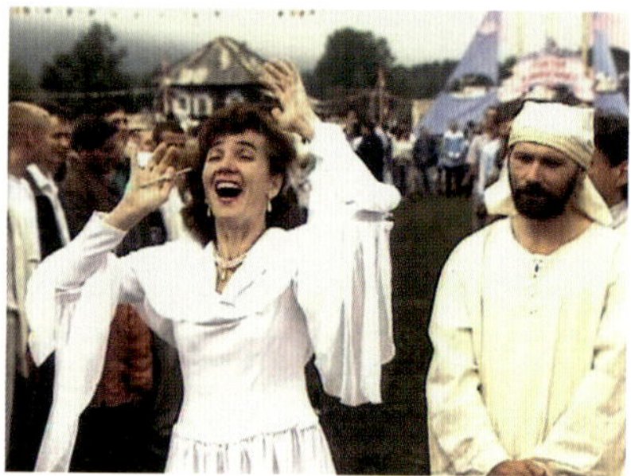

In this video lecture, the media theorist and philosopher Boris Groys combines an item on the role of religion as a medium with a collage of selected historical as well as contemporary film extracts. The video shows both the correlation with and the gap between what we hear in the media and what we see there, and in this way it furnishes insight into the relationship existing between image and word in our media-managed world. So here, the audiovisual medium of video does not serve, as is usual in mass media today, the effective distribution of information or of propaganda for ideologies, but much rather makes an issue out of video itself as a medium. The difference between the private and the public use of video becomes visible, as well as endlessly looped video as the contemporary form of a ritual.

Boris Groys
*1947 in East Berlin,
formerly German Democratic
Republic, today Federal
Republic of Germany,
lives and works in Karlsruhe,
Cologne, and New York

Religion as Medium, 2006,
video lecture on DVD,
color, sound, 25 min,
stills from a digital copy

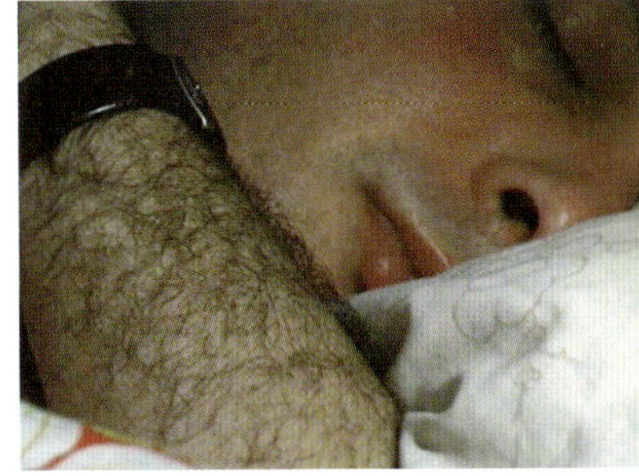
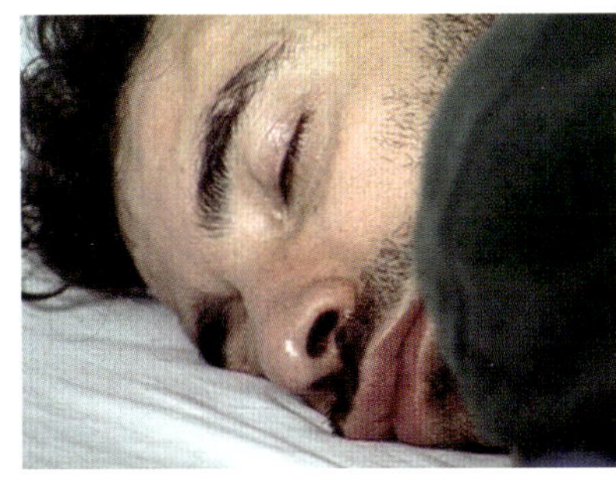
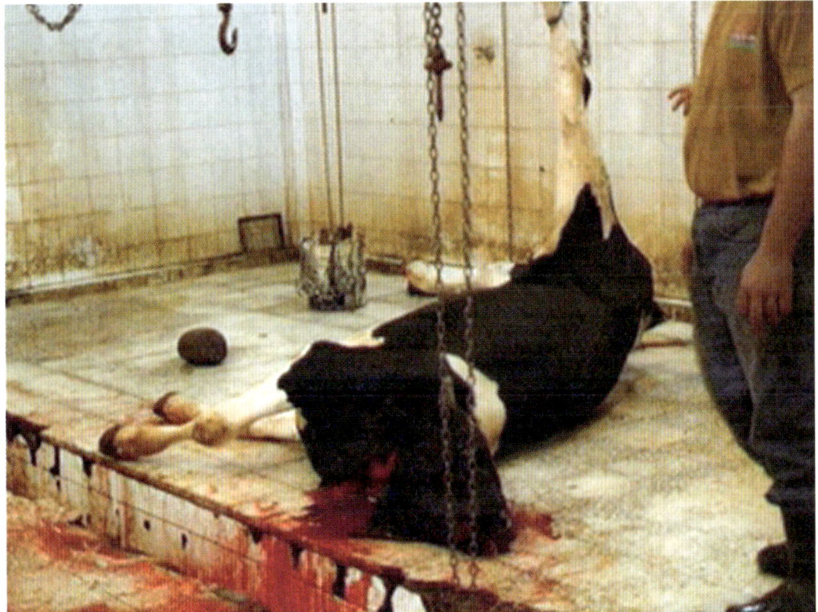
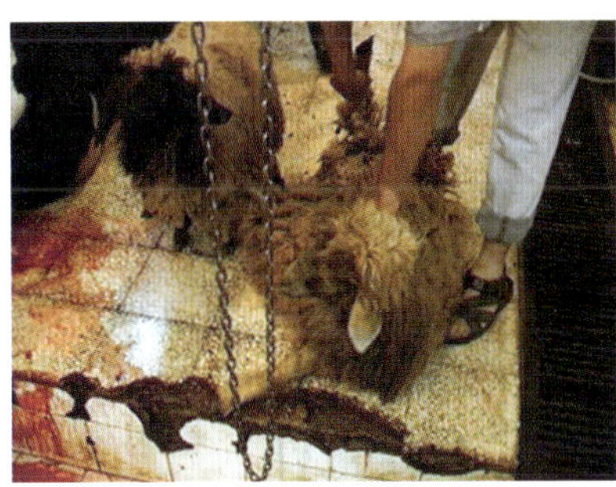
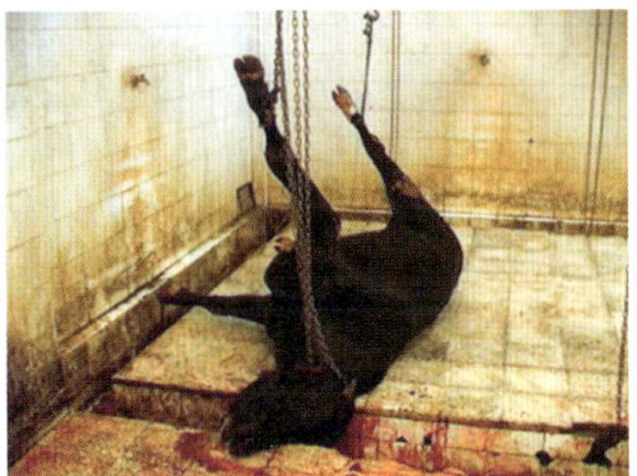
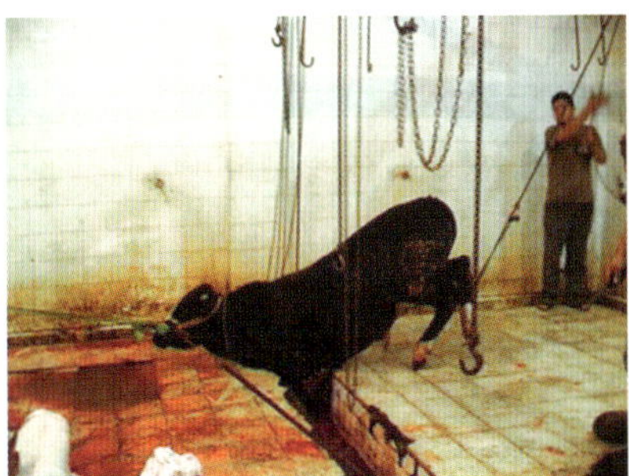
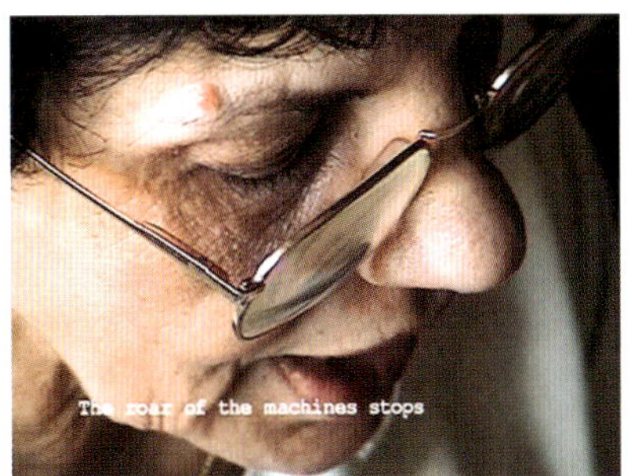

Jalal Toufic
*1962 Beirut, Lebanon,
lives and works in Beirut

*The Sleep of Reason. This Blood
Spilled in My Veins*, 2002,
video, color, sound, 32 min,
stills from a digital copy

The video *The Sleep of Reason. This Blood Spilled in My Veins* documents the ritual slaughter of two cows and two sheep, which Jalal Toufic sets in direct contrast to sequences of people sleeping. "The organic dying of a (resurrectable) human is nothing compared to that of an animal, for example, of a bull in a corrida; the only phenomenon of equal intensity is the resurrection of a human…," so Toufic comments. Attempting a religious exaltation and glorious fulfillment of basic existence through rituals of penitence, martyrdom, and sacrificial death in the religious traditions of Islam are the central motifs of his literary and philosophical texts and films.

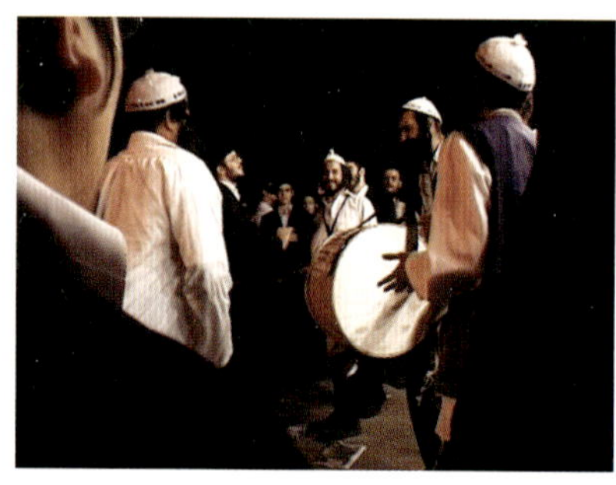
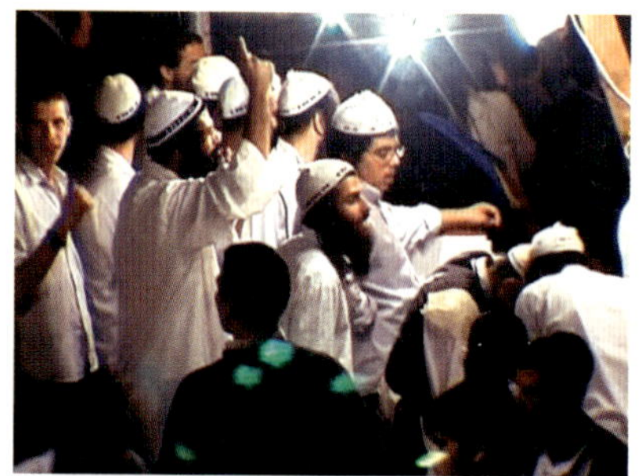
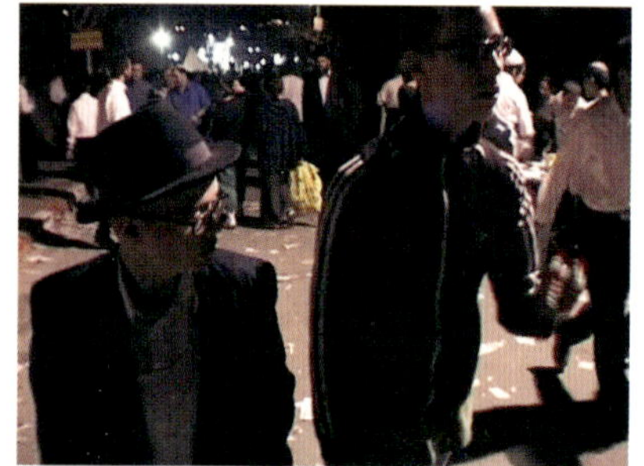
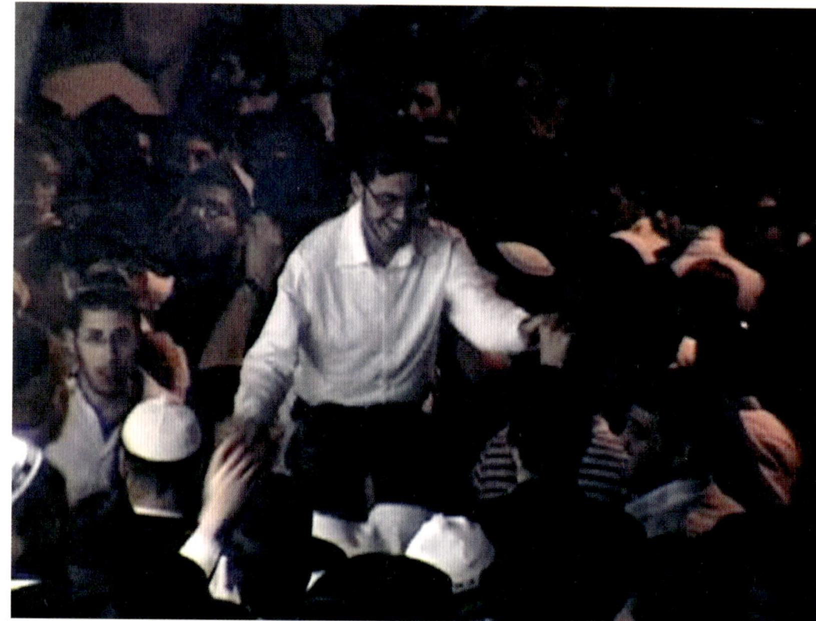
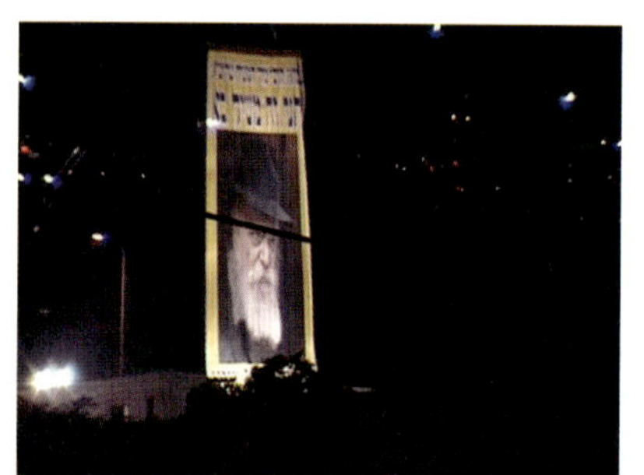
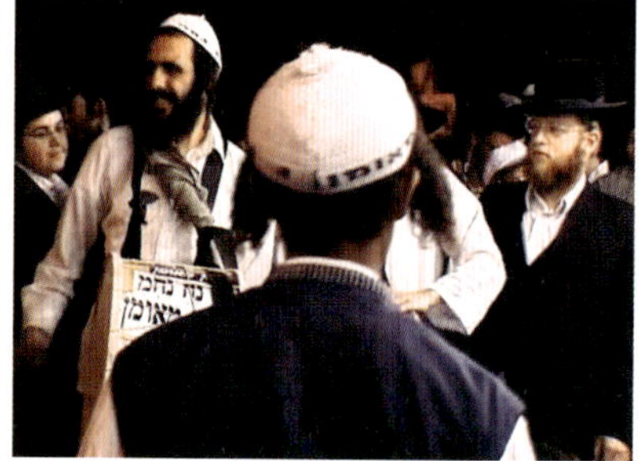
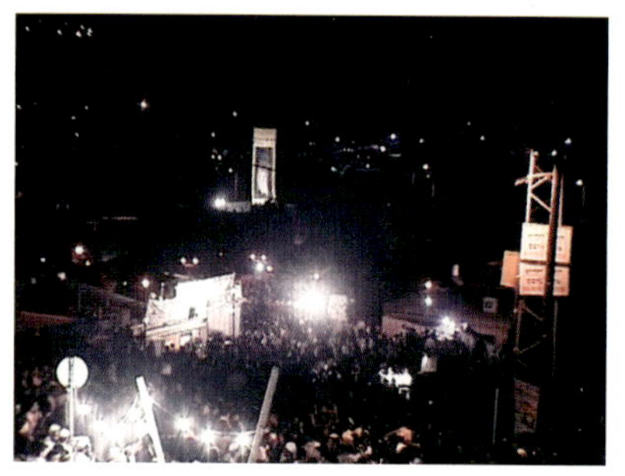
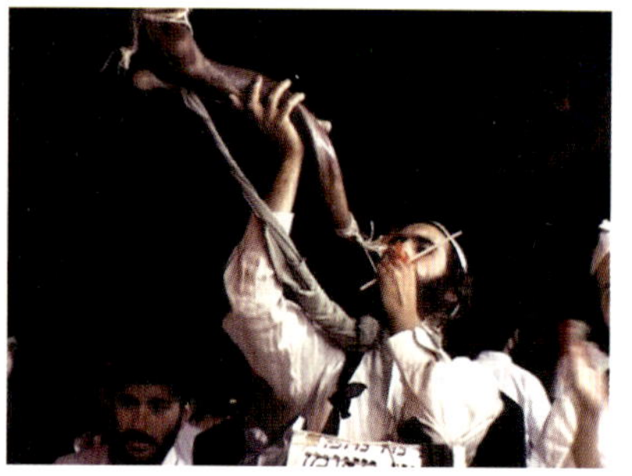

Oreet Ashery
*1966 in Jerusalem, Israel,
lives and works in London

Dancing with Men, 2003,
video, color, sound, 3 min,
stills from a digital copy

The artist describes the overwhelming feeling of belonging,
history, and home she experienced when dancing together
with hundreds of orthodox Jewish
men at the religious celebrations
of "Lag BaOmer."

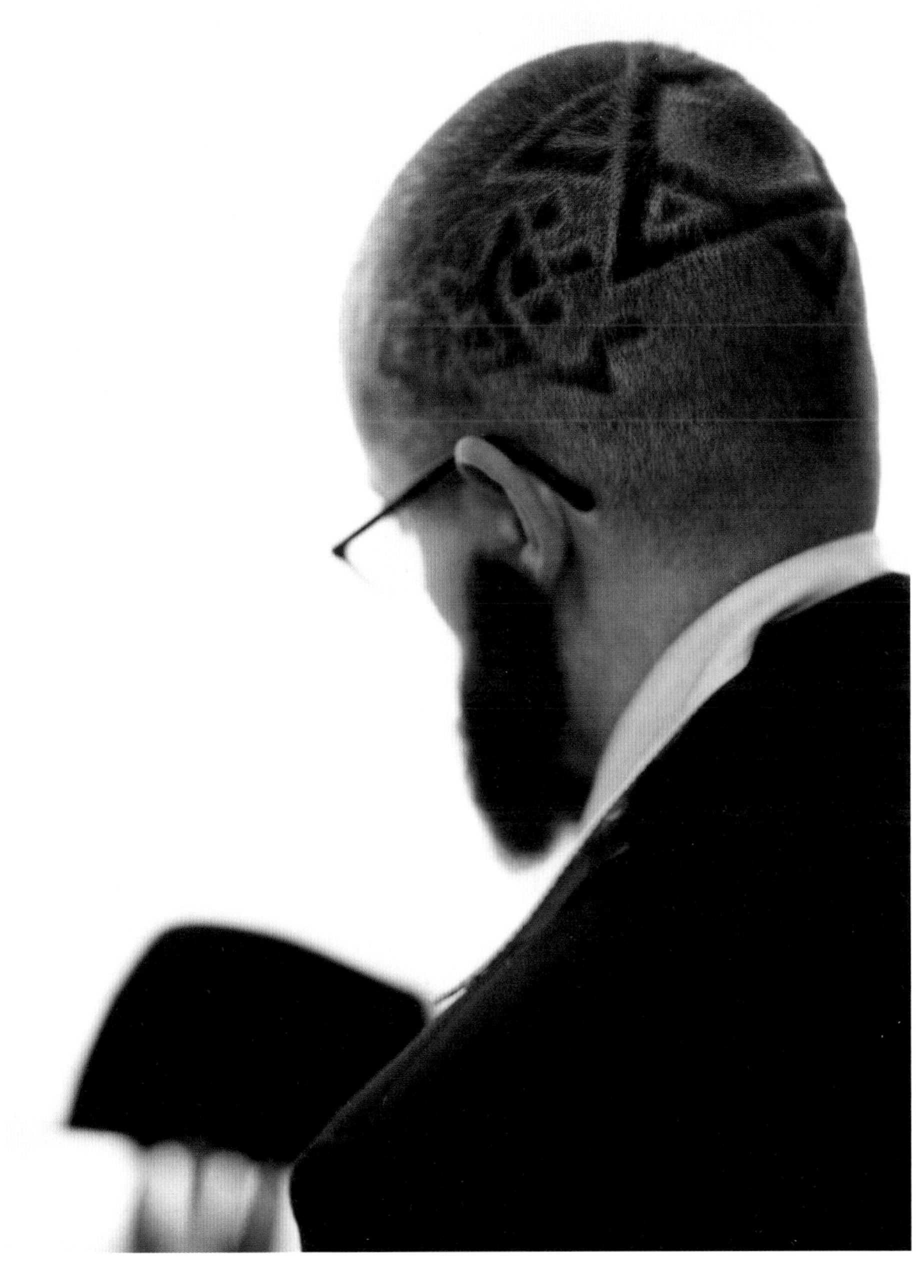

Oreet Ashery

*Self Portrait as
Marcus Fisher 1–5*, 2000,
5 photographs
(inkjet print, original: Polaroid),
101.5 × 80 cm each

In Hebrew "Mar-Cus" means
"Mr. Cunt."

By devising Marcus Fisher as her male alter ego, the London-based artist Oreet Ashery sets off a visual and performative examination of cultural, religious, and sexual identity. In her interventions as an orthodox Jew in picture-perfect attire, she confronts her secular environment with the explicitly "other," thereby probing the limits of multicultural and multi-religious societies. By confronting orthodox Jewish tradition with its own taboos, such as homosexuality, transvestism, and sexuality, Ashery simultaneously describes her own "queer" return to this very tradition.

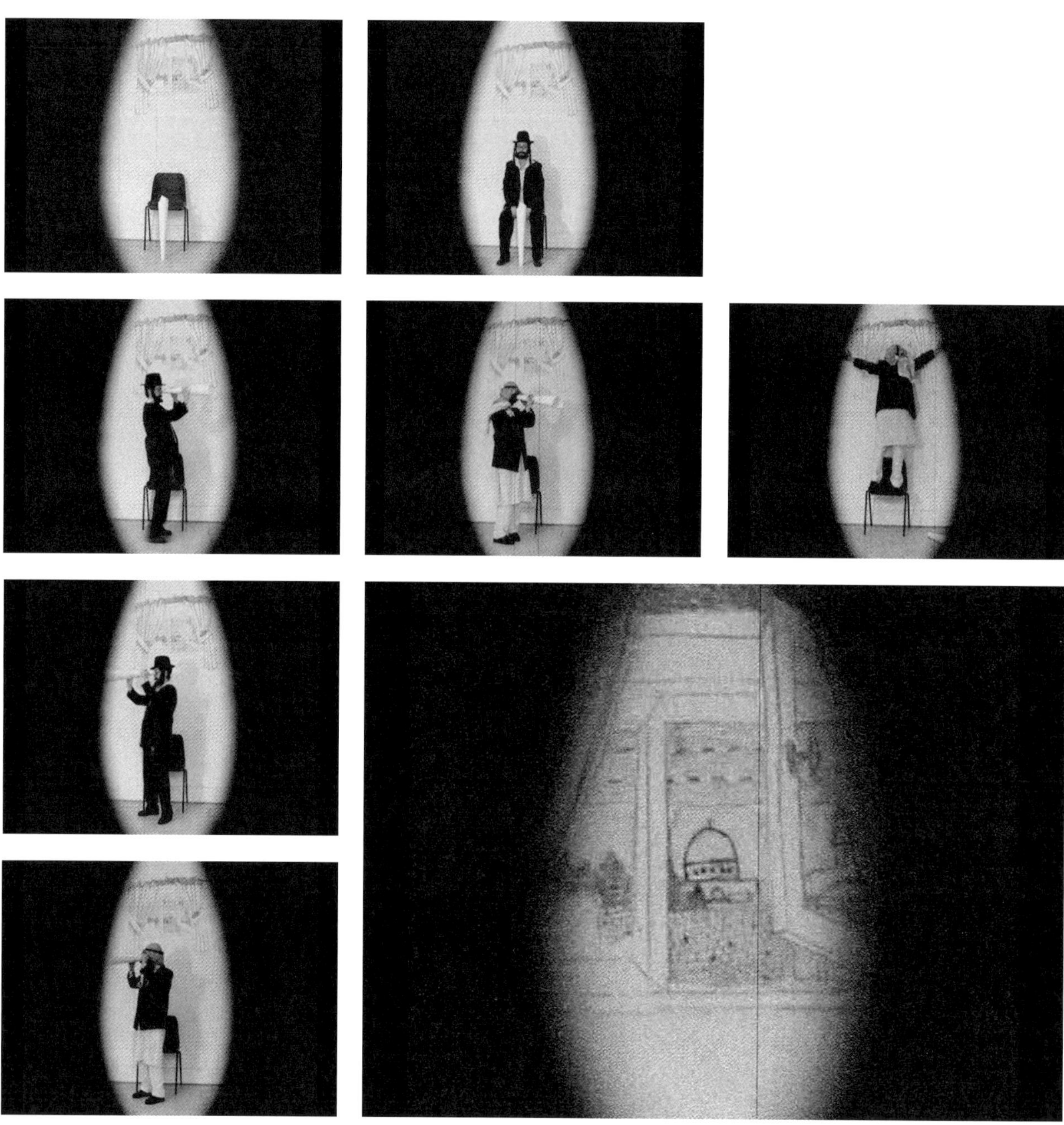

In her performances, interventions, and photographs, as well as in her video and textual works, Oreet Ashery examines questions of cultural, political, religious, and sexual identity. The video *Oh Jerusalem* shows the artist alternating between the stereotypical dress of an Arab male and an orthodox Jew. In slapstick fashion, both appear to be trapped in a loop. They sit down on a chair, spy through a large paper tube, and finally, in an excessive display of joy, they discover Jerusalem. Through a constant acceleration of the repeated actions directed towards the shared site of their longing, both figures finally merge into one. Making reference to classic silent movies, Oreet Ashery here paints a tragicomical picture of the continuing conflict between Israel and the Palestinians.

Oreet Ashery

Oh Jerusalem, 2005,
video, b/w, silent, 4 min,
stills from a digital copy

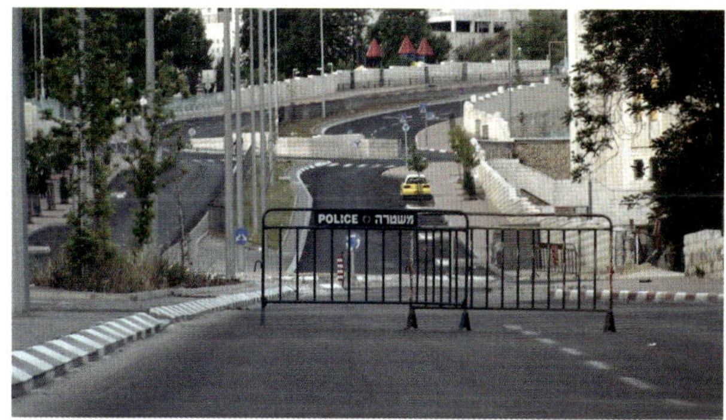

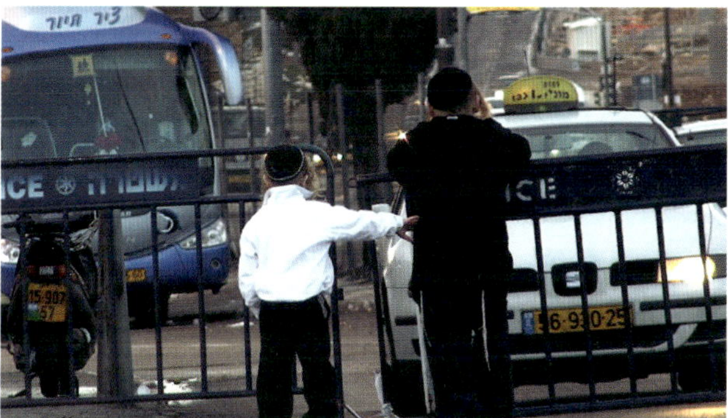

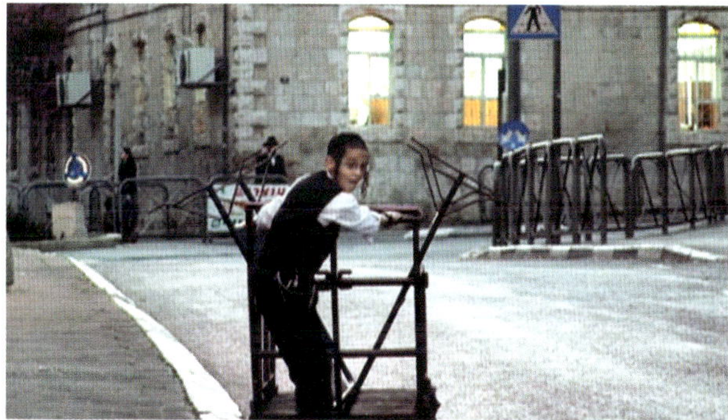

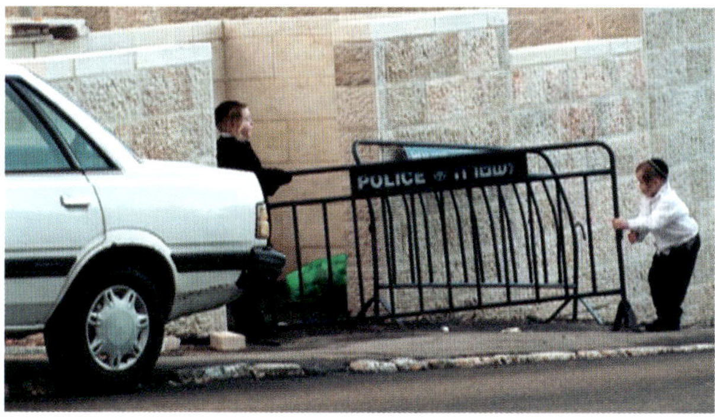

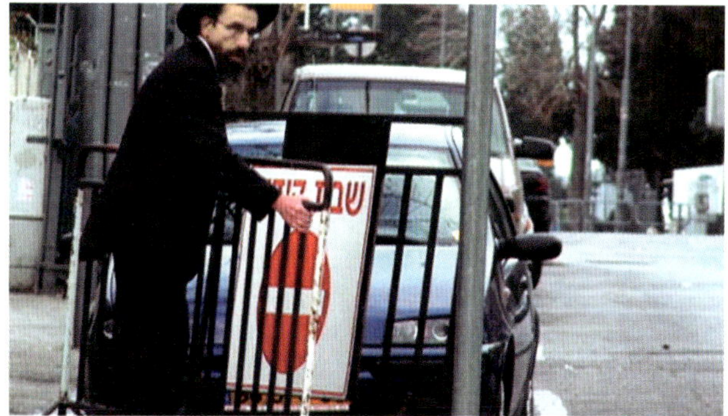

Nira Pereg
*1969 in Tel Aviv, Israel,
lives and works in Tel Aviv

Sabbath 2008,
Jerusalem, Israel, 2008,
1-channel video projection,
color, sound, 7 min,
stills from a digital copy

The work *Sabbath 2008* documents the closing of the ultra-orthodox districts in Jerusalem on the eve of the Sabbath. With the consent of police and city administration, residents erect temporary barriers in order to block vehicle access to these areas for 24 hours. During these hours, the strict rules of the religious day of rest apply – topologically, the city is transformed into two cities. Nira Pereg observes this regularly repeated ritual of putting up borders and points to its potential for conflict. In her search for the personal within a systematic ritual, she develops her own photographic and filmic ritual. From the presence of the barriers, the portrait of a city emerges, in which sacred space is firmly separated from secular space.

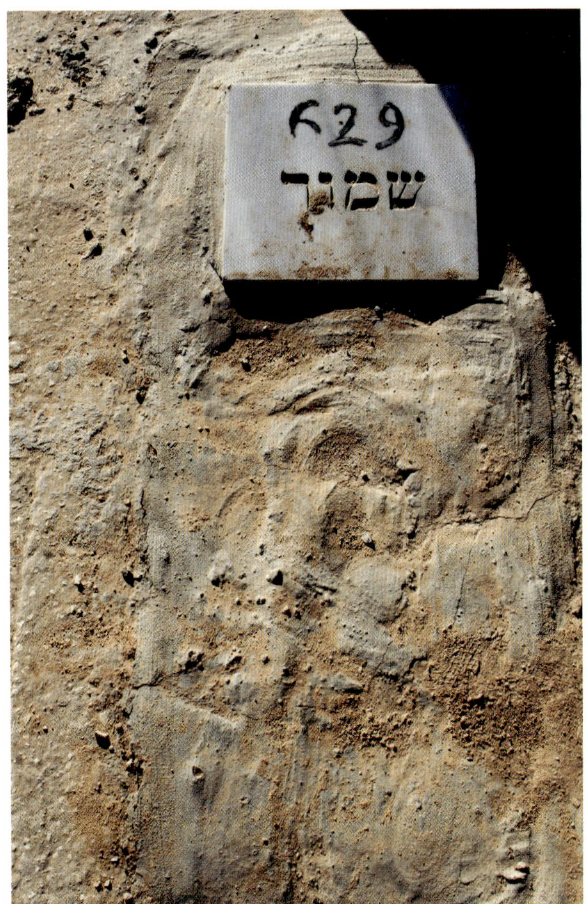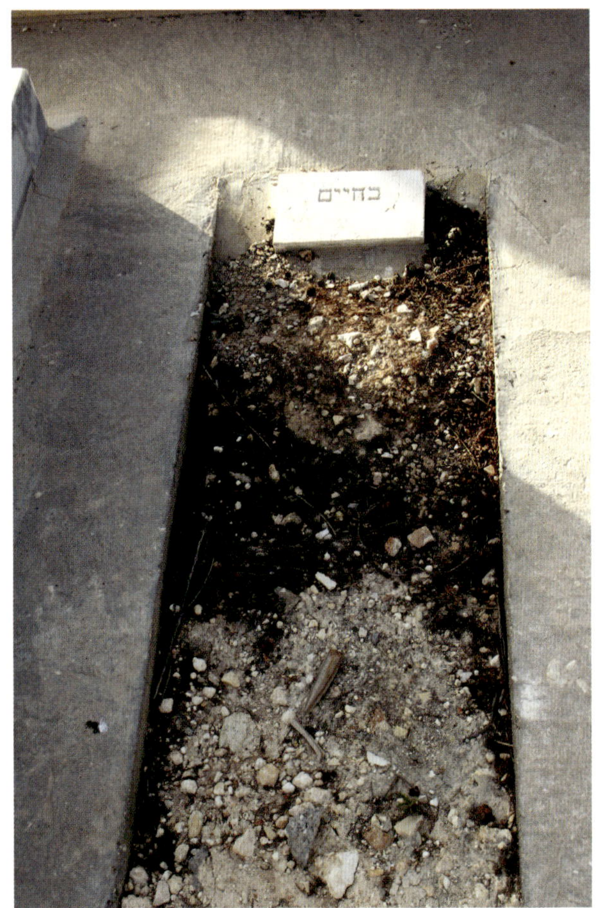

The photographs under the title *Kept Alive* focus on one of the largest cemeteries in Israel, Har Menuchot [Mountain of Rest]. This cemetery, founded in 1953, lies on a slope of the mountain along Side Road No. 1 and functions as an impressive backdrop for the main approach road to Jerusalem. The cemetery spreads across 580,000 square meters and is constantly being expanded. Therefore, it is still possible to reserve burial grounds or to buy them. Reserved graves may be marked at the buyer's request, and some people choose to mark their burial plot with the sign "Alive" or "Kept Alive." In this project, Nira Pereg continues with her search for signs of individuality within a social system and documents the burial grounds of those who are still living, yet already possess a concrete territory among the dead.

Nira Pereg

Kept Alive, 2008,
12 photographs (C-print),
60 × 80 cm each

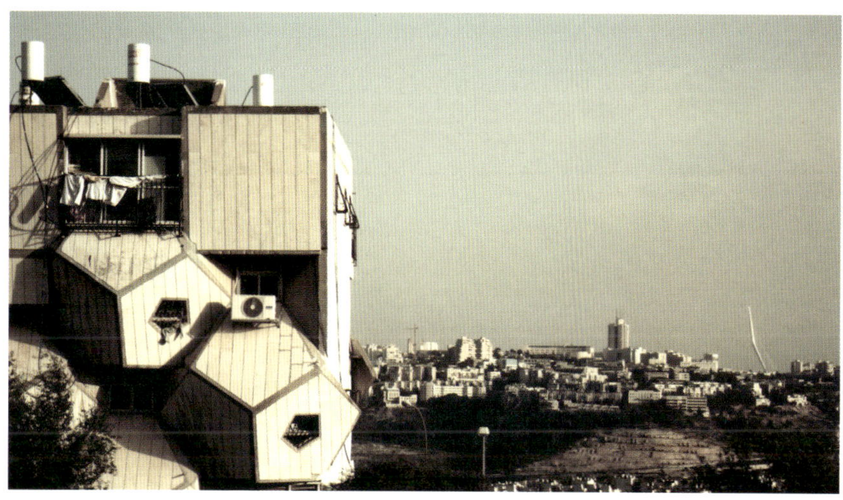

Nira Pereg

Location 8 –
Ramot Polin / Polish Hills, 2008,
14 photographs (C-print),
60 × 80 cm each

In *Location 8*, Nira Pereg resorts
to the orthodox neighborhood
Ramot Polin, located in the northern outskirts of Jerusalem, which
has also been a film location for
Sabbath 2008. Built in the 1970s to
the designs of Zvi Hecker, one of
Israel's most determinedly avant-
garde architects, Ramot Polin was
one of the few attempts by the
National Ministry of Housing to
break out of the standard architectural mold and create a neighborhood for a religious community.
Hecker created a beehive-like
structure, clattered with almost
no straight walls and windows.
In her photographs, Pereg focuses
on the relation between indoor
and outdoor, windows and wall,
humans and geometry, and comes
up with a story of a place and its
inhabitants.

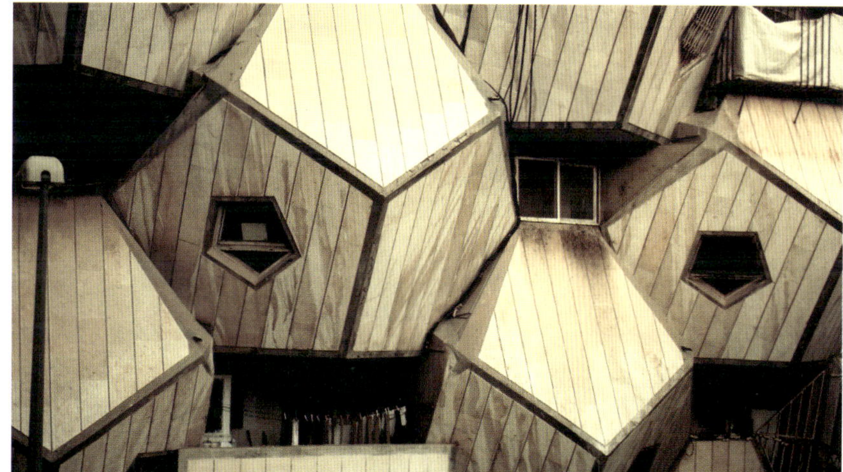

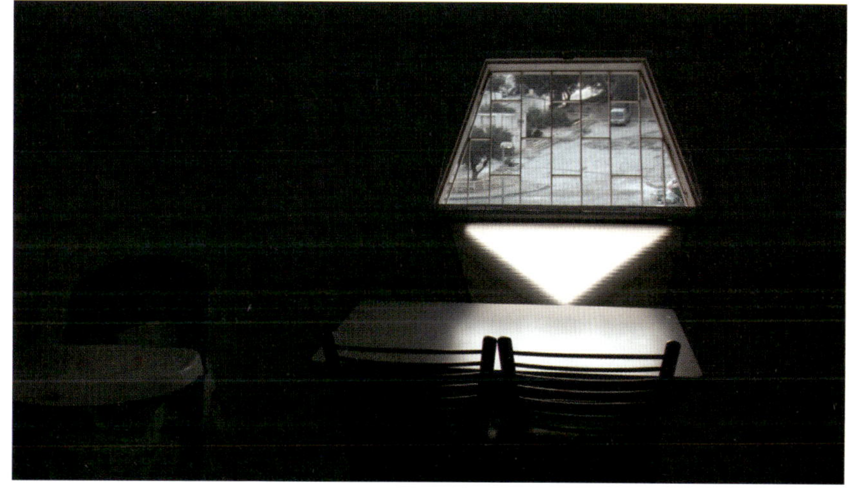

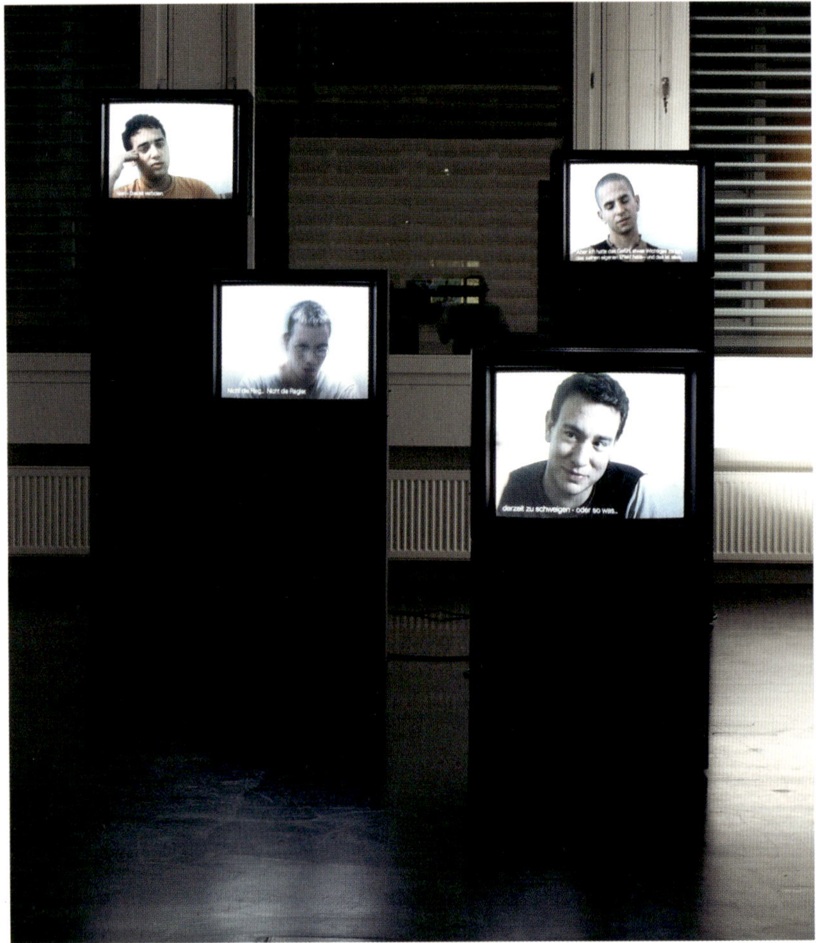

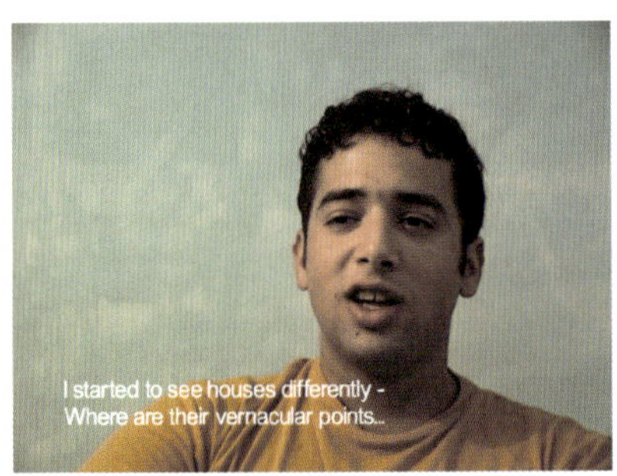

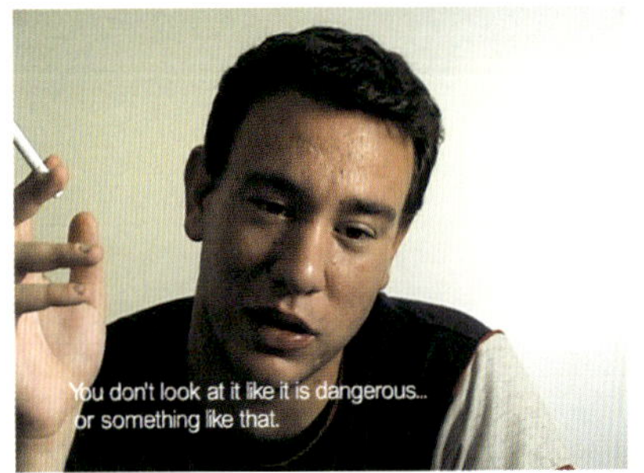

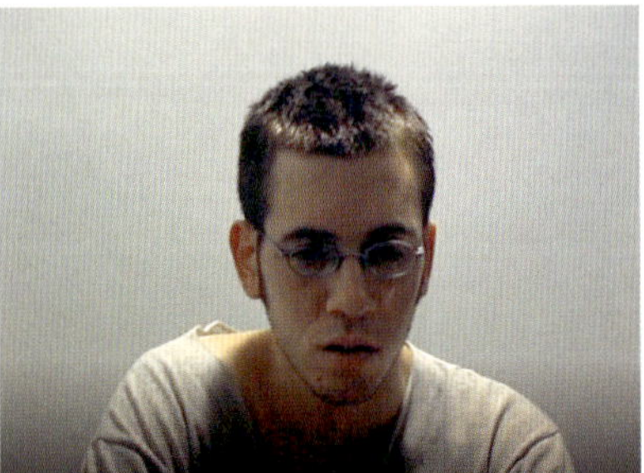

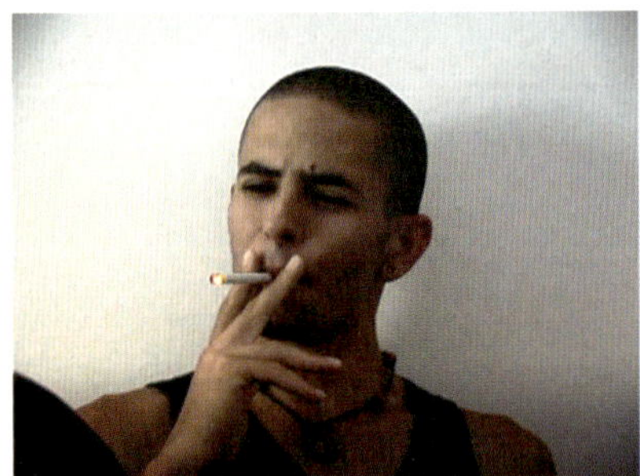

On four monitors, the installation shows interviews with Israeli soldiers from a tank crew. Analogous to the positions of the soldiers in the tank, the monitors are set up at various heights. The soldiers describe their respective personal state of mind while going into action in an armored vehicle. Omer Fast intervenes in the documentary character of the interview by manipulating the subtitles. Military expressions shift to civilian ones, individual words disappear completely, and statements are given an opposite meaning. The work shows, on the one hand, the conflict between a task ordered by the state and civilian principles, while on the other, it enquires into the boundary between a private mission and a state-ordered one and the way public media present truth.

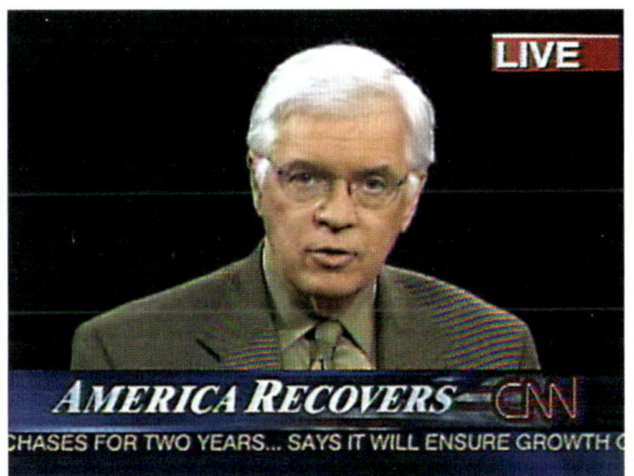
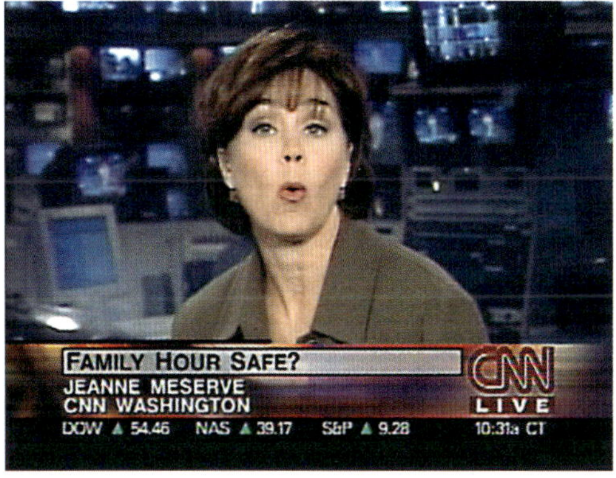

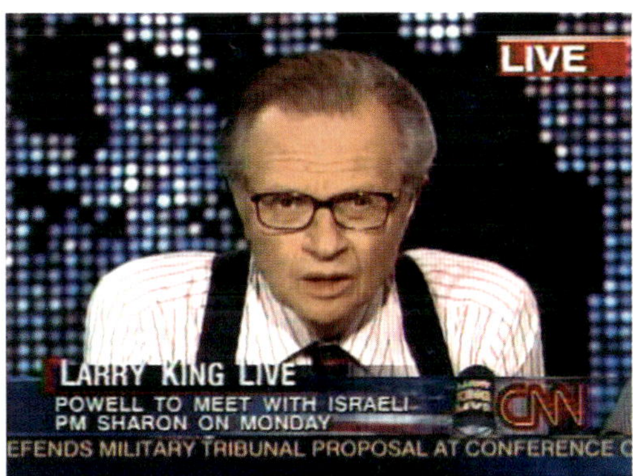
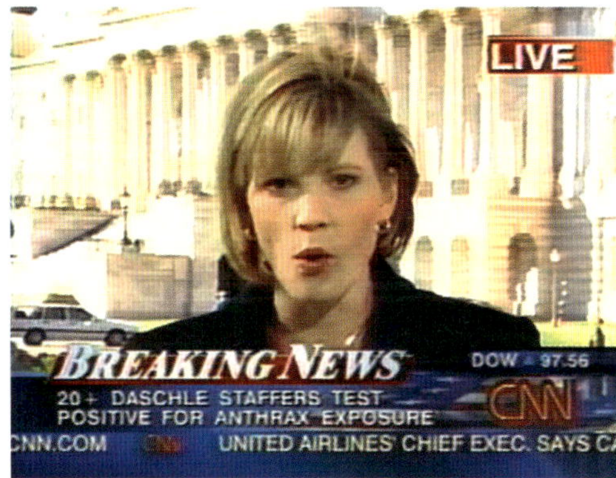

Omer Fast

CNN Concatenated, 2002,
video, color, sound, 18 min,
stills from a digital copy

CNN Concatenated is a compilation by Omer Fast from a database of 10,000 words and clips into a speech put together from individual words spoken by different news anchors. In contrast to the profusion of daily news, the artist attempts here to close the gap between the necessity to know and to understand, and the desire to see and to experience, and so provides a consistent context from which the information gains coherence of meaning. Community, intimacy, and a collective memory are created here, action and escape appear possible. The common language also forms the basis for a common framework for action.

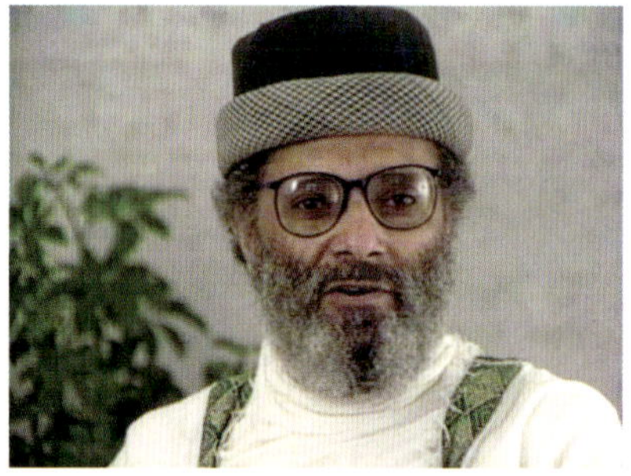

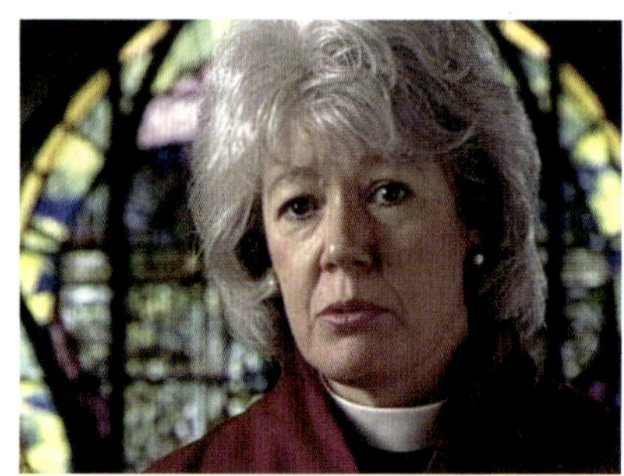

67.
Abraham was not a Jew
Nor yet a Christian;
But he was true in Faith
And bowed his will to
Allah's (Which is Islam),
And he joined
not gods with Allah.

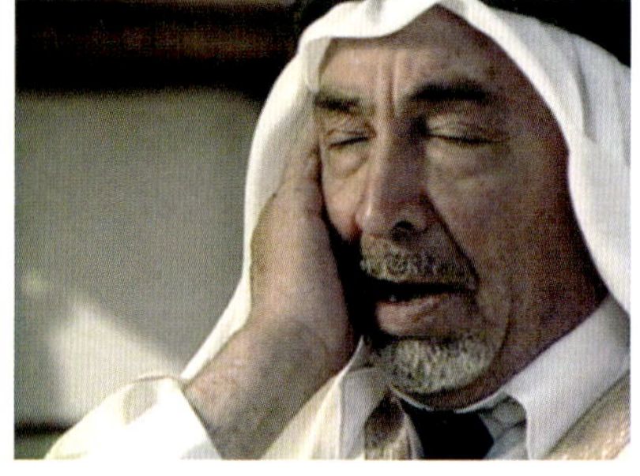

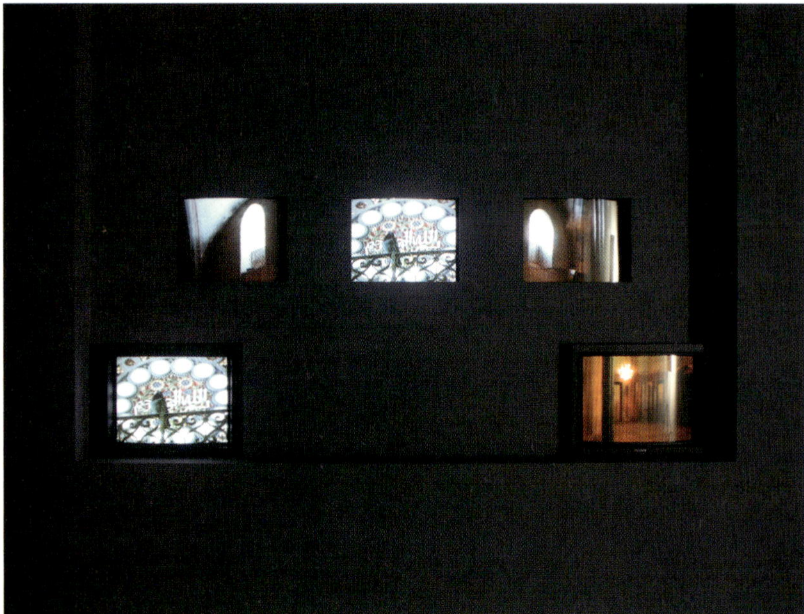

Beryl Korot and Steve Reich
Beryl Korot
*1945
Steve Reich
*1936
both live and work in New York

The Cave, 1993,
5-channel video installation,
color, sound,
installation view
ZKM | Karlsruhe, 2009,
and stills from a digital copy

The Cave denotes the Cave of Machpela in Hebron on the West Bank, in which Abraham, the common ancestor of Judaism, of Christianity, and of Islam, is supposed to lie buried. According to mystical sources from Judaism, this is the entrance to the Garden of Eden; however, until today, Machpela has been the scene of political-religious tensions and conflicts. The American composer Steve Reich and the video artist Beryl Korot devoted a video opera to the place and accordingly asked Israelis, Palestinians, and Americans about the respective significance of Abraham in their faith: Who, for you, is Abraham, Sarah, Hagar, Ishmael, and Isaac? These recordings served as the basis for the music, libretto, and scenography of the work. Alongside the original video opera as performed with an orchestra, a second version arose as a video installation.

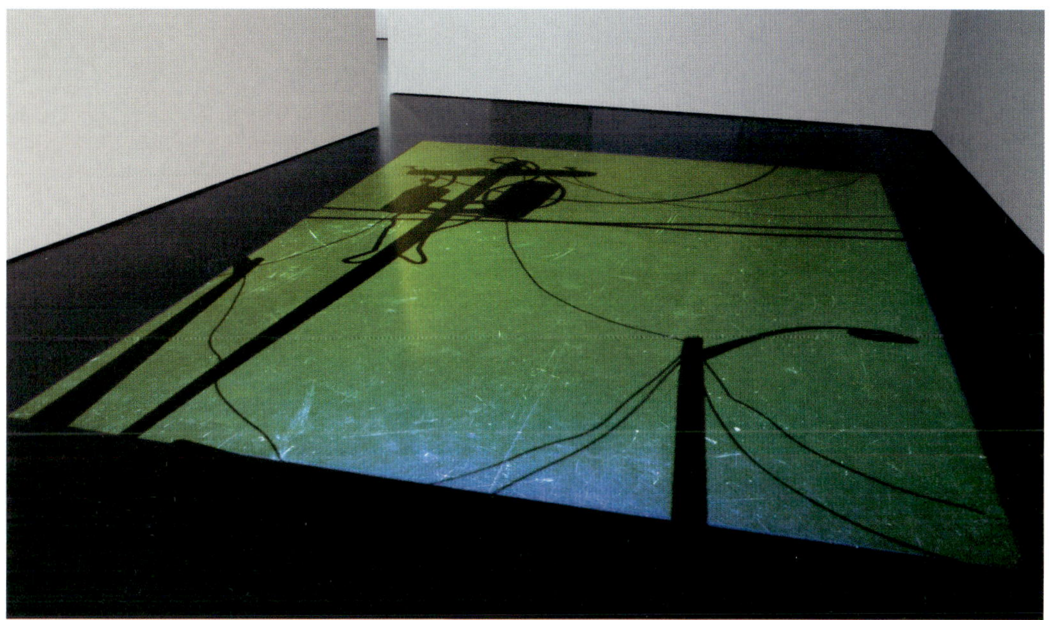

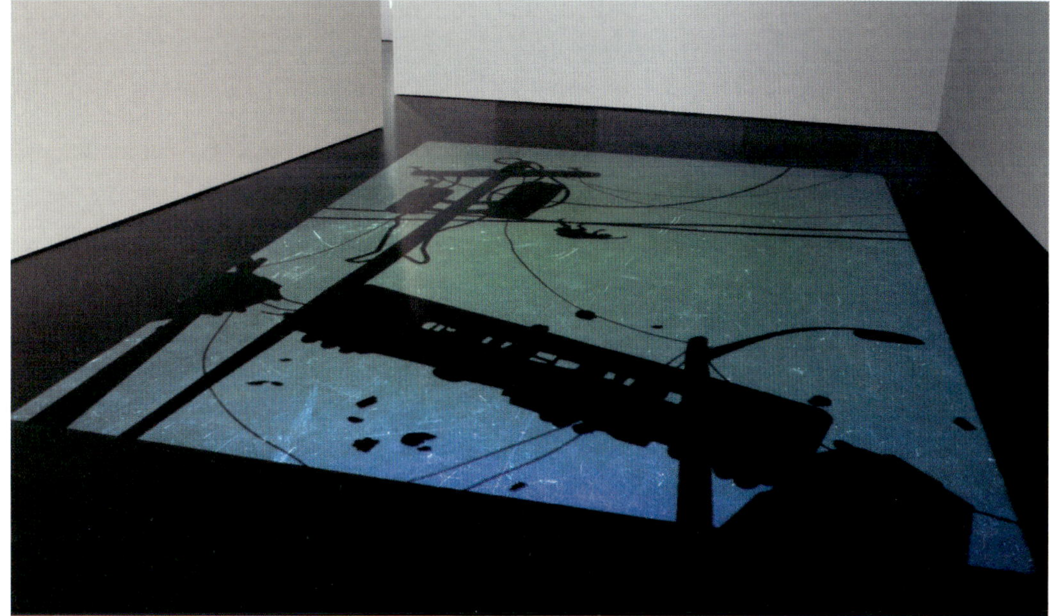

Paul Chan
*1973 in Hong Kong, formerly
Great Britain, today China,
lives and works in New York

1st Light, 2005,
digital video projection, color,
silent, 14 min, installation views
ZKM | Karlsruhe, 2009

Particularly since 9/11 and the war in Iraq, Paul Chan has become a key figure in the American art scene as well as in political activism. As part of the series *The 7 Lights*, the computer-animated video *1st Light* describes a vision of Biblical elation – the ascending of the believers to Heaven – making reference to 9/11. The floor projection shows shadowy silhouettes of bodies and everyday objects falling to the ground and equally rising towards the sky. This evokes the 1969 images of floating astronauts as much as those of bodies tumbling from the burning towers – iconic images of hope and terror, of utopia, and the apocalypse merge. They show how Chan's deconstructivist critique of civilization rests on the idea that a random happiness is possible.

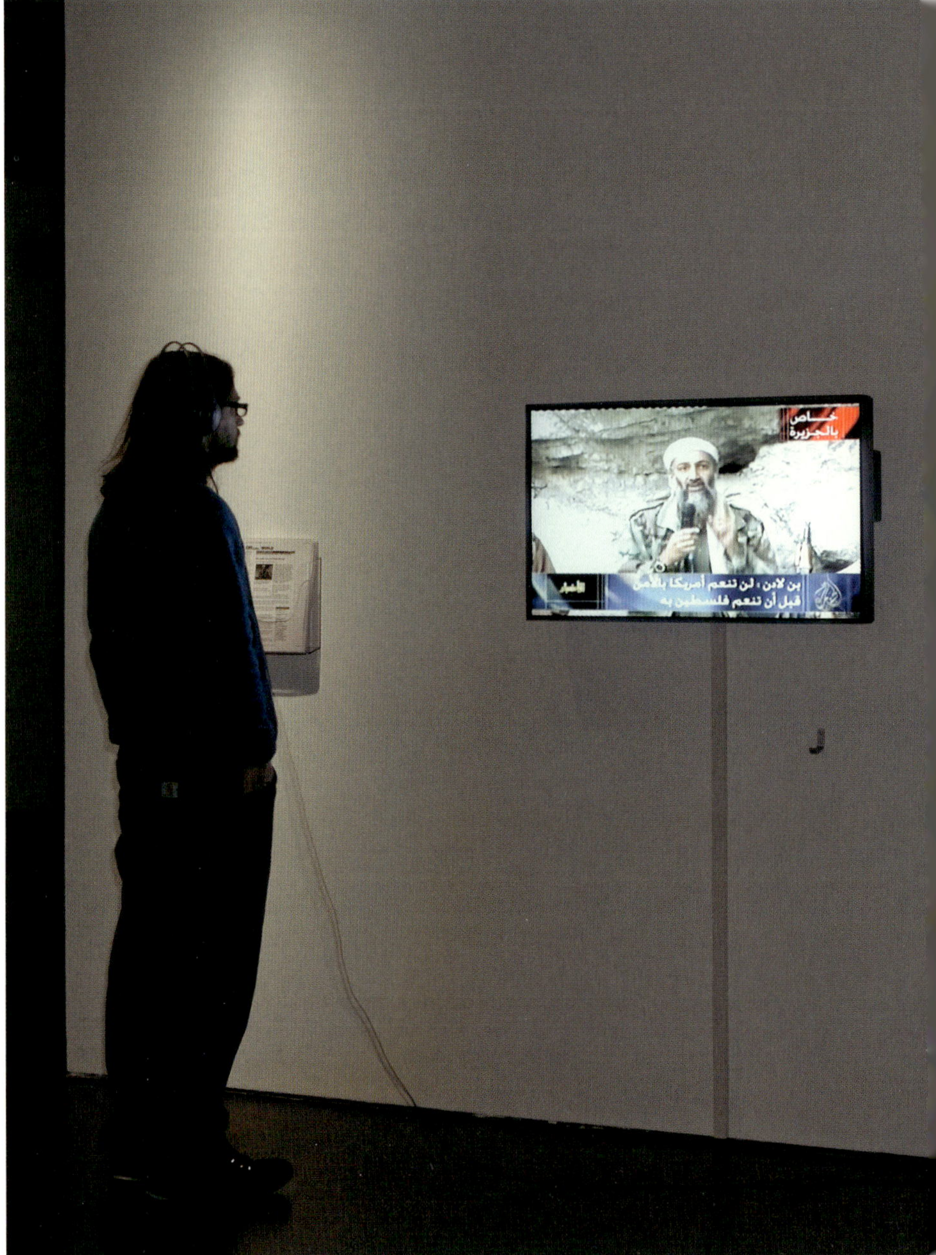
خـــاص بالجزيرة
بن لادن : لن تنعم أمريكا بالأمن قبل أن تنعم فلسطين به
الأخبار

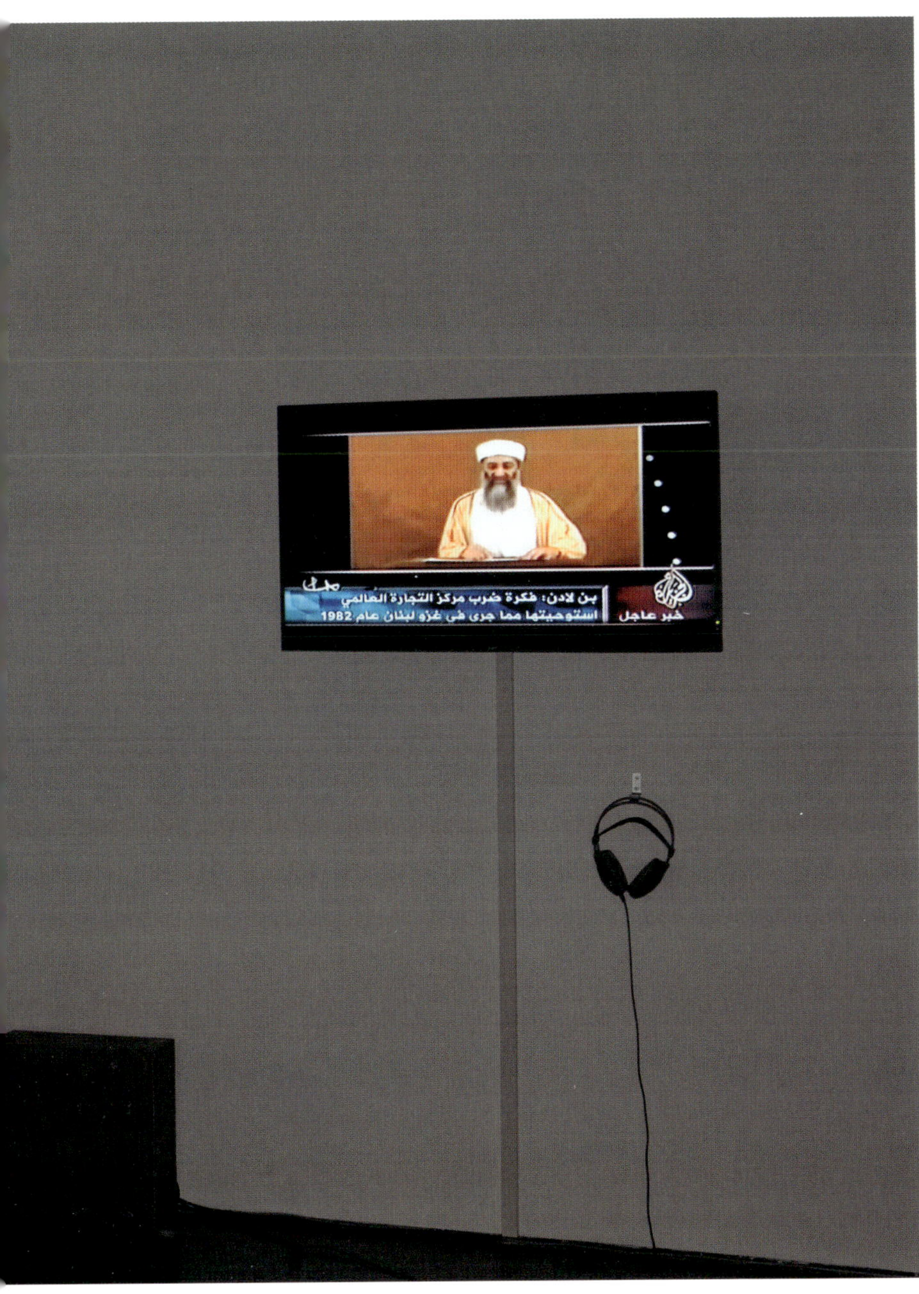

Video messages by
Osama Bin Laden
(Usāma ibn Muhammad ibn Awad
ibn Lādin), 2001 and 2004,
video, color, sound, 5 min and
5:40 min, installation view
ZKM | Karlsruhe, 2009

Osama Bin Laden utilizes the medium of video chiefly for effectively distributing his messages to the world public. Like politicians, actors, or artists, he uses his media appearances in the form of video messages to position himself effectively and strategically within the realm of the media. Viewed as a quasi-artistic production of a media spectacle under the sign of terrorism, the attack on the World Trade Center managed to involve in a virtuoso manner all the available capacities of mass media reporting. On October 29, 2004, just prior to the imminent presidential elections in the U.S., a video message from Osama Bin Laden, in which he addresses the American public, offering explanations on why he attacked the World Trade Center in New York, was broadcast on television. In this video, Bin Laden does not present himself as a *Mujahid* [holy warrior] in military uniform with a Kalashnikov as symbol by his side, but rather appears in the dress of a Saudi religious teacher, with which he stages himself as a Byzantine icon.

Joshua Simon

.The.Aesthetics.of. ..Terror.in.General.and.. ....Suicide.Bomber.... ..Videos.in.Particular..

This story again makes clear that wherever commodification reigns supreme, whether in the bourgeoisie culture of Paris or the counterculture at the end of *Weekend*, the phallus will give way to the anus. This is not the utopian sexual liberation […], but the catastrophic end of all singularity. What we might call "anal capitalism"[…].

Kaja Silverman in conversation with Harun Farocki,
from: Speaking About Godard, 1998, p. 111.

With the aesthetics of terror, our visual culture has been introduced to a new tactical apparatus of staging, framing, and distribution. This represents a set of forms and images aimed at us, thereby challenging the distance we see ourselves as having to them as viewers. In an article published by Israeli artist Roee Rosen, the author argues that the spectacle of the 9/11 attacks and the drama surrounding each new videotape of Bin Laden, prompted most theoretical commentaries to focus on the aesthetics of underground terrorism to the neglect of the imagery of state terrorism (while comments have been made with respect to the appropriation of the Twin Towers attacks by the 2004 presidential election campaigns, distinctions in the representational means employed and the images generated by Ehud Olmert, Ariel Sharon, or George W. Bush and those of Bin Laden and Palestinian suicide bombers have been overlooked). Rosen has suggested that the principle difference between representations of subversive terrorism – produced by terrorist groups – and those of state terror is the difference between figuration and abstraction. According to Rosen, the representational apparatus of state terror is based on the blurring or erasure of central figures, by replacing them with abstraction: Aerial views of bombardments taken by cameras inserted into smart bombs (U.S. Army General Norman Schwarzkopf Jr.'s briefings during the 1991 Gulf War saw him marking arrows and circles on monitors much like a sports commentator. Among other images, this war produced CNN live broadcasts of Coalition Forces' cruise-missile shelling – neon-Rothko and Kandinsky-like abstractions spread through the Baghdad sky as if it were a canvas. State terror imagery also includes the blocking of visibility by grids (such as in the grid of Israel's Separation Wall). The prototype of state terror would be the image of the atomic mushrooms in Hiroshima and Nagasaki; in terms of abstract painting this would represent the stain.[1]

At the other end of the spectrum, representations of subversive terrorism strive for a central, powerful figure – the portrait of a suicide bomber, collapsing skyscrapers, and the icon of Bin Laden with his golden gown and triangular composition (this is an icon in the religious sense: a human, semi-divine person whose very appearance defies the divide of life and death).

The framework of abstraction/figuration proposed by Rosen facilitates discussion of terror as an image production machine. Nevertheless, there is a gap in this basic binary. An intermediate realm of ambivalent images which includes the cellular phone documentation of Saddam Hussein's execution and the photos from Abu Ghraib. The reason for the pictures having surfaced and for having been produced at all remains uncertain: In both cases, the digital photos of molestation and degradation and the cell phone video segment of the execution with its humiliating exchange and swift conclusion. The ambivalence of these images derives not only from their content, but also from the question of authorship. As their producers participate in criminal acts, these constitute both criminal pieces of evidence and part of the crime itself. The images appear to occupy opposing roles; they represent both amateur means of enjoyment and moral denunciation. The unresolved reasons for their initial production and distribution comprise part

Note:
An early version of this text generated the exhibition *The Aesthetics of Terror* co-curated by Joshua Simon and Manon Slome at the Chelsea Art Museum in New York City (November 2008 – January 2009). The exhibition was canceled at the very last moment due to disagreements between the exhibition curators and the hosting institution regarding the content and framing of the show.

1 See: Roee Rosen, "*Basic Instinct* Meets the War in Iraq," in: *Maarvon – New Israeli Film Magazine*, issue 1, 2005.

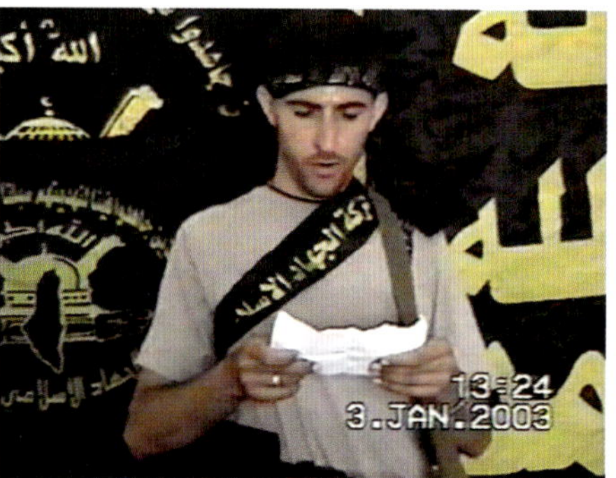
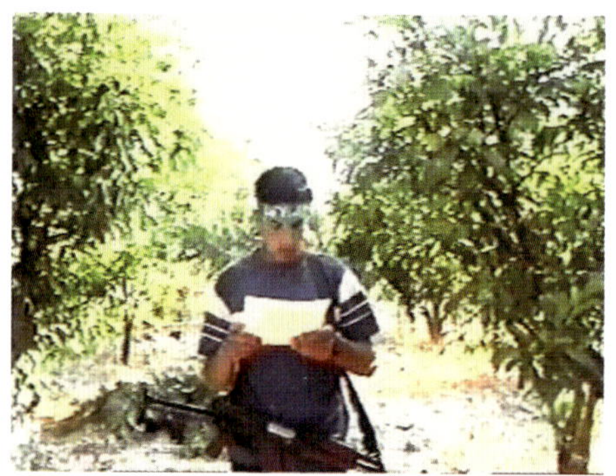

of their significance. These unauthorized, low- to mid-resolution images function both as images denouncing state terror and as actual examples of state terror. It is agreed that since the image is not in the hands of the producing agency when distributed, its meaning and effect shift. But this is true for images of state and group terror alike.

The beginning of the 1990s introduced into our visual culture a new, enigmatic and macabre set of images: the videotapes of Palestinian suicide bombers – the Shahids. Shahid (in Arabic plural, *Suhada*) is an Islamic religious term, which translates as "witness," or more commonly, as "martyr," and is used as a designation for Muslims who have died fulfilling a religious commandment, or waging war for Islam. These videos capture the moments before the suicide bomber is about to carry out his or her attack and, as such, function both as suicide notes and a form of death mask – documentations of those about to die. The Shahids' use of video technology incorporates certain formal properties of framing, color, self-portraiture, and duration. By tracing these formalistic aspects of the suicide bombers' videos and by placing them within the context of contemporary video works, photography, and painting, one can explore the tension they sustain within the politics of representation and find in them both subjective and objective usage of the image as a critical tool in the apparatus of terror.

Terrorist Groups and State Terror

Prior to the 1990s, most attacks Palestinian resistance groups carried out against Israeli civilians were chiefly aimed to draw attention to the Palestinian problem among international media organizations and to secure the release of Palestinian prisoners jailed in Israel. The Palestinian groups hoped to bargain and negotiate with the Israeli government, which up until the 1993 Oslo Accords, refused even to recognize Palestine as a nation. The quadruple hijackings of Dawson's Field (1970), and Air France flight 139 hijacked to Entebbe (1976), carried out by the Popular Front for the Liberation of Palestine (PFLP), and the kidnapping and execution of Israeli athletes by the Black September organization during the 1972 Summer Olympics in Munich – to mention just a few of the attacks – were all executed by highly trained fighters. While these were all media spectacles they did not include operating suicide bombers.

On February 25, 1994, Baruch Goldstein, a Jewish settler and extreme right-wing activist, entered the Mosque of Abraham, located in the Cave of the Patriarchs in Hebron, in the occupied territories. Standing in front of the cave's only exit and positioned to the rear of the Muslim worshippers, Goldstein opened fire with his assault rifle, killing 29 people and injuring a further 125. Forty days after the Hebron massacre, on April 6, 1994, nineteen year old Ra'id Zaqarna, a Palestinian suicide bomber, member of the Abdel el-Rahman Hamadan cell of the Hamas Izz ad-Din al-Qassam Brigades exploded himself in the northern Israeli city of Afula, killing eight people. His car was loaded with seven gas cylinders, five anti-personal hand grenades, and a bomb wrapped in a backpack containing 1,100 carpenter's nails. Since Zaqarna's suicide attack, dozens of Palestinian suicide bombers have been operating in Israeli cities. In the Palestinian revolt, coined the Second Intifada (2000–2005), 161 suicide bombers carried out 144 attacks, killing 515 Israelis and injuring a further 3,428. All of these suicide bombers were video-documented before they set out on their mission.

Two opposing points of view dominate the ongoing debate on the origins for the phenomenon of the Palestinian suicide bombers. The Israeli Defense Force and Secret Service endorsed Samuel Huntington's clash-of-civilizations paradigm[2] which focuses on Islam's holy war or jihad as the main source of this trend, going on to determine Islamic fundamentalism to be its cause. Activists opposing aggressive Israeli military tactics against the Palestinians in the occupied territories and refugee camps in neighboring countries, regard Israeli occupation and the very existence of Israel itself to be the cause for the killings in this region, including the phenomenon of the suicide bombers. From this perspective, suicide bombers are seen either as active agents who challenge Israel's monopoly on violence and oppose Israeli occupation – or as the tragic, but inevitable, reaction to the extreme conditions of repression and oppression endured by the Palestinian people on a daily basis.[3]

A close reading of the images produced by the Shahids enables us to gain a better understanding of the means by which these videos of the suicide bombers function as terror imagery and the specific formal aspects which have become their unique signature.

As Don DeLillo states in his novel *Mao II*[4], by the killing of others, the terrorist asks to live. Bill, the protagonist, laments that novelists are rapidly becoming obsolete in an age in which terrorism has supplanted art as that "raid on consciousness" which jolts and transforms culture at large. Just as the writer fundamentally rejects the givens of reality, so does the terrorist, claims DeLillo, and like the writer, the terrorist looks for ways to create a discourse that captures the imagination of society through which its transformation will be inevitably effectuated. In this respect, as DeLillo goes on to assert, the terrorist and the writer may be considered adversaries, and where, currently, the writer loses ground to the terrorist: no contemporary writer can compete with the effect generated by terrorist action.

In his *Welcome to the Desert of the Real: Five Essays on September 11 and Related Dates*, published a year after the 9/11 attacks, Slavoj Žižek presents terrorists as the agents of the real. He contrasts this real with the virtual lifestyle of the West, and goes on to suggest that the terrorist commands over a greater degree of "real" life than do those who lead monotonous urban existences, who live and work in skyscrapers, go on leisurely jogs, and surrender to the general injunction just to enjoy themselves.[5] In Žižek's polemic, the terrorist, who is obligated to die for something greater than himself, challenges the West's repressed notion of death. Warfare, as waged by the suicide bomber, he argues, attempts to break the logic of the postindustrial plasma-screen variety characterized by the use of anonymous weapons – aerial bombardment, helicopters, cruise missiles, smart bombs, and surveillance radar – and seeks to annul the distance by which these state-of-the-art killing machines operate. The suicide bomber demands the clash of flesh against flesh.

Conceptualizing the act of taking one's life and the lives of others by removing it from the political arena can be useful up to a certain point, beyond which what remains are videos, and their specific aesthetics.

Media

In 1978, as protests against the Shah of Iran reached their zenith, Michel Foucault traveled to Tehran as special correspondent for *Corriere della Sera* and *Le Monde*. Writing from a turbulent Tehran, Foucault noted that Islamic revolutionaries and various anti-Shah groups used audio cassettes to disseminate their beliefs among the Iranian people. This soon proved an especially

2   See: Samuel P. Huntington, *The Clash of Civilizations and the Remaking of World Order*, Simon & Schuster, New York, 1996.

3   See: Amira Haas, *Reporting from Ramallah: An Israeli Journalist in an Occupied Land*, Semiotext(e), Los Angeles, 2003; Tanya Reinhart, *Israel/Palestine. How to End the War of 1948*, Seven Stories Press, New York, 2002.

4   See: Don DeLillo, *Mao II*, Viking, New York, 1991.

5   See: Slavoj Žižek, *Welcome to the Desert of the Real. Five Essays on September 11 and Related Dates*, Verso, London, 2002.

effective weapon against the Shah's hegemony.[6] Foucault suggests that by virtue their content, format, and distribution strategy these cassettes triggered a direct revolutionary reaction.

The early 1990s and the first Gulf War introduced the 24-hour live news coverage known as "the CNN effect." This global real-time aspect of contemporary media set the stage for the suicide bombers.

To characterize suicide bombers' actions as merely challenging the state's monopoly on violence would be misplaced. Their tapes force us to recognize that the battleground has shifted. Since their first appearance in nineteenth-century tsarist Russia, terrorist activity has sought to capture the imagination of society and to dominate public opinion. Contemporary terrorism is not a form of guerilla warfare; it does not use violence to occupy or defend geographic territory. The terrorist challenges the media's monopoly on the imagery of violence. The eminent interrelation between media and terror is fundamental in this context.[7] In that spectacle is the locus of medial sovereignty, terror cannot be conducted other than by and through media.[8] With terror we no longer encounter a revolutionary attempt to usurp the means of production, but to penetrate the means of representation.[9] It is worth noting in this context that in his *The State and Revolution,* Vladimir Ilyich Lenin did not understand terror as a revolutionary act, as it was not the weapon of the masses, but of individuals.[10]

Shahids

The Shahids are young men and women, who choose not only to kill themselves and others, but also to document themselves before doing so. In this statement of purpose and farewell to the world, they attempt to present to the camera the pride they take in their act, providing the viewer with a glimpse at their whole, healthy, and intact bodies before death. From the dozens of such videos, I will be discussing here a selection of four that may be considered representative of the genre.

Shahid Ahmed Hiari Fathi Yahie

At twenty two years old, Ahmed Hiari Fathi Yahie, from the town of Jenin, was part of the Jerusalem Brigade – the militant arm of the Islamic Jihad. On July 7, 2003, he entered a home in the village Yavetz in the Sharon region of Israel, before blowing himself up (leaving one person dead – Mazal Afari). In his videotape, he is seen in a neon-lit room, standing with a rifle held across his chest, against a backdrop of posters, slogans, and flags spread over the wall, indicating his affiliations. The rich green of the fabrics and the gold captions that stand out against the black background, immediately catch the eye. His initial pose is leisurely, he raises his eyes to the camera to make sure that it is running, adjusts the strap of his gun, glances at a piece of paper held in his hand, and starts reading the contents out loud. It seems that the filming serves as a phase in his preparation for death – he becomes alert. On his head there is a green band with a caption. He is unshaven and slightly perspiring. He wears a silver ring on the fourth finger of his right hand. He speaks about independence in Arabic, about Allah, Ariel Sharon, the Israeli Minister of Defense at that time, Shaul Mofaz, Palestine and jihad. All the while he does not raise his eyes from the paper. He concludes by stating his name – Ahmed Hiari Fathi Yahie. His gaze is now raised to the camera. It seems as though he is in great haste to begin the mission he has set for himself. He turns around and bends over. The cameraman shifts position accordingly and places the camera on his shoulder – the camera shakes. Ahmed then raises himself again to face the camera; he clasps a grenade in his left hand and the gun in his right. He poses for the camera with ammunition and a gun, trying to assume a determined appearance. He then exits to the right side of the frame. Cut to a new shot. Ahmed moves around and prays in a standing position. He looks at the camera, drops to his knees, prays on the floor, and then stops. He looks up toward the camera to make sure he is still being filmed. He stands up and takes the gun now propped against a chair. He positions himself in front of the camera – lifts

6   See: Janet Afary and Kevin B. Anderson, *Foucault and the Iranian Revolution: Gender and the Seductions of Islamism*, University of Chicago Press, Chicago, 2005.
7   See: Bethami A. Dobkin, *Tales of Terror. Television News and the Construction of the Terrorist Threat*, Praeger, New York, 1992; Ariella Azoulay, *Death's Showcase. The Power of Image in Contemporary Democracy*, The MIT Press, Cambridge, MA, 2001; Jean Baudrillard, *The Spirit of Terrorism and Requiem for the Twin Towers*, Verso, New York, 2002.
8   See: Boris Groys, "The Fate of Art in the Age of Terror," in: Bruno Latour and Peter Weibel (eds.), *Making Things Public. Atmospheres of Democracy*, ZKM | Center for Art and Media Karlsruhe, The MIT Press, Cambridge, MA, 2005, pp. 970–997.
9   See: Guy Debord, *The Society of the Spectacle*, Zone Books, New York, 1994.
10   See: Vladimir Ilicz Lenin, *The State and Revolution* [1917], Penguin Classics, London, New York, 1993.

the gun to a diagonal position and holds it in a demonstrative manner. He directs his gaze to the camera, which then zooms in for a close-up of his facial features. The lens moves towards and away from him in a zoom-in / zoom-out motion: From his face back to a poster caption, from a shot of his upper body holding the gun, to the background. The filming is unsteady – the take is over. Ahmed sits on the chair. The camera slowly fades.

Shahid Abdel Muati Shabna
Eighteen years old, Abdel Muati Shabna belonged to the Hamas Izz ad-Din al-Qassam Brigades in Hebron. On June 12, 2003, he blew himself up on a bus in Jerusalem leaving seventeen people dead. In his tape, he is pictured in a sunlit orchard, dressed in a blue T-shirt, with a rifle strapped across his chest. He reads aloud from a note held in his hand. He is in haste and does not raise his eyes to the camera. He is very young and slight in appearance; he wears a wristwatch on his left hand that glitters in the light. The camera is adjusted to automatic shutter and automatic white balance (the setting of the light – artificial light / sunlight); because of the daylight in the background, he appears very dark. Zoom-in and the shutter changes to reveal his soft face; a green headband is attached to his forehead. One can see that he uses gel to fix his hair, which is meticulously combed. He explains that his mission is to retaliate for the Israeli attempt to assassinate Abdel-Aziz al-Rantissi, a key leader of Hamas. He talks of an armed struggle and of the Palestinian people, turns the page, and continues reading.

Shaheeda Unknown
A Shaheeda (a female martyr), whose name I was unable to learn, is sitting behind a desk in a room in a frame that gives her the appearance of a news anchorwoman. A rifle is positioned on the desk in front of her, along with a big, decorated Koran, ammunition, and a grenade. She is reading aloud from a page and faces the camera. Only the tone of her voice discloses her gender: She is veiled and her face covered with a Keffiyeh. Her eyes can be seen through a small slit in the veil. Zoom-in and zoom-out across to a poster of a Shaheeda in the background. Without uttering a word, the martyr patiently waits for the cameraman to complete his shot. Through the veil, her eyes can be seen wandering, waiting.

Shahid Abdel Hamid Misk
Raad Abdel Hamid Misk, a twenty-nine-year-old man from Hebron, was a former student of the An-Najah National University and served as an imam [prayer leader] at a mosque in his hometown. Abdel Hamid belonged to the Hamas Izz ad-Din al-Qassam Brigades also in Hebron. On August 19, 2003, he blew himself up on a bus in Jerusalem transporting people back from prayer at the Western Wall. Twenty-two people died. In his tape, he is seen seated on a chair in an empty room, the camera is in a fixed position (perhaps placed on a tripod and located slightly lower than him. It is possible that Abdel Hamid was alone in the room and that he operated the camera himself). In one hand he holds a rifle and a book in the other. He is a large, bearded man with glasses. He talks in Arabic and then in English, explaining that he chose this mission because Ariel Sharon did not fulfill his part of the Hudna (Arabic for quiet, a period of agreed ceasefire between Israel and Hamas): "This is a first reaction to the blood of our Shahids in Nablus, and a revenge dedicated to Mohammed lob Sider." [Sider was head of the Islamic Jihad in Hebron and was killed by the Israel Defence Forces a few days earlier]. By stating his reasons in English, Abdel Hamid is addressing a third party in the conflict – the international English-speaking media as well as the actual mediators of the conflict – both American and European. He looks calm. It is not clear if he is reciting out loud or reading from a board located behind the camera. He concludes: "The Israelis need to finish with Sharon – what happened to Rabin will also happen to him."

Video

The fact that Shahids refrain from saying anything personal beyond their names and the somewhat similar choreography of events and props, makes these videos appear as reenactments – as formulas or rituals rather than an expression of individual purpose. The locations fall into two categories: Either an exterior setting such as an orchard, backyard, or field, or an interior such as a basement, a studio or a non-descript room. The lighting is either natural daylight or normal fixtures, with no additional professional lighting included. The setting always includes posters, flags, green drapes (the color of Islam), and black fabrics adorned with images and patterns (such as that of the Dome of the Rock and the map of Palestine/Israel), quotes from the Koran, and slogans. A handheld camera is used. The photography is direct, mainly of a one-shot sequence. The shutter, focus pulling, and white balance, are all on automatic mode with extensive usage of zoom-in / zoom-out techniques. The sound is monotonous, text-based (sometimes one hears Arabic pop music from a CD player); no additional sounds are added to enhance what was recorded on location. As far as editing is concerned, there are no apparent cuts beyond those made by stopping the recording during the shooting.

This amateur style of documentation shares essential formal characteristics with videos taken at weddings, birthdays, bar mitzvahs, family vacations, and surprise parties – the very stuff of home video. When an extraordinary event is captured on camera, these home videos occasionally provide materials for television shows such as *Bloopers* and *Funniest Home Videos*. The Shahids' videos, by contrast, find their way to TV after they have completed their missions. As a format, the framing and presence of young people in these videos showing themselves on tape, resembles the tactics of commercial video dating services. The fact that the Shahids recite, more or less, the same text brings to mind ventriloquism and karaoke.

In Vito Acconci's *Theme Song* (1973), the artist is lying on a carpet in a living room and asks the viewer to join him, be his lover, and overcome the barrier of the screen. Music is playing, and so, after a while, Acconci provides dubbing for songs playing in the background and uses some of the lines for his own

text. The Shahids, like Acconci, transform themselves into a tool for uttering formulaic or scripted speech and, like him, they seek to overcome the barrier of the screen.

Self-Portrait

In Israeli artist Roee Rosen's *Martyr Paintings* (1991–1993) martyrdom is examined with regard to iconophilia and self-portraiture and considered in its relation to suicide. The series is made up of portraits of friends and self-portraits of the artist as Christian martyrs. Rosen reactivates in the series the anachronistic mix of death and faith. These multi-layered paintings all involve young women and men offering themselves for the cause. In this catalogue of religious icons, Rosen shows himself and his friends as figures who undergo excruciating pain and torment caused by the pulling out, tearing off, and plucking of limbs. The series gained great relevance when first shown in Tel Aviv, in 1995, in the wake of the first wave of Palestinian suicide bombings in Israeli cities. The martyrs of early Christianity were brought into the context of the martyrs of late Islam.

Suicide bombers' videos function as self-portraits. In many ways, they answer the challenge Edward Said presented in *Orientalism* (1978), when appropriating a passage from Karl Marx's *Eighteenth Brumaire of Louis Bonaparte* (1852): "They cannot represent themselves; they must be represented."[11]

Left with the opposition of victim/terrorist, the Palestinian suicide bombers seek to transgress this dichotomy. Their videos are a macabre mix of a suicide note and murder confession. When we see the suicide bomber praying and preparing for his or her death and the death of others on TV, the events occur after they died. When we see them on TV, in other words, the suicide bombers are being brought back from the dead. One could argue that when filmed, the suicide bombers are, in fact, already dead even before carrying out their mission: From this perspective, the filming could be interpreted not as an act of terror, but as an actual death. Roland Barthes' association of death and photography in *Camera Lucida*[12] is, of

11 Karl Marx, *Eighteenth Brumaire of Louis Bonaparte* [1852], available online at: www.marxists.org/archive/marx/works/1852/18th-brumaire/ch07.htm, October 7, 2010.

12 Roland Barthes, *Camera Lucida: Reflections on Photography*, Hill and Wang, New York, 1981.

course, the most useful reference. But at a more practical level, when filmed, the Shahids do sentence themselves to death, simply because the existence of tapes in which they are seen swearing to die as martyrs in Israeli cities makes them what military intelligence calls "ticking bombs," meaning they will be tracked down and targeted.

The Palestinians document their struggle, and their self-documentation is a form of liberation; the self portrait of the Shahid is a means of emancipation. There, on screen, the Shahid is not only avenger or terrorist – the Shahid succeeds in acquiring a face. But the ownership of the image is taken away the moment it is broadcast on television with commentary and titles provided by mainstream media. In Lebanon, Hezbollah controls not only the documentation, but also the airing of its operations. Hezbollah's TV station, Al-Manar, produces live-action films of the organization's operations against Israel. Using several cameras, the directors of Al-Manar cut between a handheld camera accompanying the fighters and a steady camera positioned further away and shoots an open frame of the scene. At home, the viewer witnesses a live simulation of war.

Framing

In the first Palestinian Intifada (1987–1993), Israeli photo journalist, Miki Kratsman, took black-and-white photos of the Palestinian popular revolt including youths throwing stones, women demonstrators, and men rallying others to their cause. Kratsman's photographs echoed Christian iconography – a Palestinian Pietà of a mother embracing her dead baby boy; a Palestinian staging of Doubting Thomas – a man pointing toward a hole in the stomach of a corpse left lying on the ground. Stylized as they are, these images are loyal to the popular aspect of the First Intifada. The photographer's engagement and sympathetic leanings could be felt in the black-and-white contrast that charges these photos with sharpness and strength. A clear correlation exists between the photographer's distinctive moral spectrum of just and unjust and his composition and manipulation of the negative. The photographer's agency was present in the composition and contrast.

In the context of the first Palestinian Intifada, the question of authorship is again complicated – after all, the news images of this revolt may have been framed and shot by Israeli and international crews, but the production and staging belonged to the Palestinians, who created the images of stones versus tanks, women versus soldiers, and masses versus military vehicles. In this sense, Kratsman's images, as important as they were, were not nearly as influential. And so, the inability to represent one's self as Palestinian, found its way out through Israeli and international lenses.

But suicide bombers in the Second Intifada did not need someone from the outside to document them, nor did they operate within the limits of black-and-white still photography: they exist in the highly saturated world of video. As the medium of video is used by rivaling political agendas such as antagonistic radical-democracy activism and extreme right-wing ideologies, we assume it is indifferent to the images projected through it. But this assumption calls for a close examination of the medium's specific qualities. Compared to still photography's sentimental allure, video is much more ambiguous. Realistic photography is still characterized by the notion that "this really happened," whereas video exists as a flow, disrupting the balance between cause and effect, between past and present. Black-and-white still photography is, in itself, an unambiguous testimony, not only because it seems to validate the claim that "this happened," because of the clear contrast between the black and the white, and the definite outlines of the subjects within them. Video, on the other end, consists of much doubt, in its smeared colors and jumpy frame. These video testimonies present us with many uncertainties – where do they come from, who took them, and for what reason? How were these people recruited? The images of the suicide bombers returning from the dead in their videos, contribute even more to the moral ambiguity of the medium.

Color

"The man is the center of the drama. Not flowers, not gardens, not dresses. The face is the center of the man and the eyes are the center of the face. If this process is not sharp enough to show the white in the eye of the man from reasonable distance, it's not worth a thing."

Technicolor's coloring technology tried to meet with the needs expressed in this quote by a 1930s Hollywood producer.[13] But in suicide bombers' videos, color strives to have a much bigger role. In these videos it seems that color is the center of the drama; the reds lash out, the blues float on aimlessly, the greens are smeared. The use of color in television broadcasting, even when showing material that was originally shot in black-and-white film stock, is devoid of the contrasting outlines of film. Here, any attempt to differentiate the just from the unjust on aesthetic terms is futile. The amorphousness of color is a moral amorphousness.

Johan Grimonprez's 1997 *Dial H-I-S-T-O-R-Y* (which incorporates DeLillo's *Mao II* for its narrator's voice) compiles a variety of archival material: Spectacular footage of televised airplane hijackings is juxtaposed with TV commercials, segments of feature films, and original recordings taken by Grimonprez himself. It is obvious this work concerns spectacle and the interrelations of terror and media. It seems the film examines the color of these interrelations. *Dial H-I-S-T-O-R-Y* is saturated with colors in a manner almost bordering on exaggeration. It is as if the excess of color is there to mock all attempts to differentiate between terrorists and victims, state violence and terrorist groups, political resistance and commodification. While the film, made prior to 9/11, seems to suggest a nostalgic reference to airplane hijackings and an affinity with Marxist-Leninist staging à la May 1968, the footage used in the film, seems to state that color is essential for terror; airplane hijackings were born the same time TV began broadcasting in color. The flow of images, the remixed feel of channel changing, the excess color; we see an airline hostess and a terrorist, an expert in sexual

repression, and a camera crew, all blending in with one another.

Suicide bombers can be said to endanger culture with saturated color, for excessive color has been affiliated with the primitive, barbaric, and corrupt.[14] Vivid and vibrant colors were considered the predilection of children, uneducated people, and savage nations.[15] While theories of color show that Western culture suffers from chromophobia, thereby aiming to repress color, terror mashes and exploits the red, green, and blue lights of television's color spectrum.

Duration

The option of limitless duration and endless continuity, which video allows, distinguishes it from any former technology of filming. Surveillance cameras, taping public and private spheres 24/7, offer non-event, non-narrative videos for non-viewers. As internet cameras and "real time" websites broadcast without editing, and maximize to infinity the duration potential of video representation and surveillance cameras by producing endless hours of footage, these technologies somewhat negate the role of the viewer. They exist without agent or audience until the catastrophe has already occurred.

Andy Warhol's *Empire* (1964) introduced the duration of surveillance cameras, and so predated the actual omnipresence and infinite duration of this technology. Shot on 16 mm film, this 485 minute static filming of the Empire State building in New York City depicts ongoing state terror. Conceptually, this piece was ahead of its time in terms of the continuity that videotaping allows. Even before filming on computer chips, videotapes recorded hours of footage. Before the introduction of video as a widespread technology, Warhol's reflections on the photographic image and its morbid hold on the modern imagination enabled him to foresee this phenomenon and to trace its temporal experience and aesthetics. As a landmark Manhattan skyscraper, the image of the Empire State Building resonates for many the Twin Towers, but it is the formalistic quality of this piece – its never-ending fixed frame

13 See: David Bordwell, Janet Staiger, and Kristin Thompson, *The Classical Hollywood Cinema. Film Style and Mode of Production to 1960*, Columbia University Press, New York, 1985.

14 See: Adolf Loos, "Ornament and Crime," in: *The Architecture of Adolf Loos*. An Arts Council Exhibition of Great Britain, London, 1985.

15 See: David Batchelor, *Chromophobia*, Reaktion Books, London, 2000.

on a still object (a building in this case) – that gives it such prophetic significance.

As shopping centers and government buildings are controlled by security checks at every entrance, until proven otherwise, these measures are aimed at us: we are all potential terrorists. A few days prior to the 9/11 attacks, Mohammed Atta, the head organizer of the hijackings, was documented in an ATM video camera. This was his suicide tape, so to speak. In this respect, not only are we all terrorist suspects, but are all potentially caught by surveillance cameras, too. As potential terrorists, our tape is already set.

Harun Farocki's video *I Thought I was Seeing Convicts* (2001) is composed of footage taken from surveillance devices at a high security prison in Corcoran, California. The cameras are aiming from the point of view of the gun.[16] In his video, *War at a Distance* (2003), Farocki examined state terror's internal and external manifestations through footage produced by "smart bombs" and surveillance cameras. In this piece, automated assembly-line footage, traffic control computer models, security cameras, aerial photography, and the smart bomb's self-documentation, all manifest the new form of non-human image-making by unmanned cameras. Opening the piece with an actual aerial footage of a bombing in the First Gulf War, the viewer encounters an image of annihilation that is in itself annihilated – no figure, perspective, scale referencing, or color are present to help us with a possible narrative, context, time, or location. No human beings, no story, no drama, no war. All we are left with are stains and grids. Like the production process, warfare has been abstracted and with it, the images it produces. Coining the term "suicide cameras" with regards to "smart bombs" armed with recording devices, Farocki is personalizing this otherwise anonymous form of warfare.

Pornography

Terror and pornography both share similar ways of using video. Although prostitution is illegal in most of the United States, pornog-raphy is protected by the First Amendment of the Constitution. Hence, when soliciting for paid sex, the presence of a running video camera can make it legitimate. For the terrorist, as for the pornographer, the presence of the camera makes all the difference.

Apart from the narrative climax a specific video may or may not pursue, the format itself entails a limitless extension of duration. The pornographic time frame is endless – ad infinitum, as Roland Barthes repeatedly emphasizes in relation to Marquis de Sade's literature.[17] The nature of video, it appears, adheres to this pornographic time frame. The "home video" of family events and the Shahid's video echo the all-inclusive pornographic aspect of video time. A long, and essentially endless dying, a state between life and death, replaces the decisive singular moment of death as captured in the still photo. For Barthes, de Sade's greatness did neither lie in his ability to glorify crime or perversion, nor in his radical language, but rather in the invention of a wide discourse based entirely on its own repetitions and prolongation. Contrary to what we expect of a pornographic film, namely, that it aims towards a fulfillment of the situation – the pornographic time frame relies on repeating certain positions and lectures – a certain order of never-ending confessions. De Sade's pornography does not require climax, but the sustaining of repetitive, didactical duration. The pornographic time frame relies on repetitive, didactic duration, Barthes claims. For him, de Sade's pornographic literature, does not address passion or sex, but rather fantasy, prolonging, and repetition. As the sadist's apparatus entails an elimination of the self as well as of the other,[18] so does the suicide bomber, who ascertains self-elimination and the elimination of others.

As Kaja Silverman put it, in our era of "anal capitalism's catastrophic commodification," only material goods are capable of eliciting passions[19] – the Shahids' videos are a passionate fantasy of death and destruction; their monologues consist of Sadean repetitions; their assault is never ending – a perpetual death.

16 See: Harun Farocki, *Imprint*, Vorwerk 8, Berlin, Lukas & Sternberg, New York, 2001.
17 See: Roland Barthes, *Sade, Fourier, Loyola*, University of California Press, Berkeley, 1989.
18 See: Pierre Klossowski, *Sade My Neighbor*, Northwestern University Press, Evanston, IL, 1991.
19 See: Kaja Silverman and Harun Farocki, *Speaking about Godard*, New York University Press, New York, 1998, p. 111.

Dorna Safaian

.After.the.Machine:.
...The.Economy.of...
..Innovation.and.the..
Iconotechnics.of.Islam

Innovation, Information, Image, Interdiction

God can only consistently show himself in the objects of the world when there is no doubt as to who created them. If creativity could also be claimed for those products formed by human beings, then God's monopoly on information and innovation would break down with each newly created product. However, according to Islam, mechanically produced and reproducible pictures do not intervene innovatively in the closed information space of the world; they do not make the claim of creative uniqueness, do not defy the creator with reference to one who calls himself *author* and one who wishes to imitate him. The flourishing production of reproducible images proves that a radial interdiction of pictures can no longer be upheld, but must be rather dismissed in favor of innovative economic considerations.

Islam and postmodern discourse correspond at the medial junction of traditional models of authorship, the dearth of transcendental production, the lack of an index of the mechanical, as well as in the subsiding of innovative heat, which had hitherto adhered to picture production. Having now become a mundane maximum, with Muhammad at the end of the prophetic line, visuality is a documentary means to codify the "thisness" of the world: independently of the author, independently of gesture, as pure information mediated by the world itself in estimation of a saturated picture of world information.

Muhammad and Pure Mediality

Muhammad radicalized monotheism by abolishing its pictorial multiplication, purified godliness from symbolic practice and claimed the position of consistent unity in distinction to Trinitarian Christianity, which describes the presence of the divine spirit through *approximation* and pictorial *appearance*. The fossilization of biblical linguistic tableaus "face to face"[1] in everyday language may conceal the fact that the truth as the modus operandi of the religious becomes active through approximation. The consistent concealment of the sacred has still been maintained 610 years after the Christological revelation in the flesh, since "Allah is the sole, unique, and only God (the unvarying). He creates and is not created, and no being is like him."[2] The God of Islam does not reveal himself, he is *unvarying*, conceals himself, with the exception of the revelation, and thus remains constant in form. The prophetic form is alone attributed the function of a "blind" ecstatic mouthpiece, into which are whispered the Koranic letters. It is precisely this model of communication between divine knowledge and profane receptacle, which forms the process of the cultural-historical navigation of Islam as a primary structural reference of medial mechanization. Here, Muhammad is neither an enigmatic figure, which could claim the veneration of his body, nor intrinsic messianic body, but an activator of his own ability for conception, which permits him to become sensitive to Koranic signs. His Christian predecessor, by contrast, became an iconic body, as modification of the aggregate state of a formable divine spirit, which can also let itself into a body so as to honor the thaumaturgic promise ("Through his wounds you have become whole"[3]).

In Islam, spirit is sublimated to the nonpictorial. Prophethood becomes an activity of pure mediality without being modified by its own share of bodily participation. The Islamic concept of the prophet negates the participation of sacral moments of Muhammedian life and defines it as profane life, which, only due to an initial consecrational purification, articulates itself as exclusive. According to the historiographer Ibn Ishaq, as a child, Muhammad was sought out by two men clad in white, who then took his heart from his body, split it in half, and removed a black lump.[4] The operative purification of the body separates *pure* from *impure*, thereby bringing forth the two spheres of the profane and the sacral as a founding act of the religious. At the same time, this narrative points to prophethood not as apriori sacral, since it is not the fact of being chosen which expands within the body, but to predestination selection, that is

[1] Gen 32, 31; 1st Kor. 13, 12, in: *Bible*, based on the translation by Martin Luther, Deutsche Bibelgesellschaft, Stuttgart, 1991, translated from the German by Justin Morris.
[2] Sura 112, 2–3, in: *Koran. Das Heilige Buch des Islam*, Goldmann, Munich, 1959, translated from the German by Justin Morris.
[3] 1st Petr. 2, 24, in: *Bible*, 1991.
[4] See: Ibn Ishaq, *Das Leben des Propheten*, Spohr, Kandern, 1999, p. 34.

5 Ibid., p. 46.

6 Great Ayatollah Sayyed Ali Khamenei, "Lessons from the Nahjul-Balaghah," available online at: http://www2.irib.ir/occasions/rahbar/nahjul.htm, June 10, 2009.

7 Ibid.

8 Sahī al-Buchārī, *Nachrichten von Taten und Aussprüchen des Propheten Muhammad*, Reclam, Stuttgart, 1991, XXXV, 31 (al-Buchārī is quoted according to chapter and paragraph).

9 Ayatullāh al-'Uzmā'As-Sayyid Ali al-Husaynī al-Khamene'i, *Antworten auf Rechtsfragen. Die Handlungen*, section I, part 2, Tehran, Iran, 2002, p. 65, translated from the German by Justin Morris.

10 Author unknown, "Hanging pictures," access via the online archive *Islamweb*, http://english.islamweb.net/ver2/Fatwa/Show Fatwa.php?lang=E&Id=82040&Option=Fatwald, December 6, 2010.

11 Author unknown, "Islamic Views on Erecting Statues," access via the online archive of the INFAD World Fatwa Management and Research Institute, Islamic Science University of Malaysia, http://infad.usim.edu.my/modules.php?op=modload&name=News&file=article&sid=6617, December 6, 2010.

consummated on the body as a process. It is evidently not Muhammad's physical ability to know the word of God, but his passive talent for being addressed by this language. Islam insists on the radical purity of religious mediatory activity, as liberation from the losses or additions of attrition. It implements Muhammad's bequeathed illiteracy *(an-nabi al-ummi)* as the guarantee of a pure transformation of information of knowledge, which is why it must be reviewed and presented by Archangel Gabriel. The angel surprised Muhammad during the night with a shawl the sign of which he was to decipher. "Read!" Gabriel commanded him, whereupon, as proof of optimum medial requirements, the surprised one then countered: "I cannot read."[5] The message is thereby shielded from profane impurities, since it cannot be modified by scholarly reproduction. Mediality hardens into a profession, which Seyyid Ali Khamene'i defines according to the tradition as handed down by Imam Ali, the so-called *Nahjul-Balagha*, under the title *How Are Prophets Chosen?*, based on a selection according to "better spiritually trained,"[6] whose representatives were called upon, "… not to mix their personal views with the divine message."[7]

Since 570 AD – the year of Muhammad's birth – the precarious unity of sender, message, and medium has been annulled and, by means of transcendentally protected prophethood, deiconized. With Muhammad, Islam pursued an initial aniconism, which precludes the divine medium as pictorial medium. With the necessary absence of God on earth, the suspicion of an ubiquitous presence is enforced all the more. Allah's name does not become plastic with reference to the body, but distances itself from the bodily image by means of the artificiality of the etiolated textual body. The significance here is that the Koran – as an exception in Arabic written culture – is consistently printed with all vowels. In order to understand a reference text without vowel signs, experience is required which attaches to the life of the *language game*, whereas the combination of letters and vowel signs allows the text to be sufficient in itself, beyond phonetic knowledge as an absolute entity.

The Author's Index

The use of reproductive media does not run counter to the aniconic and asymbolic culture of Islam: On the contrary, these are included in its position as a structural foundation. Muhammad's iconophobe bearing – "Those who paint these pictures will be severely punished on judgment day. To these it will be said: 'Bestow life to what you have created!'"[8] – represents an objection of the blasphemic idea of rivalry by means of mimesis, but formally refers to the indexical added value, the intelligibility of the madeness of the work: to traces of the author. The objection here is not that a picture has been created, but far rather that it has been created by a human being.

And yet with the machine, the hubris-like complicity of work and hand expires and gives way to the benefit of the smooth surface, which lends credibility to the fact that nobody wishes to use his hand for pictorial creation. Hence, it must appear as a cultural caesura and seem surprising that in a *Fatwa* [Islamic legal decree] al-Khamene'i permitted the production of sculptures of living beings animated with souls by means of mechanical reproduction "in so far as such production is not dependent on the direct action of the human being."[9] The severest penalty may be avoided as long as the body does not interact.

What al-Khamene'i does not tolerate is the trace of the author in the work, which becomes noticeable through indexicality; this is because, as a sign-theoretical eye of the needle, indexicality links the sphere of the living with that of the dead in the object. "Rough materials"[10] and "substances that last for a long time, wood, metal, or stone, for example,"[11] testify to the heterodox approach of the two rooms as a recorded trace. Resistance and immunity are intractable conditions with respect to the temporal facts of the world. By contrast, that which is in a state of decay and decomposition directly subordinates itself to spatial and temporal laws. This is why a *Fatwa* commends the use of video images, since as hard matter, these do not make the claim of having the status of an object: "[…] if a person was to look at the videotape itself with the naked eye then he would not see anything until he placed it in a device (video player) which (would then) project the images within the video tape (onto the screen for viewing) […]."[12] Only the secondary act of replaying makes the video image visible, which is a coded, secondary, temporary, and thus controllable existence, since offensive material is taken out of the world in the act of withdrawing the video. The negative bearing towards pictorial representation relativizes itself as soon as no indexical structure is perceptible on the surface, namely, as soon as the author, as one who acts with the hand, withdraws in favor of a codification.

Ban on Innovation

"[…] that one turn towards the path of the Sunna
and not turn towards the innovations by the human Satans,
who wish to renew the laws of religion."

Abū Hāmid al-Ghazālī [13]

Religious systems define a greater space of reflection which, in view of the primary act of creation, annuls the creativity of its earthly dwellers. Creativity and the claim of the new, position themselves in a precarious place, on the informational periphery of the "once given frame of the divinely established significance of being."[14] The Koran is that which is in itself complete since "we have left nothing out of this book."[15] Thus, Islam delimits the world space of the religious in an original and final division of information, which, with the spirit of the *Ummah* [original community], is saturated with the objects of creation and the letters of the Koran. That about which it is permitted to have knowledge and which may be touched for use, is the knowledge representing that which is modification information and that which is information modifica-

tion. Everything in the world is measurable by the yardstick of the ontological proficiency of the world. Authorship must also place itself on the innovation scales of the original counterweight, and thus, with the claim of the new, the unique, and the individual, desires only to disrupt the balance of the "thisness" of final information. This is because, in itself, it is a provocative counterpoint to the theological *Bid'ah* [innovation], the motto of which implies that God is everything innovative. Namely, "Islam […] has doctrines for everything concerning people and society. […] There is nothing that exists about which Islam has not passed judgment."[16] However, so as to avoid taking informatively mistaken steps, the life of the Prophet serves as leitmotif orientation, especially in the sunna [custom, habital modes…]: "The best guidance is the guidance of Mohammed. Of all matters the worst are innovations, and everything new is an innovation, and every innovation is a deviation, and every deviation leads to Hell-fire."[17]

As an expression of a satiated image of world information, the *Bid'ah* represents a cultural fortification for the protection of integral-original information, which realizes itself in the repetitive cycles of the religious against the dynamics of history. Here, Islam energizes this poise through the consciousness of being entrusted with the youngest and most recent grand religious project, namely, of adopting the final position in the prophetic order of the Judeo-Christian-Islamic sequence – to represent the target group of the latter of its prophetic revelations and to provide the receivers with the final dissemination of divine information. The standpoint of absolute knowledge is constituted such that Islam presupposes the beginning of belief not, as is the case in Christian-Jewish genesis and its religious writings, by referring to the Koran, but in presupposing antecedent monotheisms, and thus leaving unformulated a constitutive beginning or a genesis. Consequently, the Koran begins "without beginning"; only in this way is it the optimization of the

12 Shaykh Ibn 'Uthaymeen, "We exchanged the television for a computer," access via the online archive *Fatwa-Online*, www.fatwa-online.com/fataawa/creed/pictures/0070725.htm, December 6, 2010.

13 Abū Hāmid al-Ghazālī, *Die kostbare Perle im Wissen des Jenseits*, Spohr, Kandern, 2003, p. 112, translated from the German by Justin Morris.

14 Gotthard Günther, *Beiträge zur Grundlegung einer operationsfähigen Dialektik*, Meiner, Hamburg, 1976, p. 3.

15 Sura 6, 39, in: *Koran*, 1959.

16 Ayatollah Khomeini, *Meine Worte. Weisheiten. Warnungen. Weisungen*, Moewig, Munich, 1980, p. 19, translated from the German by Justin Morris.

17 Author unknown, "Who are innovators?," access via the online archive *Islamweb*, http://english.islamweb.net/ver2/Fatwa/ShowFatwa.php?lang=E&ld=82606&Option=Fatwald, December 6, 2010.

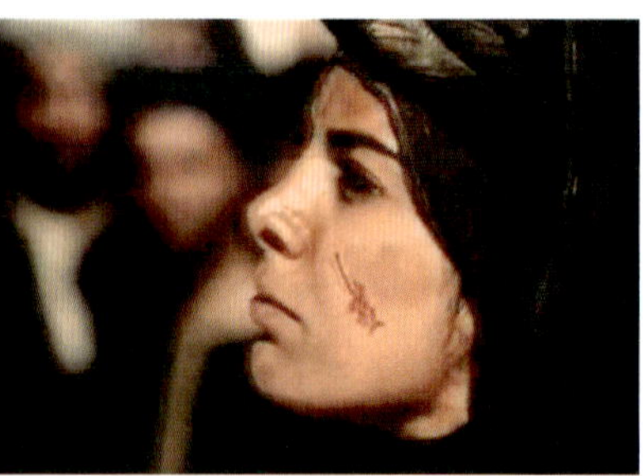 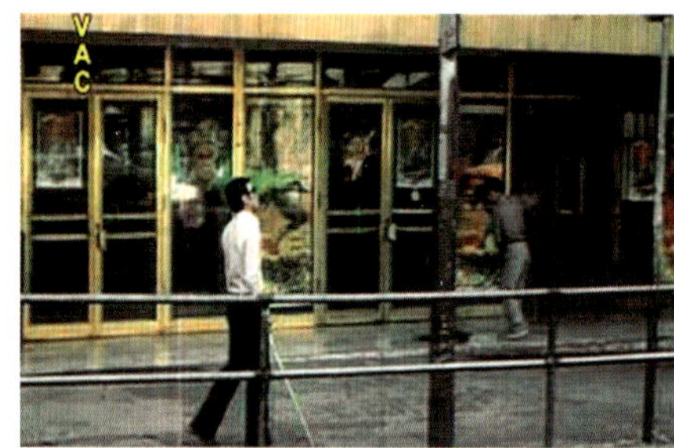 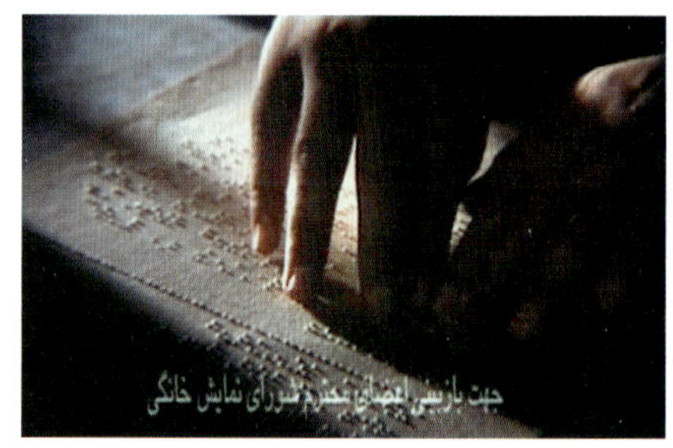

previously prophetically enriched. In this connection, al-Khamene'i asserts that in a condition of possible mundane maturity, God sent down Muhammad for this last prophetic case with all "(knowledge and awareness) that could be contained in the human mind"[18] and so set the limit to what God deemed it possible to pronounce upon about earth. In view of the integrity of the world and the human nature of its heralds, the best believer may be described as the most consistent tautologist, for whom no questions must remain open, whether in this world or in the hereafter. Even the *Fatwa* as legal institution serves to incorporate possible states of emergency within the framework of Islamic legitimacy. In a *Fatwa*, for example, one encounters the question as to whether women may also look forward to similar pleasures in paradise with angel-like partners of desire *(Hoor)* as can men, or whether there exist other facilities for this. The mufti intimates that for women who have been married several times, a paradisiacal partnership of desire may be assumed with the last or the best of their men, whereas unmarried women choose one of the paradisiacal men "who died before getting married or whose wives did not enter the Paradise with them."[19]

The Muslim does not demand proof of God by symbolic exertion, but the order and conclusiveness of a relevant system armed against emergency conditions. According to Christian revelation, once the prophetic contract has matured, it then evidently becomes unnecessary to symbolically or iconically affirm the existence of the transcendental addressee. The

earth can become a place of pure action. In orthodox Islam, actions which do not necessarily appear essential are considered as being impartial and thus questionable. However, authorship is de facto and a priori that sphere which the *Bi'dah* stimulates, and which is thus independent from what also expresses itself in the products of action: for Islam something that must remain a questionable figure.

Icono-technology of the Inanimate

"If living beings are a classification, the plant is best able to express its limpid essence; but if they are a manifestation of life, the animal is better equipped to make its enigma perceptible."

Michel Foucault[20]

As an innovation, the image dialectically touches the border with the living since, by referring back to the physical existence of an author as something artificial, it is already a passive participant in vital space. A specific icono-technology opens the navigation along this precarious line between the highly charged space of the living and the dead. On the threshold between the inner and the outer space leading to Muhammad's apartment – according to the sources of a *Hadith* [prophetic accounts] – the Archangel Gabriel introduced icono-technic practice: "I came to you yesterday, and there was nothing to prevent me entering (your house), other than the illustrations (tamatil) on the door. [...] Arrange things such that the illustrations are positioned (like this!) on the door of the house,

18 "God deputed His Last Messenger to provide them with all (the knowledge and awareness) that could be contained in the human mind and to complete the culture of prophethood, fulfilling the divine promise and overcoming all religions and man-made schools of thought." See: Khamenei, "Lessons from the Nahjul-Balaghah."

19 Author unknown, "Hell and Heaven as Eternal," access via the online archive of the INFAD World Fatwa Management and Research Institute. Islamic Science University of Malaysia, http://infad.usim.edu.my/modules.php?op=modload&name=News&file=article&sid=3788, December 6, 2010.

20 Michel Foucault, *The Order of Things. An Archeology of the Human Sciences*, Tavistock, London, 1974, p. 277.

< **Dorna Safaian**,
After being interpreted by a machine (the blind; the dead; realism), 2008, video installation, color, sound, duration variable, stills from a digital copy

> **Dorna Safaian**,
After being interpreted by a machine (the blind; the dead; realism), 2008, video installation, color, sound, duration variable, installation view, ZKM | Karlsruhe, 2009

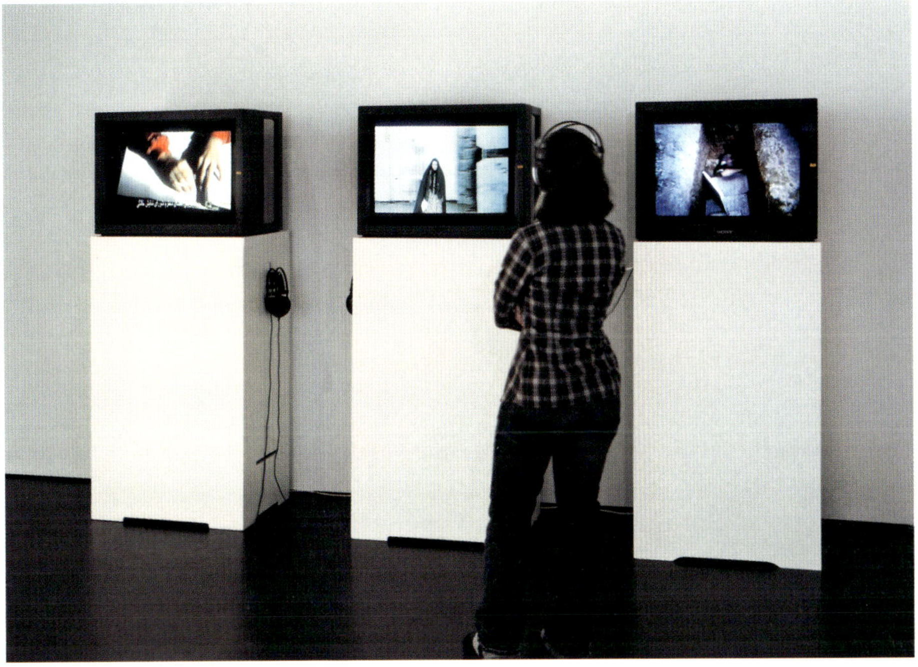

with the head detached, and that they appear like trees! And arrange things such that from the curtain (sitr) two (carelessly) thrown cushions […] are torn (or cut) on to which one then treads! […] Since, whatever resembles trees is like script or ornamentation […]. And whatever is placed on the wall or a curtain in the form of a living being, is like an idol (sanam). That upon which one treads however, does not resemble an idol. This is because it is not highly valued."[21]

Not to enter a space because of an object means that one has opened a space, and thus the passage, through to the Archangel Gabriel who does not cross the threshold, containing as supplement a picture-strategic offering, namely, the legitimization of the presence of pictures through their symbolic and semantic debasement. By seating oneself on the cushions, the potential danger of the desire to be seen, which is essential to pictures, is thereby annulled. However, what is more astonishing is why the angelic entity does not perceive vegetative life as miasma of his appearance.

The categorization of that which is apostrophized in Islam as living in the medium of the pictorial seed – via the distinction between plants and trees on the one hand as well as the mobile living entities on the other – is based on an idea, which leads this definition of vitality to the limits of representation. Furthermore, that which is permitted to be represented is decided by the existing vitality of the object; but planetary objects and plants could also be worshiped, as can be proved in the history of humanity. And yet this argument is encountered by the scholar Hanafit Ibn 'Abidin around the middle of the 19th century so that thereby "each time the thing itself [is] worshipped, and not the copy thereof."[22] Thus, he concludes that illustrations of the planetary and the vegetative cannot be worshipped, since their mode of being does not necessitate a fixation in the picture, whereas animate-living entities must first be "arrested" in the picture. In itself, the static is already an opaque picture, whereas the mobile makes a pictorial added value necessary. By a reverse logic: that which requires no representation withdraws from the concept of the living. But to illustrate something living – in this connection the

21 Quoted after: Rudi Paret, "Textbelege zum islamischen Bilderverbot," in: Josef van Ess (ed.), *Schriften zum Islam. Volksroman, Frauenfrage, Bilderverbot*, Kohlhammer, Stuttgart, Berlin, 1981, pp. 213–225, translated from the German by Justin Morris.
22 Ibid., p. 221.

innovative economic hindrance –, impedes the world by means of an additional piece of information, since it signifies no artificial alteration, namely, the fixing of the object in the picture. Characteristic of this is that the Arabic language does not differentiate between *forming* and *copying*, but both are expressed by the word *sawwara*. Vitality has to do with a deficiency of the moved, flexible, and non-pictorial – it requires representation in order to be seen intensively. As such, the inanimate-static is already complete and does not add anything new to the world as information, since it is the soul as *turgor vitae*, which makes the picture a risk. Vegetable being, the existence of which can only be presupposed in the border area of the "invisible" and "experienceable," relinquishes mobility and *turgor*, which leads from *life* into *living*.

The motif of death in the picture mediates itself in Islam in the icono-technological dead. As a condition for this, Gabriel demands that Muhammad's images be tolerated, their symbolic decapitation. This is further elaborated upon in Islamic legal literature by the option of represented life-endangering damage to the copied body. According to the *Kitab al-Mugni*, an Islamic legal canon of the Ibn Qudama (541–620 A.D.), the picture of a represented entity after decapitation from the torso is no longer considered a living being.[23] The non-vital, as an exception to this, could also be made effective. With respect to wearing clothes with pictures in the case of war a *Hadith* [records of the deeds and pronouncements of the prophet Muhammad] maintain s: "I asked Abū' Abdallāh (VI.) about clothes made of silk and brocade. He said: in war there is nothing to object to, even if pictures are on them."[24] The case of war as provocation of death carries the pictures of living entities with it into the zone of possible death. The wearing of the picture becomes a legitimate possibility of destruction through the threat of its existence. Islam focuses not on the complete abolishment of the body from the picture, or even the elimination of the picture itself, but on a deformation or (foreseeable) destruction of the pictorial body such that it cannot be claimed to have a soul. The significance of the soul-infused body gives an indication of the basis of the symbol-critical content of Islamic thought through its interpretation relating to the pictorial idea. The symbol as a psychic insignificant element – no less than a vegetative being – can assume no mediating position as illustrated agency. The central contact point of vital-energetic exchange remains the *acheiropoieton* Koran. The killing of that which is represented as icnono-technical impossibility of intended psychic life is thus the unconditional productive condition of the picture.

The Photography and the Freedom of the New

The photographical picture is already lifeless; it is that which complies with recognized limits of information. Islam understands photography as the possibility of picture production, including the iconoclastic gesture and excluding the psychic life of the object. The *Fatwas* on photography make clear that the photographic picture of the soul of the living object is not transformed within the medium. Here also, it is the "non-vitality" which opens the way to the picture, since it is emphasized that the act of photography – independent of the composition of the object, excepting hostile and immoral subjects – is not a form of new creation ("[…] while photography means capturing the reflection of a creature. Thus, this act is not considered as imitating Allah's creation."[25]) Furthermore, the act of photography is not understood as an individual recontextualization of an object: "Photography is fundamentally permitted. They are only then *haram* [forbidden, taboo], if their object is *haram*."[26] A surface of media theory now appears, making it clear that the structure of Islamic attitudes to pictures corresponds with the techniques of reproductive media. Hence, as the medium guarantees, Islam demands the distance towards the illegitimate constitution of objectness to the benefit of the icono-technicity of "pure" given

23 Ibid., p. 224.
24 Ibid., p. 228.
25 Author unknown, "Owns Photo Shop in America," access via the online archive *Islamweb*, http://english.islamweb.net/ver2/Fatwa/ShowFatwa.php?lang=E&Id=84269&Option=Fatwald, June 10, 2010.
26 Yūsuf Qaradāwī, *Erlaubtes und Verbotenes im Islam*, SKD Bavaria, Munich, 1989, p. 107.

information, which neither wishes to be original nor new. The fact that photography is intrinsically precise, illustrating point for point with the human hand on the release button, is something which reconciles the picture with the Islamic world. To represent something imprecisely by hand illustrates mimesis as hubris, exact illustration by machines duplicates without duplicate picture.

Islam not only points to the annihilation of vitality through the reproduced multiple pictures, but also to a temporal theoretical aspect, through which the legitimacy of the camera apparatus as *medium of redundancy* is recognized. Here, the information economic emphasis in relationship to time and innovation is once again actualized. It is the author's ability to make time visible by acting on material, which becomes his undoing. As author, he leaves traces behind and thereby time signs and thus refers to his presence at the interface of an obvious being and reaction *on* and *from* a time axis, which a priori characterizes his profession. The legitimation of photography dissolves the entanglement of the author from the point of this temporal theoretical problem. Those temporal signs mediated by hand are eliminated and facilitate rescue from the hardest punishment by God. Authorial attitude – this is the fundamental skepticism of Islam towards creative people – is temporally and indexically parasitic, since it does not retract itself entirely before the God-given reality. Everything that did not previously exist is doubtful and intentional. This argument was introduced to the discussion on photography, among others, through Yūsuf Qaradāwī, founder of the Faculty of Islamic Law at the Quatar University and president of the European Council for *Fatwa* Research. Hence, it speaks for itself that photography is that which creates pictures with ideal parameters, namely, from something which anyway exists.[27] In Islamic thought, photography is therefore not media-specific, such that through the act of recording, whatever is illustrated becomes transformed. It is understood as a pure recording surface from which it is

less the camera that speaks to nature in a centrifugal-transformational manner, but far more nature, centripetally, to the media recording surface. The camera is not a mode of perception, but only the recording. As William Henry Fox Talbot attests in a letter to the editor of the *Literary Gazette*: "[…] it is not the artist who makes the picture, but the picture which makes ITSELF."[28] Talbot petrifies photography as the exposure of an object which, via the processual route object–machine–material–picture, is neither affected nor, through transformation, sign-theoretically revalued. According to this view, the picture is not semiotisized: "And the picture taken by the machine is the same thing created by Allah and not its resemblance."[29]

Real Time and the Precariousness of the Moving Picture

The foundations for legitimation with respect to the theme of photography are adapted for transfer to the genre of *moving pictures* of film, television, and video. In general, the specificity of the three types of picture is not accounted for in the *Fatwas*, or no distinctions are made between them. Due to the ubiquitous acceptance of these media, the decision with respect to the interdiction is made solely on the basis of the use and the represented context, and the same goes for computer-generated pictures: "The ruling concerning the mass media such as television, video and computer depends on their use."[30] What is decisive for these pictorial media is the assumption of an ontological foundational equality with the genre of photography since, "as for photography, which is similar to the image one sees in the mirror, it cannot be included in the prohibition. The same argument applies to video filming."[31] The filmic picture legitimizes itself as reproduced, unoriginal, multiplied, as well as ontologically past and, at the same time, space-time present: The Islamic concept of reality, which is derived from the cosmic entity of the *Tawhid* [belief in the unity of God, the notion of a space-time

27   Ibid., p. 104.

28   William Henry Fox Talbot, letter to the editor of the *Literary Gazette* from January 30, 1839, quoted after: Gail Buckland, *Fox Talbot and the Invention of Photography*, David R. Godine, London, 1980, p. 43.

29   Author unknown, "Professional Photography," access via the online archive *Islamweb*, http://english.islamweb.net/ver2/Fatwa/ShowFatwa.php?lang=E&Id=83020, June 10, 2010.

30   Author unknown, "Playing computer or video games," access via the online archive *Islamweb*, http://english.islamweb.net/ver2/Fatwa/ShowFatwa.php?lang=E&Id=83778, June 10, 2010.

31   Author unknown, "Video of a Wedding," access via the online archive *Our Dialogue*, www.ourdialogue.com/answers/articles.php?action=show&showarticle=1131, June 10, 2010.

continuum], is anchored in the categorical and stabile-homogenous space-time axis, which describes the "thisness" of the condition of the world with information contained within it as God-given. The disregard of its coherence as infraction against the divine foundation of being is also worthy of discussion within the framework of the ontology of the filmic picture. This is because the moving picture assumes its status in the world, which, as construed by Islam, must be thought as one, which must be described as temporally neutralized. It makes reference to reality due to its visual orientation, aligns itself with the space-time continuum and yet at the same time denies this in that – during the observation – it plays back past information as present information. At the same time however, it does not make the claim of being something special and new in the present space-time continuum, but always defines itself as something bygone. Thus, in terms of temporal theory, the filmic picture is a paradoxical medium, which is temporally neutralized at the interface between past and present reference. As medium, it operates in the present, always with recourse to pictorial reference. Consequently, it is thus safeguarded both in reference to the *Bid'ah*, as well as to the coherence of the *Tawhid*. It is anchored in space-time, but nevertheless leaves this not through the creation of an innovation, since it adheres parasitically to the God-given thing world. Accordingly, medial precision of the ontological status of the moving picture in Islam can only be read *ex negativo* by means of a criticism, which operates on a temporal-theoretical level: The criticism of live or direct transference of perception allows for the moving picture, as one which locates itself as a multiplicational outside life, to become clear. This form of transference assumes a temporally ambivalent role, in that due to its real-time status, it scratches at the periphery of vitality (even if there are only minimal temporal delays). Al-Khamene'i decreed in [*Answers to Legal Questions*]: "If the observation is connected to the presence in the wrestling arena and with the direct observation of that which is directly transmitted by the television or the like [...], then it is not permitted, otherwise it is admissible."[32]

In that direct transmission of the actual moment brackets out the reproductive aspect, it facilitates no extraction from the space-time continuum. The fixation of the illustration on the technical surface through temporal delay – which provides the conditions of reproduction – does not facilitate the perception of the vitality of the illustration from the continual space-time. The cultural emphasis of the reproductive in Islam has its source in the automated and particularized character of the reproducible medial surface as a result of the encapsulation of real time. The reproductive refers to past circumstances and thus extracts it from the continuum according to time. At the same time, the direct transmission not only points to the real references, but mediates these within the closed space-time continuum. The actual legitimation of the medium within Islamic thought, namely, that visuality expresses itself as unoriginal reproduction, is disrupted in the moment of real-time transmission. This is why al-Khamene'i points to the essential difference between a delayed and a direct transmission of the medial picture. In the wrestling match *Fatwa* he remarks that the viewing of the body in delayed time is permitted, where the reasons for this are to be found in the problematic immediacy, or temporal logic of simultaneity in the represented bodies. As medial pictures, these cannot be dehumanized in the sphere of the unloving if they at the same time duplicate themselves as real. It is not clear in the live transmission whether the picture produces life, or whether the life in the picture becomes visible as reproducible. The reciprocity of the relationship generates a mistaken perceptual procedure, which does not clearly mediate to the television viewer a disembodied and dehumanized medial surface. This is why al-Khamene'i examines the temporally delayed observation of the

32 Al-Khamene'i, *Antworten auf Rechtsfragen*, 2002, p. 52, translated from the German by Justin Morris.

wrestling match not from the point of view of appetitive soul, but treats it independently from the seductive impression of a direct body. This divergence between the observation of an unmediated body and a medial encoding may be compared to the difference in the pictorial preparation of corpse and body. Thus, just as the body annuls the relationship to place,[33] so does the picture annul a spatial-temporal localization and fixation. Maurice Blanchot describes corpse and picture as the presence of an indefinite *here* and *nowhere*, which makes human action absurd and turns it into a simple picture resembling his previous self. The dead as a picture is far removed from itself, as mere reference to that which the shell had hitherto made living. The picture as something frozen embodies the corpse-like being in rigidness, which "sets nothing, constructs nothing,"[34] whereby its localization must remain forever questionable and speculative.

In the course of direct transmission, the distinction between the space of life and death in a moment of temporal symbiosis is blurred. The real-time transferred picture is a delicate interface, which contextually cancels the radicality of the reproductive picture and catches up with this as originally divergent from the time of expiring life. However, the dual temporal structure points to the Islamic legitimation of moving pictures due to the temporal distance between shot and transmission time, which is effective in terms of religious law, if the medium approximates lived time. The foundation, on which the analysis of the photographic treatment of pictures is based, is augmented in the context of the moving pictures around the space-time coordinates of the *Tawhid*, and measured against these. Here, the temporal interval, which eliminates the explosiveness of the represented, can be captured in real time.

This stands in contrast to postmodernist critique of the media. When comparing the two, it becomes clear that in Islam transmission in real time is criticized by means of that argument, which defeatist postmoder-

nity refers to as the object of its demand: the appearance of the real. For Islam, the lack of body in real-time still has too much reference to life.

Repetition or the Conditions of the Picture

Neither the zeitgeist nor strategies of political agitation alone cause Islam to affiliate itself to reproductive cultural technology: it is the theological religion itself, which lays the foundation of visual extension in media pictures; and thus, it is due to the inherent dialectic of Islam that the basic grid of its contemporary visual picture strategy of iconoclastic gesture is subject to the iconoclastic gesture or the oscillation between iconoclasm and aniconism. On the one hand, icono-skepticism and innovation bars separating them from primary picture production, while thereby preparing the optimum fertile ground for the reproduction of pictures, which make no claim to a connection with *a* human being. Here, one is confronted with a phenomenon, whose visuality requires a medial twin in order to be visible and to redeem the enigmatic complicity of religion and the mechanical. This is because, if the picture is realized by means of a mechanized apparatus, it cannot be said of it that it is a spectral, repetitive, and multiplicative picture with a discreet gaze towards vitality. Where life has been animated and represented by God, then the attempt to approximate it, even if only by means of representation, cannot be tolerated. The Islamic icono-skepticism nourishes itself from the attenuation of innovative impulses and leads the original avisual space back towards the pragmatically unnecessary encumbrance of the closed, mundane circle with pictures. The traceability of the human being as index is one auctorial presence too many; however, this is balanced out through the flat surface of reproducible pictures. The approximation to the Islamic conception of the picture demands change to the surface of the medium itself: not to the iconic reference to the picture, not to the medial necessity of the picture, but to the pictorial necessity of the medium.

33 Maurice Blanchot, "Die zwei Fassungen des Bildlichen," in: Thomas Macho and Kristin Marek (eds.), *Die neue Sichtbarkeit des Todes*, Fink, Paderborn, Munich, 2007, pp. 25–36, here: p. 27.
34 Ibid., p. 30.

Rabih Mroué

..The.Fabrication..
.....of."Truth".....

This text was first published in: *Tamáss. Contemporary Arab Representations. Beirut/Lebanon 1*, Fundació Antoni Tàpies, Barcelona, 2002.

Contemporary Arab Representations is a long-term project directed by Catherine David. The series includes seminars, publications, performances, and presentations of works by various authors – including visual artists, architects, writers, poets, and intellectuals – the aim of which is to encourage production, circulation, and exchange between the various centers of the Arab world and the rest of the world.

In Arab countries, political powers, parties, religious communities and various official institutions continue to celebrate and praise martyrdom and collective death. This is done in the name of "the fatherland," "the soil," "liberation," "Arab blood," "Islam," and other such slogans. Yet these same societies swiftly forget their heroes, who are later relegated to the status of names that merely lengthen the list of martyrs.

In the following pages we will attempt a reading of the videocassette recorded by a member of the Lebanese Communist Party and combatant for the National Resistance Front, Jamal Satti, in 1985. The recording was made just a few hours prior to carrying out the suicide operation against the Israeli army, which was occupying Southern Lebanon at the time, and was broadcast on the news program of Lebanese national television, as is often the case with such operations.

Elias Khoury and I happened to come across the original, uncut videotape. Here, Jamal Satti repeats his testimony three times in front of the camera before finally opting for the best version to present to the public. However, the differences between these three versions are virtually without consequence. The public was supposed to see only one of his attempts: an incontestable, unequivocal document. When viewing the original cassette, we immediately fell under the spell of these repeated attempts; we gave into temptation despite ourselves, and we decided to present the unedited version of the tape to the public. We even made it the subject of our theatrical performance, *Three Posters*. We were well aware that in so acting we were exposing ourselves to the severest of moral accusations:

1. We allowed a public "foreign to the party and the family" to witness the martyr's emotions before his death.
2. We presented a videotape that does not belong to us.
3. We exploited this videotape to develop an "artistic" performance from which we will draw both moral and financial profit.
4. We allowed ourselves to violate the sacred space of the martyr in order to critique the concept of martyrdom and,

therefore, the powers which nourish and encourage such ideologies (official or otherwise; in this case, the political party to which Jamal Satti belonged).

Here, we are neither concerned with responding to these accusations, nor of discussing the problems they raise. Our interest rather lies in attempting to understand the meaning of Jamal Satti's repeated attempts before the camera, to elucidate the significance of these unutterable instants of that non-place between life and death, and to attempt to understand the effect produced on the public by this exceptional situation during the showing of the videotape.

To begin with, let us pause to consider more closely these repetitions in Jamal Satti's testimony, evidently induced by a state of heightened emotion. Jamal Satti was a fighter who feared no death, and his voluntary confrontation with it bears testimony to this. However, as soon as he steps before the camera to film his testimony, his words begin to fail him, stuttering and stumbling between his lips. His gaze is both fitful and focused. These different takes resemble those of an actor when preparing his role. Why does Jamal Satti see the need to act? Does his martyrdom require some other mark that could be in any way more effective than the actual suicide operation itself, intended as it is to "cause substantial damage to the Israeli enemy"? Could it be that the media image has greater impact than the act of martyrdom itself, even more than physical death?

These questions, although simple, are violent.

The young man begins by introducing himself: "I am the martyred comrade Jamal Satti…" By means of the image, he presents himself as a martyr in an undefined, non-place antagonistic to either of the known worlds, the worlds of the living and of the dead. In reality, however, his martyrdom is to be performed only after a certain period of time has elapsed, the duration of which we remain ignorant, but that extends from the moment of filming to the moment at which his mission is fulfilled.

Does the martyrdom then take place directly before us, through the film image of the videotape?

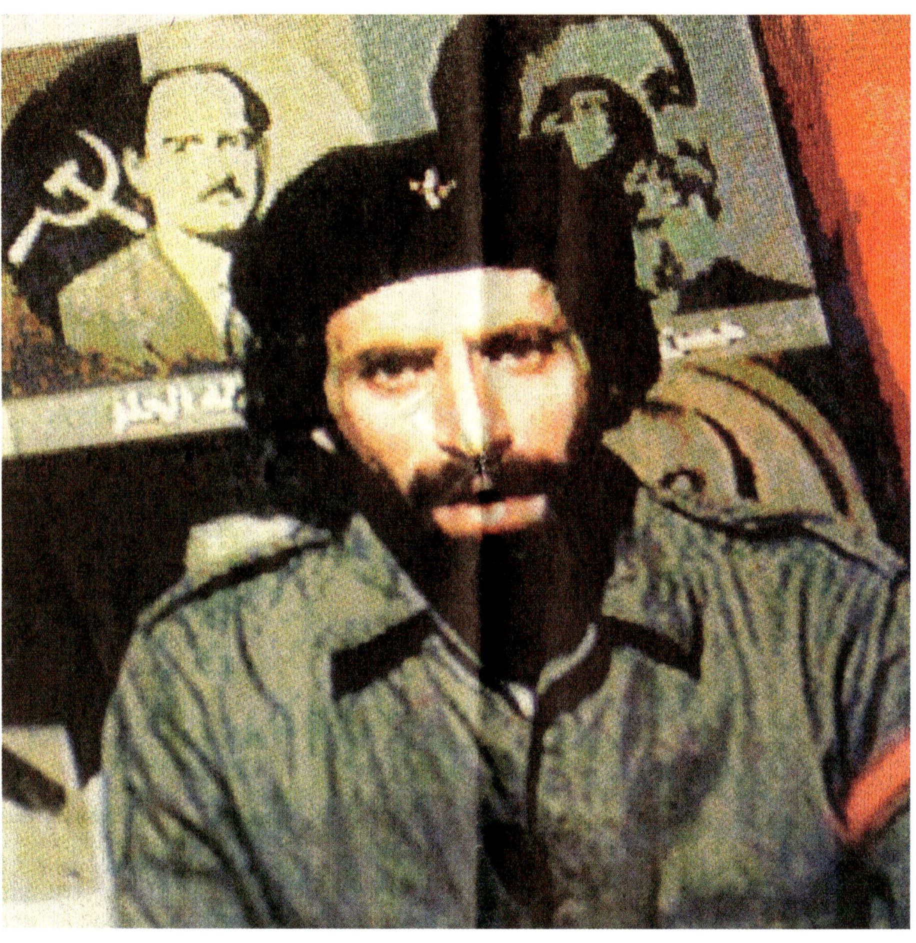

It would, indeed, appear that the martyrdom is actualized at the very instant in which the young man announces his martyrdom before the camera, by the sheer fact of this announcement. Thus, for him it is self-evident to introduce himself with the words: "I am the martyred comrade Jamal Satti…" and not "I am Jamal Satti, soon to be a martyr…" The martyrdom has taken place before the suicide mission. The question as to whether or not this operation has been executed remains immaterial. When declaring, "I am the martyred…," what I am really saying is, "I am the dead man…" However, as yet, I am still alive, and it is quite possible that I will not become a martyr. In spite of this, viewers acknowledge the declaration of the martyr's death without hesitation. But if I repeat this declaration once again, and for a third time, then doubt begins to set in. It would seem that the powerful effect of these repetitions is induced by the refusal of life and the announcement of "departure" even by a deferral of the act of death to a later, unspecified point in time. I would argue that emotion is evoked neither by the mere calculated desire to gain the audience's sympathy, nor simply by a belated awareness of what will become of the martyr after death. The emotion, above all, attaches to an unarticulated desire, a desire, moreover, impossible to formulate, and which seeks to defer death coincident to the withdrawal from life. Hence, the repetition signifies this twofold desire for deferral and withdrawal…

I dream that I am facing a camera, and that I am unable to finish filming my testimony before going out to execute a suicide operation against the Israeli occupation. I repeat the same text over and over again on the pretext

> **Rabih Mroué**, *On Three Posters. Reflections on a video-performance*, 2006, video, color, sound, 18 min, installation view, ZKM | Karlsruhe, 2009

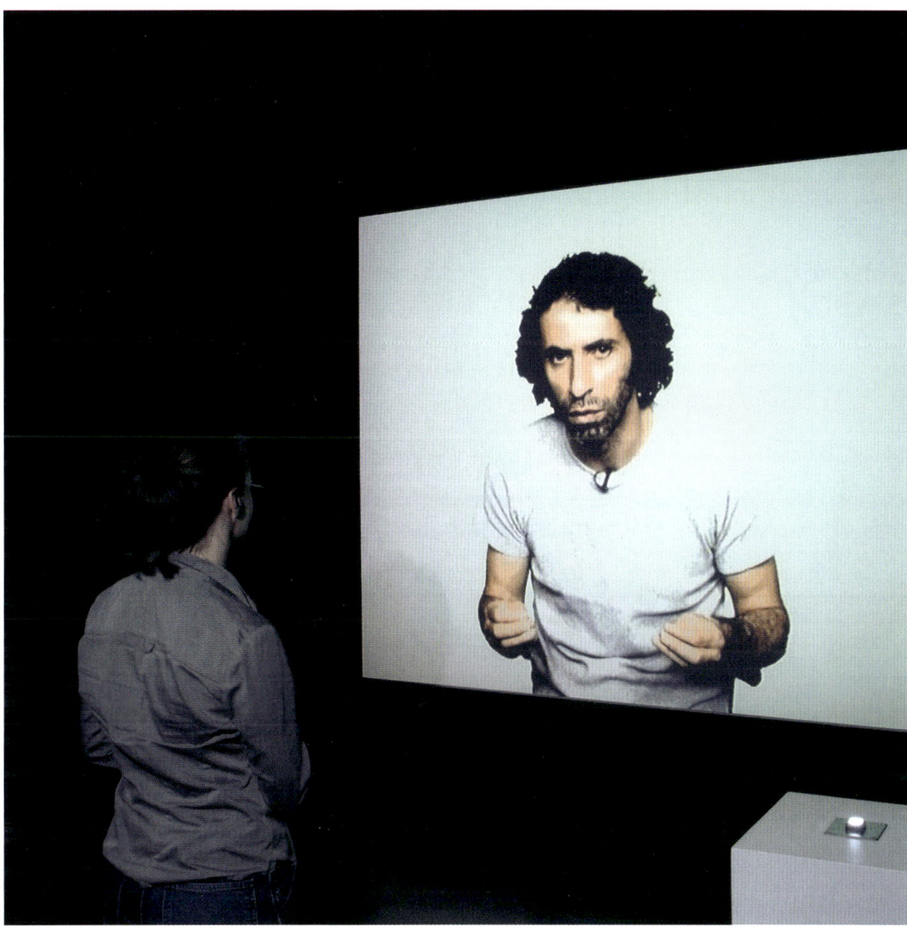

of trying to obtain a better version. Twice, ten times, a hundred times… while it is easy to see that all the takes are the same, I am unable to stop myself… A repetition ad infinitum… Repetition for the sake of killing time, just to gain time… Time passes; I grow older and continue repeating my testimony before the same camera… Suddenly, my military superior appears… He is dressed in civilian clothing… He tells me, smiling, that the Israeli army has withdrawn from Lebanese territory and that the operation is now unnecessary.

During a performance at a theater festival, an actor wounded his eye which began bleeding profusely, an occurrence troubling to the audience as well as his fellow actors. The latter suggested that he leave the stage as discreetly as possible, unnoticed by the public, but he refused. Yet he was truly suffering, his condi-

tion was critical. The performance continued, and the actor's bloody eye became a spectacle in itself, a unique commingling of reality and fiction so as to feed the public's voyeurism with a rare and curious spectacle to which they were certainly intent on being privy. At the end of the show, audience and fellow actors gave their unreserved applause, thus expressing their admiration for his self-denial, their gratitude for his sacrifice; a salute to the risks he had deliberately run just so as to ensure the play's success. As it lay prone on the stage, detached from its rightful place, the eye's fixed glare at the audience went unnoticed.

The actor was awarded the jury's special prize for several reasons: for the public's compassion and empathy evoked while continuing to act out and interpret his role even while in the throws of excruciating pain.

What does acting and dramatic interpretation coupled with real suffering mean for the public? What is the relation between this meaning and the martyr's repeated takes in front of the camera?

The injured actor did not leave the stage; his colleagues continued the performance, while the public appreciated its privileged position in being witness to the spectacle of blood. Taking the significance of this act to its logical conclusion, we arrive at a crime participated in by all. No one is aware of the severity of the injury. Will it kill the actor? Will he lose his eye for good? Will he collapse in a fit of nervous convulsions which will end in complete paralysis? No one knows… And yet the desire for death has been declared before our very eyes, and we accept it as a seldom encountered object of voyeurism, something that enflames our desire. While this tacit pact to contemplate death in cold blood is an expression of the refusal of life and a revolt against its logic, it is no less a desire for the deferral of death until the end of the performance.

Why does the actor accept the experience of death during the performance? Why does the martyr accept the experience of acting and representation, in the dramatic sense of the term, even while preparing to die? Is it the temptation, the idea of immortality? Perhaps…

However, it is no less probable that such sacrifices are the expression of a desire to enter history without the encumbrance of a body, of one's own body. In other words, through the actor's declaration of his readiness to die, a promise is made of a paradise where all martyrs dwell in a single, ideal body, an image-icon without a past or personal history.

Thus, whether or not the actor's announcement of his decision to withdraw from theatrical life represents a desirable end to this story is something I cannot say: It would doubtless be the most logical one, no less than it would be for the martyr, if ever he decided not to carry out his suicide mission after his testimony had been broadcast. I suspect he would have no other choice than to retreat into isolation and withdraw from life. This is actually what happened in the case of one resistance fighter, in May 1986: After the broadcast of his testimony on an official TV station, rumor had it that the operation had not taken place, that the martyr was not dead. What is more, Israel had announced no incident inside the Lebanese territories it was occupying at the time. What happened? We will never know. What is more, and most importantly, we also know the body of the fighter will never be found. The fighter disappeared, and to date no one can say what became of him or what actually happened.

In my opinion, the degree of truth in this story is immaterial. Jamal Satti's repeated attempts before the camera raise a further question, namely, the significance of the mediated "truth" when broadcast to the public as an exceptional moment at which "truth and fiction" merge. Similarly, his repeated attempts pose the question as to whether it would be possible to construct an artistic work that critiques the notion of "truth," a work claiming to convey the unedited "truth" even while itself remaining a "fabricated truth."

In *Three Posters*, the image of the martyr Khaled Rahhal appears to the public alongside his actual embodiment in flesh and blood. Hence, a crucial discrepancy emerges between these two forms of presence, which reciprocally cancel each other out. The image no longer functions as the residue, or representation of the real body, just as the presence of the real body ceases to function as an alternative to the image. This mutual interference denounces before the public not only the usurped identity of the martyr by his appearance in flesh and blood, but goes so far as to denounce his identity as a stage actor, an actor who reads his own real name, date of birth, and a few other details of his "personal life" from a piece of paper, before giving up his playacting to sit down alongside the public and watch the videotape on which the image of the "real" martyr, Jamal Satti will appear.

I cannot help but interpret Jamal Satti's repeated attempts as a desire for the deferral of death, in these depressing lands where the desire to live is considered a shameful betrayal of the state, of the nation state, of the fatherland or motherland.

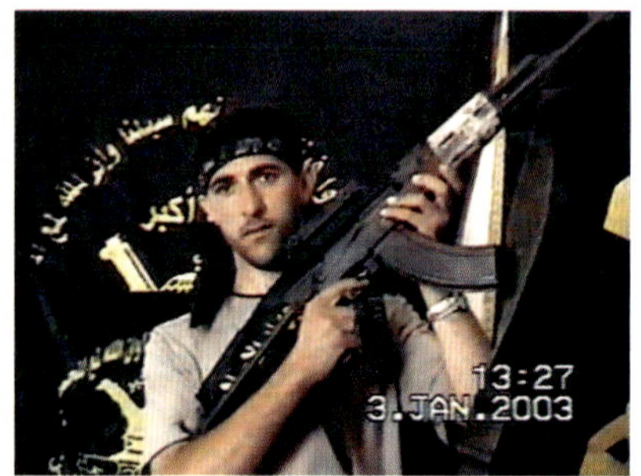

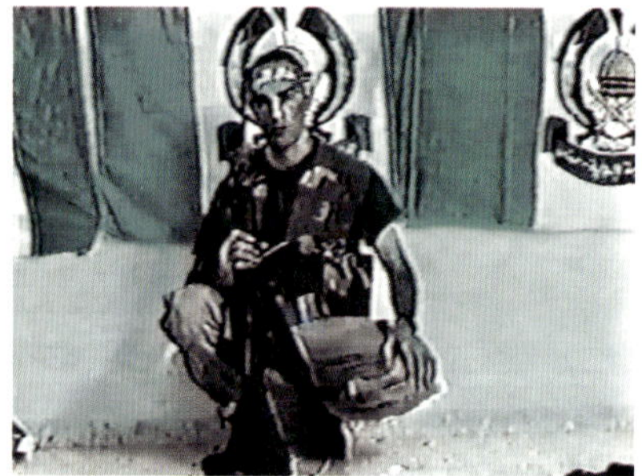

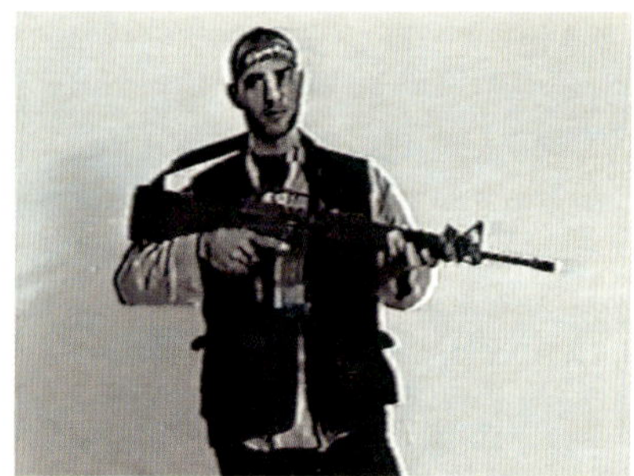

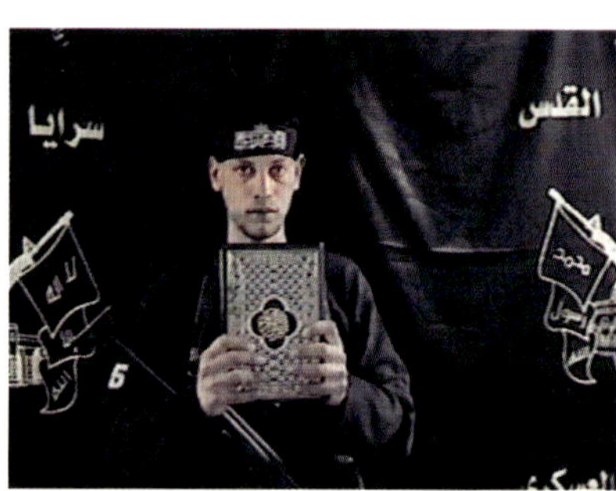

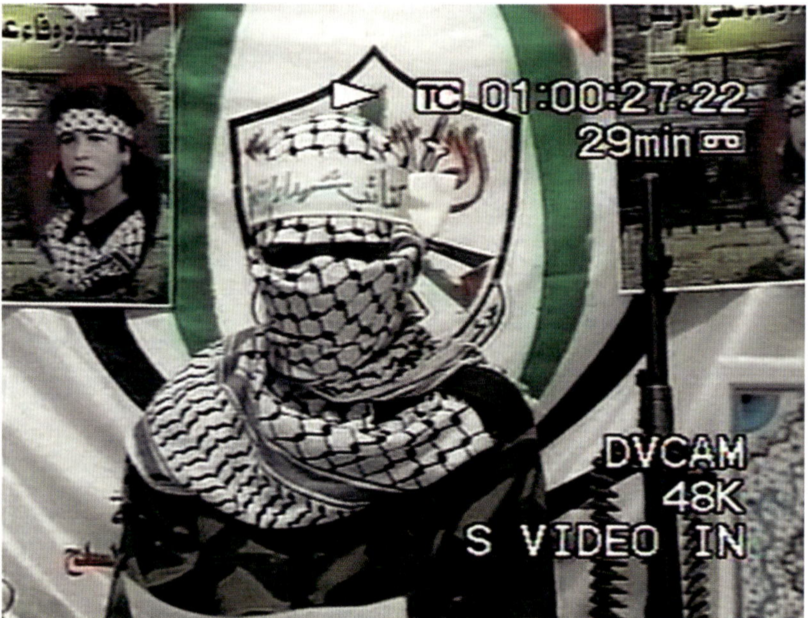

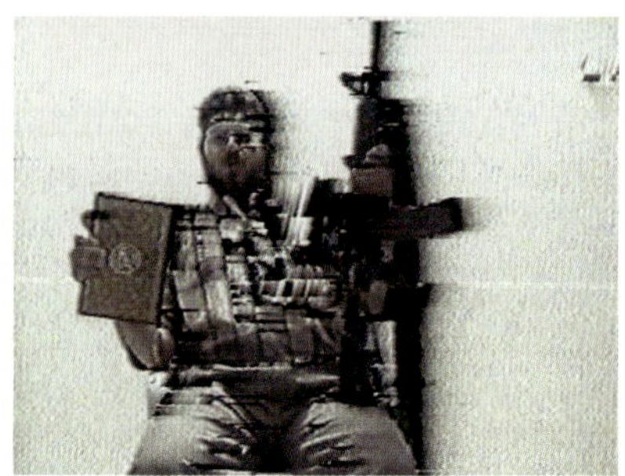

Joshua Simon
*1979 in Tel Aviv-Jaffa, Israel,
lives and works in Tel Aviv-Jaffa

Shahids, 2003–2008,
video collage, color, sound,
20 min, stills from a digital copy

During the Palestinian revolt known as the Second Intifada and beginning in autumn 2000, 161 suicide bombers carried out 144 attacks in which 515 Israelis died and a further 3,428 were injured. All of the suicide bombers allowed themselves to be videoed before they set out on their mission. As examples, the documentary video collages show six Palestinian videos of suicide bombers. The videos record the moment before the act and are at the same time a confession of murder, a farewell letter, and part of a strategy of terror aimed at claiming media coverage. By the time we see these young men and women, as they pray and prepare for death, they are already dead, the anticipated act has already been committed. All of the confessional videos also distinguish themselves by a common aesthetic with respect to lighting, camera use, and editing.

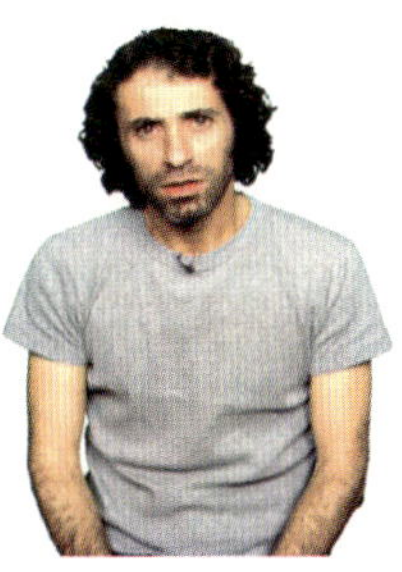

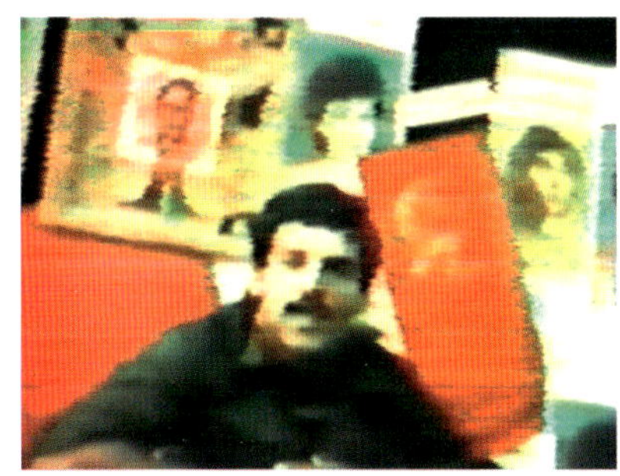

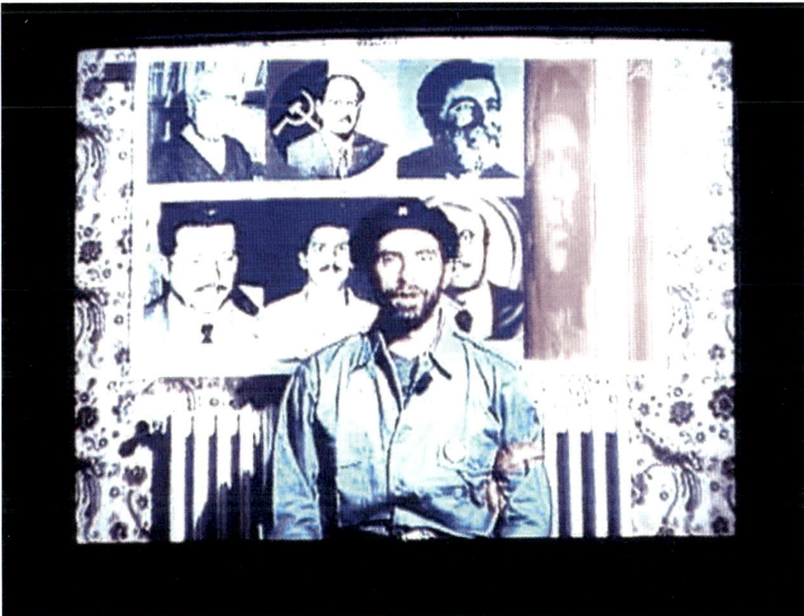

Rabih Mroué
*1967 Beirut, Lebanon,
lives and works in Beirut

*On Three Posters. Reflections
on a video-performance*, 2006,
video, color, sound, 18 min,
stills from a digital copy

In this video commentary, the
performance artist Rabih Mroué
depicts how a video confession by
a Lebanese resistance fighter,
killed in 1985 on one of the first
suicide attacks on the Israeli occu-
piers of South Lebanon, came
about. The chance discovery of
the video material shows that the
freedom fighter had tried, like an
actor, to depict himself in various
versions as one already dead and a
martyr. This inspired Mroué and
the Lebanese historian Elias
Khoury to analyze which artistic
and political aspects intersect in
the production of such a video. In
addition, they look into the question of why such a document,
which was developed originally in
a secular struggle for freedom,
could establish itself as an Islamist
strategy of the Hezbollah.

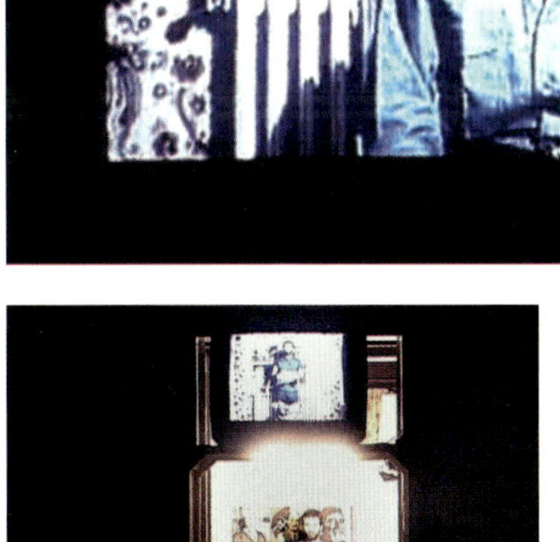

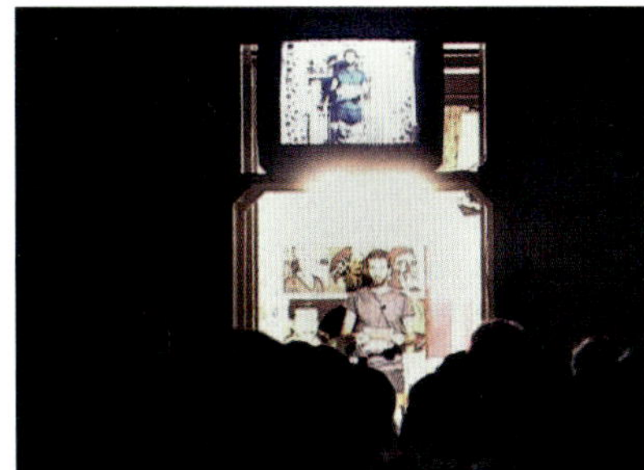

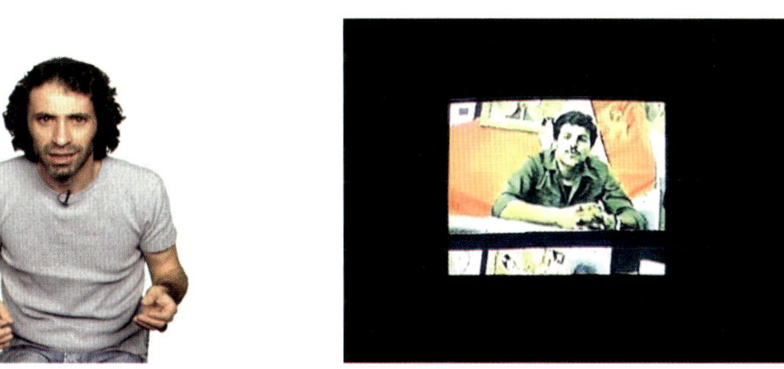

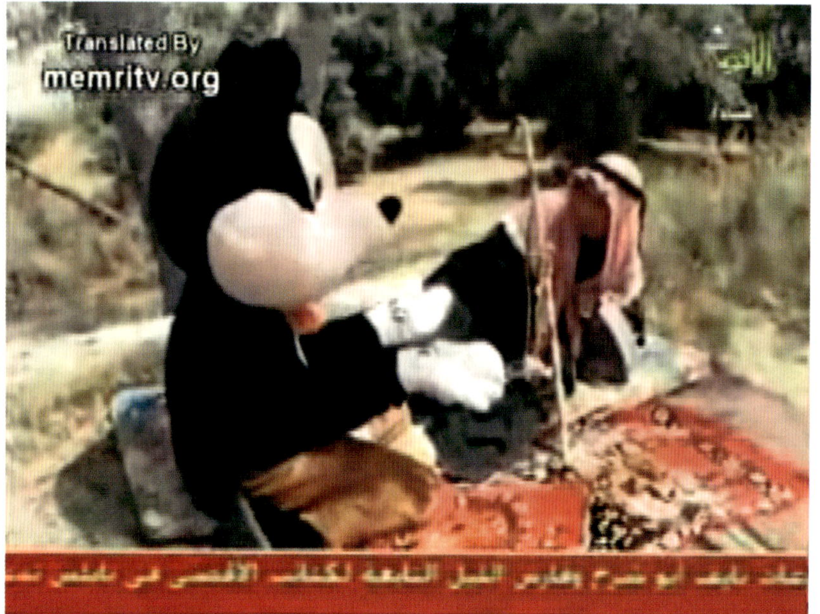

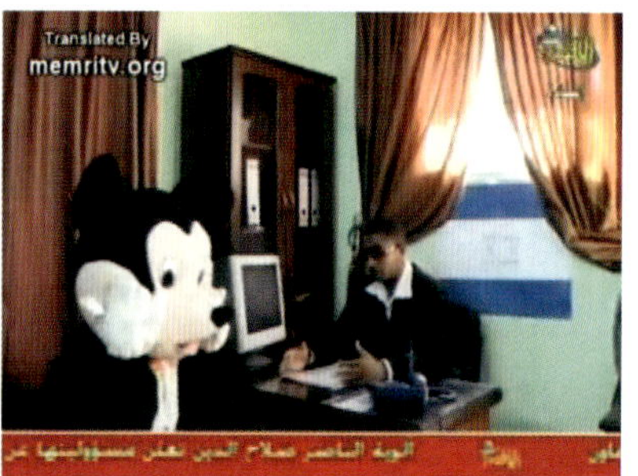

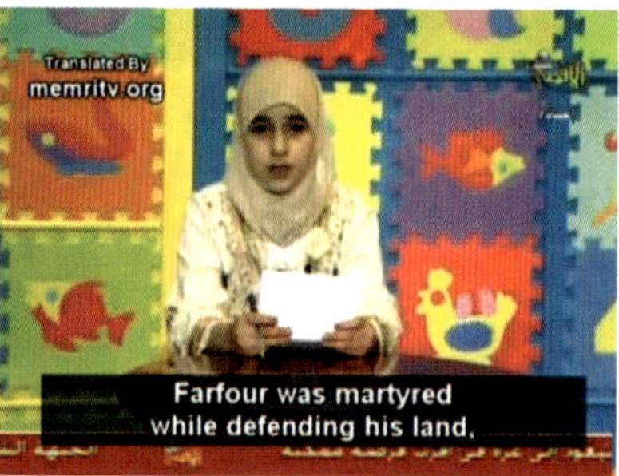

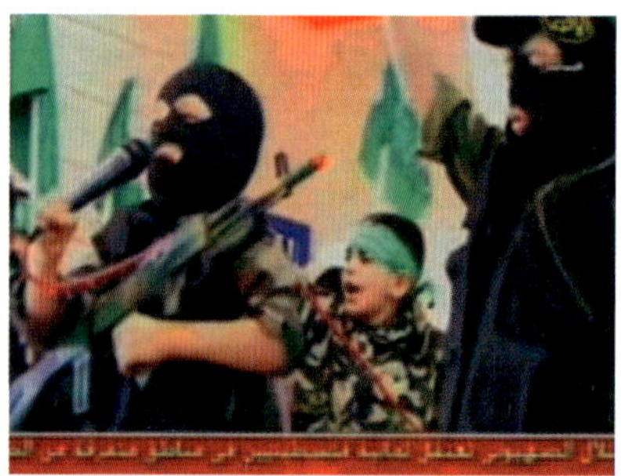

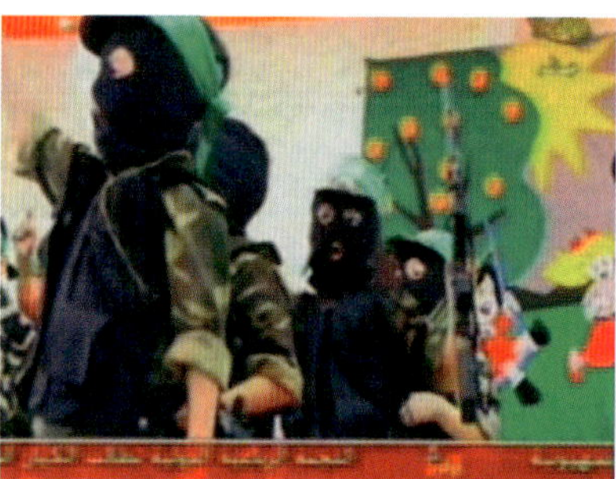

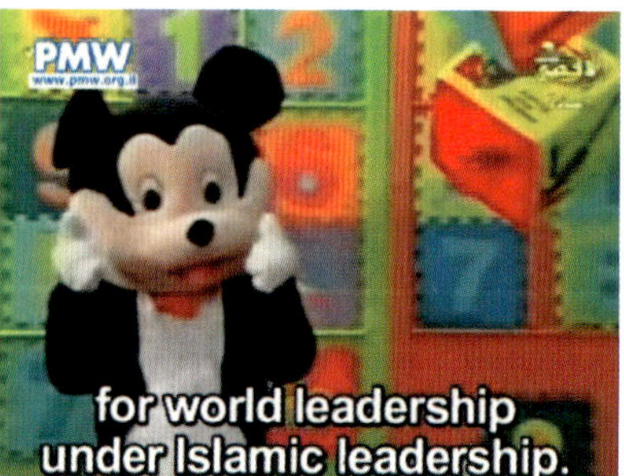

Christoph Büchel
*1966 in Basel, Switzerland,
lives and works in Switzerland

Tomorrow's Pioneers (Farfour),
2007, video, color, sound,
10:59 min, stills from a digital copy

Tomorrow's Pioneers is an interactive TV series for children,
broadcast weekly by the official
television station of the Hamas,
Al-Aqsa TV. Christoph Büchel uses
this medial ready-made to comment ironically on the religious
political propaganda by the media.
Its main protagonist is Farfour,
a mouse twin of the Western
Mickey Mouse. As a member of
the Palestinian Islamic resistance
movement, this character's lively
and entertaining manner indoctri-
nates its very young audience with
hatred directed towards Israel and
American imperialism. Büchel's
medial ready-mades are often
not immediately recognizable as
pledges of reality – their laconic
presence is simply too much of a
surprise in the cultural context of
this locality (and still more in the
context of the exhibition), where
they deploy their eccentrically
provocative, disturbing impact.

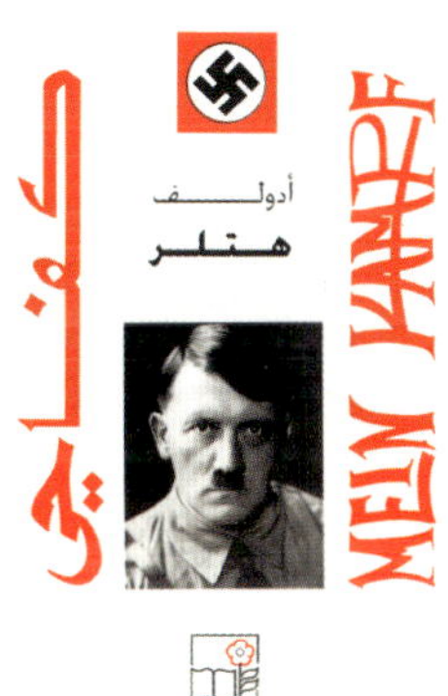

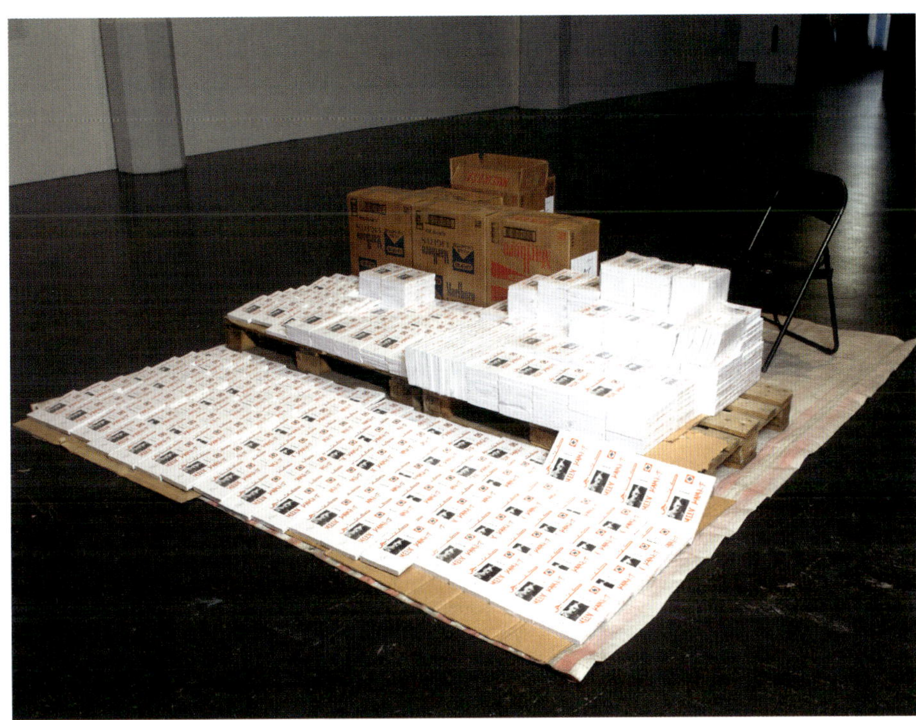

Christoph Büchel

كفاحي [My Struggle], 2006,
1,000 copies of Adolf Hitler's
Mein Kampf (Arabic translation),
tarp, cashier box, chair, pallets,
boxes, installation view
ZKM | Karlsruhe, 2009

In his works, the artist Christoph Büchel often makes use of artifacts from the mass media, like military propaganda videos, political pamphlets, or original knotted carpets, which show motifs of the attack on the World Trade Center, for example. Büchel's 2006 work كفاحي [My Struggle] consists of 1,000 copies of the Arabic edition of Adolf Hitler's *Mein Kampf* [My Struggle], which are arranged in an improvised sales setting on simple Euro pallets and in the original U.S. Marlboro shipping cartons used by the Arab publisher. The book has been a bestseller in Arab countries and points to the relations of the National Socialists to the Arab world reaching back to the 1930s. A key figure in this connection is Haj Amin Al Husseini (1893–1974), a driving force of Palestinian nationalism and an honorary member of the SS. As the founder of the Bosnian-Muslim SS Division Handžar, he was centrally involved in the genocide against Serbian and Jewish populations. His nephew and political protégé Yasser Arafat actually set the name Al Husseini aside, yet demonstrably paid his uncle great political respect all his life. كفاحي [My Struggle], was originally planned in 2006 as a provisional memorial for the Residenzplatz in Salzburg, on the very site of the first burning of books in Austria, as organized by the Nazis in 1938, and was rejected in the context of the international controversy surrounding the (Muhammad) caricatures in 2006 and of the Salzburg Festival.

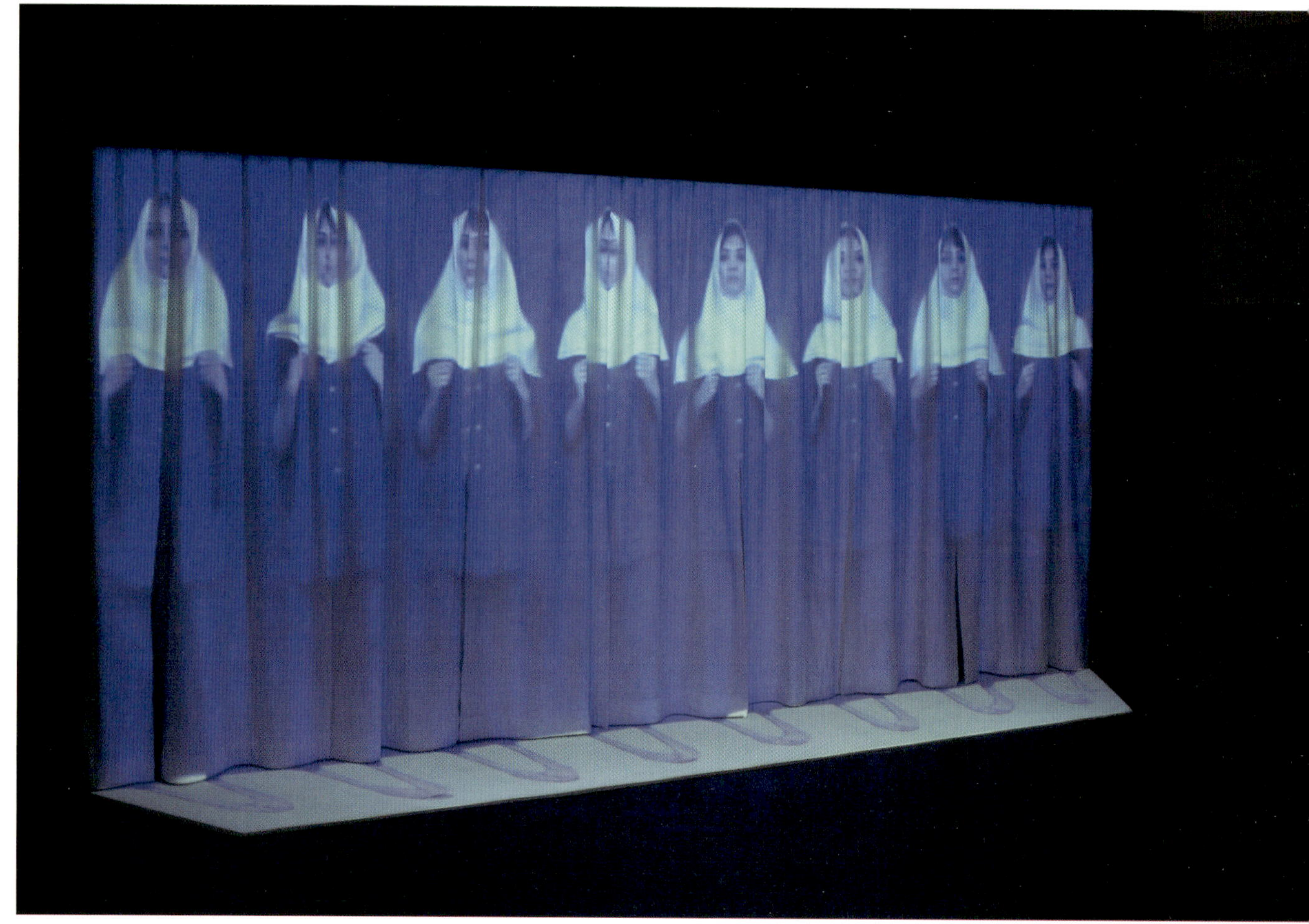

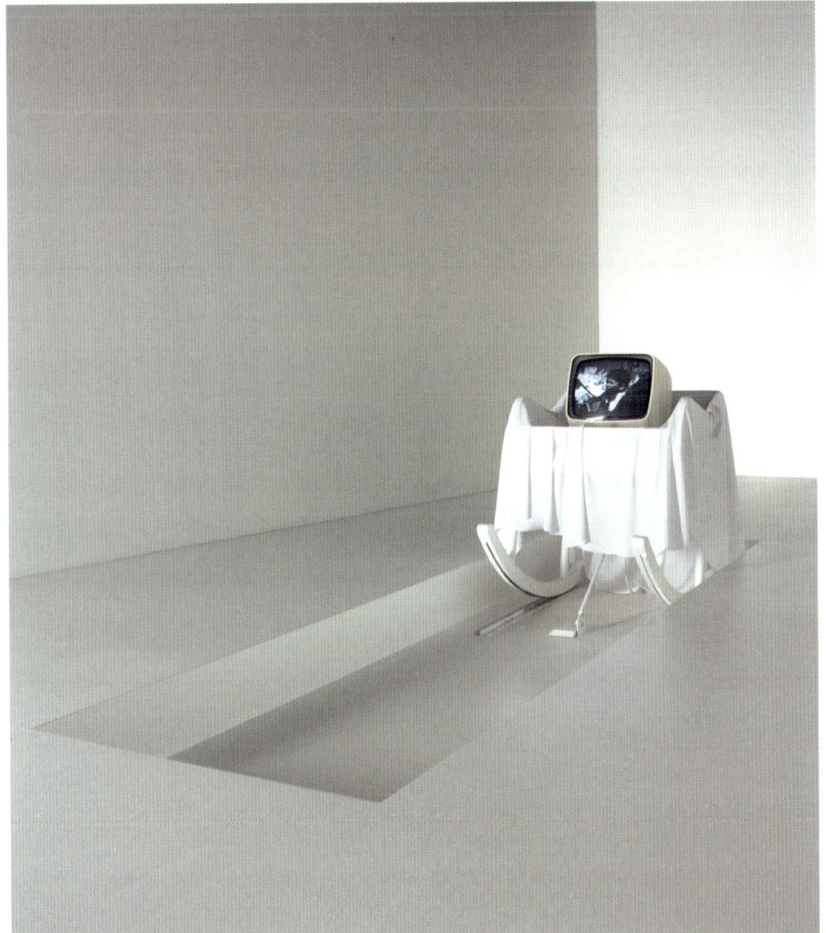

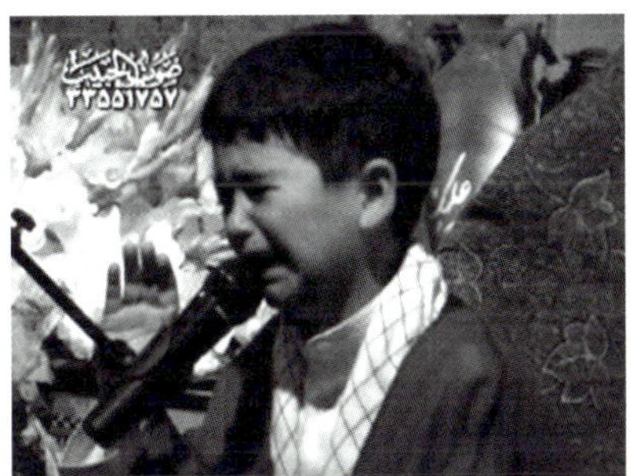

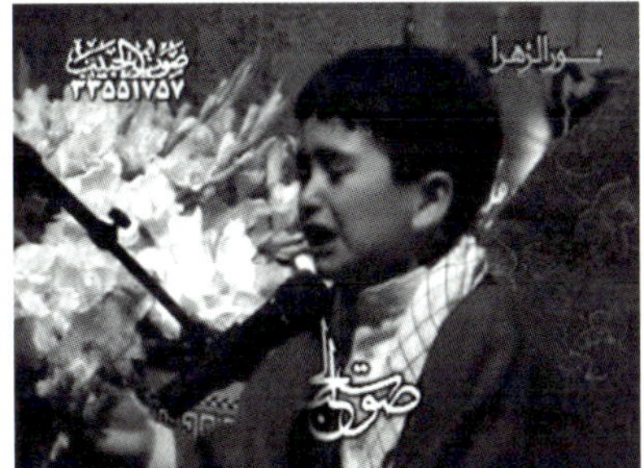

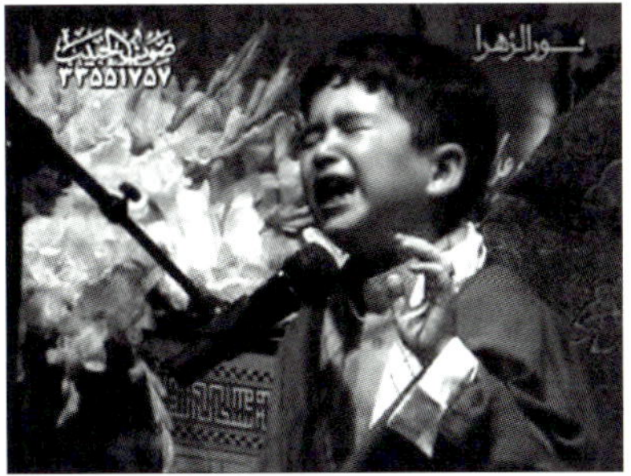

Barbad Golshiri
*1982 in Tehran, Iran,
lives and works in Tehran

mʌmı, 2008, video installation, color, sound, mixed media,
dimensions and runtime
variable, installation views
ZKM | Karlsruhe, 2009,
and stills from a digital copy

The exterior projection of mʌmı shows eight young women in Iranian school uniforms standing in a row before a blue backdrop. They slowly close their eyes and dissolve into the blue of the curtain. The rocking chair in the interior of the installation is a play on an unadorned "throne," and the television set shows a six-year-old professional mourner weeping bitterly. mʌmı reflects the role of the media, and television in particular; how it has generally, in an almost maternal fashion, substituted religion and particularly the pastor, and how religion, once considered as "the opium of the masses," has become the opium of a religious, media-based state and its masses. The Persian word for curtain, *pardé*, carries equally the meanings of screen, hymen, and shroud. The blue *pardé* refers both to the blue box technique and various mise-en-scènes used in Iran's political-visual system of representation. The installation mʌmı faces Mecca.

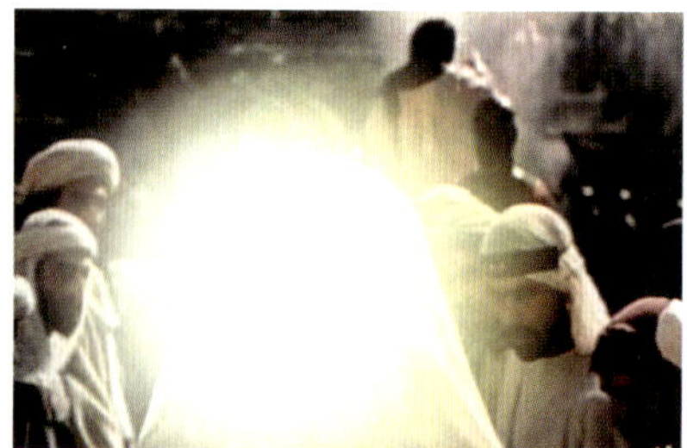
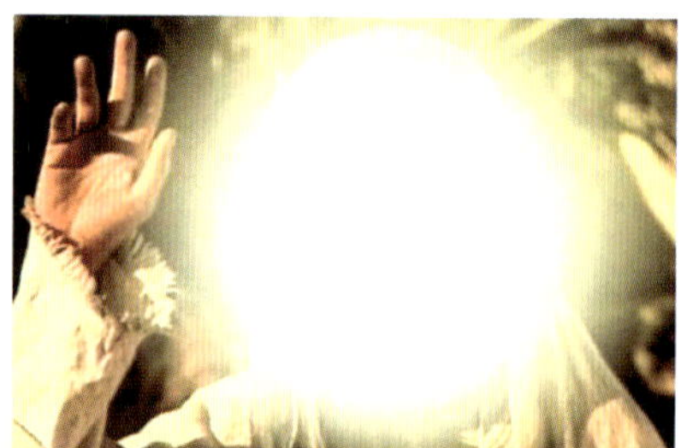
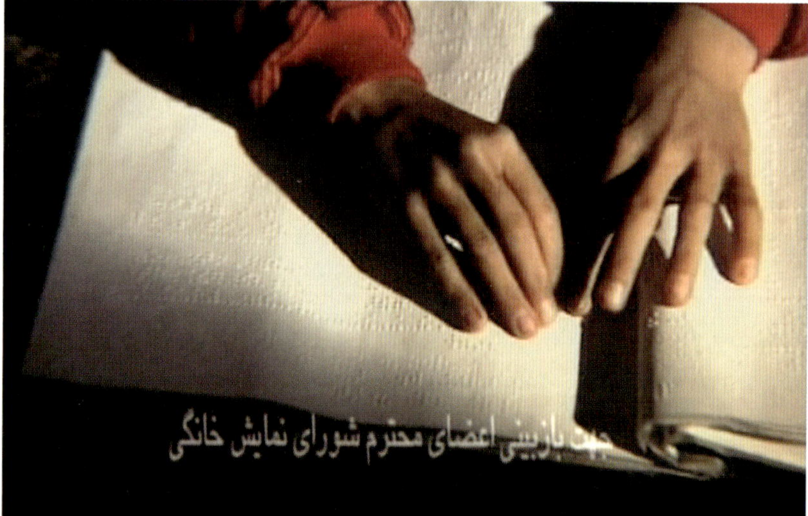

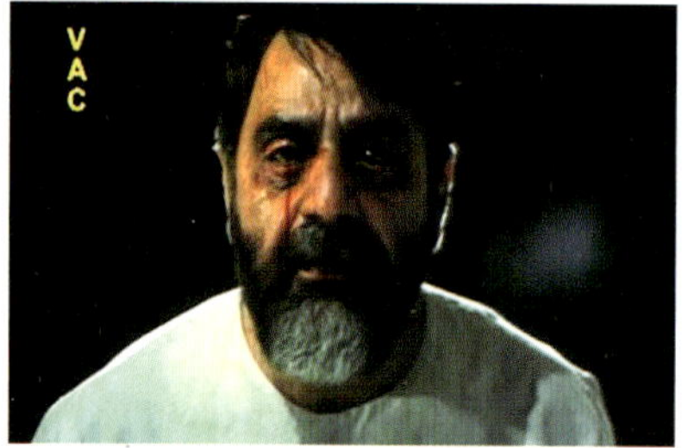

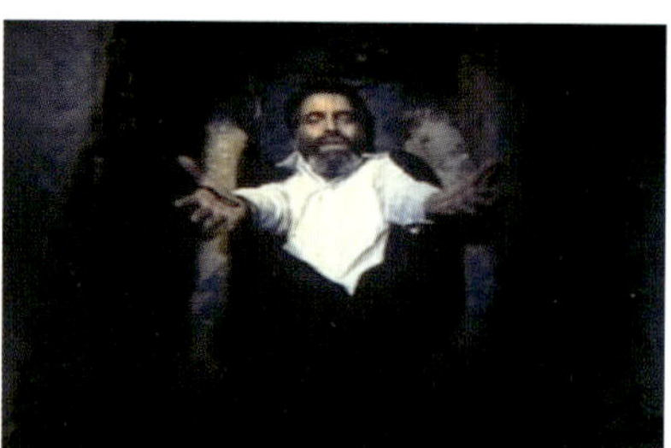
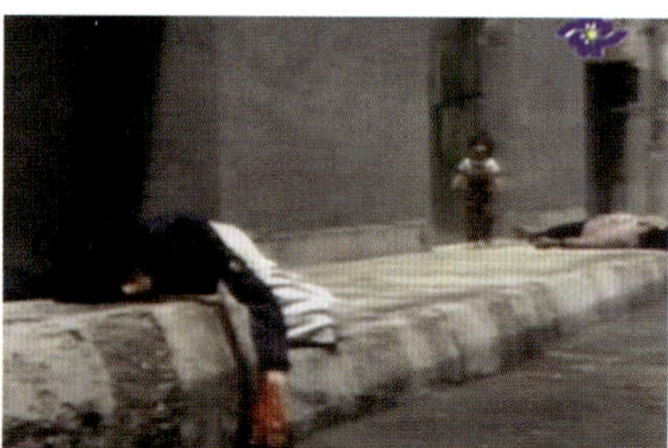

Dorna Safaian
*1984 in Tehran, Iran,
lives and works in Berlin

*After being interpreted by a
machine (the blind; the dead;
realism)*, 2008, video installation,
color, sound, runtime variable,
stills from a digital copy

The work entitled *After being
interpreted by a machine* is the-
matically devoted to the overall
complex of Islamic strategies
of imagery. Taking origins in aniconism as starting point, Islam
develops its own idiosyncratic
technique of imagery, which
orientates itself according to the
divine framework of information.
The three documentary videos,
respectively entitled *the blind,
the dead*, and *realism*, show the
filmic consequences of the Islamic
technique of iconography by
means of religious films from Iran.
Alongside the iconographic perspective of forbidding imagery, the
video *After being interpreted by a
machine* focuses on the specific
impact on media of Islamic images
the production of which is legitimized by their technical reproducibility.

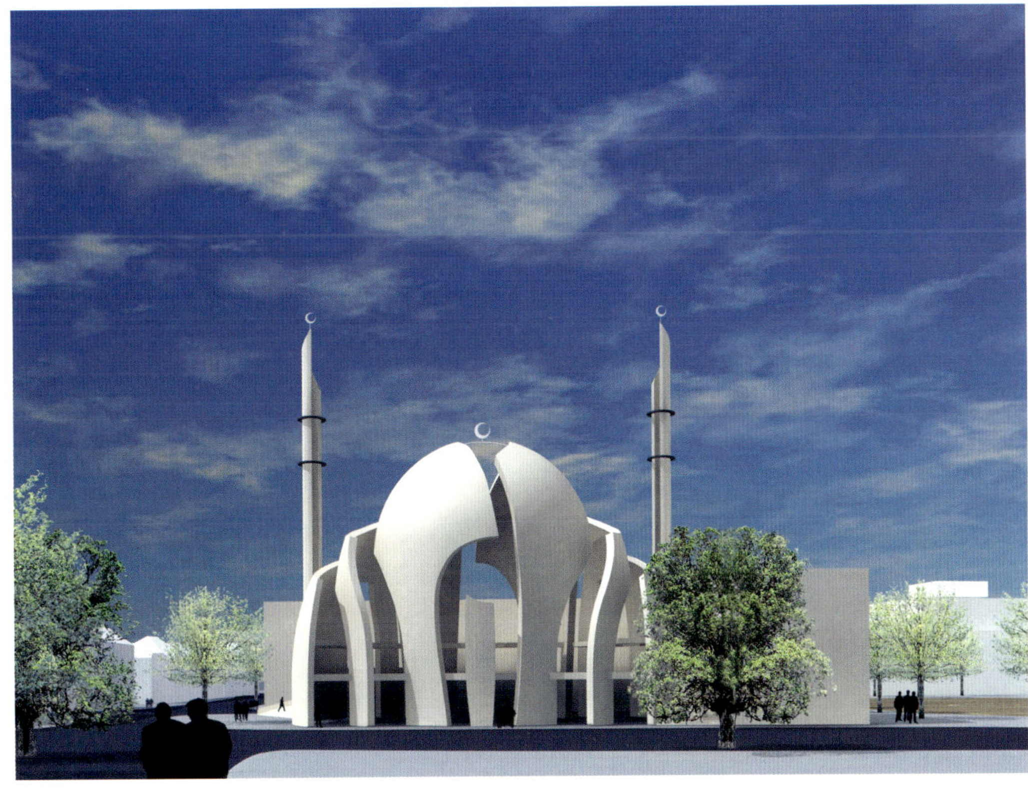

**Debate on
Cologne Mosque project**
documentary material
(architectural designs,
photographs, graphics, texts)

The structures on the Temple Mount in Jerusalem reflect the changing history of Judaism, Islam, and Christianity; at the same time, together with the city of Jerusalem, it is the best-known symbol of the long-standing, politically and religiously motivated conflict in the Middle East. A similar conjunction of religion, politics, and architecture has also been on view in Cologne. Out of their concern about a growing islamization, citizens' initiatives have been trying to prevent the planned erection of a central mosque there: the mosque has become the metaphor for a general fear of foreign infiltration, which fails to recognize that Islam has long since become a part of German identity. Cologne cathedral, the historical trademark of the city, is one of the largest gothic cathedrals and is crucially important for the Catholic Church; however, it is also an early symbol of a German national consciousness, which formed in the nineteenth century. Therefore, it displays the arguably perfect antagonist in the debate on the building of the central mosque, in which houses of prayer furnish symbols for ways of looking at the world and for political programs, as well as flashpoints for cultural conflicts.

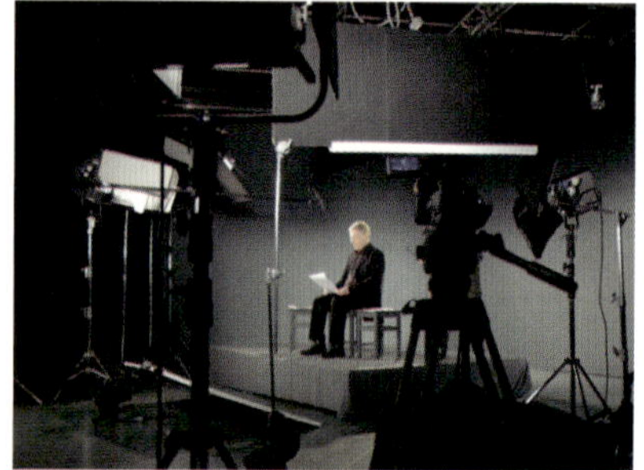

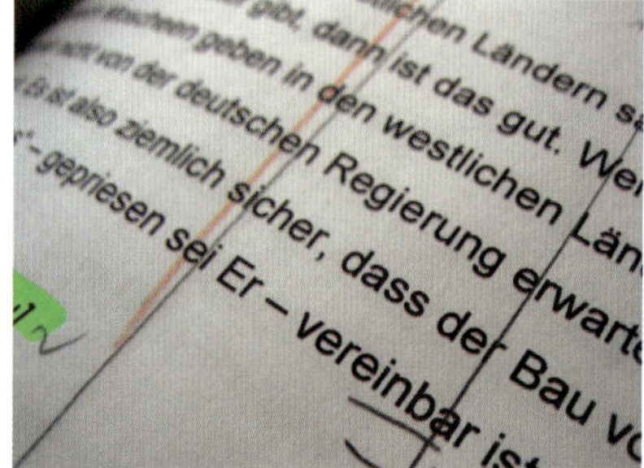

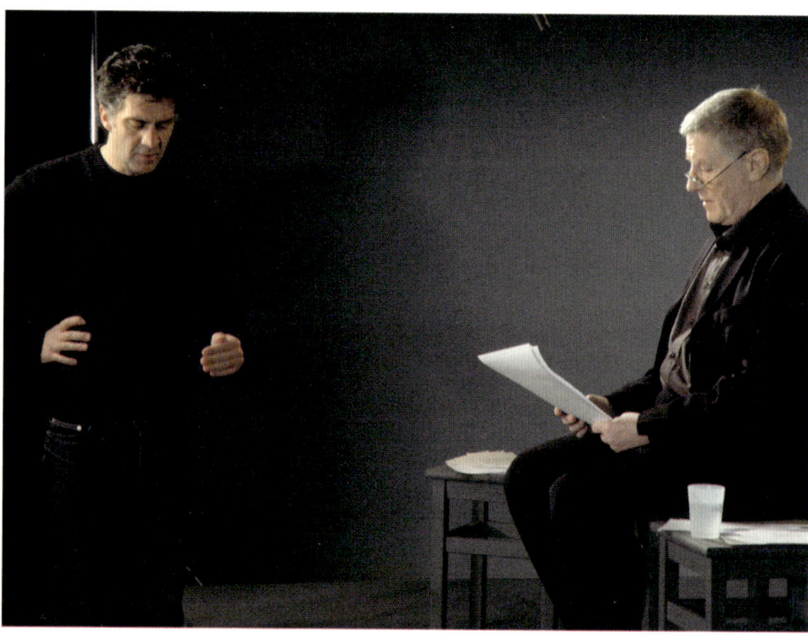

In his film *Hamburger Lektionen* [Hamburg Lessons], the German film-maker Romuald Karmakar takes up the issue of the inflammatory preaching of the imam Mohammed Fazazi in the Hamburg Al-Quds Mosque in 2000. In his preaching, the imam gives answers drawn from the *Sharia* to questions of everyday life and elucidates Islamic dogma whilst totally rejecting, for example, basic democratic rights. In the film, the actor Manfred Zapatka performs the transcribed texts. The subtitles occasionally hint at background noises emenating from the mosque, which both illustrate the erstwhile sociocultural surroundings and neutralize the anonymity of the studio setting. In this abstract presentation, the propaganda material becomes a document, which demonstrates the internal structure of inflammatory preaching and the radical rejection of rules drafted in any way differently.

Romuald Karmakar
*1965 in Wiesbaden, Germany, lives and works in Berlin

Hamburger Lektionen, 2006, digital projection, color, sound, 133 min, photographs

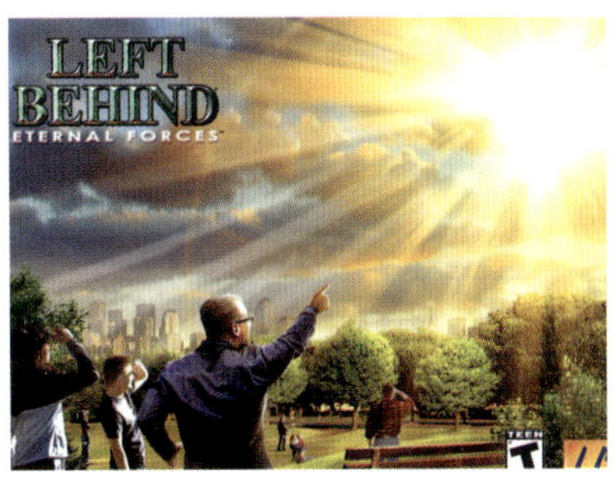

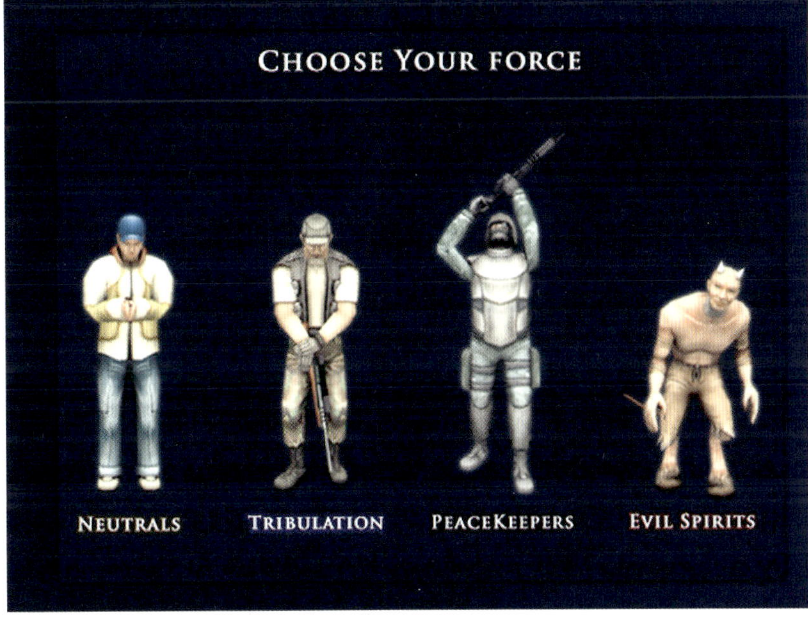

Jerry B. Jenkins & Tim LaHaye:
Left Behind. Eternal Forces, 2006,
computer game,
video collage, 12 novels,
screenshots

The computer game *Left Behind* is
based on the eponymous series of
novels – very successful among
the evangelical movement in the
U.S. – by the Christian authors
Jerry B. Jenkins and Tim LaHaye,
a one-time pastor of a Baptist
megachurch. Players find themselves in the scenario of an apocalyptic final battle between good
and evil after pious Christians have
already ascended to Heaven. The
goal of the game is to prevent the
Antichrist taking over the world.
To do this, players must build
churches, reach people with missions, and, if necessary, kill them.
After every bloody deed, players'
so-called "soul points" diminish
and have to be restored by prayer
in order to carry on the fight for
Christian righteousness.

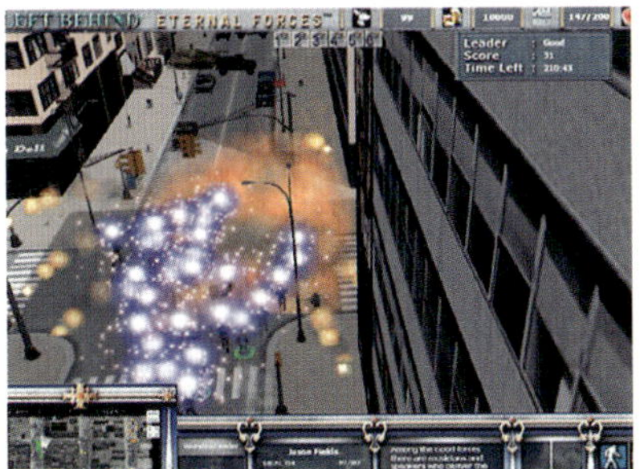

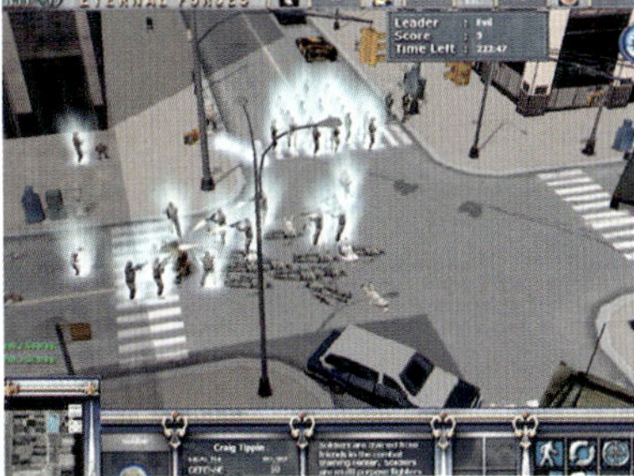

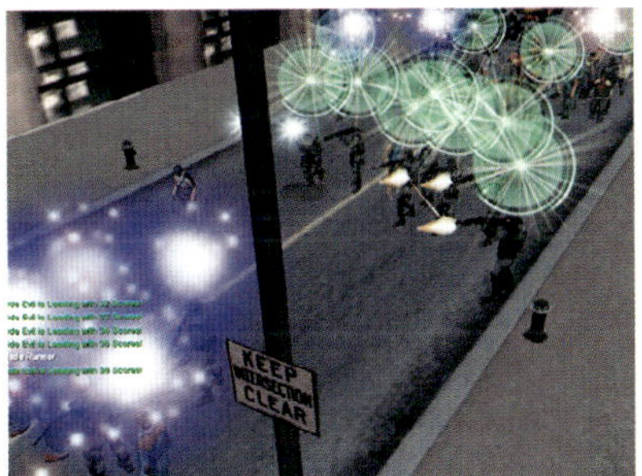

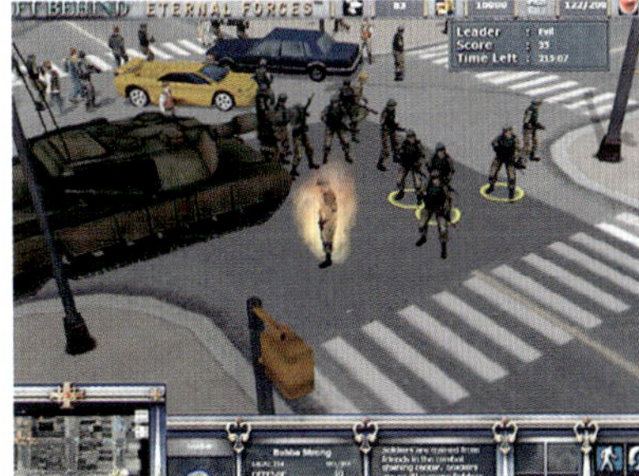

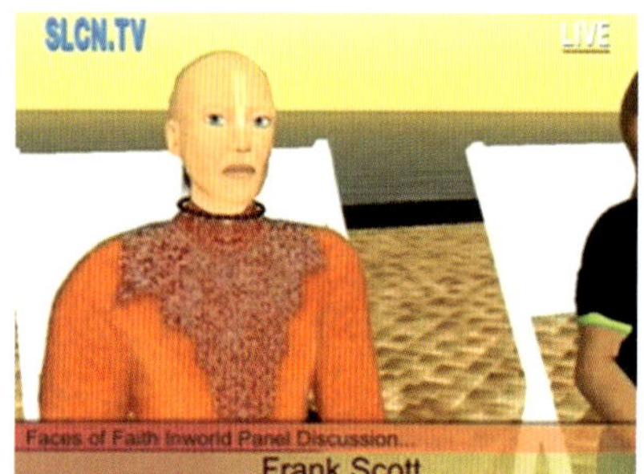

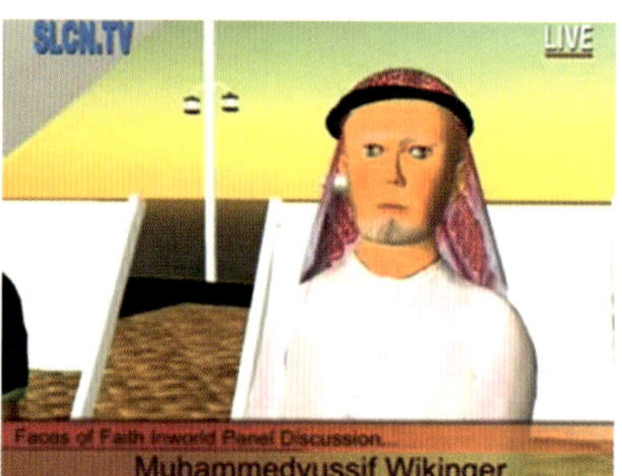

Frank Scott

Muhammedyussif Wikinger

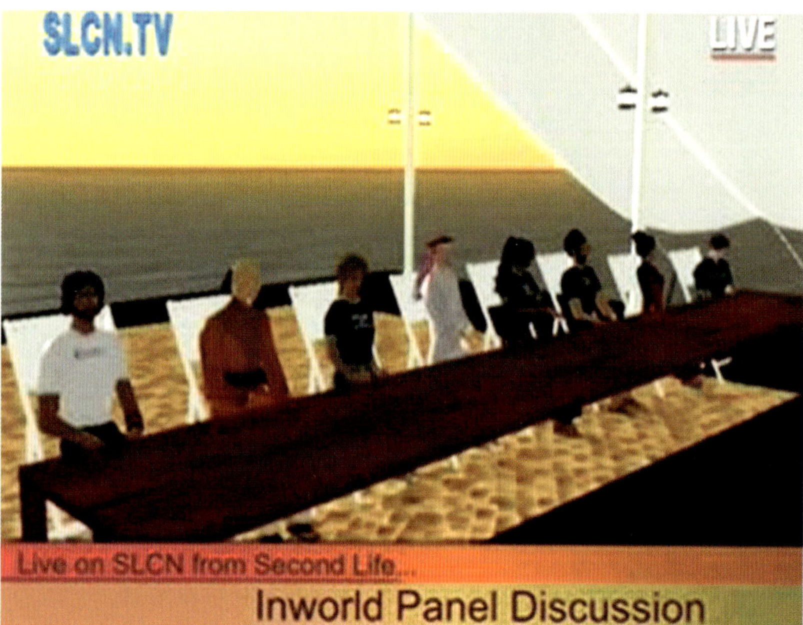

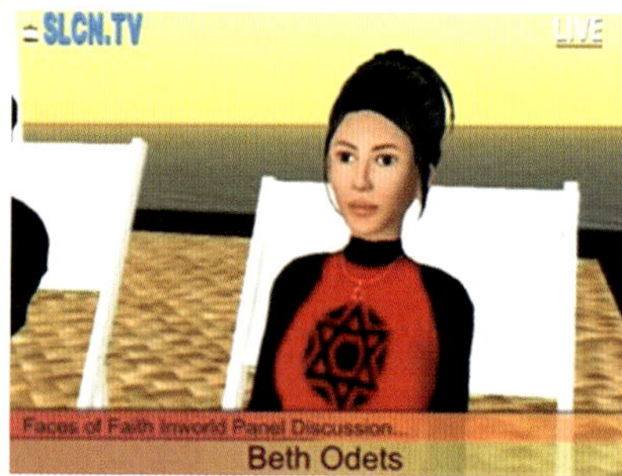

Beth Odets

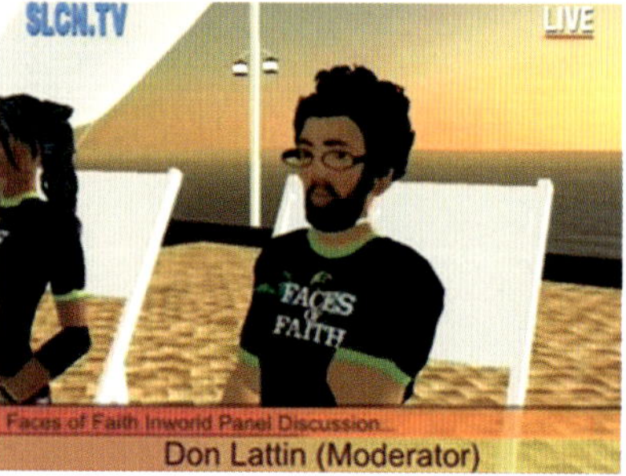

Don Lattin (Moderator)

**UC Berkeley
Journalism Project**

Faces of Faith, 2008,
Second Life panel discussion,
recorded 3-D animation, color,
sound, 76 min, screenshots

With the project *Faces of Faith*, journalists of the Graduate School of Journalism of the University of California, Berkeley enter the virtual world of Second Life. The panel discussion involves both spiritual leaders and scientists from the "real world" and experts and practitioners in matters of Second Life as avatars in exchanges on experiences of spirituality in the virtual space and illuminates the most varied aspects of the relationship between religion and the new media.

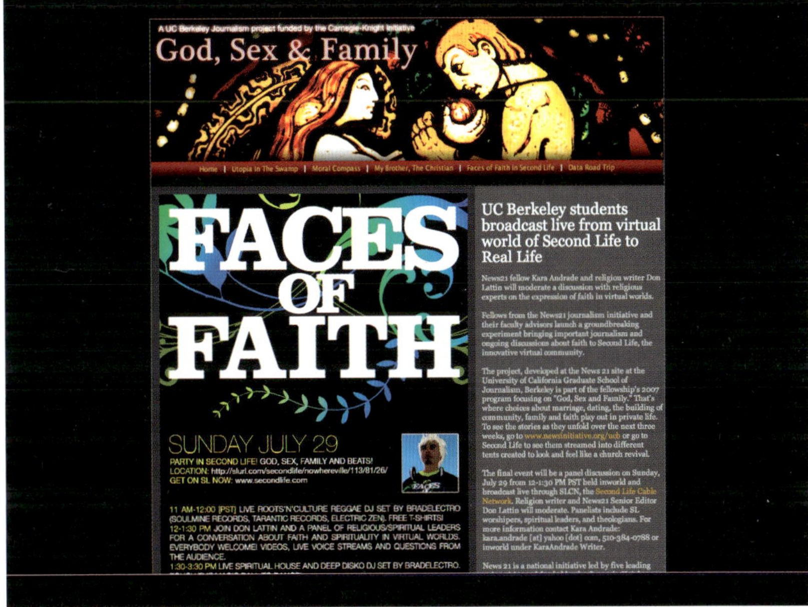

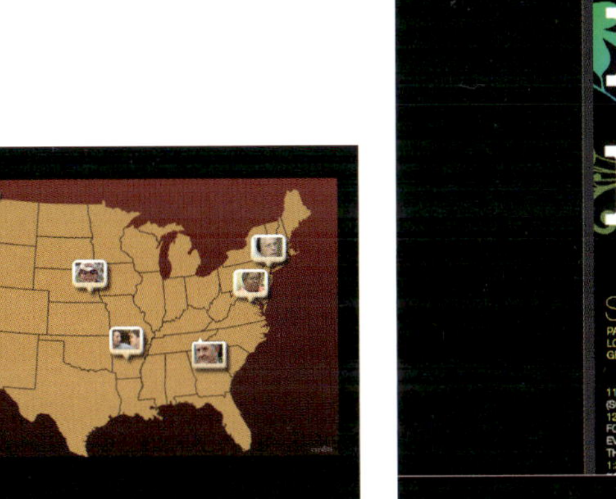

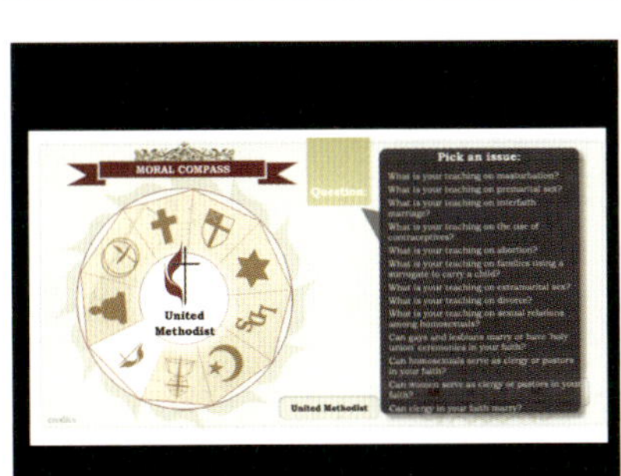

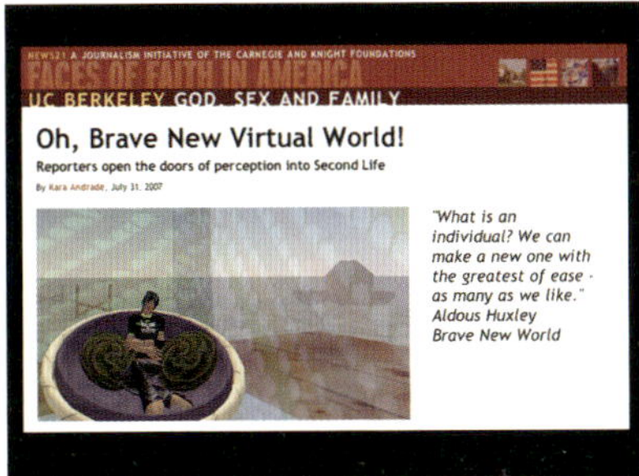

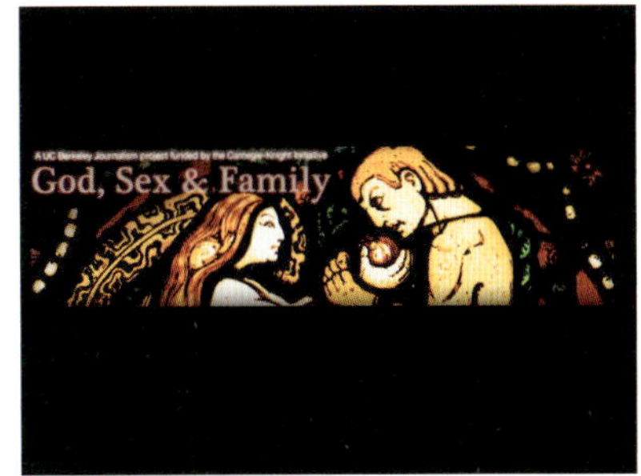

**UC Berkeley
Journalism Project**

God, Sex & Family
website, screenshots
http://newsinitiative.org/ucb

The website *God, Sex & Family*, created by journalists of the Graduate School of Journalism of the University of California Berkeley, deals with current social questions on sex, marriage, faith, community, and family by means of discussion forums and interactive hands-on applications. Thus, the project demonstrates how the Internet today, to a certain extent, has assumed the social function of the church.

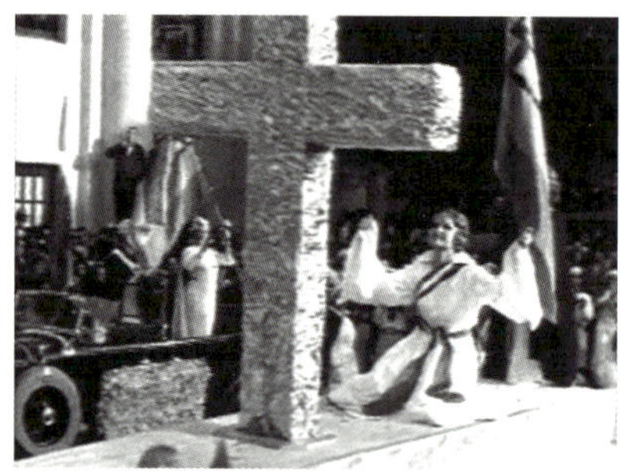

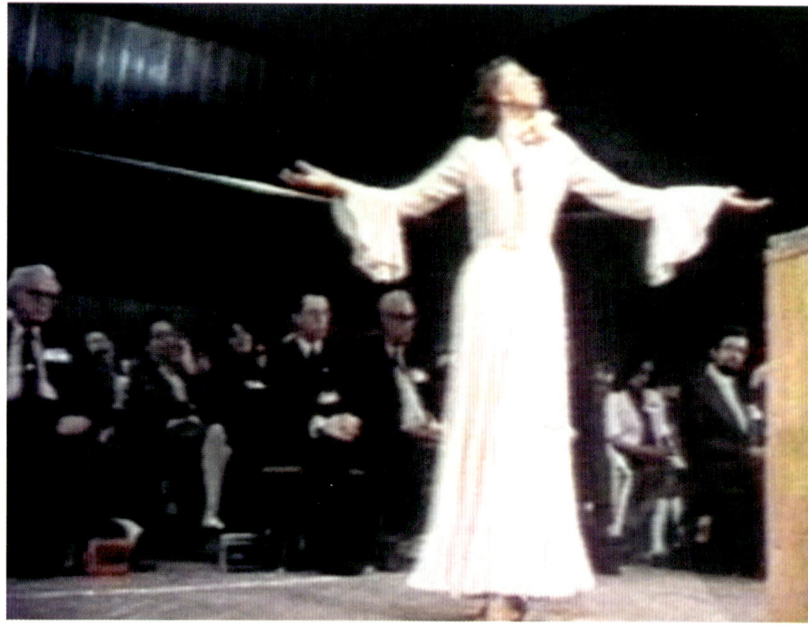

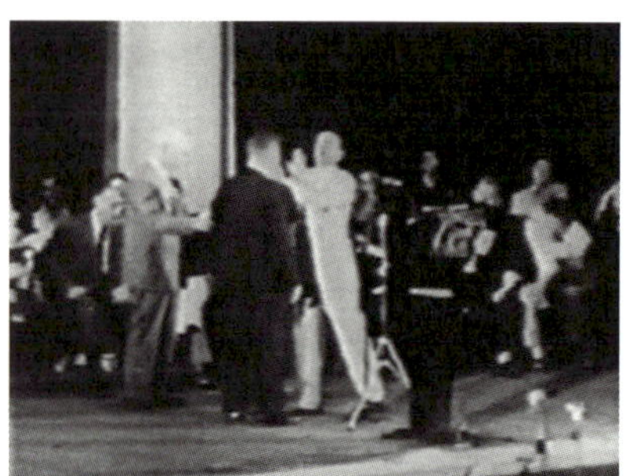

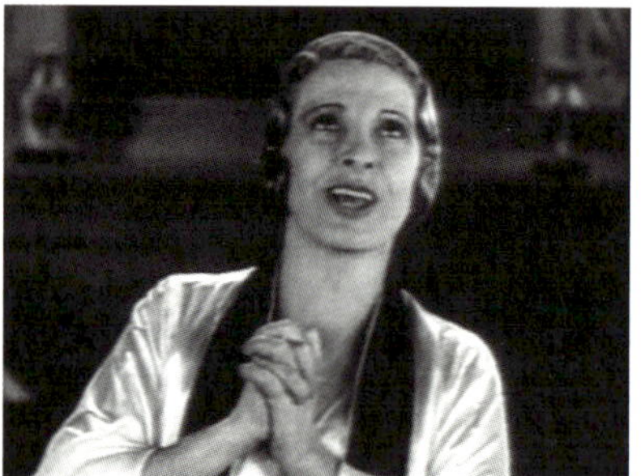

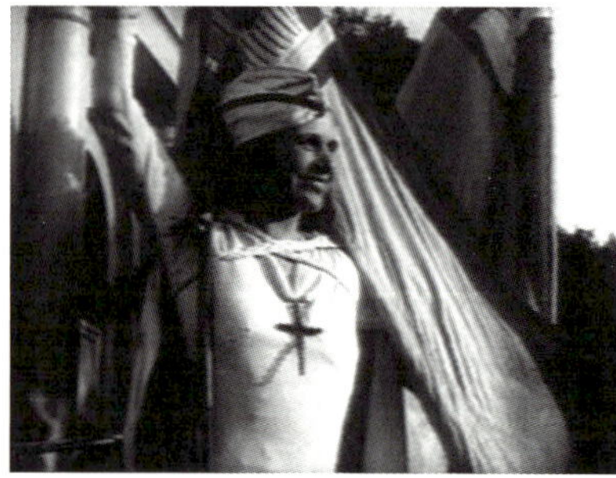

God's Generals, 2008,
documentary video
material, found footage,
color, sound, 15 min,
stills from a digital copy

What we see here are extracts
taken from historical documentation of American itinerant
preachers and faith healers. These
charismatic personalities, who
filled entire halls and circus tents
with people at once hopeless and
expecting salvation, reveal themselves here in their gestures and
actions as being curious or even
grotesque, as preachers, saviors,
and manipulators of hysterically
devout masses. These self-
declared "God's Generals" style
themselves in the spectacle of
mass events as direct agents of
God, as the way to healing and
redemption.

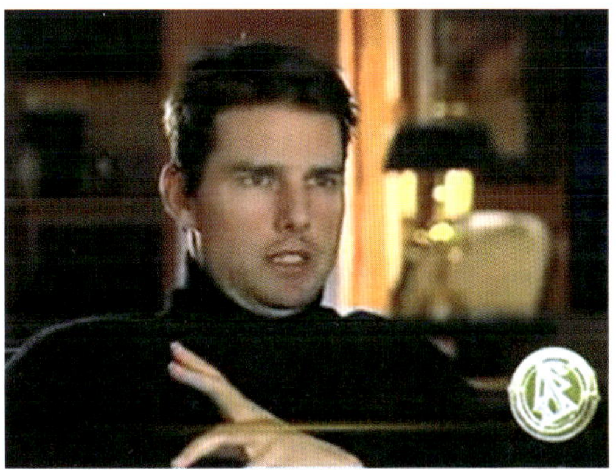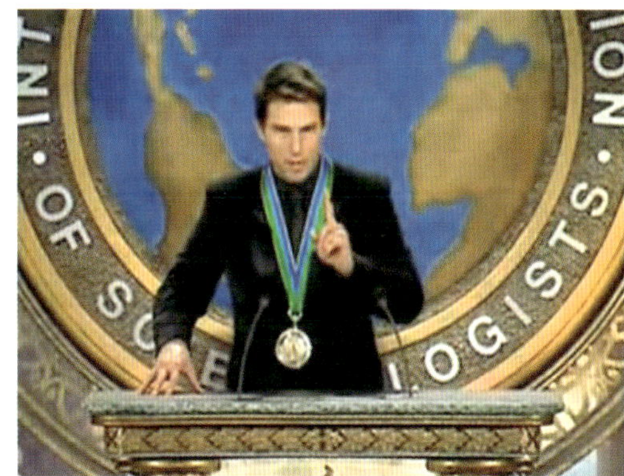

Internal Scientology Videos

Tom Cruise Scientology
[Medal of Valor], 2008,
and *Tom Cruise Scientology Video*
[monologue], 2004,
videos, color, sound, 0:53 min
and 9:35 min, video stills

The Church of Scientology bases its activities on the book *Dianetics* (1950) by its founder L. Ron Hubbard, the cult figure in his own strategic design for a religion. How Scientology denotes its practices, such as auditing, processing, or "clear" process, is reminiscent of technical functions, such as those of a video or tape recorder. This demonstrates how close is Scientology's understanding of human beings as a medium to media technology and to psychological techniques. The video to be shown is an internal training video, in which the actor Tom Cruise advocates the "knowledge about knowledge" [etymological for Scientology] to the rhythm of the music for his film hit *Mission Impossible* (1996/2000). It did the rounds in the Internet at the beginning of 2008, but generated anti-propaganda by dint of such a context outside of the sect. A further video from the Scientologists shows the actor being awarded a "Medal of Valor" by the sect. Cruise harangues his audience in a frenetic speech of thanks. Using popularity for advertising products and ideologies is not new, but these videos do show particularly clearly how these areas are becoming increasingly blurred – the person of the actor, his film roles, and his religious convictions are inextricably interwoven: the actor becomes the medium for his faith.

Peter Sloterdijk

...Scientological... ...Enlightenment.–. On.the.Civilizational .Use.of.Artificial. .....Religions.....

A nyone wishing to found a new religion can essentially only do so under two if different premises. The first says that although there are already many religions, the true one is still not among them. New insights now make it possible and necessary to call it into being. Using this scheme, Paul distinguished Christianity from Judaism, just as later Saint Augustine distinguished it from Manicheanism and from Roman cult, and even later Muhammad distinguished Islam from the two preceding monotheisms. The Enlightenment took an analogous approach, seeking as of the seventeenth century to justify the "religion of Reason" by setting it off from the historical religions.[1] Such new foundations start with the progressive revelation of truth – they state the new substance to be uncovered and endeavor to find the form appropriate to it. The new substance stems from the insight that intrinsically possesses more salvational power than the content hitherto known. This type of foundation of a religion can thus be termed substantively religious. Its actors are as a rule naive, using the word non-judgmentally, and believe that they believe what they believe. They are not naive, but would gladly be so, and rue their skepticism.

The second premise under which a new religion can be kick-started says that the previous forms of religion are inadequate because they stick too strongly to content, whereas in the future the form of religion is what will count. Hand in hand with this turn toward the form goes a drastic bifurcation: Either the new religion arises as a free-floating meta-religion that no longer knows dogmatic sentences and yet aspires *bona fide* to preserve the dimension of the religious "per se" while remaining neutral to its substance (this is the stance taken by most modern confessionless, who believe that there is something after all to that which they do not believe in). The advantage of this position is that it takes the sting out of the tension between salvational and secular knowledge. Or the new religion exclusively addresses the formal side to religion in order to transport different substance with and in it. This was, among others, the case with Pierre de Coubertin, who tried to couple the substance of sport to the form of religion – and we have seen what the results are.

If one takes a further step down the formal-religious path, then religion can be used as a mere vehicle to realize *mala fide* external content. The inevitable example here are the recently much discussed "political theologies" thanks to which religion is resorted to as a psychosocial tool to help assure the state's success. Anyone wishing to provide examples to visualize this stance thinks invariably of popes who at the head of their troops expand the Papal States, or the cynical French cardinals who entered into pacts with the Islamic Turks in order to damage the Christian rulers of Austria to the greater glory of France. And the empirical political world of the twentieth century provides examples ad nauseam of the fact that peoples and nations who in the past or of late have occasionally donned the garb of communities of salvation, and of how revolutionary movements can dress themselves up messianically. Where the formal religious stance takes a radical turn, abstraction extends to the point at which potentially any random *content* can assume a religioid design to the extent that the person undertaking the effort so wishes. Religion then becomes a rhetorical/ritual mode and presentation principle that can serve as a means of self-dissemination for any project, be it political, artistic, industrial, sporting, or therapeutic.

In the following I would like to show how L. Ron Hubbard's entrepreneurial and technical/literary/quibbling genius made fruitful use of the formal-religious principle when proceeding with the campaign promoting the product he launched in 1950 under the name of *Dianetics*, in order to transform the same by means of religioid upgrading into a scientological "church" only a little later. The basis for Hubbard's campaign: the cultural crisis of the later 1940s also a period of profound personal crisis for the author. At that time, the author could assume there to be a market for counseling/self-help literature, indeed one with great growth potential. In

1   See: Hermann Cohen, *Religion der Vernunft aus den Quellen des Judentums*, Fourier, Wiesbaden, 1988 (first published in 1919); Mark Lilla has most recently described the modern religion of Reason as a cult of the stillborn: *The Stillborn God. Religion, Politics, and the Modern West*, Knopf, New York, 2007.

this field, psychoanalytical motifs got all mixed up with those from the philosophy of life, from the Samaritans and from management consultancy, not to mention psychagogical, religioid, and dietetic elements as well as fitness psychology. Hubbard's ingenious approach entailed bringing these disparate realms of demand together in a single point. In this way, he took his place in the tradition of modern charlatans, again using the word in a non-judgmental sense, who provide a single antidote to all illnesses – to put it more abstractly, who wield a single solution to all problems. It is a practice that is to be seen in countless concrete forms from the sixteenth to the twentieth century, from the notion of a *tabula rasa* and zero point to the idea of the total revolution and the concentration on the One that is needed. According to the great charlatans, the art of all arts has always consisted in distilling the one means, the panacea, the universal agent, be it in a physical or a mental test-tube. As a rule, the distillation produces a simple substance or one final element and/or a simple action and final operation. He who possesses it or is able to use it, can do anything and possesses everything.

Hubbard's new product was devised as a mental panacea and launched on the agitated market for self-help articles. His "Dianetics"[2] of 1950 appeared at first sight to be nothing more than a new means, lavishly advertised, of cleaning the dimmed lens of consciousness – after all, it was a product, which as a very successful seller in its first year, proved that the Americans, five years after dropping the first atomic bomb, were ready on a broader front to take up spiritual proposals for the simplest solution to the world's problems. There was no time, the author suggested, for sophist esotericism, it was time to swiftly transform the world from the bottom up "before we're beaten to it by the Bomb."[3] *Survival* became the main word in casual counseling. It provided the U.S. counterpart to early Christian metanoia in the face of ever less time. Given the nascent nuclear race between the United States and the Soviet Union, dianetics offered an alternative armaments race – between itself and the world system of war, mental illness

and criminality. If we assume that in this second Cold War no one gladly got stuck in the "problems camp," then we can understand why it suffices to accept the scenario in order to prefer to be in the "solutions camp."

The solution lies in the name of the method itself: Dianetics is said to derive from two elements from Ancient Greek *dia* (through) and *nous* (mind), and thus to mean the science of that which occurs "through the mind" (occasionally a word such as *dianoua* is cited as the source, but it does not actually exist in Greek). We can easily imagine why everything is to occur through the mind – whereby the meaning of "through" shall remain a moot point. We cannot yet discern how the system reassembles the old opposition of mind and matter – seen superficially it does so "scientifically," at a deeper level it does so gnostically. Bereft of any false modesty, Hubbard's new hyper method claims to be the "modern science of spiritual health" and promises to offer the simplest solution to all the problems that had hitherto seemed insoluble. Like a Californian avatar of Johann Gottlieb Fichte, Hubbard praises the science of knowledge as the end of the era of mere prior attempts. While previous solutions themselves became part of the problems, regardless of whether they took the stage as religions, therapies, or politics, dianetics proclaimed the solution of problems with definitive clarity in a manner that would no longer become part of the problems – thus, so the argument, only the mentally infirm could have an interest in preventing dianetics. Consequently, from then on a new criterion was at hand to swiftly diagnose someone's state of mind: indifference or animosity towards what dianetics offered. An immoderate polemic against what Hubbard terms conventional psychiatry runs like a red thread through all his writings – and that of his higher-level students. Without doubt he sensed what the specialists would say about him and his endeavor. And he made them pay heavily for what he sensed.[4]

In substantive terms, dianetics initially no longer offered a simplified and technified version of the basic psychoanalytical assumptions: It gaily replaced the Freudian distinction between systems and/or field states *cs* and *ucs*

2 L. Ron Hubbard, *Dianetics. The Modern Science of Mental Health*, New Era, Copenhagen, 1950.

3 L. Ron Hubbard, *Die Wissenschaft des Überlebens. Vorhersage menschlichen Verhaltens*, New Era, Copenhagen, 1983, p. xlviii.

4 From documents whose authenticity I see no reason to doubt, we find that in 1943, when serving the U.S. Navy at a desk, he suffered from psychotic states in the form of severe depressions and thoughts of suicide and therefore sought treatment from a military doctor. He is said to have been severely wounded shortly before the end of the war by a grenade; he is said to have as a consequence been blinded temporarily but to have healed himself. It has not been possible to find out any greater detail on his reconvalescence and the methods of self-treatment he used; they are said to have helped found his conviction that mind forms matter. A report compiled by an Australian specialist in the 1960s confirms Hubbard's premonition: It states that he had an abnormal personality structure with clear paranoid and schizophrenic traits. Just how Nietzsche would have judged Ron Hubbard is as easy to guess as are Hans Würtz's possible opinions on him. It does not take much imagination to construe what virtual diagnoses that Würtz would have reached in the case of Hubbard. Whether E. M. Cioran ever passed comment on his American contemporary (they were both born in 1911) I do not know, but his possible commentary is as good as unforeseeable given the high irony factor one would expect to be involved.

(conscious/unconscious) with Hubbard's distinction between analytical mind (with its clear memory base) and the reactive mind (with its pathological memory base). Beneath the surface of the latter lie the sum of all problems, while the former offers the solution of all solutions. Given this starting point, the task that would seem natural for the analytical mind would be to dispel all the sullying in the reactive mind until it reaches complete clarity. Anyone who has emptied their pathological memory can be reached by the sole rule of the analytical mind and can call him/herself *clear*. Nothing other than the creation of such clarity is the task tackled by dianetic "processing," during which the clients, irrespective of what complaints they feel they suffer from, are led via inner "time orbits" back to the "engrams" of their pathological memory – to this end, the *locks* in front of the pathogenic memorized content have to be unlocked. Such trips back are undertaken in the more or less mystical assumption that the old engrams can be "deleted" by *recall* and the "aberrations" they cause eliminated – it is an assumption that at the time when Hubbard started writing had been popularized by psychoanalysis, cathartic therapies, and Alfred Hitchcock, although it was never able to prove more than that it was purportedly plausible. All "processing" is made in line with the maxim that: Where the reactive mind was, an analytical mind shall reign.

If this summary of Hubbard's approach were truly to have covered everything, then we could close the book now and state that dianetics is a more or less amusing chapter in the epic of the Americanization of psychoanalysis. In that chapter we can read how the partisans of Ego psychology adhered carefully to the psychology of the unconscious – or how the healthy psyche of the esoteric West Coast won a victory over the morbid psychology of the Jewish East Coast. In truth, the dianetics/scientology episode needs to be seen in the context of a far broader intellectual current that I would like to term the techno-gnostic turn in Western psychology. It is typified by a new technological alienation of the traditional intellectual and emotional stocks down to the very last details. The alienating

energy is triggered by an event in the history of technology that we can consider the most profound caesura in intellectual history since the assertion of vowel-based writing around 700 B.C. The development of computer culture around the middle of the twentieth century compels a revision of the classical body/mind distinction by constructing computers, "intellectual machines" and thus showing that a good part of the phenomena that had hitherto been ascribed to the mind-and-soul side of existence in its entirety in truth were part of the mechanical/material side. Since then, the redistribution of the world under the pressure exerted by this new cybernetic center has defined the drama of contemporary thought. The philosophy of cybernetics now enables us to formulate a general theory of the twilight of the gods.[5]

The Hubbard phenomenon must unmistakably be placed in the context of the turbulence triggered by cybernetic's invasion into the domain of the metaphysical classics. What he wanted to achieve with his dianetics and scientology can only be meaningfully evaluated if we view these systems as the turbulent vortex in the wake of the epoch-making emergence of cognition technology. As a contemporary of the first generation of cybernetic scientists and as the author of sci-fi novels (indeed, the cognoscente of the genre held him in quite high esteem) Hubbard had the privilege of exposure at an early date to the new world of the inner technologies. One should guard here against drawing the wrong conclusions and considering Hubbard's "prior life" as a sci-fi author as a taint. Gotthard Günther, still one of the most important philosophical interpreters of the computer as a new event, has with good cause suggested that the genre of the sci-fi novel should be considered the lab that generated the real philosophy of the technological age – a hypothesis that would seem legitimate in light of the oeuvre of authors such as Stanisław Lem and Isaac Asimov, to name but the two greatest.[6]

Everything would seem to suggest that Hubbard never changed genre, but only expanded it. It is extremely logical that his

5   Gotthard Günther, "Seele und Maschine," in: idem, *Beiträge zur Grundlegung einer operationsfähigen Dialektik*, vol. 1, Meiner, Hamburg, 1976, pp. 75f.

6   Ibid.

first step beyond the borders of science fiction takes him to dianetics, which in terms of cognitive status is nothing other than psychology fiction. This fits with the fact, reported by people close to him, that Hubbard wrote the 500-page *Dianetics* in Bayhead, New Jersey, in merely one month – and exclusively *off the top of his head*, without any recourse to scientific research. The experimental basis which he cites in his book, namely the "hundreds of case studies" are part of the overall invention. This type of writing sheds light backwards on the systems devised by Sigmund Freud and C. G. Jung. Once the scheme has been clearly outlined, one can discern the characteristics of psychology fiction in the other versions, too. Admittedly, the Europeans' respective projects remained less dogmatic and more open to empirical findings owing to their slowness and the decidedly therapeutic ethic. What Hubbard, Freud, and Jung share is their resolve to break through the limits of scientifically-inspired literature into the realm of applied fiction. What divides them is the tie back to moral criteria. There can hardly be talk of such a tie with regard to the founder of Scientology, while for the two European deep psychologists, on balance the work of fiction and the work of conscientious research were in balance.

In our context it is Hubbard's second step out of the genre of science fiction that is informative: It is the move that raised dianetic psychology fiction to the status of scientological religious fiction. Anyone observing this transition will witness the premiere of a "religion" of the technological age.[7] When the success of his *Dianetics. The Modern Science of Mental Health* gave Hubbard feedback from the real world that applied fiction "functioned," he read this as the green light for his ambitions. With the same elan that had prompted his first transgression of sci-fi, he took the second, and in doing so established not just the psychotherapeutic but also a religious front line. The feedback from the real world indicated that this, too, "functioned" – the religion fiction material-

ized in the briefest of time spans and took the form of a real, existing "church." Without doubt, there was an element of forward flight in this play, as following the success of his self-help/therapy book, Hubbard had to fear the response that would be forthcoming from the medical profession. To the extent that the guild denied that his "magic" methods had any impact and accused him of irresponsible abuse of the hopes of those suffering, including cancer patients, an obvious move was to sidestep things and enter the religious sphere. Incidentally, in the inner circle of the organizers back then, no one made any secret of the fact that the religious camouflaging of the new anti-professional method of healing was a way of misleading the tax authorities.

When giving flesh to the Church of Scientology after 1954, Hubbard made use of the strategies of formal religious practices by shrouding the content of Dianetics®, and later of the Hubbard books, Hubbard speeches, Hubbard counseling techniques etc. with the usual apparatus of religious techniques. The foundations were an unlimited cult of the founder – the celebration of the master as universal genius and the man who showed humanity the light firmly imbues the entire scientological media sphere. It comprises what is without doubt one of the most densely self-praising systems of recent intellectual history, and within it, as if in a spaceship, the system's own operating data are constantly recycled. Added to which, a fierce propaganda campaign of urgency was launched – the strategic answer to notions of the apocalypse: It outlined for the clients the choice between Scientology or suicide. Moreover, Scientology created countless internal functional roles, "auditors," "registrars," "Ethics Officers," and any number of new important levels in the form of supervisory and control tasks (the imaginative responses to a church hierarchy), not to mention seminars, business centers, clinics, and even universities that offered heterodox academic degrees including that of Doctor of Theology. One could not claim that the new officers and

7 That this was by no means a premiere is shown by analogous and often far more ingenious projects in the avant-garde movements of the Russian Revolution, in particular the writings of the Immortalists and Biocosmists. See: Boris Groys and Michael Hagemeister (eds.), *Die Neue Menschheit. Biopolitische Utopien in Russland zu Beginn des 20. Jahrhunderts*, Suhrkamp, Frankfurt am Main, 2005. They can incidentally be read as proof that Communism itself was a form of applied social science fiction.

those who wished to join them were not catered to. An insider language was developed for internal communications, the use of which gave the gap between the in-crowd and the non-members the necessary depth. A system of mutual controls and the discrete surveillance of members to identify skepticism at an early date rounded out the package of measures that imitated those of the Church. Above all, the design of the scientological community was truly original: It envisages that with every new believer a new client is acquired – one needs to go back to the Catholic trade in absolution in the sixteenth century to find a similarly close-knit and elegant relationship between matters of salvation and those of money.

Hubbard must be highly praised for these achievements in reconstructing the Church phenomenon, as with his formal religious imitation process he offered invaluable insights into the general conditions of "religion formation," be it historically over time or synthetically. He evidently was not troubled by the possibility that his religious artifact might lose its aura. What the new church lacked in old reverence, it offset by the carefree approach with which it presented itself as the late, but nevertheless timely pinnacle of humanity's search for the truth. Baldly, the scientological theology concedes the religious founders of the past the status of looking up to L. Ron Hubbard, the perfecter – Buddha, Lao Tzu, Jesus, Muhammad, not to mention authors such as Aristotle, Immanuel Kant, Arthur Schopenhauer, Sigmund Freud, Henri Bergson and whoever else can compete for a place in the colorful list of forebears. Hubbard is the epitome of what the predecessors aspired to – with more or less unsuitable means. And a certain dharma is supposed to have come very close to the truth back in the past, ostensibly a monk in ancient Asia. A rascal is he who thinks evil of this approach – yet do we not encounter in the New Testament entries that do not stand up to historical critique? I am not sure whether we can suspect Hubbard of having wished to show with his less accomplished statements that a complete Church likewise had to exhibit manifest signs of fallibility.

The question whether Hubbard in addition to psychology fiction and religion fiction also wished to create a kind of applied politics fiction shall remain unanswered here. Depending on one's views and mood, the master's corresponding statements (in particular his equation of democrats and monkeys) can be rated either pre-fascistic or Dadaistic.[8] What counts is that all scientological themes are from the outset permeated by a radically parodistic trait that did not cease to strongly affect everything Hubbard ever tackled. Whatever he touched from the symbolic tradition then cropped up again as a technically iterable phenomenon. Evidently nothing is as suited as "religion" to be translated into the universe of technical images.

Hubbard achieved great things parodying religion, in particular when parodying the principle of hierarchy (one need think only of his amusing "Operating Thetans," levels one to eight), but also as a creator of parodies of the mythical notion that at its heart the soul (more recently *Thetan*) recognizes God. Hubbard deserved a Nobel Prize for his insight that weak minds could be replaced by high-grade Thetan implants. And Scientology's treatment of those who turn their back on it is also of great value as a parody – here we find a travesty of the classical condemnation of those who deny the existence of God in the systematic harassment of ex-Thetans. It would be comical if it did not also imply real terror for those attacked. If translated into current conditions, the principle of the old missionary cults that converted a people by converting the king spells the insight that you first have to woo the celebrities.[9] Thus Hubbard used unlimited quotations to create a Las Vegas of intellectual history. The discontent given this complex of exposing imitations may be one of the reasons why members of the original religions preferred to avoid crossing swords with him. All the more thorough the attention that the Constitutional Protection Agency in Germany has paid to the ambiguous organization (in the USA, the FBI at one time had Scientology in its sights). Its very design makes it inevitable that it seems suspicious, for it is very open about the principle underlying it.

8   The expression "politics fiction" was first used, in a different context, by Philippe Lacoue-Labarthe. See his *Die Fiktion des Politischen. Heidegger, die Kunst und die Politik*, Ed. Schwarz, Stuttgart, 1990.
9   Dana Goodyear, "Château Scientology. Inside the Church's Celebrity Centre," in: *The New Yorker*, January 14, 2009, available online at: www.thenewyorker.com/reporting/2008/01/14/080114fa_fact_goodyear, November 15, 2010.

This has to be the case, as Scientology offers the pattern for staging in the form of religion contents that come from elsewhere.

The European Court of Human Rights confirmed in April 2007 that Scientology had the right to act in public as a religious community, despite its at times far-from-serious, indeed at times manifestly criminal economic activities.[10] This judgment deserves attention because, despite appearances, it includes no statement on the religious content of the sect. It merely states the inalienable right of every person to profess to membership of a functioning fiction. The judges took the scientological organization's claim to realizing religious, spiritual, and humanist goals at face value. Seen in the harsh light of day, the judgment passed down by Strasbourg is nothing more than a statement by the court on itself, namely that it cannot pass judgment on matters of parody. According to a similar logic, the security officers at airports are obliged categorically to refuse to allow any joker who claims to have a bomb in their hand luggage from access to the departure area, as the controllers cannot be assumed to understand any statement other than in the words it is said.

The highest court has therefore decreed that today, a religion can be considered to be such if an enterprise enduringly claims that it is a religion. Whosoever has religion in their hand luggage may go to the gate. The notion that Jesus would not have been able to submit a petition for admission as a man of religion before the Court of Human Rights because he did not know the word "religion" was something that did not occur to the judges. Jesus also did not know the concept of human rights, especially not modernity's notion of an inalienable right to free expression of an illusion. The Strasbourg judges did not sense how close they are to Ron Hubbard: If he was able to found a religion, then they were also able to approve it. It is hard to say who is more misguided. At least the judges (assuming there were no disguised scientologists among them) sought to pass down bona fide right given that Hubbard founded his "church" over an abyss of functional ironies. Incidentally, Scientology's attorneys have for decades been working to transform the legal systems of their host countries into a venue for jurisdiction fictions – as one can see, with successes that are quite striking. Without the American penchant for law suits, which is starting to spill over into Europe, Scientology would no doubt have long since disappeared from the market.

By contrast, I deduce from the dispute over whether this group of psychotechnical practitioners have the status of a religion that it conclusively shows that there is no religion. If we study the fundamentals of the fetish that is religion, then we will only identify anthropotechnics (the same applies analogously to the second major fetish to today, "culture"). The expression "religion" is, here and elsewhere, a password on the inside in order to open up the more pliable zones of the mind, those that are most as risk of exploitation (see the above-mentioned four modules of religioid inner operations), and on the outside a badge that one shows to gain entrance to the world of seeming respectability.

To summarize, let me say that the indirect enlightening dynamism of Hubbard's scientological doctrine, and to an even greater extent its practical organization, are connected with the unprecedented brashness of his eclecticism. In this point, Hubbard even steals the show from Rudolf Steiner, who was anything but bashful. His quite ruthless eclecticism bears the signature of an age that he completes with the transition from "the truth of thought to the pragmatism of action."[11] What traditionally was termed the spirit or soul is grasped in Hubbard's system only to the extent that it is treated as a terrain that offers scope for *survival*. For Hubbard, the notion of *survival* has permeated the thereafter and has seized control of everything that previously at some point was considered the intellectual/spiritual surfeit that went beyond physical life. Thus, Scientology offers pragmatism from there for here and vice versa. In accordance with this, it provides the metaphysical justification for the thirst for higher positions in the pyramid-structure game of life. Typical of such pyramid games is that the newcomers pay the price for the ascendancy of their

10 L. Ron Hubbard himself was sentenced by a French court in absentia to four years' jail in 1979 for fraud. The FBI also uncovered material in the sect's business files. In the 1970s, Hubbard's wife was sentenced to several years' imprisonment.

11 See: Gotthard Günther, *Die amerikanische Apokalypse*, edited from the estate and with an introduction by Kurt Klagenfurt, Profil, Munich, Vienna, 2000, p. 277.

elders. The danger insight Nietzsche propagated, namely that the evil can also directly be the good, comes fully to bear in such games. In them we find the grounds for gnostic irony, according to which everything is only a game with games. In Los Angeles, where Scientology has its deepest roots, this gets translated into the hypothesis: Everything is only a movie that refers back to prior movies. What counts is to be on the side of the producers.

If we trace this "religion" back to its essentials, then three complexes emerge that cannot be further reduced, and of which each has a clear reference to the anthropotechnical dimension. First, on the dogmatic side: A strictly organized association for practicing illusion, whose members become ever more deeply impregnated with the milieu's concepts as time progresses. Then, on the psychotechnical side: A training manual for the exploitation of all opportunities in the transcendental struggle for survival. If we then lastly turn to the tip of the movement, then we find all manner of things, but no "founders of a religion." What stands before us is a radically ironic business trainer and producer of illusions willing to do anything and who shows his ambitious but still uncertain successors what techniques can be used to survive in the jungle warfare of the egos. This does not exclude that there is also a charming side to it all. Here, benevolent and clever people can find a home for a while. From the systemic viewpoint, this proves the rule according to which a perverse whole can appropriate the integrity of its parts without fully absorbing them.

To end with an argument *ad personam*, let me remark that in more recent intellectual history there have only been three figures who one could place alongside Hubbard from the typological perspective: Marquis de Sade, the pioneer of philosophy fiction, who championed the liberation of a sexualized will to power; the Russian miracle healer and bohemian monk Rasputin, whose maxim was "power is the truth"; and British occultist Aleister Crowley, who spent his life with excessive drug abuse and experiments in evil and claimed to be Satan, the Antichrist, the animal of the apocalypse, the animal whose number is 666. Whether Crowley's games with occult traditions can themselves not likewise be understood as a feral version of the rehabilitation of *matière* is something I shall desist from investigating further here. The analogy between black magic and historical materialism is quite evident here at any rate.

Without doubt, the youngest member of this infernal quartet was the most successful. According to a statement by Hubbard's eldest son, Ron Hubbard, Jr., Crowley had early on fascinated his father. Through one of his pupils, rocket scientist Jack Parsons of the Californian Institute of Technology, Hubbard the elder was introduced to Crowley's infamous Ordo Templi Orientalis and initiated into the thought of black magic.[12] It is here, so the son suggests, that his father learned that the will is everything and is permitted to do anything. And it was this school that gave him the most secret of all secret insights that his system offered: No one need die, everyone can win and become God after a few sessions. Hubbard knew firsthand that the voice of the animal spoke from the depths in these sentences – or, to translate it more freely: the revenge of matter for 2000 years of being ignored and slandered. After Crowley's death in 1947 LRH is said to have believed that the latter's place was now vacant and awaiting a worthy successor.

Ron Hubbard, Jr., a knowledgeable if not always impartial witness, claims moreover that his father, with whom he worked on everything in the founding years of the "Church," was a psychological and physical wreck as of the mid-1960s. He had evidently fallen victim to his own fictions and was ruined by his addiction to drugs and medicines and, during the closing years of his life was caught in the trap he had himself built, lost like a prisoner in an exploding fireworks factory, plagued by hypochondria, overwhelmed by choleric attacks, filled with the wish to destroy "repressive persons" who dared to criticize his oeuvre. He is reputed to never again have shown his face in public in order not to reveal to his disciples just how far you could go with his methods of practicing illusion.

12 See: John Carter, *Raumfahrt, Sex und Rituale. Die okkulte Welt des Jack Parsons*, Hadit-Verlag, Albersdorf, 2003.

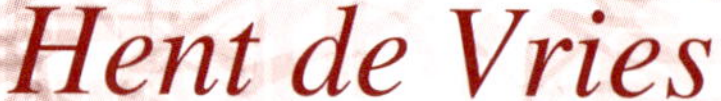

Hent de Vries

..Causes.for.Wonder:..
...Religion,.Media,...
..and.the.Miraculous..

Why, who makes much of a miracle?
As to me I know of nothing else but miracles,
Whether I walk the streets of Manhattan,
Or dart my sight over the roofs of houses toward the sky,
Or wade with naked feet along the beach just in the edge of
    the water,
Or stand under trees in the woods,
Or talk by day with anyone I love, or sleep in the bed at night
    with anyone I love,
Or sit at the table at dinner with the rest,
Or look at strangers opposite me riding in the car,
Or watch honey-bees busy around the hive of a summer
    forenoon,
Or animals feeding in the fields,
Or birds, or the wonderfulness of insects in the air,
Or the wonderfulness of the sundown, or of stars shining so
    quiet and bright,
Or the exquisite delicate thin curve of the new moon in spring;
These with the rest, one and all, are to me miracles,
The whole referring, yet each distinct and in its place.

To me every hour of the light and dark is a miracle,
Every cubic inch of space is a miracle,
Every square yard of the surface of the earth is spread with the
    same,
Every foot of the interior swarms with the same.

To me the sea is a continual miracle,
The fishes that swim – the rocks – the motion of the waves –
    the ships with the men in them,
What stranger miracles are there?

Walt Whitman, Miracles[1]

Walt Whitman's poem captures the central intuition informing the type of inquiry which, in the present day and age of mediatized religion and, we should add, apparently religionized media is more necessary than ever. Such an inquiry would have to start out from a simple hypothesis, namely that the historically most remarkable, yet seemingly singular, idiosyncratic, and for many now obsolete, occurrences and perceptions, events and effects of miracles and miracle belief, could be taken as *illustrative*, indeed, *exemplary*, *indicative*, and *regulative* for many of the most ordinary as well as most significant experiences with words and things, gestures and powers, affects and attitudes, vision and touch, sounds and smells punctuating life in modernity, in the so-called "secular age" and, who knows, beyond.

This is an insight which may not only bear in on the present or on the immediate future, it may also, retroactively, shed light on the most distant past, an era not yet affected by media in the strict, technical and, indeed, technological sense currently attributed to the term (in contrast, for example, to mediums for spirit possession, but also to classical mediums of direct oral transmission, the invention of writing, hieroglyphic and alphabetic signs, etc.). Thus, more broadly speaking, reference

<hr>

1   Walt Whitman, "Miracles," in: Michael Moon (ed.), *Leaves of Grass and Other Writings. Authoritative Texts, Other Poetry and Prose, Criticism*, Norton Critical Edition, W. W. Norton & Company, New York, 2002, p. 327. Whitman's poem was originally entitled "Poem of Perfect Miracles" in the 1856 edition.

to the mediatic aspect of religion and the religious aspect of modern media may illuminate the domain of the social and the political, just as it may extend to the intimate spaces of private existence. In fact, all of these temporal and socio-spatial as well as psychic-existential axes, however distinct ontologically and conceptually, can no longer be distinguished in any rigorously explicit (i.e., criteriologically determinable) sense, especially where miracles, events, and special effects manifest themselves in increasingly comparable and, all too often, interchangeable ways.

Taking Whitman's insight further, we may surmise that the impression and impact that *signs*, like *wonder*, make on us has become an increasingly *special* feature of our experience, just as it has been progressively mediated by technological means, many of which acquire a virtual, some would say religious life of their own. Through the proliferation of photographic, cinematic, and televisual technologies in the nineteenth, twentieth, and twenty-first centuries, initially engaging visual (in black-and-white, in color, in small or large format, and in two or three dimensions) and later auditory as well as other sensory faculties (from silent through to sound films to films that use Dolby quality sound), our perception has been shaped in remarkable ways. In a second, more recent wave, we have also witnessed the multiplication, diversification, amplification, and dissemination of digital and other media in the broadest possible sense – the Internet and cellular telephony, cable networks and YouTube, personalized talk radio, cassette sermons, but also the blogosphere or vlogosphere, being only the most recent and salient among them. These undeniable quantitative and qualitative leaps in technological development, of its expanded use as well as enhanced capabilities and refinement, may well have produced a qualitative, some may argue, ontological shift or transformation that affects each single one of us in virtually every private and public aspect of our lives. What results is a process of simultaneous intensification and generalization or,

indeed, trivialization of cultural meaning that requires an altogether different hermeneutic or critique.

As Jacques Derrida observed, there are now "so many miracles transmitted live (most frequently healings, that is to say, returns to the unscathed, *heilig*, holy indemnifications) followed by commercials [...] So remarkably adopted to the scale and the evolution of global democracy, so well adjusted to the technoscientific, economic, and mediatic powers of our time, the power of all these phenomena to bear witness finds itself formidably intensified, at the same time as it is collected in a digitized space [...] The ether of religion will always have been hospitable to a certain spectral virtuality."[2]

I have argued elsewhere that this hospitality can be explained by religion's ontological, or rather metaphysical, status as a virtual archive, which shares certain conditions with the virtuality produced by mediatic effects.[3] However, what ought to be included is a more comprehensive and phenomenologically compelling description and analysis of the ways in which religion and its media – or, more specifically, miracles and special effects – take shape and, however fleetingly, manifest and materialize themselves as genuine events in real time and space as instants and instances epitomizing and punctuating the pace, rhythm, and direction of modern secular life.

While there is exponential growth in the number of interchanges, or interfaces between religion and (its) media, miracles have from the very beginning coexisted with the "ether" that both transmits and betrays it. In other words, although technology could not be said to belong to its very definition or essence (nothing does), religion, paradoxically, opens itself to artificial media at each of its successive stages, using them as necessary stepping-stones while at the same time discovering them to be inevitable stumbling blocks.

But why is this? The hypothesis from which I started out not only implies that the history of religion and its key notions – namely, creation, revelation, epiphany,

2   Jacques Derrida, "Faith and Knowledge. The Two Sources of 'Religion' at the Limits of Reason," in: idem, *Acts of Religion*, Gil Anidjar (ed.), Routledge, New York, 2002, p. 62.

3   Hent de Vries, *Religion and Violence. Philosophical Perspectives from Kant to Derrida*, The Johns Hopkins University Press, Baltimore, 2006, chapter 4. Hent de Vries, "Introduction," in: idem (ed.), *Religion. Beyond a Concept*, Fordham University Press, New York, 2008, pp. 1–98.

and testimony *by way of* miracles (is there any other?) – still, or once more, casts its long shadow over modern experience, but also that it achieves this especially in the present technological and computerized, digital, and informational era in which "mechanical reproduction" (to use Walter Benjamin's well-known expression) has entered a dramatically new phase: a post-secular age, in which "idols" and "icons," "spirituality" and "secular magic," the return of "aura" and the emergence of new mythologies and not so new superstitions are not so much anomalies (or side effects), but serve as illustrations of the theoretical and practical difficulty of contemporary existential choices and political problems. As important as these two viewpoints are, the hypothesis above all suggests that so-called current affairs stand under the aegis of theological issues now mostly forgotten or repressed, whose stored insights we should once again begin to mine, if only to give our most urgent and pragmatic needs a certain dimension of depth which they now often sorely lack.

Conversely, we should explain how it is that the modern technological, that is to say, the automatic, artificial, and all too often theatrical crafting and spinning of events and effects in the current phase of global expanse and exponential growth of markets and media, sheds light, both *retroactively* and *prospectively*, on theological concepts and ritual practices of the miracle and, more broadly, on "religion," in its past, present, and, perhaps, future possibilities of articulation.

We have far from exhausted, let alone understood the *archival* and *mediatized* resources of expressing and blocking experience (history and temporality, spatiality and embodiment, the public and the private) *at its deepest* or, put differently, in its most marked instants and instances. "Religion," and especially the age-old and modern tradition of miracle belief, is replete with semantic and metaphorical, argumentative and rhetorical, visual and figurative, visceral and otherwise sensory repositories, whose

essentially *pragmatic* value cannot be overestimated and whose ontological status – as a "virtual memory" always with us – needs to be spelled out and redeployed to better effect than hitherto. We have not yet learned to use the best of religion against the worst of its violences.

I believe this task to be all the more urgent now that it is becoming increasingly apparent that current affairs and, more specifically, political events often reveal themselves as effects of undetermined ulterior causes, as unintended consequences, just as, in more protracted ways, the most deliberate attempts to pursue certain causes may have the most unexpected of reverberations – often confusingly called "side effects" – which, in turn, may or may not create events, indeed, small miracles, in their own right. Needless to say, crises or catastrophes – negative miracles, as it were – can be their effects or side effects as well.

This claim, if plausible and sufficiently demonstrated, has important repercussions for our interpretation of and dealings with contemporary political events, but also for the increasing technological production of special effects and their spin control. By the same token, it will help us assess the now exhilarating and outright disturbing intermingling between these two strands that are together *constitutive* of our world. Miracles, events, and effects comprise the many causes for wonder in the present day and age in which an ever more "global" manifestation of "religion" not only proves its unexpected resilience, but also its serious toll. For there is a curious sense in which near complete mechanization and computerization go hand in hand not with greater transparency and predictability, but with the opposite, that is to say, obscurity and randomness or arbitrariness (yet another dialectic of Enlightenment and rationalization, albeit one whose consequences seem less dire and, in any case, less fated than the one studied – deplored and exaggerated – by Max Weber, Max Horkheimer, and Theodor W. Adorno at their more pessimistic moments).[4]

4 For an analysis, see: Hent de Vries, *Minimal Theologies. Critiques of Secular Reason in Adorno and Levinas*, The Johns Hopkins University Press, Baltimore, London, 2005.

Neither naturalism nor secularism, I contend, can explain why and how this aleatory mixture of trends came to reveal its now salutory and then devastating consequences. And appeals to the postmodern and post-secular can offer only the vaguest of clues as to what new directions conceptual and empirical analysis should take to provide answers to these questions. An altogether different perspective – a "dual aspect theory of reality," as Stuart Hampshire, drawing on Spinoza, called it, as a new form of "seeing aspects," as Wittgenstein intimated, as well as a new conception of pluri-dimensionality and infinity, which could be articulated with the help of Gilles Deleuze and Alain Badiou – is required in order for us to venture well-prepared into what remains largely uncharted territory. Unfortunately, this is not the place to elaborate such a perspective in all necessary detail.

Put more succinctly, in order to analyze the modes, modalities, and moods implied (and unfolding) in the process leading to the present situation, the "secular age," one would need to establish a dialogue between a selection of representative ancient, medieval, and early modern *theologies of the miracle*, nineteenth and twentieth century *philosophies of the event*, and contemporary *media theories of the special effect*, all of which are referred to and, as it turns out, dependent on each other as elements and forms of belief and religious practice, ritual and faith, disarticulating and reconstellating themselves in and for the twenty-first century.

This, in many ways, unlikely conjunction of intellectual tools and requirements offers fruitful insights in all three of these traditions with their, admittedly very different, respective discourses, imageries, and disparate levels of conceptualization, argumentation, and demonstration. In spite of their undeniable historical and empirical, rhetorical and analytical specificity, which are both indications of and responses to entirely distinct sets of metaphysical, ontological, and aesthetic-technological, not to mention political and social as well as cultural and existential problems and preoccupations, it might nonethe-less be contended that their vocabularies and intuitions, strategies and solutions can be translated into each other – even *to the point of virtual indistinction*. Indeed, paradoxically, it is just at that point at which we are no longer able to tell them apart or determine their specificity that miracles, events, and effects come into their own. Taken to extremes, this insight confronts us with a genuine aporia, whose peculiar nature teaches us more about current affairs and their corresponding mental states than any naturalistic or otherwise reductionist attempt in liberal or radical democratic theory to flatten things out, that is, to dispel the riddle.

The increasing realization of this remarkable juncture, where miracles, events, and effects – "signs and wonders," as the Christian New Testament has it (Heb. 2:4) – become *all but interchangeable*, is the moment and momentum at which we find ourselves in contemporary modern, secular, and post-secular societies, and in the North-Atlantic West, perhaps, no more than elsewhere. No Eurocentrism, no Orientalism, nor, for that matter, Occidentalism is involved in this claim. In fact, the impossibility of distinguishing these phenomena, their "saturation" no less than their being void of meaning and sense, is precisely what characterizes "global religion" – as well the political theologies that vehicle, embody, and institutionalize its potentials and perils – in the most extensive and intensive of ways.

It is a junction whose apparent confusion, that is to say, empirical indiscernability, conceptual undecidability, existential impasse, and, perhaps, ontological *indifference* holds at least as much promise as it is based upon unanticipated, novel uncertainties and scarcely veiled threats. And this largely because mediatically driven events have taken on almost miraculous (some would say, magico-mythical, in any case, theatrical) qualities, whose sufficient causes and accompanying immersions increasingly elude us, in spite of the fact that they are more and more construed and fabricated (fabulated, fictionalized, and virtualized) as effects of a special kind, whose man-made qualities must remain hidden – and then also forgotten – for them to have their, all too often, disproportionate impact: that is to say, their "shock" and their *very* marginal and subliminal, though no less efficient "distraction."[5]

For while the signs and wonders of our world are of a *minimal* – and, at times, virtually negligible – difference, their subsequent effects are, paradoxically, of *maximal* consequence. Conversely, it has escaped no one that the maximal posturings of relentlessly advocated political-theological strategies, military might, and terrorist tactics have, for all their grandstanding, the least enduring repercussions. They somehow inform but do not necessarily justify, or even shore up, let alone warrant, the fulfillment of the actual agendas they seem to declare with so much clarity and fervor. Most of all they are a whistling in the dark, barking up the wrong tree, preaching to the home crowd, full of empty rhetoric and "performance violence" (as Mark Juergensmeyer wisely noted).

By contrast, seemingly innocuous statements and minimal events can have the direst, maximum effect. We cannot tell beforehand which result to expect and should weigh many other factors as well, beyond the obvious semantics and hermeneutics involved. And the task is hard enough. Most of us have forgotten how to interpret signs, or read between the lines, and have lost sight of the fact that the intended meaning often counts for nothing, whereas the unsaid – or what was not done, or did not happen – may well come to determine everything. Such are the signs of the times which, I would argue, only the putative wonders of "religion" and its multiple archives allow us to read. But why and how exactly? An outline must suffice here.

One cannot study, describe, and analyze, let alone comprehend, an "event" without immediately tapping into historical sources and intellectual registers that claim what – in the language and imagery of religion or, as it were, theologically – constitutes a "miracle." Nor is it possible, although this may seem somewhat far-fetched, to understand either one of these notions, namely "event"

and "miracle," without addressing what, in the language of cinema and so-called new media, is called a "special effect."

It is important to realize that this does not only, or even primarily, hold true for so-called major events, shocking historical events, for example, the determining or effective causes of which elude us. The comparison can also be made with what we take to be ordinary events or the eventfulness of the everyday. The religious testimony of the miracle – the very phenomenon or set(s) of phenomena for which it stands – might epitomize and flag, but also condense or magnify, bring into foreground and highlight, the most down-to-earth, profane, and secular difficulty in our coming to terms with virtually *any* culturally mediated and, indeed, ever more mediatized given. As Walt Whitman noted, "We hear of miracles. – But what is there that is not a miracle?"[6]

Further, one cannot theorize "the political" or concrete contemporary forms of "politics" without drawing, once again, on their theology, more precisely, their "political theology," just as one can hardly assess the contemporary forms and re-shaping of the political without reference to media, old and especially new. This is particularly clear in the ways that violence, in random terror no less than so-called justified wars, is differently – and never fully or convincingly – legitimated but always clings to grounds and motivations that remain transcendent to any cause. "No violence without religion, no religion without violence."[7] True, the clips, sound bites, public religion spin, and its political theologies differ greatly, and so do their calculated and incalculable effects, leaving, once again, no alternative but to learn to read the signs, to read between the lines, to see what is not visible, to hear what is not said, unaided by certain criteriological means or by rules for their interpretation. Minimal differences have maximal import; the grandest events may go unnoticed or peter out without a whisper. An hour of zapping or surfing confirms this point.

The uses and abuses of religion for political causes – and hence the need for a critique of

5   See: Naomi Klein, *The Shock Doctrine. The Rise of Disaster Capitalism*, Picador, New York, 2008.
6   Whitman in: Moon 2002, p. 327, note 1.
7   De Vries 2006

"political idolatry," as the French political scientist and contemporary of Jean-Paul Sartre Raymond Aron once called it – remains as relevant today as it was in the days of Henri Bergson, who in his last major work, *The Two Sources of Morality and Religion*, wisely noted that all too often "nations at war each declare that they have God on their side, the deity in question thus becoming the national god of paganism, whereas the God they imagine they are evoking is a God common to all mankind, the mere vision of Whom, could all men but attain it, would mean the immediate abolition of war."[8]

We know that things do not always work out in this manner and that these two contrasting yet complementary political theologies – say, the pagan and the Christian or, more broadly, the Abrahamic, for example – can be equally damaging. Weighing theological motifs, motivations, and movements, exposing their intrinsic and structural ambivalence, or even self-contradiction is thus *de rigueur*.

That the discourse on miracles can have an even more direct bearing upon the question of the theologico-political also seems clear. A hint in this direction is given in a remarkable passage from Sari Nusseibeh's autobiography. At the time of writing to the president of the Al-Quds University, the Arab university in East Jerusalem, Sari Nusseibeh, a respected historian of medieval Islamic philosophy, discusses his life-long passion for Abu Hamid al-Ghazali's "new way of conceiving miracles" and teases out its political significance:

"The followers of Aristotle denied the possibility of miracles. If the essence of an object – say, a drop of water – is inherent and immanent, that is to say, if no matter how deeply you explore the drop you will always find 'waterness,' then there can be no way of turning water into wine. Or, to use a political example, if two sides of a conflict have essential differences, even God can't bridge their differences. If nothing else, as the creator of all natural laws, God must be consistent. If Q inherently contradicts P, it will always do so.

To account for miracles al-Ghazali adopted atomism. Borrowing from the ancient Greek thinker Democritus […], he argued that the world and all the objects within it including our soul are composed of discrete, featureless, and interchangeable 'atoms.' These atoms take on various shapes, so if God chooses to turn water into wine, all he has to do is shift the atoms around a bit. Or, going back to politics, hatred may seem as immutable as Dr. Johnson's stone, particularly in the Middle East, where blood feuds can keep it going for generations. Yet, emotions are not Aristotelian essences, but can be transformed through an act of will. It's up to us to turn hatred into understanding. No matter how hopelessly entrenched two parties seem, their feud can be solved through an act of human will."[9]

Could this be a possible conclusion for the proposed meditation on miracles, events, and effects, even as other historical points of reference – beyond Aristotle and atomism, al-Ghazali, and Middle-Eastern stalemates – are taken into consideration? And, when all is said and done, could "understanding" and an "act of human will," or some equivalent for these loaded philosophical terms, do the trick? Does everything depend on how we, as spectators and agents, or both, are able and willing to take phenomena, to call them by their name, if not for what they are?

Moreover, what underlying metaphysics of so-called possible worlds and their, in principle, free configuration or rearrangement of elements, as atoms, monads, or other, or some equivalent for this conception (which Nusseibeh traces back to Avicenna no less than Leibniz), would we need for theoretically backing up such an alternative view, together with its correlative critique of inherent properties and hierarchically ordered natural kinds, now seen as a mere "dynamic function of the will, whether that will be that of the self or of the nation"[10]? What, in other words, would it mean, here and now, to assume as Avicenna did, that "with a shift in perspective the concrete world, so immutably

8   Henri Bergson, *The Two Sources of Morality and Religion*, University of Notre Dame Press, Notre Dame, 1977, p. 215.
9   Sari Nusseibeh with Anthony David, *Once upon a Country. A Palestinian Life*, Farrar, Strauss, and Giroux, New York, 2007, pp. 127–128.
10   Ibid., p. 149.

familiar, can become animated by the will, as if the inner and outer worlds, instead of being opposed to each other, join into one"[11]? No easy answers to this question are readily available.

Again, to have any chance of answering it would require that we establish a dialogue between traditional *theologies of the miracle*, modern *philosophies of the event*, and contemporary *theories of the special effect* (in cinema and visual culture, to be sure, but also, more broadly, in political spin and its deceptive tactics as well as military strategy and planning). I submit that it is in these three historically richly documented and systematically thoroughly elaborated domains with their respective fields of inquiry that the clash and confusion between the old and new – and the emergence of the old-in-the-new or the old-as-new, but also the new-in-the-old or the new-as-old – comes most prominently into view.

This clash is not so much one "between" cultures supposedly more or less adapted to the exigencies of the modern world of markets and media or to the moral and legal demands of political liberalism, to parliamentary democracy and the free exchange of ideas (as some, more notably Samuel Huntington, have suggested), but rather a source of tension and creativity, a threat no more than promise that resides "within" any one culture or mix of cultures (as Martha Nussbaum has countered). Its ambivalent and, indeed, Janus-faced aspect may well form the determining characteristic of globalization and its accompanying and enabling phenomenon – namely, "global religion" – whose general tendencies and overall significance, let alone local impact, we have only barely begun to register and assess.

Historical and, more broadly, empirical (economical, sociological, and anthropological or cultural critical) work will not suffice to unravel its internal logic, whose paradoxical, indeed, aporetic nature commands another kind of attention. Indeed, it requires quite a bit of philosophical speculation and phenomenological acuity to bring out, let alone understand, the enigma of why and how it is that religious and, in fact, any testimony must be seen and experienced as increasingly *interfaced* with media technologies. That this circumstance is not simply a sign of historical, let alone democratic, regress (which is often decried) should be clear. Not only are "modern conversions" and "public religions" themselves just as much products of modernity as they oftentimes protest against it. "Religion" also offers multiple resources and has come to represent both the best and the worst of possible answers to the predicaments of the modern world in all of its economic and political, cultural and existential dimensions. And these extremes of the best and the worst all too often trade their places unannounced.

It is precisely this flipping over of one perspective, attribute, or aspect into the other – *its* other – which catches us unawares and unprepared. Highlighting its paradoxical rhythm, conceptualizing its logic, and evaluating its impact offers, in my view, a far more helpful account of the fateful existence and essence of "religion" in the contemporary world than has been provided by threadbare, yet endlessly recycled or revived, sociological and cultural theories of secularization and disenchantment, privatization and trivialization. With few exceptions, the latter are based on progressivist versions of historical teleology and dialectics or based on their negative inversion, that is to say, on pessimistic and all too often nostalgic or reactive accounts of religion's decay and decline as a process that is imagined to be either unilinear and irrevocable or cyclical and reversible.

But what if "religion," indeed, the whole virtuality of its past and present archive was a *standing possibility* for humanity or, more precisely, a risk and chance, whose option or even "optionality" has lost nothing of its relevance in the world of today? What if this *roaming virtuality* has now all the more occasion and reason to come to the fore as a *deus ex machina* and at the most unexpected of moments and places? What, moreover, if "religion's" continued (renewed

[11] Ibid., p. 156.

or increased) role in the public domain today were almost perfectly consistent in what past theologies and philosophies all along tended to view as its peculiar metaphysical "existence" and "essence" in the general scheme of things (to the extent that we could now feel justified, if not to rehabilitate then at least to reinhabit these intellectual categories of old)?[12]

To say this is not to advocate an ahistorical and even less an anachronistic view of the religious phenomenon as it presents itself to us here and now. For it might well be that a long and sinuous historical process delivered to us – and delivered us unto – a conception that only now, retroactively, reveals a "possibility" or "virtuality" that we could not perceive or imagine earlier and for which we had, pragmatically speaking, no use until very recently: a past, present, and future "possibility" or "virtuality" that is thus only now set free for all, with all the "global" repercussions we have come to know in recent years.

The exhibition *Medium Religion* demonstrates the conceptual and empirical difficulties involved in addressing these issues. It places central focus on the increasingly complex, yet intricate relationship between the phenomena of so-called global religion and the new technological media that make them apparent and – all too often, unknowingly – "known" (giving a new sense to the meaning of traditional theological notions such as revelation, epiphany, grace, apocalypse, mysticism, and the like), but that, it should be added, also tend to increasingly obfuscate their more specific historical (situated or embodied) reference. Consequently, as we observe, these phenomena's present significance and wider relevance mostly eludes us.

It is, indeed, undeniable that contemporary – and, especially, technological – media are the main source and vehicle for a wide range of psychological, cultural, and notably political *affects*, which are ever more prominent and, indeed, dominant in determining the guiding motifs, moods, and motivations of individuals and collectives, nation states and non-state actors, non-governmental agencies and multinational corporations, informational networks and terrorist cells, international elites and business lobbyists, think tanks as well as public opinions. Yet it is also apparent that their precise and overall short- or long-term *effects* on our perception and sensibilities have become less and less predictable, let alone traceable or controllable – nor should they be. Indeed, that these phenomena and their agents (namely, their actors and spectators, victims and witnesses, bystanders and militants) strike us in a variety of novel, mediatized ways and, more importantly, cannot be preempted or framed by any anticipatory preparation on our (or anyone's) part, is, in sum, *a net gain* of the modern technological world. It has taught us to live in "global contexts" (which is nowhere more evident than in so-called "global cities") which are characterized by their potent mixture or, rather, alternation of excessive control and irreducible randomness, the measurable – or computable – and the immeasurable, near total transparency and the total lack thereof. We somehow find our way around, or in-between, these extreme, contemporary instantiations of the age-old metaphysical contrast between the general and the particular, the universal and the singular or the unique. But how, exactly, do we succeed? And why does this happen only in the most unlikely and rarest moments?

Visibly and audibly displayed for all those capable and willing to see and hear, the globally propelled affects and effects, notably those with a religious signature, form, paradoxically, the *decisive near-indiscernibles* of our times. They have acquired such stunning – and, by now, almost numbing – prevalence that they often no longer even take us by surprise, but invade and saturate us quietly and seemingly innocuously. Most of the time, they catch us unawares, influence us subliminally or unconsciously, and, when exposed to analysis and interpretation, leave us virtually at a loss. At such

---

12 See: Hent de Vries, "Introduction," in: idem 2008, pp. 1–98.

moments, which are now all too common, it becomes clear that we have largely forgotten how to read the signs or, when we do, to decipher the writing – the *menetekel* – on the wall (see: Daniel 5: 1–31), to say nothing of whatever it is that conceals itself between the lines.

What historical and conceptual resources could we access to interpret the immense amount of data, of unexpected input and ever newer output that continue to stockpile itself around us, and which do so with exponential growth, at ever increased speeds, and whose expanse, density, and intensity eludes the grasp of both theoretical knowledge and practical know-how, yet does not, thereby, render them unintelligible per se?

While it is in precise elements and formal features of the so-called *religious archive*, rather than, say, the narrative universe of magico-mythical thinking, that we can find keys to understanding the peculiar nature of what seem – albeit from opposed perspectives and under different aspects – aleatory, elusive, and, at times, obscure *miraculous* events, we also find artificially, technologically, or digitally mastered *special effects*. The historical and analytical distinction between these two phenomena, which are not as different in their *structure* and *content* as might initially seem to be the case, enables us to organize, systematize, and reassess a whole range of topics and problems that puzzle and trouble philosophical, theological, as well as political and no less theologico-political thinking in our time. Being able to tell the assumed difference between miracles and special effects and, more importantly, being aware of the putative difference they make in our individual and collective lives is of the greatest importance. Failure to do so means that we risk missing out on the very minimal nuances that, in the end, may turn out to have maximal impact and, hence, should matter – and be scrutinized – more than anything else.

To study these phenomena, their affects and effects, is not a mere academic exercise. It regards the electoral process in modern democracies where the issue is no longer "the issues," no longer "the force of the better argument" (to use Jürgen Habermas's expression), but a far more opaque "defining moment" – or, more precisely, "YouTube moment" – that, together with bodily gestures and grimaces, is valued above all else; it also regards the genuine or feigned sense of indignation whenever the accusation of idolatry and blasphemy enters the world stage triggered by, apparently, no greater event than the publication of some cartoons.

Events in their own right, special effects mimic and reinstantiate the register and regime of the miraculous – of signs and wonders, of amazement no less than fear and trembling – and, in the present day and age, do so with peculiar force. Conversely, the theological, concept of the miracle, of miracle belief (including its, often sophisticated, inter-theological, and extra-philosophical critiques), enables us to assess the mediatic version of the special effect and its hidden – now invisible and unobtrusive, then overwhelming or even shocking – workings. A peculiar "saturation" as well as "banality," to adopt Jean-Luc Marion's evocative terms, governs both "events" and makes it impossible to treat as straightforward historical or, more broadly, empirical "givens" or "facts." Instead, they are singular phenomena that do not obey standard criteria for scientific or common experience and operate, manifest, or reveal themselves with a remarkable and unique temporality of their own.

Miracles and special effects thus filter and direct the ways in which events, both in our private and public as well as political lives, enable and alter or, conversely, obstruct or destruct our perception and experience of things and their world, of images and their words, of sounds and their silences, gestures and their petrification, selves and their others. That this should be so is neither a blessing nor a curse, unless it is both; it is neither out of the ordinary nor ordinary, unless it is both. In a sense, to call things miraculous or specially effected is just to describe and judge *the way things are*, that is to say, *must* or *can* and, in some cases – where normative judgment is required – *should* be. In short, it is our way to picture or envision events in their difference from non-events, that is to say, those determinable facts and occurrences, transformations or processes, which, in traditional metaphysical parlance, have effective causes. Indeed, calling historical or empirical eventualities "events" is the first such special *act of naming*, just as our subsequent fidelity to such "events" is not so much a thought, however detailed our level of sophistication and acting upon them may be.

The problem of religion and its at once age-old, modern, and contemporary mediations and mediatizations thus poses itself in an entirely new light and requires fresh attention. No longer mere obstacles (as the letter to the spirit or writing to memory were once deemed to be) and far from being simple vehicles, let alone "the message" (Marshall McLuhan) themselves, new technological media enable and diffuse, propel and produce, invent and create "religion" on a global scale. More precisely, they follow an altogether remarkable, if not fully novel logic of *now maximizing, then minimizing* effects, according to a dynamics and rhythm whose conditions and implications elude our existing theoretical tools.

The question of miracles leads us to understand several of the most relevant historical and systematic aspects of the constellation of religion and media, whose wider spectrum runs from the ancient pictorial medium, through writing, modern mass publication, all the way up to the most advanced – televisual, digital, and virtual – of the technological and computerized mediums. But to exploit its potential to the full, we would have to explain why the modern – and largely Protestant – interpretation of "religion" as a set of propositional beliefs or doctrinal statements and moral imperatives held to be revealed and true (or false!), descriptive and natural or normative hardly captures the meaning of the religious and miraculous, as understood by representative Church Fathers and the more sophisticated among the modern philosophical theologians, including their critics (or only does so in part): authors as different as Friedrich Nietzsche and Ludwig Wittgenstein have argued as much.

Further, we would have to modify the Christian interpretation of the concept of the miracle as a unique, *one-time*, or *once-upon-a-time-only*, *one-of-a-kind* event by exposing it to non-Christian, non-theistic, and post-secular equivalents of miracle belief, that is to say, analogues or parallels, and their often only slightly different understanding of the extraordinariness of the ordinary and the everyday. These formal or functional equivalents, I contend, provide us with a better understanding of the miracle's repeatability or iterability, which reduces nothing of its novelty, but inscribes a different effect, each time, within the eventual change. In fact, fidelity to the event, heeding its call, as it were, has all the features of the performing – or seeing – of a miracle (and, hence, the miracle + n) in turn.

It is true that miracles were mostly seen as "an act or event that in some way repeats or echoes previous miracles within the same tradition" and that, hence, "what constitutes a miracle within each religious tradition is determined to a great extent by the tradition itself."[13] But then, while this structure of repetition somehow guarantees the miracle's *sui generis* character – that is, its irreducibility to anything besides this religion's own specific concerns – it does not exclude its comparability with other religious as well as non-religious formal equivalents and analogues. As is so often the case, other than into the relevant tradition's proper idiom and storytelling, the miracle's untranslatability does not prevent its translatability *tout court*; paradoxically, its absolute singularity and generality, or even universality, just like its principled orthopraxy and no less possible counterfeiting, always go hand in hand. Yet, when and where we find this to be the case, it is no longer possible to interpret miracles by relating them to their respective traditions

13 Kenneth L. Woodward, *The Book of Miracles. The Meaning of the Miracle Stories in Christianity, Judaism, Buddhism, Hinduism, Islam*, Simon & Schuster, New York, London, 2000, pp. 23f.

alone. Even though they are not derivative of things beyond them, they venture almost automatically into the comparison and competition with other classical and modern, contemporary, and future elements and forms of belief, whose phenomenality and commonality or ordinariness offer as many occasions for saturation, propensity to signify, and extraordinariness. We neither could nor should prevent this. "What is there that is not a miracle?"

The traditional theological discourse on miracles and the belief they require or inspire, together with their seemingly secular counterparts, spelled out by modern philosophies of the event as well as by contemporary theories of the special effect, provides a rich vocabulary and, indeed, conceptual-imaginative repository – or, indeed, archive – which may help us to address and rethink experiential as well as political phenomena in a variety of fruitful ways.

No one knows what a phenomenon can do, even irrespective of the endless chain of its mechanical – or, as the moderns say, effective – causation. For all we know, any event that deserves its name may present itself as either a miracle or an effect, as supranatural or natural, transcendent or immanent, extraordinary or ordinary. But I would like to ask, could any such event also be both? Could it present, reveal, or manifest itself from two angles, at once or alternatively – and at a pace or rhythm that confuses our perception and eludes our attention? Furthermore, ontologically, psychologically, or more broadly, affectively, what difference would it make to say that it does?

In pursuing the proposed inquiry of religion and media under the aspect of miracles and special effects, one need not emphasize their perennial confrontation, even though this aspect is just as real and important as their convergence or parallelism and compatabilism. This inquiry rather focuses on their historical alignment as well as their perceptual and, more broadly, experiential intermingling and resonance. What is more important is to bring out and analyze *a certain point of indistinguishability and, indeed, indiscernability or interchangeability* between these important domains which tend to present themselves as opposite poles of the medium and "the immediate" even though they have much more in common than has often been claimed.

Indeed, we should not pretend to discern too quickly or too clearly between "true" and "false" religion or between religion and "religion," even between these former and *no religion at all.* Conversely, tapping into the resources of the religious archive, suspending the scholarly principle of supposedly value-free, methodological atheism and replacing them with "methodological theism" (or "post-theism") instead, does not imply that one consider every phenomenon as an instance of religion (or "religion") *per se*. In and for itself, nothing need *be*, in fact or in essence, religious for the category of religion to be able to illuminate a host of contemporary phenomena in the most unexpected – and manifestly a-religious – of contexts.

To claim that "religion" has remained a standing possibility is not to postulate a religious nature for humankind per se. We are neither religiously wired, as some neuro-theologians would have us believe, nor are we, sociologically speaking, exemplars of the species *homo religiosus*; nor, finally, do we, as certain Neo-Kantians claimed at the turn of the twentieth century, have a religious "apriori" of any kind.

In fact, precisely the opposite is the case: For the presence of the religious past and its future is, first of all, that of a peculiar and, as we called it, roaming virtuality, whose "existence" and "essence," if we may say so, has nothing "natural" and, indeed, nothing "empirical" about it. Its increasingly mediatic modes of appearance – call it revelation, epiphany, the miraculous – are neither conventional nor normal, let alone normative (in the sense of being rule-governed or criteria-bound). And yet its singular instances and momentary instants have become the very locus and modality of passionate utterance and of agency in the present day and age.[14]

14 These questions may seem abstract at first glance, but they lead to the heart of the matter, to things that – here and now – matter most, publicly no less than experientially. Indeed, revisiting certain historical stages and current concepts of what has been called *the theologico-political problem* enables us to exemplify this broader pragmatic relevance. See: Hent de Vries and Lawrence E. Sullivan (eds.), *Political Theologies. Public Religions in a Post-Secular World*, Fordham University Press, New York, 2006.

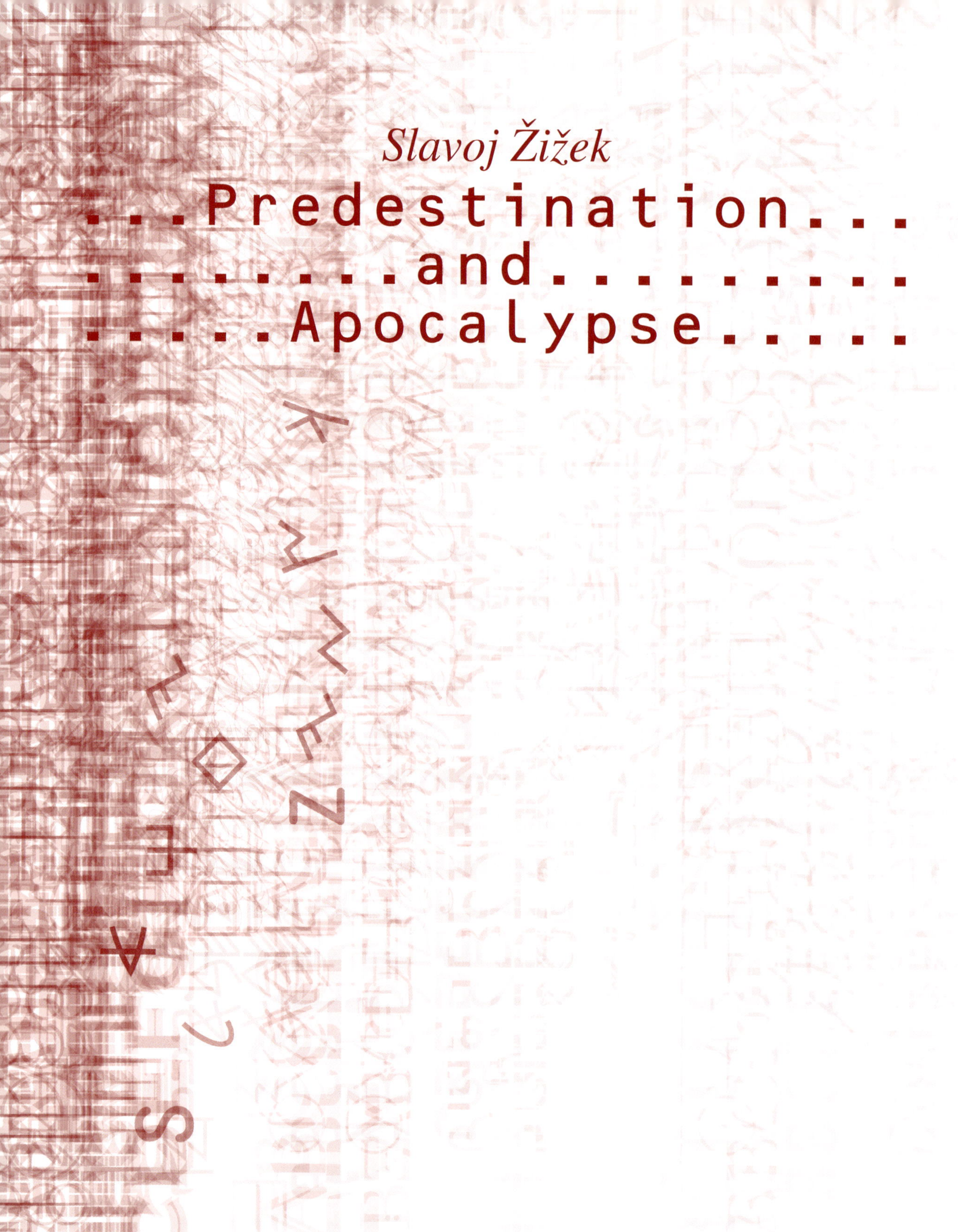

Slavoj Žižek
...Predestination...
.......and.........
.....Apocalypse.....

For all intents and purposes, we are already living in an apocalyptic era. Today, apocalypse is near at many levels, in terms of ecology, informational saturation, etc. Things are approaching zero-point, "the end of time is near." The following is as statement by Ed Ayres: "We are being confronted by something so completely outside our collective experience that we are unable to really see it, even though the evidence is overwhelming. For us, that 'something' represents a storm of enormous biological and physical proportions altering the world that has been sustaining us."[1] At the geological and biological levels, Ayres enumerates four "spikes" (accelerated developments) asymptotically approaching zero-point – the point at which the quantitative expansion will reach its point of exhaustion and will necessarily alter in quality. Population growth, mass consumption of resources, carbon gas emissions, the mass extinction of species pose a threat of such an order that, just so as to cope with it, our collective ideology mobilizes mechanisms of dis-simulation and self-deception to the point of practicing unfettered ignorance: "[…] a general pattern of behavior among threatened human societies is that their degree of blindness stands in direct proportion to their failure: The greater the crises, so the less focused does their response become."

Apocalypse is characterized by a specific mode of time, clearly opposed to the two other predominant modes, traditional circular time (the time ordered and regulated according to cosmic principles, which reflects the order of nature and of the heavens – the time-form in which microcosm and macrocosm resonate in reciprocal harmony) and modern linear time of gradual progress or development. Apocalyptic time is the "time at the end of time," the time of emergency, of that "exceptional state" when the end for which we are preparing ourselves now approaches.

At least three versions of apocalyptism are in current circulation, the Christian fundamentalist, the New Age, and the techno-digital posthuman. While all sharing the basic notion that humanity is approaching a zero-point of radical transmutation, their respective ontologies differ radically. Techno-digital apocalyptism, the chief proponent being Ray Kurzweil, remains within the confines of scientific naturalism: at the level of the evolution of human species, it identifies the contours of this species' transmutation into "post-humans." New Age apocalyptism adds a spiritualist twist to this transmutation, going on to interpret it as the shift from one to another mode of "cosmic awareness" (usually from the modern dualist-mechanistic stance to the stance of holistic immersion). Finally, Christian fundamentalists read apocalypse in strictly biblical terms, for example, they search (and find) the contemporary world for signs alluding to the proximity of the final battle between Christ and anti-Christ, that things are approaching a critical turn. Although this last version is considered the most ridiculous, it is no less dangerous with regard to content remaining the closest to "millenarist," radical, emancipatory logic.

In what ways does the digitization of our lives affect the hermeneutic horizon of everyday experience? According to a CNN report of May 29, 2008, monkeys with sensors implanted in their brains have learned to control a robotic arm with their thoughts, using it to feed themselves with fruit and marshmallows. In the experiment, conducted at the University of Pittsburgh School of Medicine, a pair of macaque monkeys were fitted with electrodes the width of a human hair that transmitted signals from areas of the brain linked to movement. Scientists conducting the experiment claim it will lead to the creation of brain-controlled prosthetic limbs for amputees, or patients with degenerative disorders. Even the well-known little finger of Stephen Hawking – the minimal link between his mind and the outside reality, the only part of his paralyzed body Hawking can move – will thus no longer be necessary: With my mind, I can *directly* cause objects to move, for example, it is the brain itself which will serve as the remote control

1   Ed Ayres, *God's Last Offer. Negotiating for a Sustainable Future*, Four Walls Eight Windows, New York, 1999, p. 98.

machine. What now looms on the horizon of the "digital revolution" is nothing less than the prospect of humans being able to acquire the faculty of what Immanuel Kant and other German idealists called *intellektuelle Anschauung* [intellectual intuition], the closing of the gap separating (passive) intuition and (active) production, i.e. the intuition which immediately generates the object it perceives – the capacity hitherto reserved for the infinite, divine mind.

Taken to this extreme, techno-digital apocalyptism thus assumes the form of so-called "tech-gnosis," and passes over into New Age apocalyptism. One of the preferred Janus-faced notions mobilized by New Age spiritualists is the notion of synchronicity elaborated by quantum physics (the instantaneous link between two events or elements, namely, faster than the speed of light traveling between the two). The precise quantum notion of synchronicity (two separated particles interconnected such that when one spins, the spin of the other is affected at a rate faster than the speed light traveling between the two) is read as a material manifestation/inscription of a "spiritual" dimension linking events beyond the network of material causality: "Synchronicities are the jokers in nature's pack of cards, for they refuse to play by the rules and thus provide a hint that in our quest for certain knowledge about the universe, we have ignored some vital clues."[2] The following is a New Age spiritualist description of the new social order expected to emerge as a secondary effect of a more substantial spiritual shift: "If we are in the process of graduating from nation states to a noospheric state, we may find ourselves exploring the kind of nonhierarchical social organization – a 'synchronic order' based on trust and telepathy – that the Hopi and other aboriginal groups have used for millennia. If a global civilization would be able to organize itself in the current chaos, it would be founded on cooperation rather than winner-takes-all competition, on sufficiency rather than surfeit, communal solidarity rather than individual

elitism, thereby reasserting the sacred nature of all earthly life."[3]

If we strip away its spiritualist coating, does this description not point to a kind of communism? How, then, are we to remove this coating? The best antidote to this spiritualist temptation is to recall the basic lesson of Darwinism: the utter contingency of nature. Why are bees dying on such a massive scale, especially in the US where, according to some sources, extinction has reached up to eighty percent? One hypothesis claims that the extensive use of fertilizers and insecticides has rendered plants poisonous to bees – is this not a poignant example of how an ecological catastrophe might look: One break of the weakest link in the chain of natural exchange derails the entire edifice? The problem here is that one cannot be absolutely sure that all we have to do is to restore nature's balance. Which balance? What if the bees in the U.S. and Western Europe have already adapted to a certain degree and type of industrial pollution? Or take the recently discovered, vast frozen peat bog in western Siberia (the combined size of France and Germany): It has started to thaw, potentially releasing into the atmosphere billions of tons of methane, a greenhouse gas twenty times more potent than carbon dioxide. This hypothesis should be read together with the report from May 2007[4]: Researchers at the Albert Einstein College of Medicine have found evidence that certain fungi have the capacity to use radioactivity as an energy source for producing food and spurring growth. The researcher's interest was aroused five years ago when a robot sent into the still highly radioactive Chernobyl reactor had returned with samples of black, melanin-rich fungi that were growing on the walls of the ruined reactor. Researchers then set about performing a variety of tests using several types of fungi. Two types – one that was induced to make melanin and another that naturally contains it – were exposed to levels of ionizing radiation approximately five hundred times higher than background levels; both of these melanin-containing species grew

2 F. David Peat, "Synchronicity. The Bridge Between Matter and Mind," in: Daniel Pinchbeck, *2012. The Return of Quetzalcoatl*, Jeremy Tarcher / Penguin, New York, 2007, p. 395.

3 Ibid., p. 394.

4 See: Kate Melville, "Chernobyl Fungus Feeds on Radiation," available online at: www.scienceagogo. com/news/20070422222547data_ trunc_sys.shtml, December 1, 2010.

significantly faster than when exposed to standard background radiation. Investigating further, researchers measured the electron spin resonance signal after melanin had been exposed to ionizing radiation. They discovered that radiation interacts with melanin to alter its electron structure – an essential step for capturing radiation and converting it into a different form of energy to make food. Ideas are already in circulation for the radiation-munching fungi to be part of the menu on future space missions: Since ionizing radiation is prevalent in outer space, astronauts might be able to rely on fungi as an inexhaustible food source on long missions, or for colonizing other planets. Instead of succumbing to terror at such prospects, cases like these rather suggest that one should keep an open mind to new possibilities, bearing in mind that "nature" is a contingent multi-faceted mechanism in which catastrophes can unexpectedly lead to positive results, much like the scene in Robert Altman's *Short Cuts* (1993) whereby a catastrophic car accident brings about an unexpected friendship.

Such openness to radical contingency is difficult to uphold – even a rationalist like Jürgen Habermas has been unable to sustain it. His recent interest in religion represents a break with the traditional liberal concern for the humanist, spiritual, etc., content concealed in the religious form. What interests him is this form itself: People who *really* fundamentally believe and are prepared to put their lives at stake for this belief, displaying the raw energy of belief and the concomitant unconditional engagement, something which is missing from the anemic-skeptic liberal stance – as if the influx of such unconditional engagement can revitalize our post-political drying up of democracy. Here, Habermas reacts to the same problem as Chantal Mouffe in her "agonistic pluralism": How to reintroduce passion into politics? However, in doing so is he not engaged in a kind of ideological vampirism, sucking the energy from naive believers without being ready to abandon his basic secular-liberal stance, so that full religious belief remains a kind of fascinating and mysterious Otherness? As Hegel had already showed apropos the dialectic of Enlightenment and faith in his *Phenomenology of Spirit* (1807, original German edition), such a contrast of formal Enlightenment and fundamental-substantial beliefs is false and remains an untenable ideologico-existential position. What should be done is to fully assume the identity of the two opposed moments, which is precisely what the apocalyptic "Christian materialism" can do with its unification of the rejection of divine Otherness and unconditional commitment.

How are we to combine such radical openness with the apocalyptic certainty of the approaching end of time? It is here that one should bear in mind the proper dialectic reversal of contingency into necessity, for example, of the retroactive nature in the necessity of the impending catastrophe as described by Jean-Pierre Dupuy: "The catastrophic event is inscribed into the future as a destiny, for sure, but also as a contingent accident: it could not have taken place, even if, in *futur antérieur*, it appears as necessary. [...] if an outstanding event takes place, a catastrophe, for example, it could not have taken place; nonetheless, insofar as it did not take place, it is not inevitable. It is thus the event's actualization – the fact that it takes place – which retroactively creates its necessity."[5]

Dupuy provides the example of the French presidential elections in May 1995. The following is the January forecast of the main polling institute: "If Ms Balladur is elected next May 8, one can say that the presidential election was decided before it even took place." If, accidentally, an event takes place, it creates the preceding chain which makes it appear inevitable: *This*, not the commonplace explanations as to how underlying necessity expresses itself in and through the accidental play of appearances is, *in nuce*, the Hegelian dialectics of contingency and necessity. In this sense, although determined by destiny, we are nonetheless *free to choose our destiny*. According to

5 Jean-Pierre Dupuy, *Petite métaphysique des tsunamis*, Seuil, Paris, 2005, p. 19.

Dupuy, this is also how we should approach the ecological crisis: not to "realistically" appraise the possibilities of the catastrophe, but to accept it as destiny in the precise Hegelian sense: Like Édouard Balladur's election, "if catastrophe is to occur, one can say that the occurrence was decided before it even took place." Destiny and free action (ignoring the "if") thus go hand in hand: Freedom is, at its most radical, the freedom to change one's destiny.

So if we are to properly confront the threat of a (cosmic or environmental) catastrophe, we have to introduce a new notion of time. Dupuy calls this time the "time of a project," of a closed circuit between the past and the future: The future is causally generated by our acts in the past, while the way we act is determined by our anticipation of the future and our reaction to this anticipation. This, then, is how Dupuy proposes to confront the catastrophe: We should first perceive it as our fate, as unavoidable, and then, projecting ourselves into it, adopting its standpoint, we should retroactively insert into its past (the past of the future) counterfactual possibilities ("If we were to do that then the catastrophe we are in now would not have occurred!") upon which we then act today.[6] Therein resides Dupuy's paradoxical formula: We have to accept that, at the level of possibilities, our future is doomed, the catastrophe will take place, it is our destiny – and then, against the background of this acceptance, we should mobilize our self to perform the act which will change destiny itself, and thereby insert a new possibility into the past. For Alain Badiou, the time of the fidelity to an event is the *futur antérieur*: Leaping over oneself towards the future, one acts now as if in the future one intends to bring about what already exists. The same circular strategy of *futur antérieur* is also the only truly efficient one when confronting the prospect of a catastrophe (say, of an ecological disaster): Instead of saying, "The future is still open, we still have the time to act and prevent the worst," one should accept the catastrophe as being inevitable, and then act so as to

retroactively undo what is already "written in the stars" as our destiny.

One should thus say of the ecological catastrophe: *If* it will happen, it will be necessary… And is not a supreme case of the reversal of positive into negative destiny the shift from classical historical materialism into the attitude of Theodor W. Adorno's and Max Horkheimer's *Dialectic of Enlightenment*? While traditional Marxism enjoined us to engage ourselves and act in order to bring about the necessity (of communism), Adorno and Horkheimer projected themselves into the final catastrophic outcome perceived as fixed (the advent of the "administered society" of total manipulation and end of subjectivity) in order to solicit us to act against this outcome in our present. And, ironically, does the same not hold for the very defeat of communism in 1990? It is easy, from today's perspective, to mock the "pessimists," of the Right and the Left, from Aleksandr Solzhenitsyn to Cornelius Castoriadis, who deplored the blindness and compromises of the democratic West, its lack of ethico-political strength and courage in its dealing with the communist threat, and who predicted that the Cold War is already lost by the West, that the communist block has already won it, that the collapse of the West is imminent. And yet, it is precisely their attitude which did most in bringing about the collapse of communism. In Dupuy's terms, it is their very "pessimist" prediction at the level of possibility, of linear historical evolution, which mobilized them to counteract it.

There is thus only one correct answer to the leftist intellectuals who desperately await the arrival of a new revolutionary agent to perform the long-expected radical social transformation – the old Hopi saying with a wonderful Hegelian dialectical twist from substance to subject: "We are the ones we have been waiting for."[7] Waiting for someone else to do the job for us is a way of rationalizing our inactivity. However, the trap to be avoided here is the one of perverse self-instrumentalization: "We are the ones we are waiting for"

6   See: ibid.
7   A Hopi saying, quoted from Pinchbeck 2007, p. 394.

does not mean that we have to discover in what ways we are the agent predestined by fate (historical necessity) to do the task – rather that there is no big Other to rely on. In contrast to classic Marxism where "history is on our side" (the proletariat fulfills a predestined task of universal emancipation), in today's constellation, the big Other is *against* us: Left to itself, the inner thrust of our historical development leads to catastrophe, to apocalypse, so that what can prevent catastrophe is *pure voluntarism*, i.e., our free decision to act against historical necessity. This is why theology is emerging once again as a point of reference for radical politics: Paradoxically, it is emerging not in order to supply a divine "big Other" guaranteeing the final success of our endeavors, but on the contrary, as a token of our radical freedom with no big Other on which to rely. Fyodor Dostoyevsky was already aware of how God gives us freedom and responsibility – he is not a benevolent master steering us to safety, but one who reminds us that we are accountable only to ourselves. This paradox lies at the very core of the Protestant notion of predestination: Predestination does not mean that we are not really free, since everything is determined in advance; it involves an even more radical freedom than the ordinary notion, namely, the freedom to alone retroactively determine (change) one's destiny.

Little wonder Blaise Pascal (or, more generally, Jansenism) was the only Catholic to have accepted predestination – predestination being a paradoxical supplement to Pascal's notion of the wager.[8] The first thing to strike the eye is that Pascal rejects all attempts to demonstrate the existence of God. He concedes that "we do not know if He is," so Pascal seeks to provide prudential reasons for believing in God. We should wager that God exists because it is the best bet: "'God is, or He is not.' But to which side ought we to incline? Reason can decide nothing here. There is an infinite chaos which separates us. A game is being played at the extrem-

ity of this infinite distance where either heads or tails will win... Which would you choose, then? Let us see. Since you must choose, let us see which interests you least. You have two things to lose, the true and the good; and two things to stake, your reason and your will, your knowledge and your happiness; and your nature has two things to shun, error and misery. Your reason is no more shocked by having chosen the one over the other, since you must of necessity choose... And your happiness? Let us weigh up the losses and gains in wagering for such a God."

Pascal appears to be aware of the immediate objection to this argument, for he imagines an opponent replying: "That is all fine and good. Indeed, I am obliged to wager; but I may perhaps wager too much." In short, if I put my wager on God, and God does not exist, then I really do lose something – when one wagers for God, one does stake something, which presumably one loses if God does not exist: truth, the respect for one's worldly life... (It is interesting to note just how utilitarian-pragmatist Pascal's reasoning is.) There is then a series of other objections:

1. Pascal assumes that the same matrix of decision and reward applies to everybody – but what if the rewards are different for different people? Perhaps, for example, there is a predestined infinite reward for the chosen ones, whatever they do, and finite utility for the rest?

2. The matrix should be more complex: Perhaps there is more than one way to wager for God, and the rewards that God bestows vary accordingly. For instance, God might not reward infinitely those who strive to believe in Him only for the utilitarian-pragmatic reasons that Pascal gives. One could also imagine distinguishing belief based on faith from belief based on evidential reasons, and posit different rewards in each case.

3. Then there is the obvious many-gods-objection: Pascal had in mind the Catholic God, but other theistic hypotheses are also possible options, i.e., the "(Catholic)

8   See: "Pascal's Wager," in: *Stanford Encyclopedia of Philosophy*, available online at: http://plato.stanford.edu/entries/pascal-wager, December 1, 2010. I rely here extensively on this entry.

God does not exist" column in fact subdivides into various other theistic hypothetical objections ([…] but the Protestant God exists, Allah exists, there is no God). The obverse of this objection is the claim that Pascal's argument proves too much: Its logical conclusion is that rationality requires believing in various incompatible theistic hypotheses.

4. Finally, one might argue that morality requires one to wager against God: Wagering for God because of the promise of future profits violates the Kantian definition of moral act as an act accomplished for no "pathological" reasons. It was already Voltaire who, along these lines, suggested that Pascal's calculations and his appeal to self-interest are unworthy of the gravity of the subject of theistic belief.

Underlying all this is the basic paradox of belief as a matter of decision, as if whether or not believing in something is a matter of decision and not of insight. So, if we read Pascal's wager together with his no less familiar topic of customs – "You would like to attain faith, and do not know the way; you would like to cure yourself of unbelief, and ask the remedy for it. Learn from those who have been bound like you, and who now stake all their possessions. These are people who know the way you would follow, and who are cured of an ill of which you would be cured. Follow the way by which they began; by acting as if they believed, taking the holy water, having masses said, etc. […]" – one can argue that the core of his argument does not directly concern belief but acting: One cannot decide to believe, one can only decide to act *as if* one believes, with the hope that belief will arise by itself; perhaps, this trust that if you act as if you believe, belief will arise, is the wager.

Perhaps, the only way out of these impasses is what, in his unpublished "secret" writings, Denis Diderot elaborated under the title of the "materialist's credo." In "Entretien d'un philosophe avec la maréchale de ***,"

he concluded: "Après tout, le plus court est de se conduire comme si le vieillard existait. […] Même quand on n'y croit pas." [After all, the most straightforward way is to behave as if the old guy exists. […] Even if one doesn't believe it.] This may appear to amount to the same as Pascal's wager apropos the custom: Even if you don't believe in it, act as if you believe. However, Diderot's point is exactly the opposite: The only way to be truly moral is to act morally without regard to God's existence. In other words, Diderot completely reverses Pascal's wager (the advice to place bets on the existence of God): "En un mot que la plupart ont tout à perdre et rien à gagner à nier un Dieu renumerateur et vengeur."[9] [In a word, the majority of those who deny a remunerating and revenging God have everything to lose and nothing to gain.] In his denial of the remunerating and vengeful God, the atheist loses everything (if he is wrong: he will be damned forever) and gains nothing (if he is right: there is no God, so nothing happens). It is this attitude which expresses true confidence in one's belief, and makes one do good deeds without regard to divine reward or punishment.

Authentic belief is to be opposed to the reliance on, or reference to another subject who is supposed to believe: In an authentic act of belief, I myself fully assume my belief, and thus have no need of any figure of the Other to guarantee this belief – to paraphrase Jacques Lacan, an authentic belief *ne s'autorise que de lui-même*. In this precise sense, authentic belief not only does not presuppose any big Other (is not a belief in a big Other), but, on the contrary, presupposes the destitution of the big Other, the full acceptance of the inexistence of the big Other.

G. W. F. Hegel was the first to indicate this: As a rule, his famous principle that one should conceive the Absolute not only as substance but also as subject, conjures up the discredited notion of some kind of "absolute subject," a mega-subject creating the universe and watching over our destinies. For Hegel, however, at its very core the subject also stands for finitude, as a cut, the gap of negativity, which is why

9   Denis Diderot, "Observations sur Hemsterhuis," in: idem, *Œuvres*, vol. I, Robert Laffont, Paris, 1994, p. 759.

God only becomes subject through incarnation: in itself, prior to incarnation it is not yet a mega-subject that rules the universe. Consequently, it is crucial not to confuse Hegel's "objective spirit" with the Diltheyan notion of a life-form, a concrete historical world, as "objectivized spirit," the product of a people, its collective genius: The moment we do this, we miss the point of Hegel's "objective spirit," which is precisely that it is spirit in its objective form, experienced by individuals as an external imposition, a constraint even. There is no collective or spiritual super-subject that would be the author of "objective spirit," and whose "objectivization" this spirit would have been. There is, for Hegel, no collective subject, no subject-spirit beyond and above individual human subjects. Therein resides the paradox of "objective spirit": It is independent of individuals, encountered by them as given, as pre-existent, as the presupposition of their activity, yet it is nonetheless spirit, i.e., something that exists only insofar as individuals relate their activity to it, only as *their* (pre)supposition.[10]

This is why Søren Kierkegaard's critique of Hegel relies on a fatal misunderstanding of Hegel's fundamental insight. The first thing that strikes the eye is that it is based on the (thoroughly Hegelian!) opposition between "objective" and "subjective" thought: "[...] objective thought translates everything into results [...], subjective thought puts everything into process and omits results – for as an existing individual it is constantly in the process of becoming."[11] For Kierkegaard, obviously, Hegel is the ultimate achievement of "objective thought": He "does not understand history from the point of view of becoming, but with the illusion attaching to pastness, understands it from the viewpoint of a finality that excludes all becoming."[12] Here, one must exercise caution so as not to overlook Kierkegaard's point: For him, only subjective experience is effectively "becoming," and any notion of objective reality as an open-ended process with no fixed finality still remains within the confines of being. Why? Because any objective reality, as "processual" as it may be, is by definition ontologically fully constituted, fully present as a positively-existing domain of objects and their interactions; only subjectivity designates a domain which is *in itself* "open", marked by an *inherent* ontological failure: "Whenever a particular existence has been relegated to the past, it is complete, has acquired finality, and is to this extent subject to systematic apprehension... But for whom is it so subject? Any existing individual cannot gain this finality outside existence, which corresponds to the eternity into which the past has entered."[13]

However, what if Hegel effectively does the exact opposite? What if the wager of his dialectic is not to adopt a stance towards the present, the "point of view of finality," viewing it as if it were already past, but to *reintroduce the openness of future into the past*, to *grasp what-was in its process of becoming*, to see the contingent process which generated existing necessity? Is this not why we have to conceive the Absolute "not only as substance, but also as subject"? This is why German Idealism already exploded the coordinates of standard Aristotelian ontology structured as it is around a vector which runs from possibility to actuality. In contrast to the idea that every possibility strives to fully actualize itself, one conceives of "progress" as a move to restore the dimension of potentiality to mere actuality, of unearthing in the very heart of actuality, a secret striving towards potentiality. Recall Walter Benjamin's notion of revolution as redemption-through-repetition of the past: Apropos French Revolution, the task of true Marxist historiography is not to describe the events the way they really were (and to explain how these events generated the ideological illusions that accompanied them), but rather to unearth the hidden potentiality (the utopian emancipatory potentials) which were betrayed in the actuality of revolution and in its final outcome (the rise of utilitarian market

10 See: Myriam Bienenstock, "Qu'est-ce que 'l'esprit objectif' selon Hegel?," in: Olivier Tinland (ed.), *Lectures de Hegel*, Librairie Générale de France, Paris, 2005.
11 Søren Kierkegaard, *Kierkegaard's Concluding Unscientific Postscript*, Walter Lowrie and David F. Swenson (eds.), Princeton University Press, Princeton, 1968, p. 86.
12 Ibid., p. 272.
13 Ibid., p. 108.

capitalism). The point of Karl Marx is not primarily to make fun of the wild hopes of the Jacobins' revolutionary enthusiasm, to point out how their high emancipatory rhetoric was just a means used by the historical "cunning of reason" to establish the vulgar commercial capitalist reality; it is rather to explain how these betrayed radical-emancipatory potentials continue to "insist" as a kind of historical specter, and to haunt the revolutionary memory by demanding its reenactment, so that the later proletarian revolution should also redeem (put to rest) all these past ghosts. These alternate versions of the past which persist in a spectral form constitute the ontological "openness" of the historical process, as it once again became clear to G. K. Chesterton:

"The things that might have been are not even present to the imagination. If somebody says that the world would now be better if Napoleon had never fallen, but had established his imperial dynasty, people have to adjust their minds with a jerk. The very notion is new to them. Yet it would have prevented the Prussian reaction; saved equality and enlightenment without a mortal quarrel with religion; unified Europeans and perhaps avoided Parliamentary corruption and the Fascist and Bolshevist revenges. But in this age of free-thinkers, men's minds are not really free to think such a thought.

My complaint is that those who accept the verdict of fate in this way accept it without knowing why. By a quaint paradox, those who thus assume that history always took the right turning are generally the very people who do not believe there was any special guiding providential hand. The very rationalists who jeer at the trial by combat, in the old feudal ordeal, do in fact accept a trial by combat as deciding all human history."[14]

Why, then, and in apparent contradiction to our aim, is there a flowering genre of what-if-histories under the aegis of conservative historians? As a rule, the typical introduction to such a volume begins with an attack on Marxists who allegedly believe in historical determinism. Their conservative sympathies become clear by a cursory glance at the list of contents of the leading what-if-volumes: The favored topics oscillate between the "major premise" – how much *better* history would have been if a revolutionary or "radical" event had been avoided (if King Charles were to win the Civil War against Parliament; if the English Crown had defeated the American colonialists; if the Confederacy had won the U.S. Civil War aided by Great Britain; if Germany had won the Great War; if Lenin had been shot at the Finland Station...) – and the "minor premise" how much *worse* history would have been if it had taken a more "progressive" turn (if Margaret Thatcher had been killed in the Brighton IRA bombing in 1984; if Al Gore had gained victory over George W. Bush and had been president on 9/11).

So how should the Marxist respond? Not, to be sure, by rehashing boring old Georgi Plekhanov's arguments on the "role of the individual in history": the logic contending that "even if Napoleon had not existed, another individual would have filled the role, because deeper historical necessity called for a passage to Bonapartism." One should rather question the very premise that Marxists (and leftists in general) are dumb determinists opposed to entertaining such alternative scenarios.

The first thing to note is that the what-if-histories are part of a more general ideological trend, of a perception of life that explodes linear-centered narrative forms and renders life as a multiform flow; up to the domain of the "hard" sciences (quantum physics and its multiple-reality interpretation; neo-Darwinism) we seem to be haunted by the chanciness of life and the alternate versions of reality – as Stephen Jay Gould, the Marxist biologist if there ever was one, bluntly put it: "Wind back the film of life and play it again. The history of evolution will be totally different." This perception – of our reality as being one of the possible, often not even the most probable,

14 G. K. Chesterton, "The Slavery of the Mind," available online at: www.cse.dmu.ac.uk/~mward/gkc/books/The_Thing.txt, December 1, 2010.

outcomes of an "open" situation, that other possible outcomes are not simply canceled out but continue to haunt our "true" reality as a specter of what might have happened – confers on our reality the status of extreme fragility and contingency, which is by no means foreign to Marxism. And it is on this that the perceived *urgency* of the revolutionary act relies.

Since the non-occurrence of the October Revolution is one of the favored topics of the conservative what-if-historians, let us look at how Lenin himself related to it. He was as far as from any kind of reliance on "historical necessity" as could be imagined. Quite to the contrary, it was his Menshevik opponents who emphasized that one cannot leap over the succession of stages prescribed by historical determinism: first bourgeois-democratic, then proletarian revolution… When, in his "April Theses" of 1917, Lenin discerned the *Augenblick*, the unique chance of a revolution, his proposals initially met with indifference or contempt by a large majority of his own party colleagues. No prominent leader within the Bolshevik faction supported his call to revolution, and *Pravda* took the extraordinary step of dissociating the party, and the editorial board as a whole, from Lenin's "April Theses" – far from being an opportunist, flattering and exploiting the prevailing mood in the party, Lenin's views were highly idiosyncratic. Alexander Bogdanov characterized "April Theses" as "the delirium of a madman," and Nadezhda Krupskaya herself concluded that "I am afraid it looks as if Lenin has gone crazy." Lenin immediately perceived the revolutionary chance as the result of unique contingent circumstances: If the moment not seized, the chance for the revolution will be forfeited, perhaps for decades. Hence, what we have here is Lenin himself entertaining an alternative scenario: *What if* we do not act now – and it was precisely the awareness of the catastrophic consequences of not acting that prompted him to act…

But there is a much deeper commitment to alternative histories in a radical Marxist view: it brings the what-if-logic to its self-reflexive reversal. For a radical Marxist, *the actual history that we live is itself a kind of alternative history realized*, the reality we have to live in because, in the past, we failed to seize the moment and act. Military historians demonstrated that the Confederacy lost the battle at Gettysburg because General Lee made a series of entirely uncharacteristic mistakes: "Gettysburg was the one battle fought by Lee that reads like fiction. In other words, if ever there was a battle where Lee did not behave like Lee, it was there in southern Pennsylvania."[15] For each of the wrong moves, one can play the game of "what would Lee have done in that situation" – in other words, it was as if, in the battle of Gettysburg, the alternate history actualized itself…

This brings us to the what-if-dimension that permeates the very core of the Marxist revolutionary project. In his ironic comments on the French Revolution, Marx opposes the revolutionary enthusiasm to the sobering effect of the "morning after": The actual result of the sublime revolutionary explosion, of the event of freedom, equality, and brotherhood, is the miserable utilitarian/egotistic universe of market calculations. (And, incidentally, is not this gap even greater in the case of the October Revolution?) However, as we have already seen, one ought not to simplify Marx: His point is not the rather commonsensical insight into how the vulgar reality of commerce is the "truth" of the theater of revolutionary enthusiasm, "what all the fuss was really about." In the revolutionary explosion event, another utopian dimension shines through, the dimension of universal emancipation, which is precisely the excess betrayed by the market reality that takes over "the day after" – as such, this excess is not simply abolished, dismissed as irrelevant, but *transposed into the virtual state* as it were, and continues to haunt the emancipatory imaginary as a dream yet to be realized. Hence, the excess of revolutionary enthusiasm over its own "actual social base" or substance is literally that of an attribute-effect over its own substantial cause, a ghost-like event waiting for its proper embodiment.

15 Bill Fawcett, *How to Lose a Battle: Foolish Plans and Great Military Plunders*, HarperCollins, New York, 2006, p. 148.

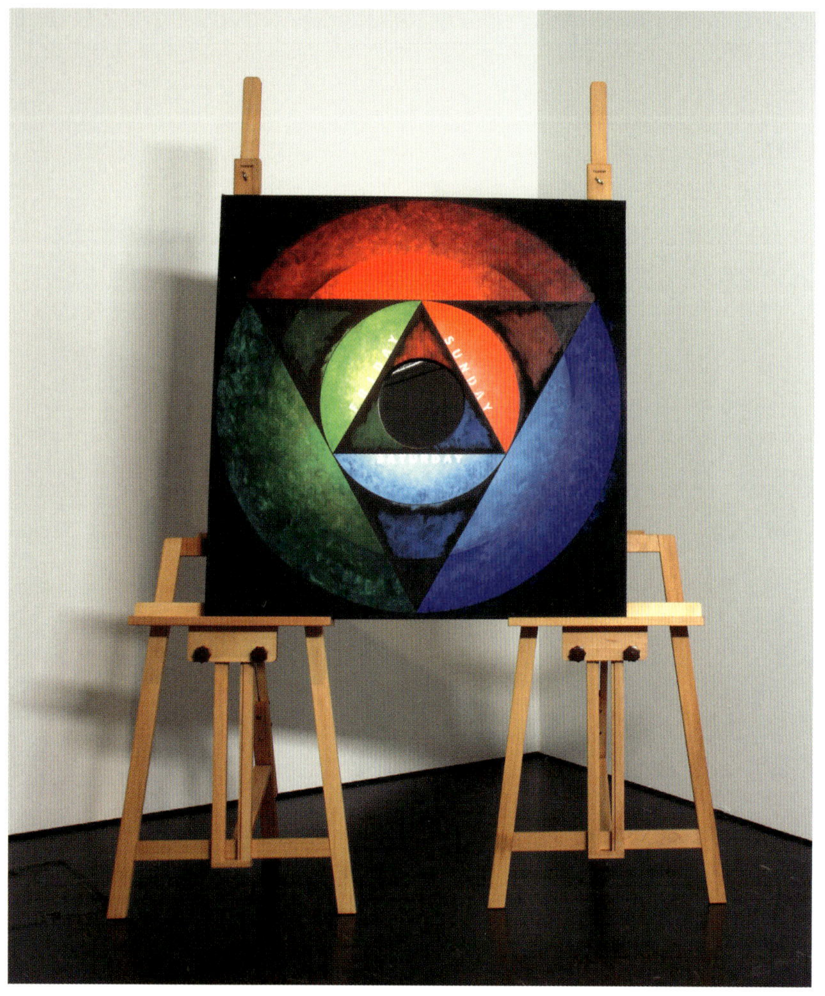

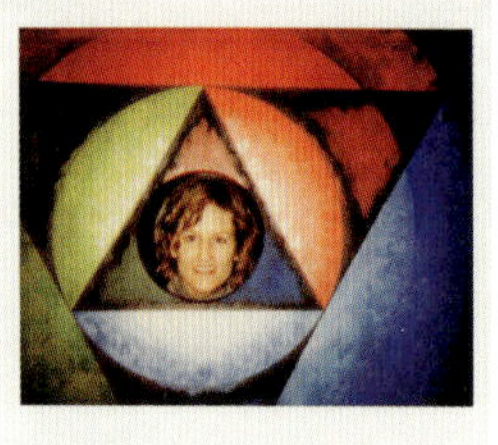

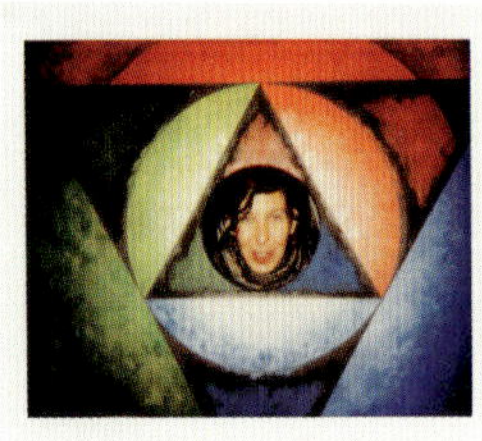

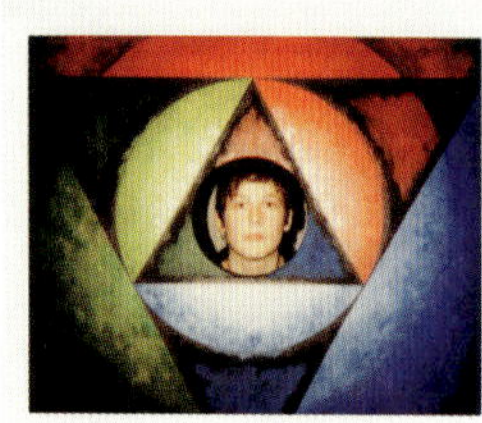

Vitaly Komar
*1943 in the former USSR,
today Russia,
lives and works in New York

From the *Three-Day Weekend*
project:
Mandala # 1, 2005,
tempera and oil on canvas,
122 × 122 cm, installation view
ZKM | Karlsruhe, 2009
Forbidden Fruit No 2, 2004–2005,
collage, 100 × 75 cm
*The Horizon at the End
of the Tunnel*, 2004–2005,
collage, 100 × 75 cm
Flashbacks, 2004–2005,
collage, 100 × 75 cm

The project *Three-Day Weekend*
(Sunday, Saturday, Friday) unites
a social dream (a 30-hour work
week) and ecumenical utopias
(peaceful coexistence of all faiths,
including atheism, within a secular
state). Vitaly Komar: "*Three-Day
Weekend* is my vision of symbolist
images which can play a role of
visual propaganda of these
dreams and utopias. Everybody is
welcome to join *Three-Day Weekend* society! All members, including artists, could send me proposals or suggestions on how to
accomplish this lofty future of
humanity."

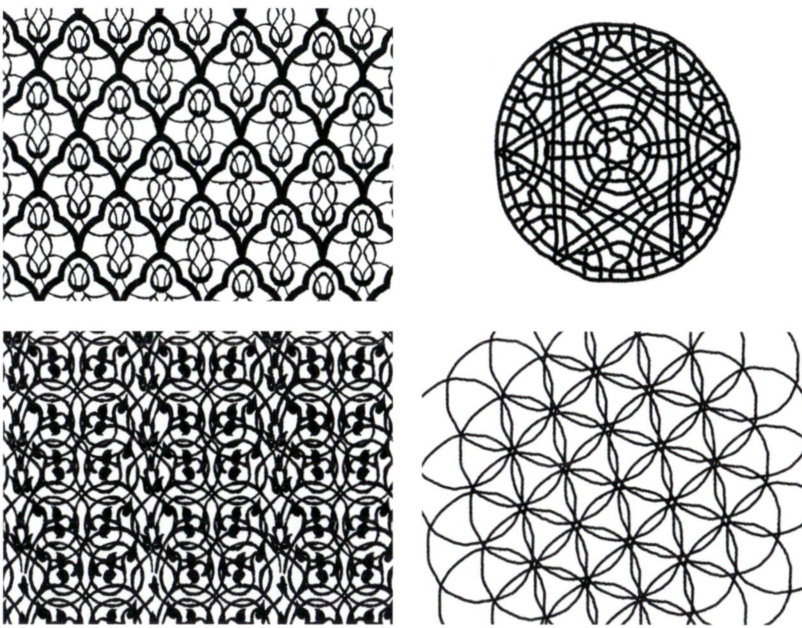

Adel Abdessemed
*1971 in Constantine, Algeria,
lives and works in Paris, Berlin,
and in the USA

God is Design, 2005,
video animation made from
3,050 drawings, b/w, sound, 4:44
min, installation view
ZKM | Karlsruhe, 2009,
and video stills

The video work *God is Design* by
the Algeria-born video and installation artist Adel Abdessemed
arose as a reaction to the xeno-
phobic climate noticeable in New
York after the attacks of September 11, 2001. Abdessemed fash-
ioned the video from more than
3,000 individual drawings of orna-
mental motifs taking up symbolism from the most varied of visual
sources: the formal canons of
Islam, Judaism, and Christianity
are as recognizable here as the
formal language of geometric
painting, of North African abstract
patterns, or of human cell structures. Abdessemed combines all
this in a kind of universal language
of form, a "visual Esperanto"
negating the supremacy or dicta-
torship of a single formal canon
in a poetical way.

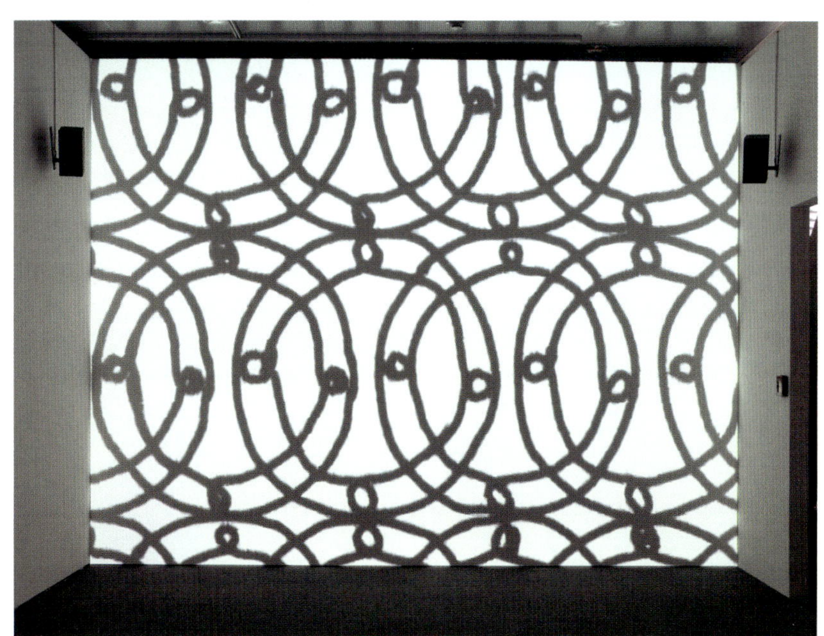

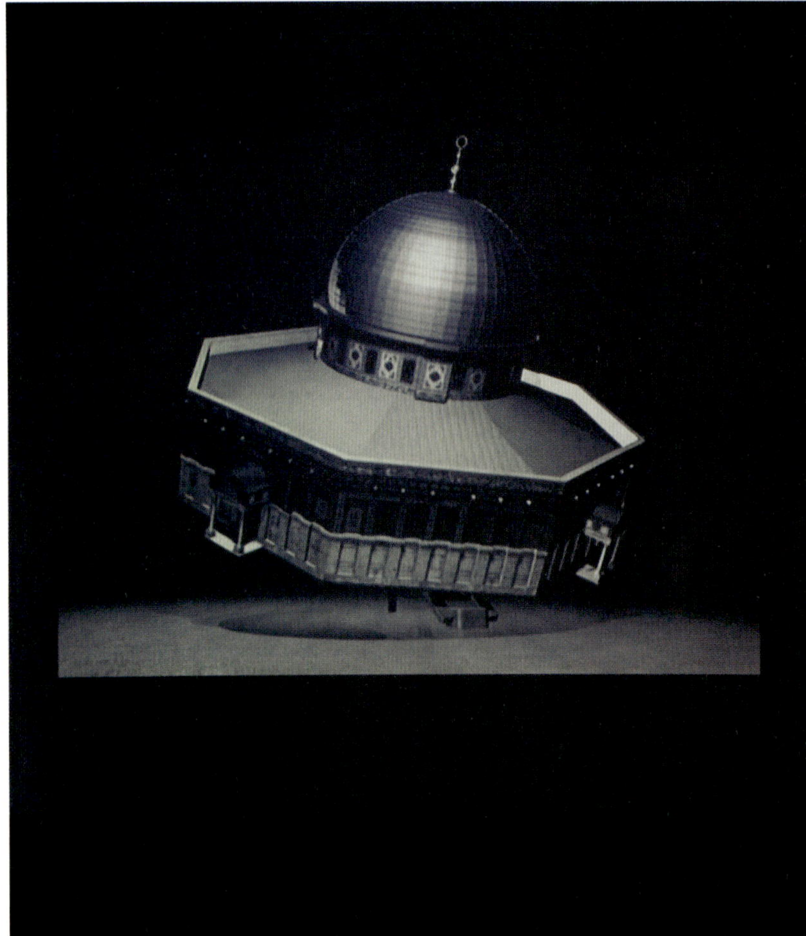

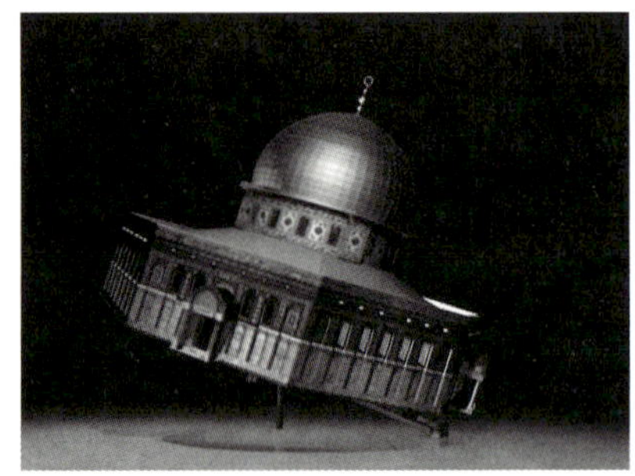

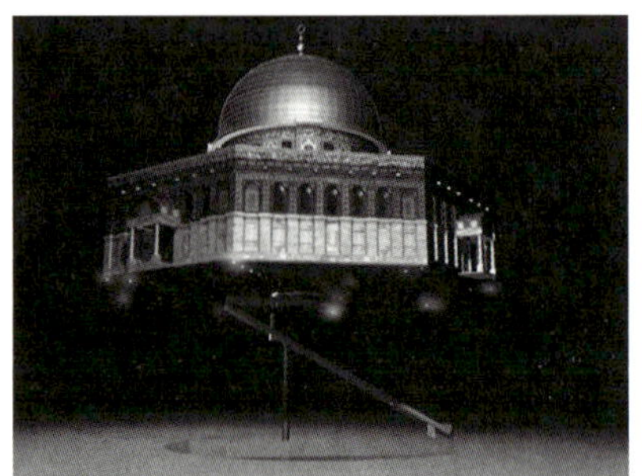

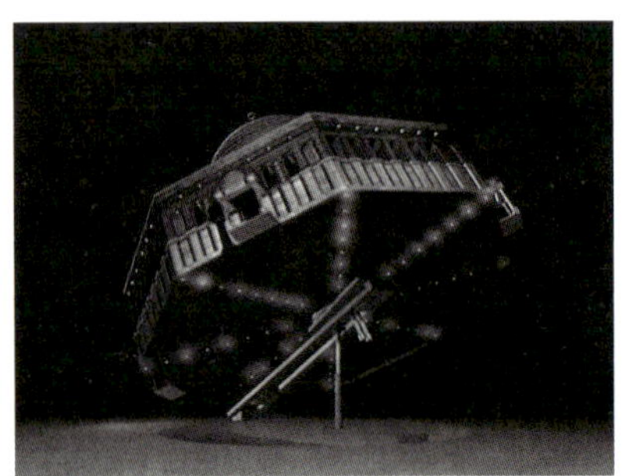

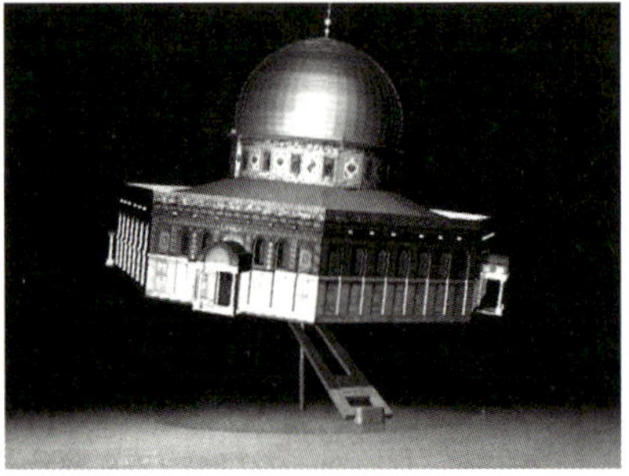

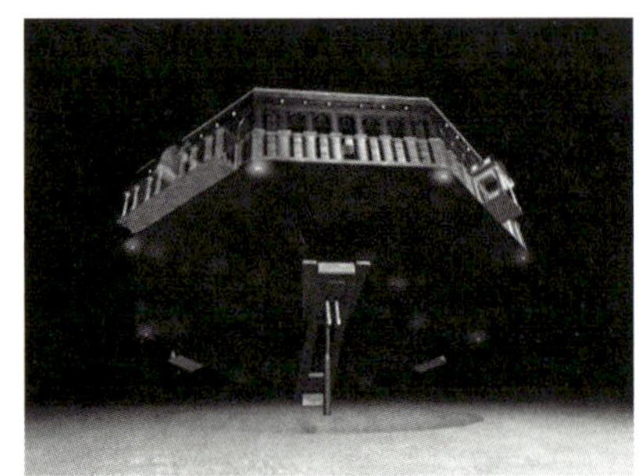

In his computer animation *Al Aqsa Park*, Wael Shawky shows the Dome of the Rock on Jerusalem's Temple Mount as a merry-go-round that has come off the rails and with its lights flashing is rotating around its own axis. Jews and Muslims make an equal claim on this holy place, as it is a site where the histories of the three Abrahamic religions intersect. By staging one of the central symbols of Israeli-Palestinian conflict as an axis of a regulated entertainment industry, the artist investigates the complex interaction of politics and religion, fundamentalism and capitalism, religious ritual and medial distribution, at the same time creating his own blasphemous version of Muhammad's ascent.

Wael Shawky
*1971 in Alexandria, Egypt,
lives and works in Alexandria

Al Aqsa Park, 2006,
computer animation, b/w, sound,
30 min, installation view
ZKM | Karlsruhe, 2009, and
screenshots

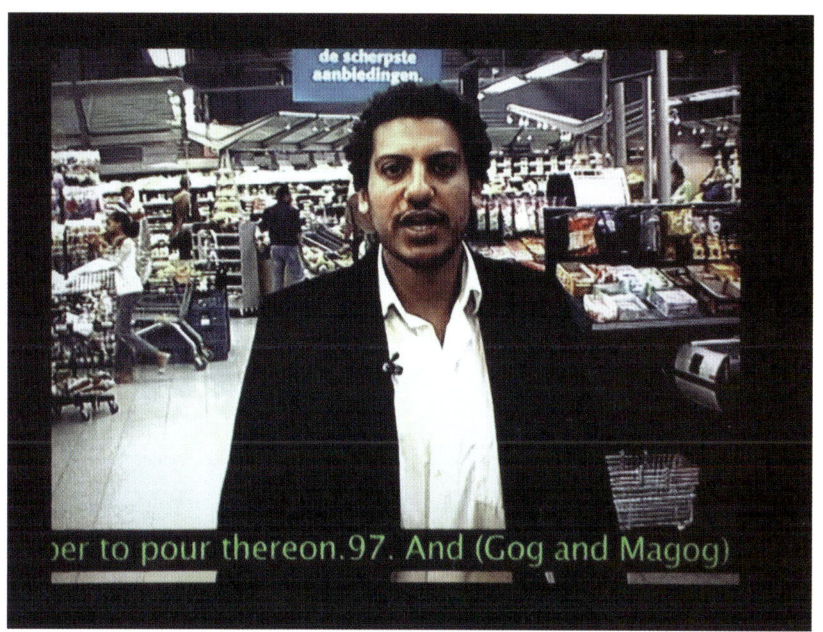

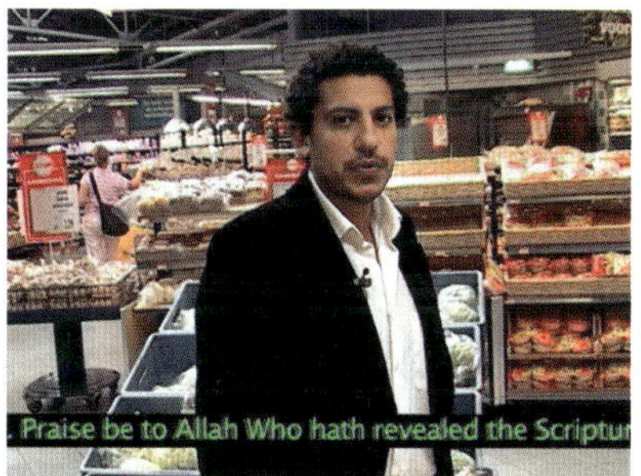

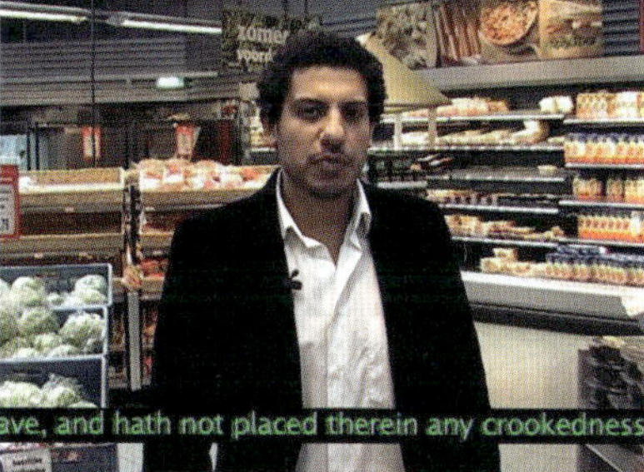

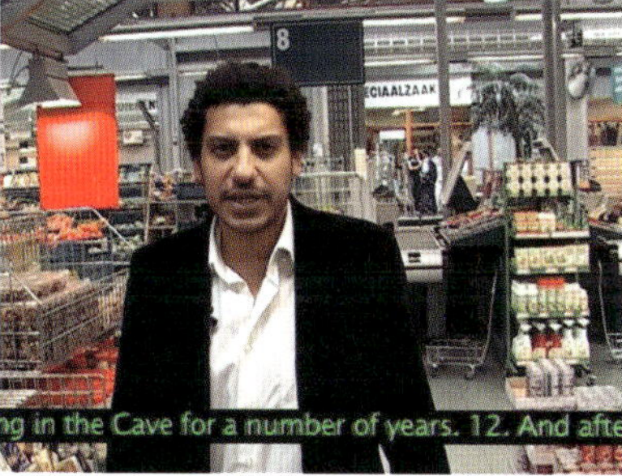

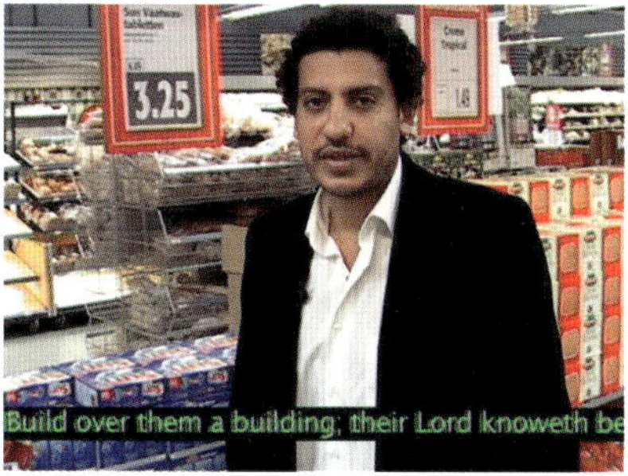

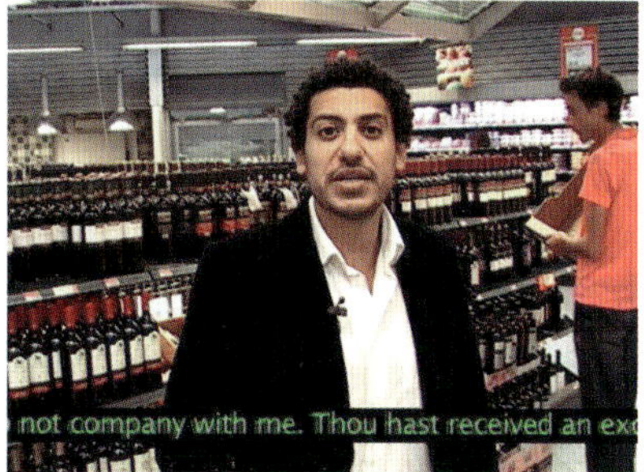

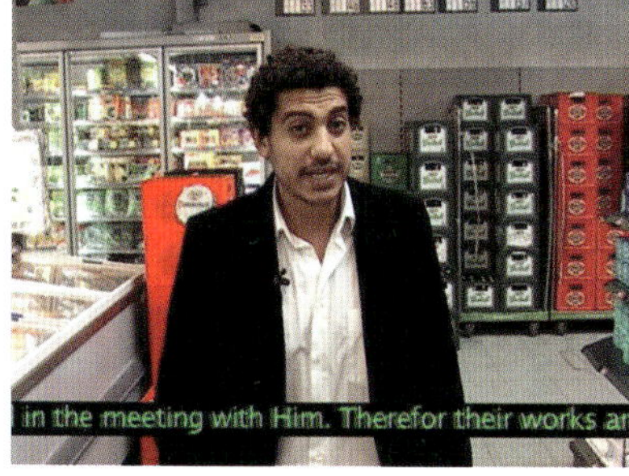

Wael Shawky

The Cave, 2006,
video, color, sound, 12:45 min,
stills from a digital copy

The video shows the artist walking through the aisles of an Amsterdam supermarket while reciting the eighteenth sura of the Koran in Arabic. Following the visual aesthetics of a news broadcast, Shawky is declaiming in an uninterrupted flow of words the legend of the Martyrs of Ephesus, who were persecuted for their beliefs and found refuge in a cave. After 309 years sound asleep, they finally awoke in a changed world now dominated by Christianity – a legend anchored in both the Muslim and the Christian faiths. In this hybrid self-portrait, the artist questions the relationship between religion and capitalism, as well as the dialectics of knowledge and power. From the neutral position of a news anchor, he counters the dominance of capitalist media with the religious speech.

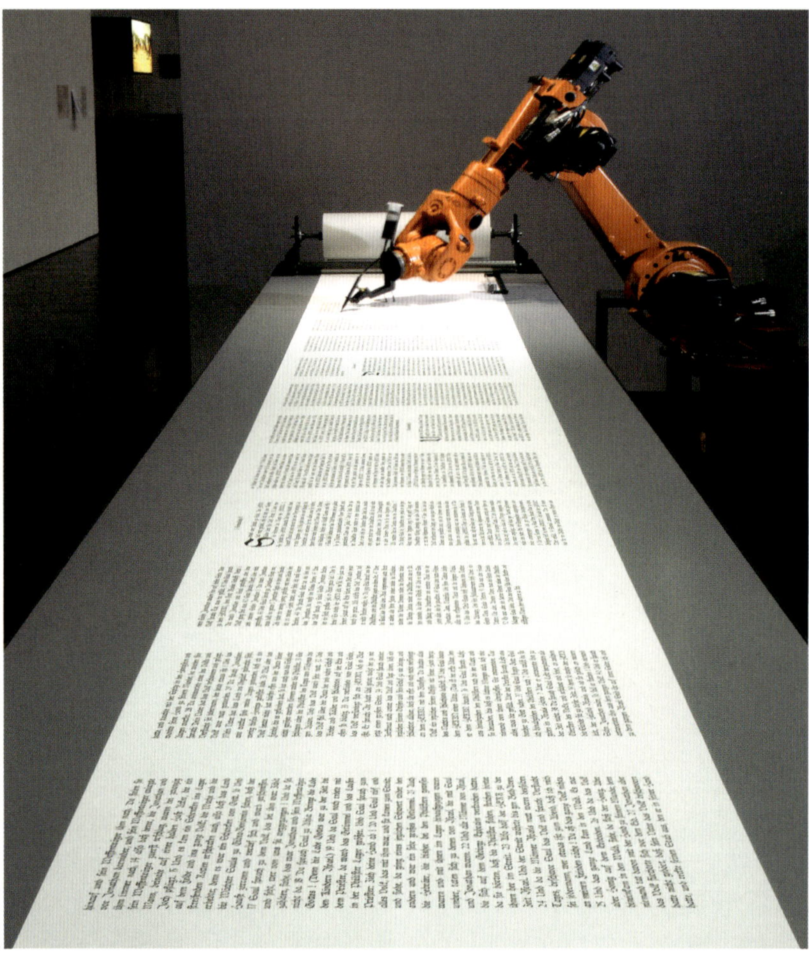

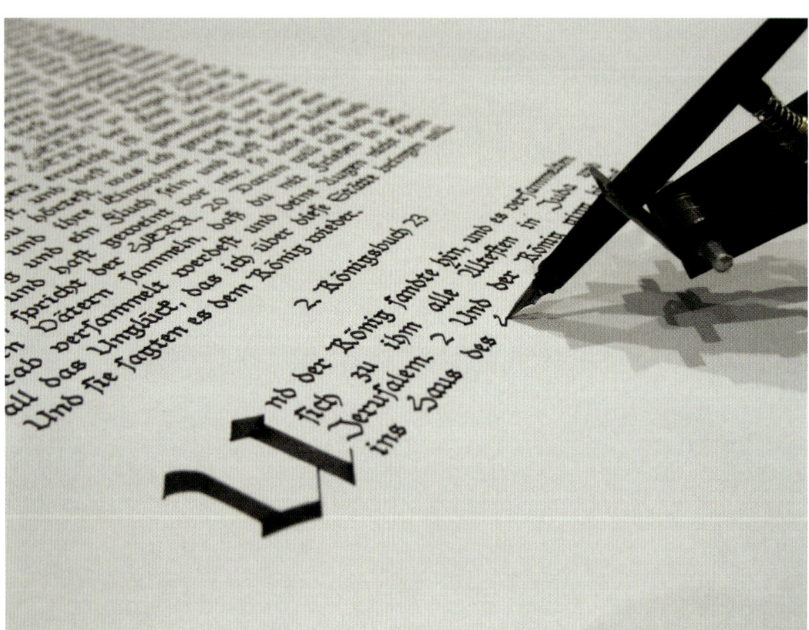

robotlab
Matthias Gommel, *1970
Martina Haitz, *1970
Jan Zappe, *1969
live and work in Karlsruhe

bios [bible], 2007,
robot installation, dimensions
variable, installation views
ZKM | Karlsruhe, 2009

The artist group robotlab takes up
the issue of how people and
machines relate: using industrial
robots, situations are deliberately
caused where the machine performs activities which are usually
subject to human culture. In the
installation *bios [bible]*, an industrial robot copies out the Bible in
"handwriting." It performs calli-
graphic precision work with a quill,
like a monk in a monastery's scrip-
torium. In this way, two fundamentally different systems are
related to each other: the formal
noting of information and scripture as a basis for religion – scientific rationality and faith. *bios
[bible]* (re-)produces the entire
Bible in seven months. The rolls of
writing are subsequently deposit-
ed in the installation's "library."

Sala

Anri Sala
*1974 in Tirana, Albania,
lives and works in Paris

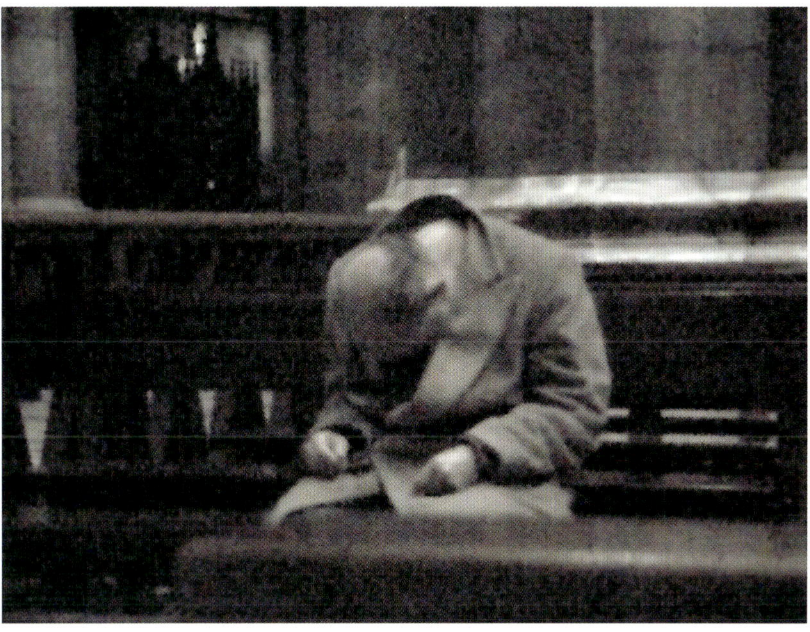

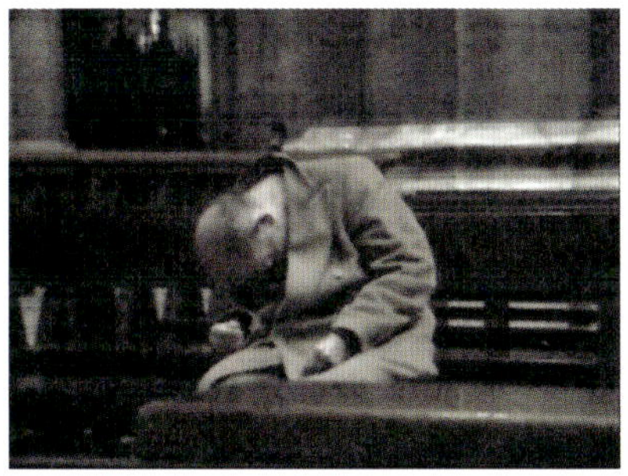

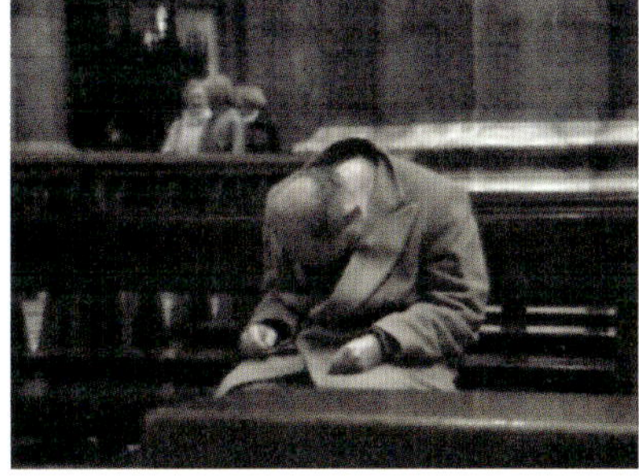

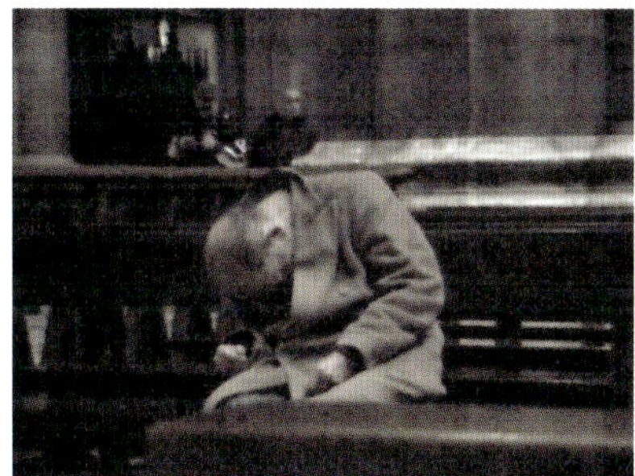

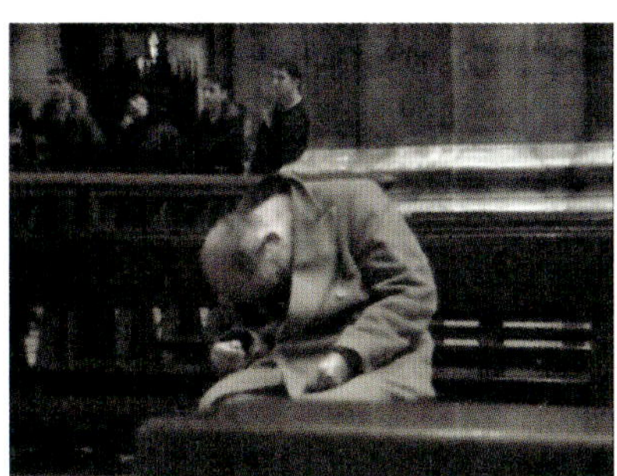

Uomoduomo, 2000,
video, b/w, no sound, 1:41 min,
stills from a digital copy

Anri Sala discovered this homeless person asleep in Milan Cathedral by chance. The biblical call to convert runs: "Awake, you who are sleeping, and arise from the dead." (Eph. 5,14) However, the person asleep in Sala's video seems unreceptive to any awakening and revelation. The sleeping person has long been a symbol for the unbeliever, to whom eternal life will remain denied and who is therefore destined for death. Homeless and only given any protection in God's house, sleeping peacefully, and with that totally vulnerable and subjected to the gaze of everyone – the existential paradox of this situation becomes manifest in this sleeping person and shows the human body as the sole revelation.

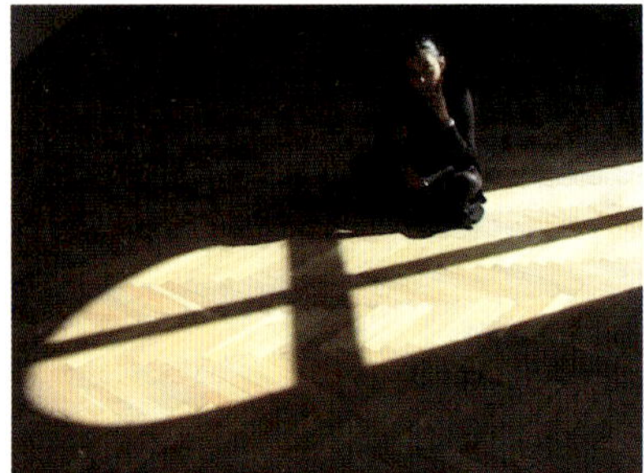 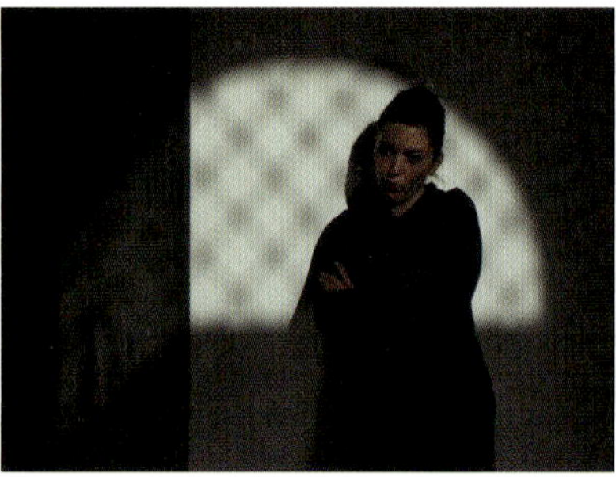 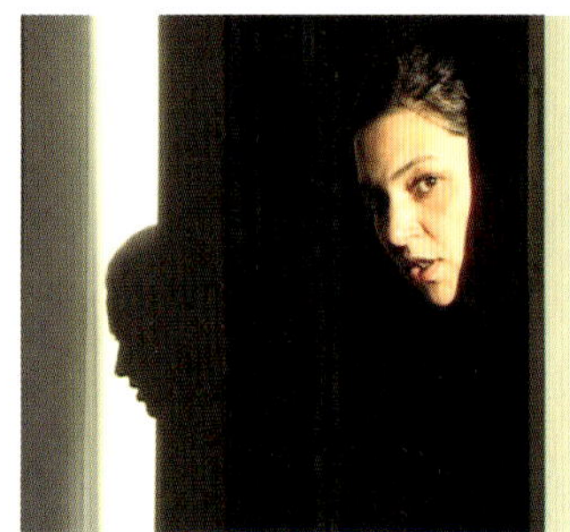

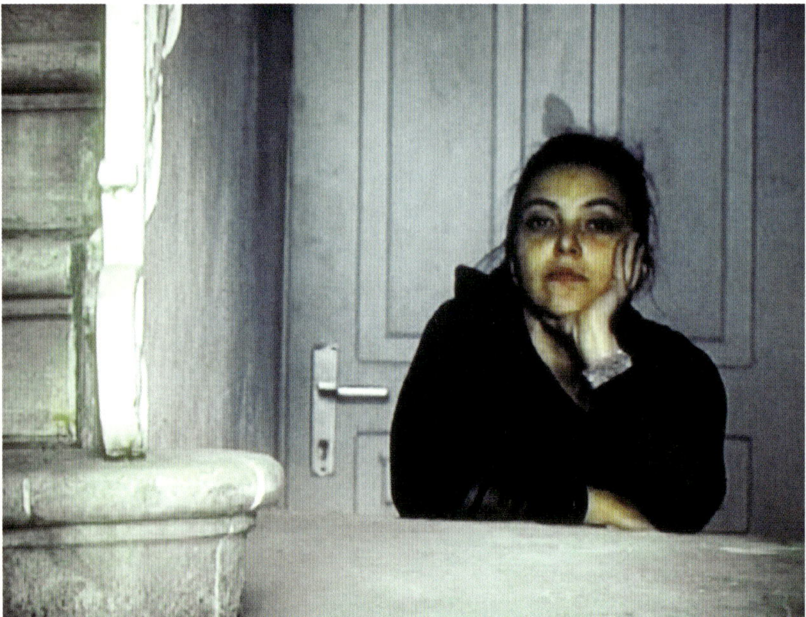

Double Bubble, a video work created in 2001 by Bosnian artist Maja Bajevic, addresses the duality of religious morals and ethics: Increasingly, political attributes are linked to particular religious confessions, while religion plays an increasingly important role in the male-dominated hierarchy of the world powers. This is the backdrop against which Maja Bajevic as a female performer utters contradictory statements such as "I have shot 55 people during prayer in the name of God" or "I free people from sins. They give me money." *Double Bubble* becomes a mirror for the misuse of power and religion.

Maja Bajevic
*1967 in Sarajevo, formerly
Yugoslavia, today Serbia,
lives and works in Paris and
Sarajevo

Double Bubble, 2001,
video, color, sound,
3:36 min, stills from a digital copy

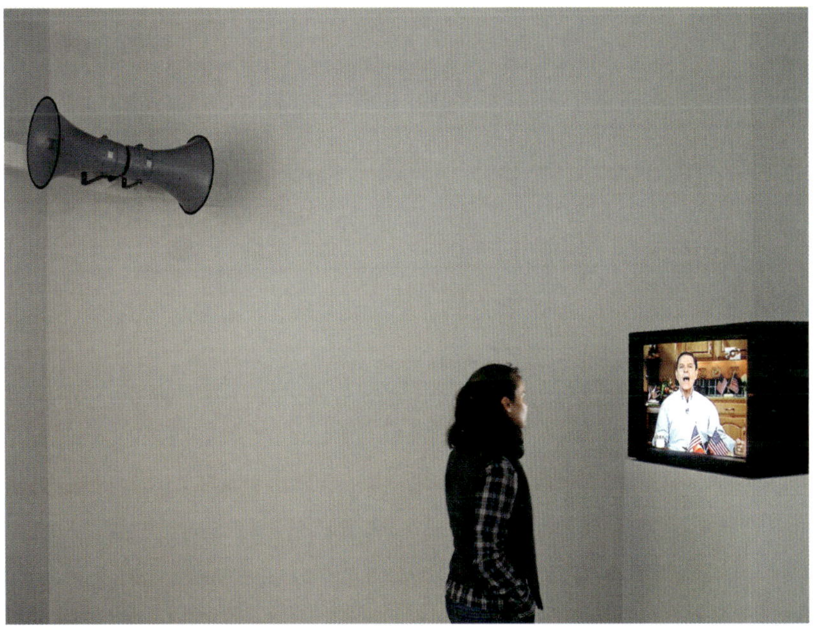

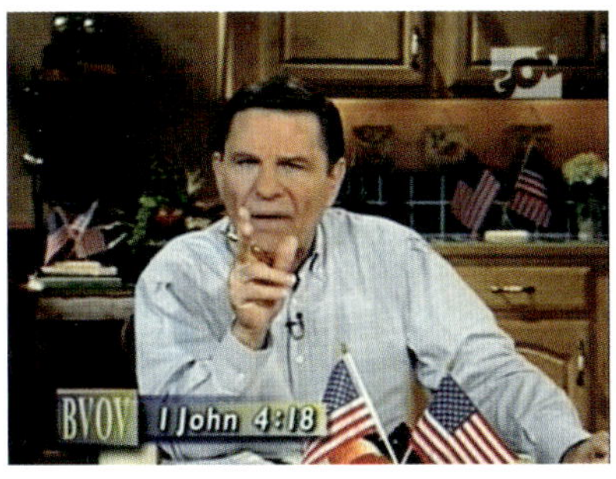

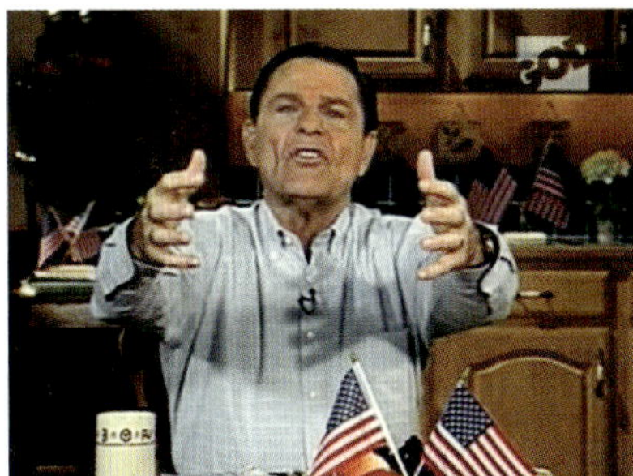

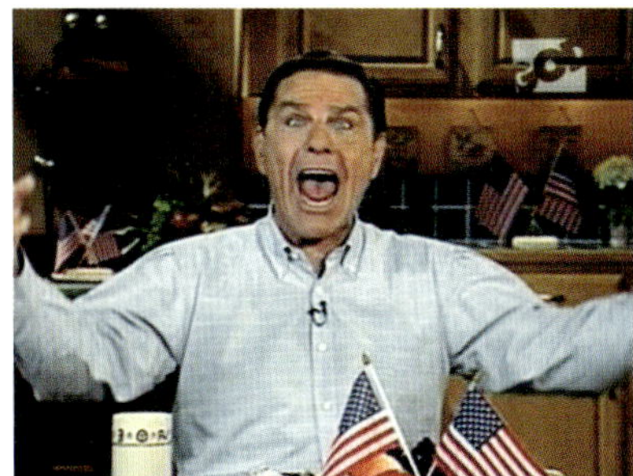

Peter Bogers
*1956 in Dordrecht,
the Netherlands,
lives and works in the Netherlands

The Secret of the Most High, 2003,
video installation, color, sound,
10 min, installation view
ZKM | Karlsruhe, 2009,
and stills from a digital copy
With the kind support of the Royal
Netherlands Embassy, Berlin.

The Dutch video artist Peter Bogers investigates the aesthetic and technical possibilities of filmic structures. Making use of his own material and of found footage, he often responds to the contemporary acceleration of visual worlds by dissecting his videos down to the individual image. In his work *The Secret of the Most High*, Bogers counter-cuts various recordings of images and sound: Sequences from a religious TV channel, in which an American TV evangelist preaches God's Word (while seated in a kitchen!), are abruptly slowed down and accompanied by sung texts from the Koran. The contrasting of both beliefs is taken to extremes, and yet their confrontation simultaneously reveals some surprising similarities.

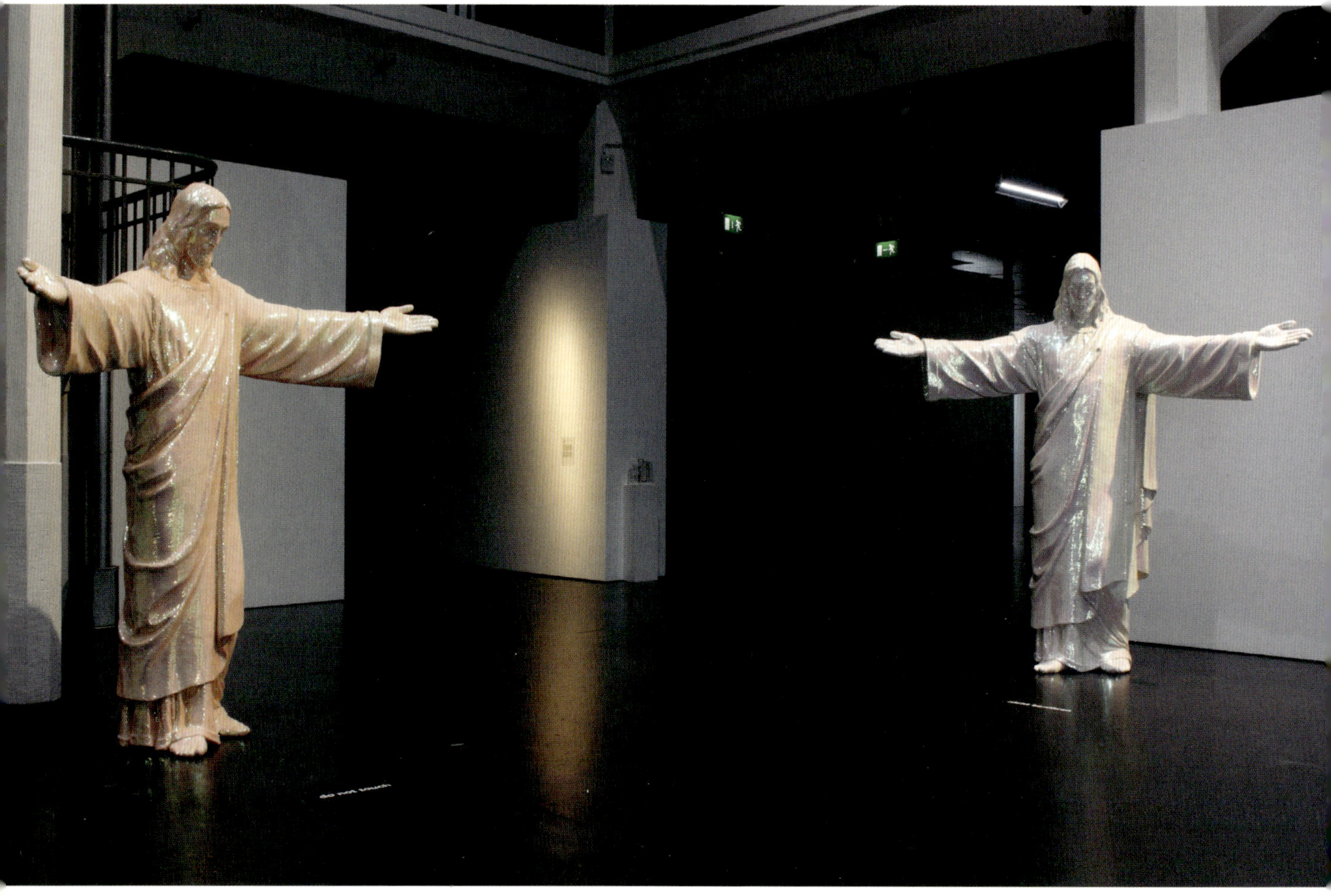

Sang-Kyoon Noh
*1958 in Nonsan, South Korea,
lives and works in New York
and Seoul, South Korea

Left
Twin Jesus Christs, 2001,
sequins on polyester resin and
fiberglass, 267 × 265 × 78 cm
each, installation view
ZKM | Karlsruhe, 2009

Right
For the Worshipers, 2008,
sequins on polyester resin and
fiberglass, dimensions variable,
installation view
ZKM | Karlsruhe, 2009

Gigantic sequin-encrusted statues, which show Jesus as an over-
sized, colorful twin figure, a deep
black Buddha projecting out of the
wall – the pictures and sculptures
of Sang-Kyoon Noh seem more
assimilated in popular culture than
in their religious origins. Behind
the unconventional treatment of
religious symbols and figures is
concealed a cynical attitude,
which invites viewers to appre-
hend the sacred symbolism differently to the way in which accus-
tomed. The Christ figure as a
double Messiah in a glittering costume points in this way to technical and medial reproducibility and
through this to the death of the
original.

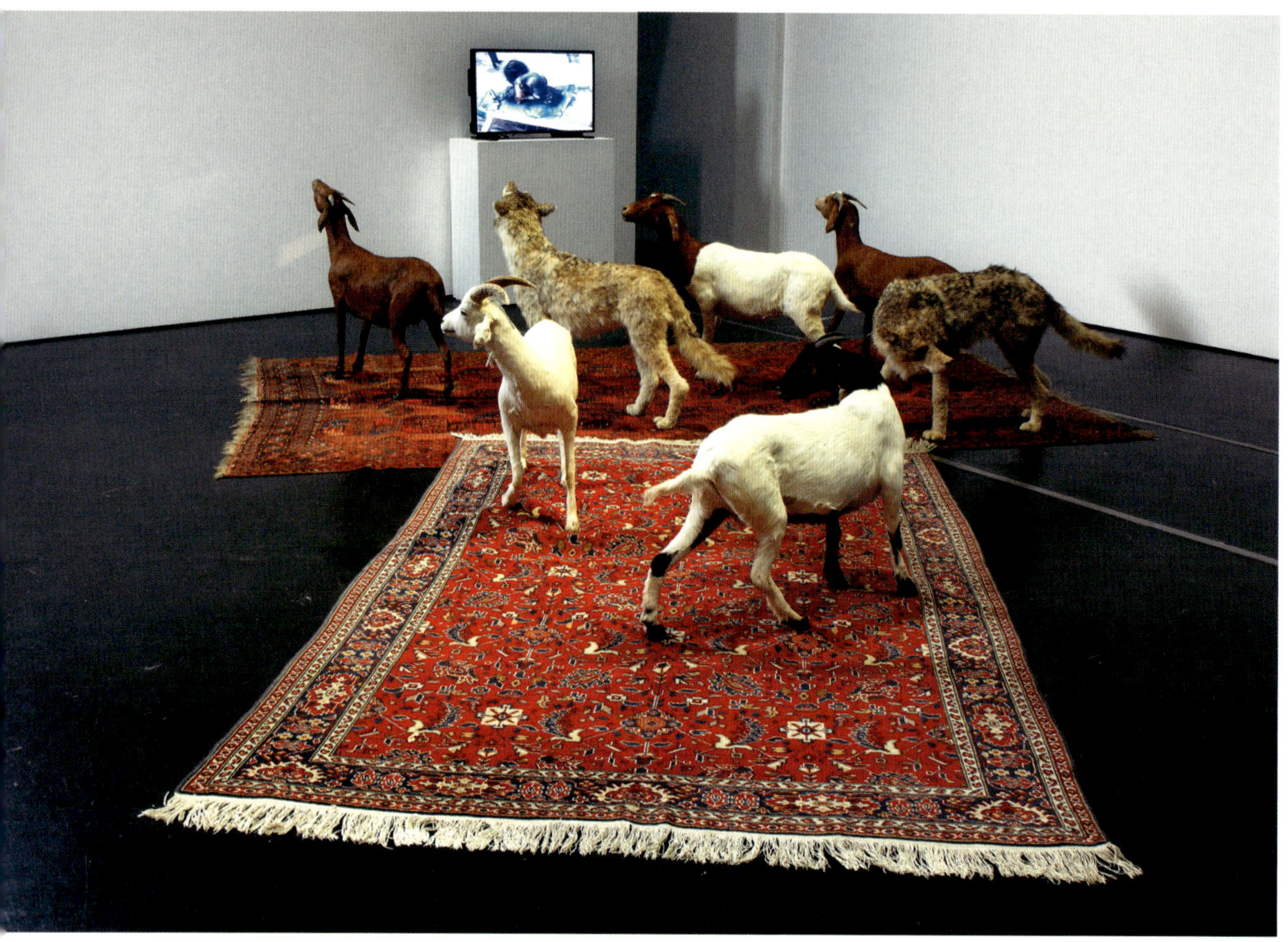

Huang Yong Ping's work stands out above all through his subtle interlinking of conceptualizing Western culture with the traditional, Far Eastern. The trademark of his mainly sculptural works is in the first instance their large-scale format, yet, on closer inspection, complexity and multi-layering reveals itself, which transports observers into a universe of situations arranged as contradictions. For his work *Loups et chèvres regardent la vidéo de Aïd-el-Kebir* [Wolves and Goats Watch the Video of Eid al-Adha], Huang Yong Ping displays laconic irony in gathering wolves and goats in familiar companionship around a video recording of the traditional celebration of sacrifice *(Aïd-el-Kebir)*, the high point of the Islamic religious year. The "great feast of the lamb" is celebrated in commemoration of the prophet Abraham sacrificing an ewe instead of his son. During *Aïd-el-Kebir* [Eid al-Adha] every family without exception and regardless of whether poor or rich slaughters an animal.

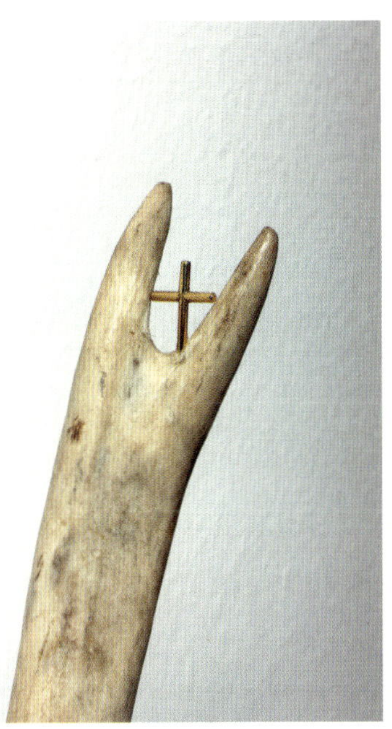

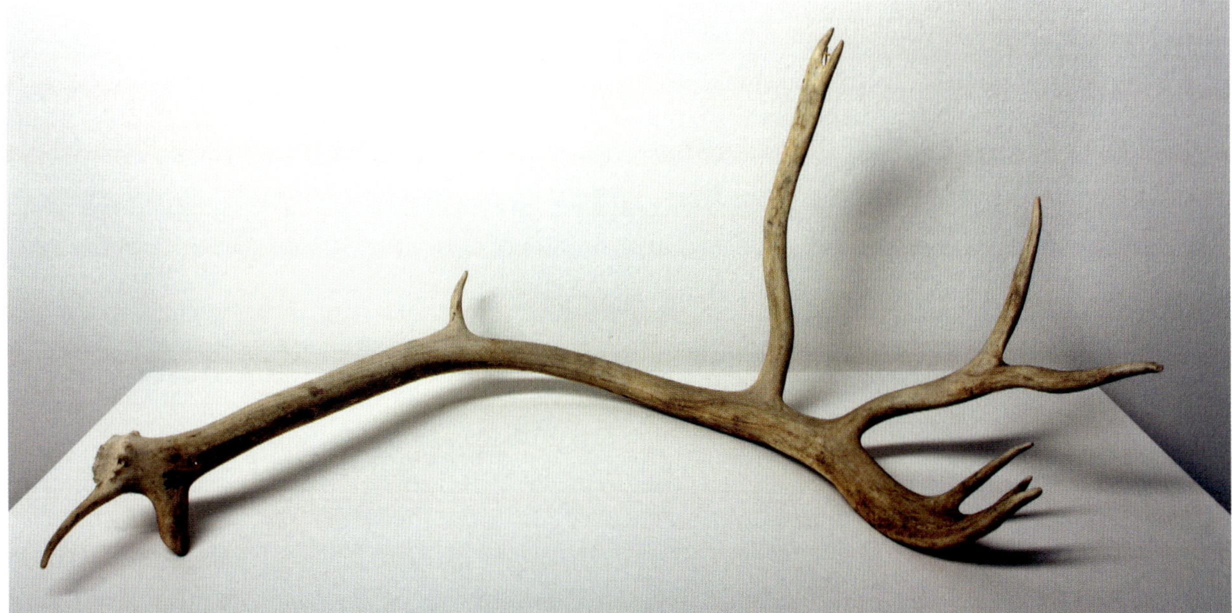

Konrad Balder Schäuffelen
*1929 in Ulm, Germany,
lives and works in Munich

Abwurfstange, 1990,
deer antler, gold, 80 × 40 × 40 cm,
installation views ZKM | Karlsruhe,
2009

Alongside publications of experimental concrete and visual poetry, Konrad Balder Schäuffelen has been creating numerous language and book objects, audiovisual installations, photographs, and sculptures since the 1960s. His work *Abwurfstange* [Launch Post] displays shed deer antlers embellished with a small golden cross. In the spring, a process of decay at the point of the bony nodule on the stag's forehead loosens the antlers and they finally fall to the ground. Schäuffelen refers here to the legend of Saint Eustace, who was one of the Roman emperor Trajan's generals and who belongs to the Fourteen Holy Helpers. One day, a stag with a cross among its antlers appeared to him, at which Eustace converted to Christianity. When Trajan's successor Hadrian demanded he make sacrifices to the Roman gods, he refused and died as a martyr.

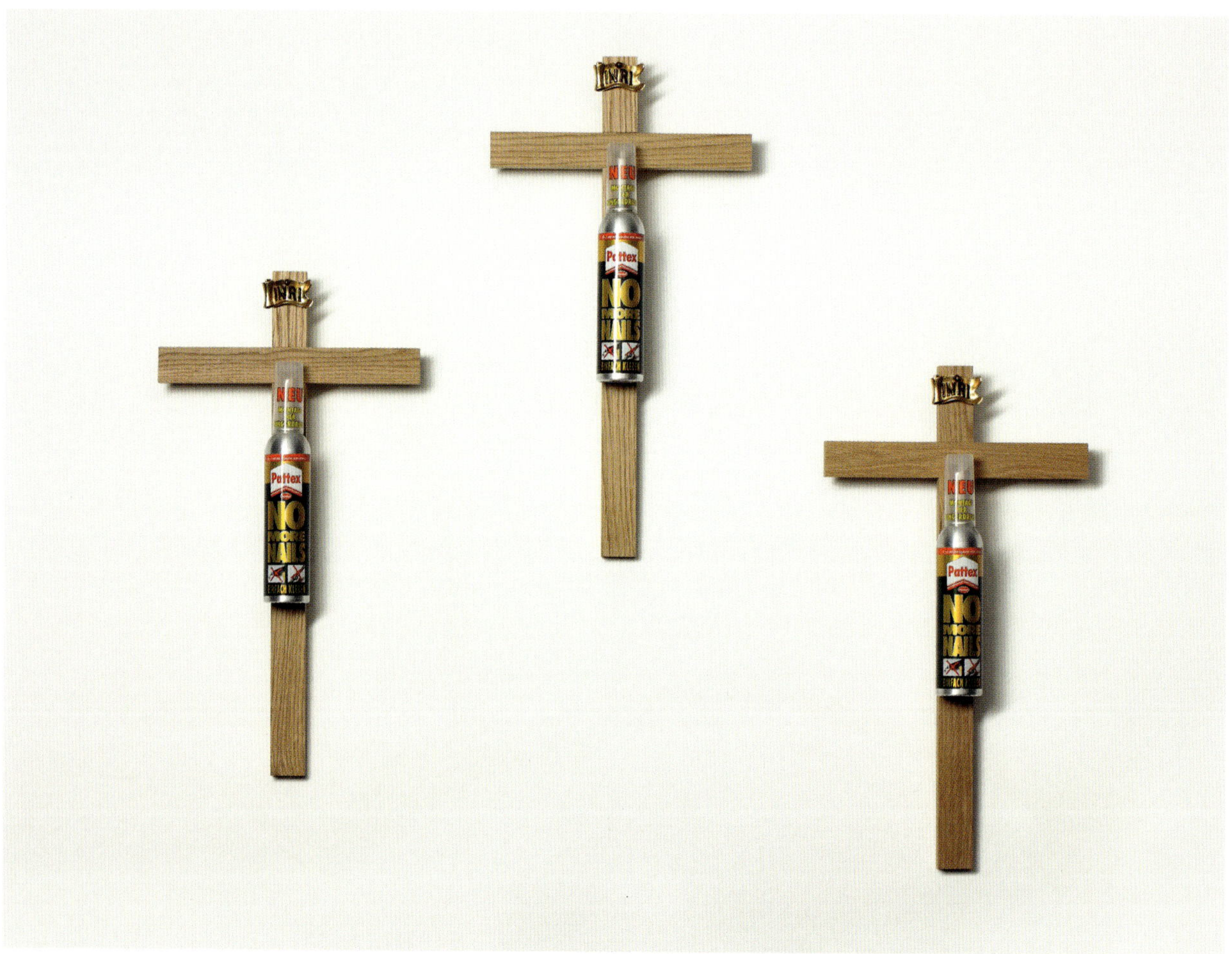

The Austrian artist Michael Schuster applies a can of Pattex spray glue with the advertising slogan "No More Nails" to three simple oak crosses, denoted by the caption INRI as crucifixes, instead of the Jesus figure. Combining all this into a readymade ironizes its individual components: the implicit hypothesis, that the Christian savior could also have been crucified without nails but solely with glue, comes over as being as grotesque as it is blasphemous. The title and the organization of the triple grouping *Golgatha* point laconically to the historical place of Jesus' crucifixion, a hill outside Jerusalem, and to his crucifixion together with two robbers – Schuster's artistic strategy is here frivolously blasphemous, if not openly provocative.

Michael Schuster
*1956 in Graz, Austria,
lives and works in Graz

Golgatha, 2008,
aluminum spray can on oak
crosses, 3 pieces, 56 × 25 × 8 cm,
installation view ZKM | Karlsruhe,
2009

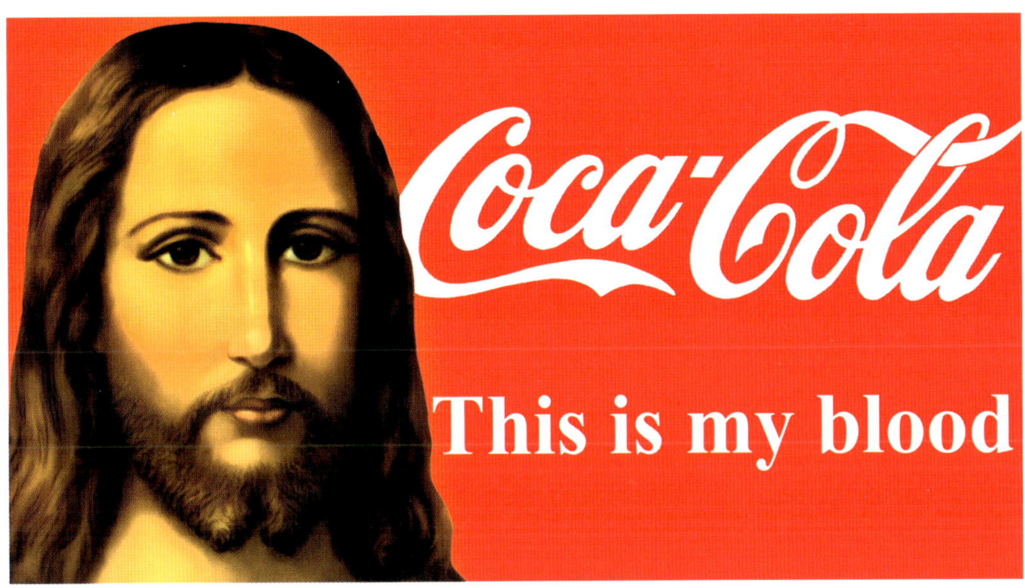

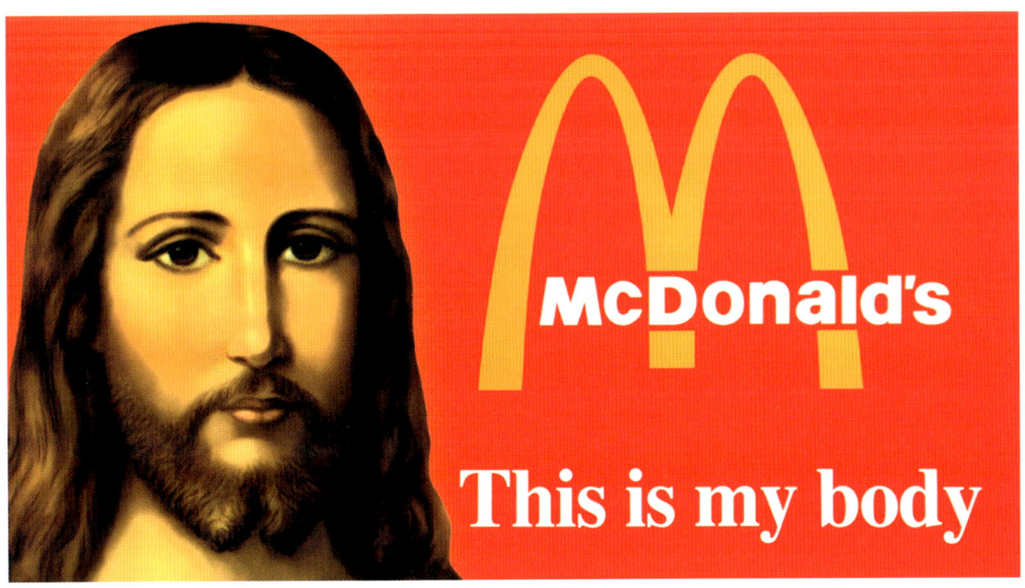

Alexander Kosolapov
*1943 in Moscow,
formerly USSR, today Russia,
lives and works in New York

This is my body, 2002,
This is my blood, 2002,
light boxes, 82 × 150 cm each

In the works *This is my blood* and *This is my body* by the "SozArt" artist Alexander Kosolapov, the standardized representation of Christ becomes a brand and the Eucharist becomes an advertising message by Coca-Cola and McDonald's. One of the fundamental questions in capitalism relates to what unites consumers – to which Kosolapov's works give one answer: religion. Both works are an ironic commentary on consumer culture, where products become fetishes and advertising becomes the Bible. Kosolapov combines Christian elements with the graphic language of commercial advertising and in this way draws attention to the parallels between the communication of religion and advertising strategies.

Kajri Jain

....Divine.Mass....
....Reproduction....

kṛtvātāvantam ātmānaṃ yāvatīr gopa-yoṣitaḥ /
reme sa bhagavāṃs tābhir ātmārāmo 'pi līlayā //
tāsāṃ rati-vihāreṇa śrāntānāṃ vadanāni saḥ /
prāmṛjat karuṇaḥ premṇā śantamenāṅga pāinā //

Expanding Himself as many times as there were cowherd women to associate with, the Supreme Lord, though self-satisfied, playfully enjoyed their company.
Seeing that the gopis were fatigued from conjugal enjoyment, my dear King, merciful Krishna lovingly wiped their faces with His comforting hand.

Bhāgavata-Purānam (Skandha 10.33.19–20)[1]

T he *Bhāgavata Purāna*, also known as the *Śrīmad Bhāgavatam* (dating from around 1300–1400 C.E.), is the most recent and most popular of the *Puranas*, a collection of mythological stories written in the form of Sanskrit verses elucidating aspects of the Vedas (regarded as the oldest Hindu scriptures) to the laity. It recounts the life of the Hindu god Krishna; the stanzas above describe his youthful dalliance with the cowherd girls or *gopis* in the countryside around Vrindavan. Krishna is dancing with the *gopis*, who have stolen away from their homes for the night. Graciously responding to the desire of each of them to have him as her partner in the *lila* (a dance, creative play or sport), he replicates himself as many times as there are *gopis*, and extends the night to the cosmic duration of a Night of Brahma (several billion years).

This scene of divine self-replication is it-self continually reproduced in many folk and "classical" performances across India, including the great community *dandiya-ras* dances throughout the course of the ten nights of Dussehra in Gujarat, or the *ras-lilas* performed by young boys in drama troupes in Mathura and Vrindavan. More importantly however were the episodes from Krishna's life; among other mythic and iconic subjects, also among the first themes to be taken up for representation and reproduction by means of new media and technology as introduced into South Asia. Indeed, in India religion, or more specifically, devotionalism (not only in Hinduism, but in Islam, Buddhism, Jainism,

and Christianity) has arguably been the most responsive arena for such new forms.[2] Over the past couple of centuries, these forms have included reverse glass painting (entering India via China where it was introduced by the Jesuits), realist painting techniques imported from Europe, proscenium theater, printing technologies from woodblocks to lithography, offset and digital reproduction, photography, cinema, video, animation, IMAX, digital media including MMOs (massive multiplayer online role-playing games), sound recording techniques, radio, audio cassettes and loudspeakers, cell phone cameras and ringtones, sculptural techniques using reinforced cement concrete (RCC) and fiberglass, animatronics, and so on.

Why this eager embrace of new techniques of expression and reproduction by particular strands of South Asian religiosity and ritual? I contend that this can be, in part, accounted for by the ongoing negotiation between institutionalized religion and traditions of personalized – not to be confused with private – devotion or *bhakti* that has informed popular religiosity on the subcontinent since around the seventh or eighth century C.E. From around the mid-seventeenth century on, with growing European trade, missionary activity, indological scholarship, colonial government, and the rise of anti-colonial nationalism, these negotiations have been further intertwined with identitarian and reformist impulses informed by post-Enlightenment European thought. In late colonial and independent India,

1 See: Śrīmad Bhāgavatam, *The Story of the Fortunate One*, Canto 10, Chapter 33: "The Rasa Dance," available online at: www. srimadbhagavatam.org/canto10/ chapter33.html, December 2, 2010
2 We must take seriously ideological critiques of the category of "religion" by scholars such as Timothy Fitzgerald, who points out its emergence as part of the post-Enlightenment project of bourgeois Europe (see, for instance: Timothy Fitzgerald, *The Ideology of Religious Studies*, Oxford University Press, New York, 2000). However, I do not believe that we can or should do away with this term altogether, as it has now taken on a discursive valency of its own. I shall therefore persist in using this term, if only to suggest that our assumptions about "religion" need to be rethought.

religion and media technologies were thrust together in an economically, politically, and, indeed, legally "parallel" cultural arena. And finally, from the late twentieth century on, these articulations were naturalized under the aegis of a neoliberal economic order. As I will outline below, there are two aspects to the de- and reterritorializing movements occurring in the region: multiplicity and novelty; the demand for multiple, personalized manifestations of the divine that, as we have just seen, is profoundly linked to devotionalism, as well as to the adoption of new visual idioms and techniques, ushering in new representational configurations that subtly dismantle existing iconographic canons and mark attendant shifts in the symbolic underpinnings of social power.

Multiplicity, Accessibility, "Livingness," Portability

Around the time image-based temple worship as mediated by priests became prevalent in South Asia, that is, by about the eighth century C.E., the region also began witnessing the emergence of popular devotional movements, initially in the south and then moving northwards during the fifteenth and sixteenth centuries. These movements, often led by charismatic gurus and poet-saints from the artisan classes, were concerned as much with social justice as with religious reform, seeking to challenge caste and other hierarchies (class, patriarchy) and to provide an alternative to the dependence on the priests or Brahmins for intercession with the divine – or, in the case of the "untouchable" castes, their exclusion from temples altogether. Thus, they emphasized direct, personal forms of devotion and a deeply affective, often ecstatic relationship to god. Eschewing both priestly textual knowledge and the need to access sanctified temple icons, the *bhakti* movements emphasized demotic forms of expression that worked in the more virtual registers of poetry, song, and dance, either to advocate the formlessness of the divine (as with the weaver-mystic Kabir, 1398–1448), or to conjure intimate visions (as with the blind

Krishna worshipper Surdas, 1479–1586). The cultural forms periodically generated by such demotic devotional movements constitute an important strand of religiosity that ran parallel to the temple- and text-based, institutional religion on the subcontinent, often coopted by the latter but also available as a resource for opposition and resistance.

The medieval *bhakti* movements' challenge to priestly privilege in some ways prefigures Walter Benjamin's argument for the redemptive potentials of mechanical reproduction and its inauguration of an era in which art might be founded on politics rather than on the cult (here I identify cult with institutionalized religion rather than with popular devotion). Of course, we are dealing here with an entirely different historical context than that exemplified in Benjamin's analysis of mass reproduction's challenge to the auratic work of art: Most crucially, the post-Enlightenment European discourse of art and the aesthetics informing Benjamin's reading had not yet entered South Asia, or even Europe, for that matter. Furthermore, there is no sense in which people had yet been subject to the processes of "massification" accompanying the pervasion of capitalist production. But, for Benjamin, inasmuch as art's aura is based on an authenticity and uniqueness derived from art's cultic origins, his insights are relevant to the displacement, or at least supplementation of unique, authentic, visible, material temple icons by dematerialized, virtual, and therefore universally accessible – that is, *proto-mass-mediated* – forms of the divine beyond priestly control. The affects unleashed by popular devotion in this ever-present arena of egalitarian potential have lent themselves to fresh expressive forms that reconfigure established canonical iconographies and create new liturgical contexts – and, in doing so, both index and facilitate reconfigurations in ways religion articulates itself in social and political power.

The *ur*-scene of mass reproduction with which I began illuminates how informal, individualized, demotic devotion (as opposed to liturgical rituals mediated by priests) might

> Fig. 1: *25 Darshan*, souvenir print sold at the main Nathdwara Temple in 1995, showing 25 views or forms of Shrinathji corresponding to his attire on various ritual occasions

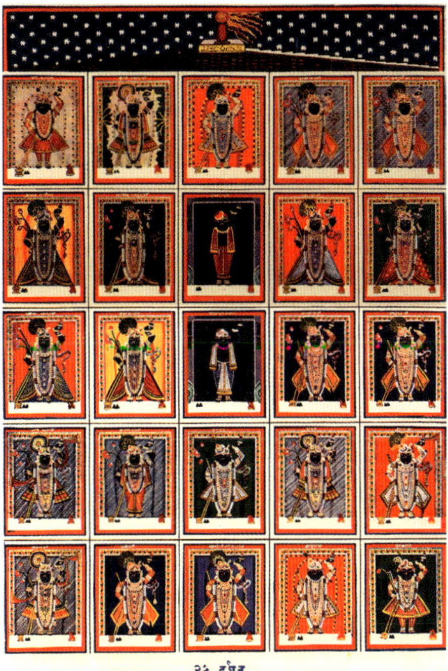

the idea of manifestations or incarnations (*roop* or *avatar*) of the divine. This is especially pronounced in the case of Vishnu worship or Vaishnavism: Vishnu has ten incarnations (including one yet to come), which he adopts when humanity is in crisis and needs salvation. These incarnations of Vishnu include Ram, Krishna, and the Buddha. Specific cults, particularly of Krishna, also generate a multiplicity of images as part of the panoply of worship, as in the case of the Pushtimarg sect in Western India, which has a highly elaborated culture of images and display. Here, the icon of Krishna as Shrinathji at the pilgrimage center of Nathdwara, near Udaipur in Rajasthan, is seen as a living being, whose *seva*, or service is the preeminent form of devotion. So the worship of this idol includes feeding him, entertaining him with music and poetry, and dressing him in an enormous range of exquisite garments appropriate to the time of the day and the season, thus generating myriad possibilities for figuration (fig. 1). Accordingly, from the late eighteenth century onward, miniature painters from the declining courts of Rajasthan and further afield were attracted to the service of the temple. Initially commissioned to paint murals, votive backdrops, and other ritual decorations for the temple, these artists also began producing pilgrim souvenirs and portable icons for one of the sect's primary constituencies, the wealthy and highly mobile mercantile communities along the northern and western trade routes.

These souvenirs – and the Pushtimarg sect's theology – demonstrate how the imperative of multiplicity is enmeshed with the treatment of an icon as a living being with whom the devotee can establish a personal relationship. Arguably, however, this also provides an instance of how the demotic, egalitarian impulses of the *bhakti* movements are subject to reterritorialization, for in this case devotion was reharnessed to the proliferation of images from the institutional locus of a temple, and thereby rearticulated with social power. This initially occurred via the legitimation of kingship in the region (as kings claimed the blessing of the icon),[4] and latterly, with the decline of princely power in the region

pave the way for – indeed, *demand* – the multiplication or replication of iconic figures, in incarnations that elicit desire rather than awe, promising intimacy rather than distance. Two imperatives are at work here: the provision of direct, unmediated access to the divine and the representation of the deity as a benign, compassionate, efficacious, responsive – indeed *living* – presence. The first imperative addresses the adoption of technological reproduction, which was prefigured in the Indian context by manual mass production, as with the inexpensive bazaar images produced as pilgrim souvenirs through the nineteenth century at the then newly-built Kalighat Temple in Calcutta.[3] Here, painters who had formerly painted narrative scrolls now began to produce rapidly executed works on paper – both religious icons and satirical images on topical themes – for sale to a new constituency of rural pilgrims and recent city dwellers: a new form for a new social configuration.

But the imperative of replication must also be understood in relation to the kinds of multiplicity inherent in many South Asian – particularly Hindu – theologies, which allow for

3   See: Ashish Rajadhyaksha, "The Phalke Era. Conflict of Traditional Form and Modern Technology," in: Tejaswini Niranjana, P. Sudhir and Vivek Dhareshwar (eds.), *Interrogating Modernity. Culture and Colonialism in India*, Seagull Books, Calcutta, 1993, pp. 47–82.

4   See: Norbert Peabody, "In Whose Turban Does the Lord Reside?: The Objectification of Charisma and the Fetishism of Objects in the Hindu Kingdom of Kota," in: *Comparative Studies in Society and History*, vol. 33, no. 4, 1991, pp. 726–754.

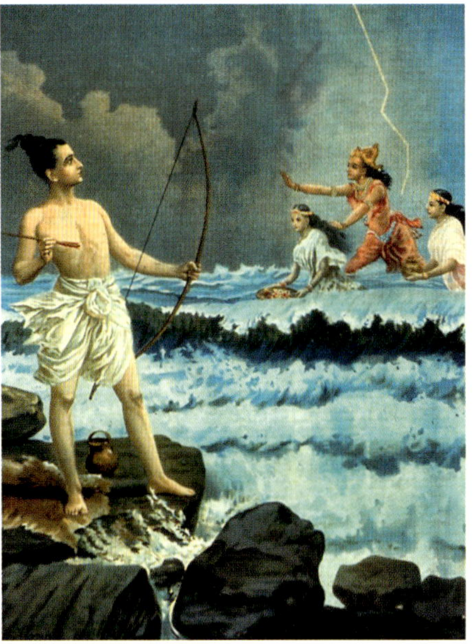

under colonial rule, through an increasingly important mercantile culture. The temple-based institutionalization of Pushtimarg and its development of an elaborate culture of images and image worship can be seen as a recuperation of *bhakti*, belying its egalitarian philosophy and inclusivity through a reinstatement of caste privilege and, significantly, by its strict policing of access to its temple icons. Up until the 1970s, only caste Hindus were allowed into the temple except on specific ritual occasions, and even now close control is exerted over the duration of viewing: There are only five viewings or *darshan* of the icon per day, and priests use cloth whips to keep the line of worshippers moving.

However, a new set of techniques and a changing social and political context, also subjected this institutionalized image culture to a further movement of deterritorialization. The colonial economy, the traditional mercantile communities of the north and west, such as the Banias or the Marwaris from Rajasthan (many of whom were Pushtimargis), took on a comprador role as middlemen or translators between the world of European trade and administration in the port cities and "native" producers and consumers in the rural hinterland, thereby amassing enough capital to

enter manufacturing. Among the early ventures of these indigenous capitalists were cultural products aimed at Indian consumers – particularly the chromolithographed mythological/devotional "Puranic" prints, which were sometimes sent to Germany and Austria for printing, but by the second half of the nineteenth century were also produced by local presses (fig. 2). These prints often adopted the visual idioms of existing devotional image-making traditions such as those of Nathdwara in the west, or Tanjore in the south, both characterized by lavish ornamentation and embellishment; indeed, several illustrious Nathdwara artists made their fortunes in the growing popular print industry.

In addition however the new genres of Puranic prints emerging in the late nineteenth century also incorporated other visual idioms and techniques, particularly photography and elements of Western painting that made for greater naturalism. Crucially, here, naturalism was neither tied to the European ideological baggage of realist painting or empiricist accuracy of scientific (or touristic) illustrations, nor to the aesthetic dictates of the picturesque – all genres in circulation at the time, to which Indian artists were exposed. Instead, these genres were selectively mined for techniques that could express the living presence of the divine (one contemporary Nathdwara artist I interviewed used the word *sajivta*, literally "living-ness"), so that the image itself would become auspicious, a source of good fortune. Here, the indexicality of photography has no special advantage over the iconicity of painting, for, aside from the impossibility of photographing the gods, in this theological schema all images have the potential, as icons, to embody the divine – while at the same time none of them will ever be adequate to the Absolute deity. Photography, painting, and printing all form part of the same image-making continuum – hence, for example, the printed postcards based on overpainted photographic images, or the more recent painted deities superimposed on photographic backgrounds via Photoshop (figs. 3, 4). For the same reason, Hindi speakers often refer to prints of painted

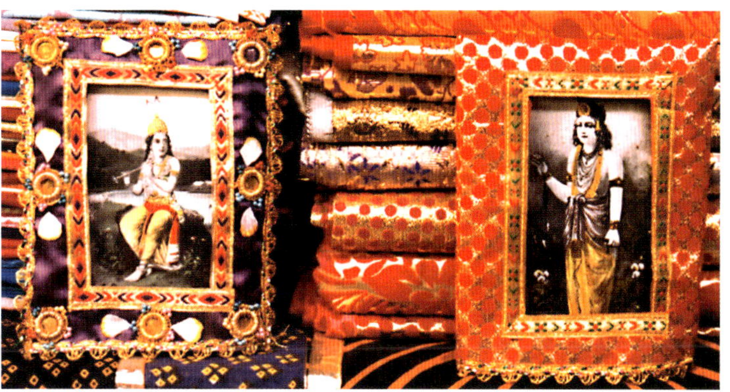

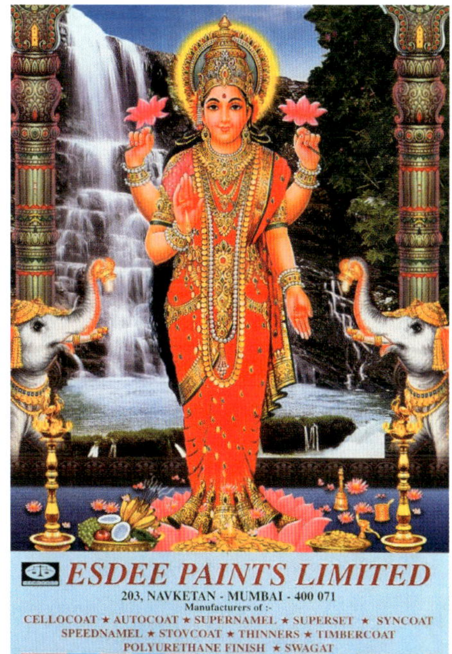

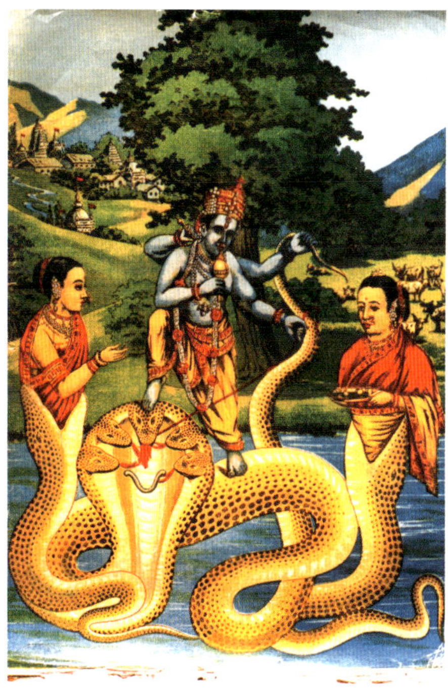

5 Hence the title of Christo-pher Pinney's book on popular Indian prints: *'Photos of the Gods.' The Printed Image and Political Struggle in India*, Reaktion Books, London, 2004.

images with the English word "photos."[5] This selective appropriation in the service of bringing the gods to life through prints is particularly evident in the naturalist depiction of divine faces, whose gently smiling benevolence and direct gaze at the devotee serve to materialize the deity's blessings.

But why does this appropriation of naturalism extend beyond divine physiognomy to the divine mise-en-scène? For the pastoral idyll of Krishna, the austerities of Shiva and the fecund blessings of Lakshmi and Saraswati unfold in idealized landscapes bearing traces of prints from Germany and Austria (fig. 5). I would suggest that this has to do with the portability of pilgrim souvenirs and printed images. Icons that are no longer moored to a particular ritual location in a temple require their own portable settings, for which artists draw on the well-known narrative contexts of the Puranas. Yet, these images do not necessarily invoke the narrative temporality of the miniature painting traditions of the region, for they are objects of worship rather than of narrative "reading." The perspectival "stilling" of the viewer in Western landscapes proves

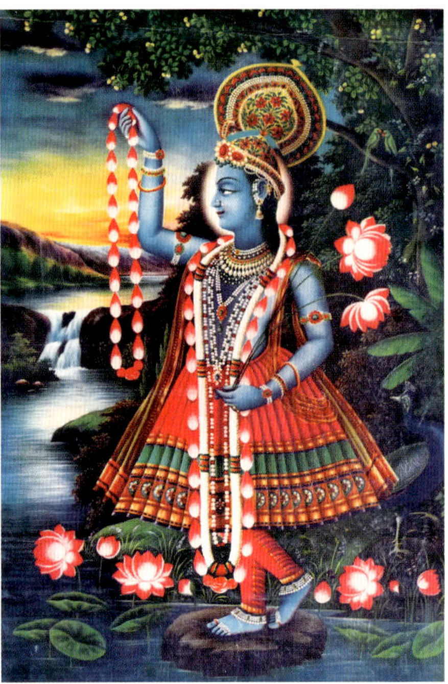

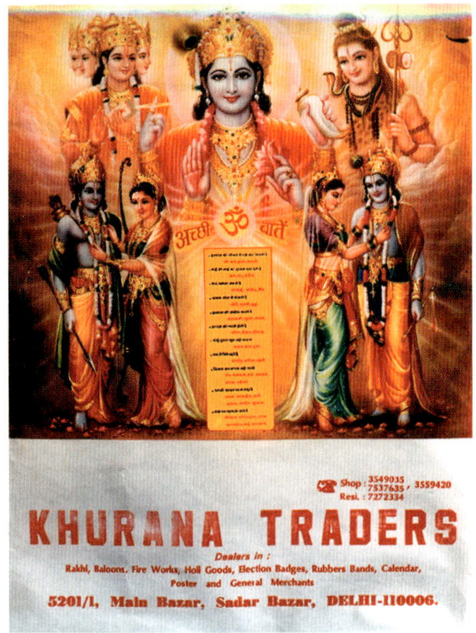

a ready-to-hand device to provide a way out of this representational impasse posed by the nomadism of the iconic image. Thus, for instance, it is the process of arriving at this new arrangement that produces an image like Shri Yamunaji (fig. 6), where Krishna is depicted in profile in accordance with the Nathdwara miniature tradition, against a background informed by Western landscapes. This profile view quickly gives way to more frontal depictions of deities, following the more ritually-driven idea that the gaze of the deity in the image is a means of blessing for those who fall under its purview.

Print Capitalism in the "Bazaar"

If the portability of icons was at first a response to the mobility of pilgrims and traders, by the second half of the nineteenth century, with the establishment of Indian chromolithographic presses targeting a wide, pan-national (and indeed diasporic) audience, it also clearly and explicitly lent itself to the identity-building agenda of the anti-colonial nationalist movement. While the role of print in the process of nation-building was consistent with Benedict Anderson's "print capitalism"

thesis (1991), these were images rather than literary texts, and the cultural unification they engendered was not based on the creation of a secular national imaginary. As Christopher Pinney and Sumathi Ramaswamy have convincingly demonstrated, in Indian popular prints, as well as other vernacular cultural forms such as poetry, theater, and cinema, national belonging had a distinctly sacral or messianic element.[6] Ramaswamy locates this sacrality in images of the new mother goddess Bharat Mata or Mother India, and in the prominence of themes of martyrdom and sacrifice to this goddess, while Pinney reads the fecund landscapes surrounding the gods as an equally potent site of resistance to the disenchanted bureaucratic-technological grids that are evident in popular depictions of colonial administrative spaces.

In Pinney's account, the sacrality in popular prints is associated with an inferior constituency marginalized by the elite, a secular-modernist nationalism informing the Nehruvian state. However, it is important to keep in mind that popular prints were themselves aligned with specific constituencies, which had been asserting their own hegemony within the vernacular arena: in particular, as I have described

6 See: Christopher Pinney and Sumathi Ramaswamy, "Maps, Mother/Goddesses, and Martyrdom in Modern India," in: *The Journal of Asian Studies*, vol. 67, no. 3, 2008, pp. 819–853.

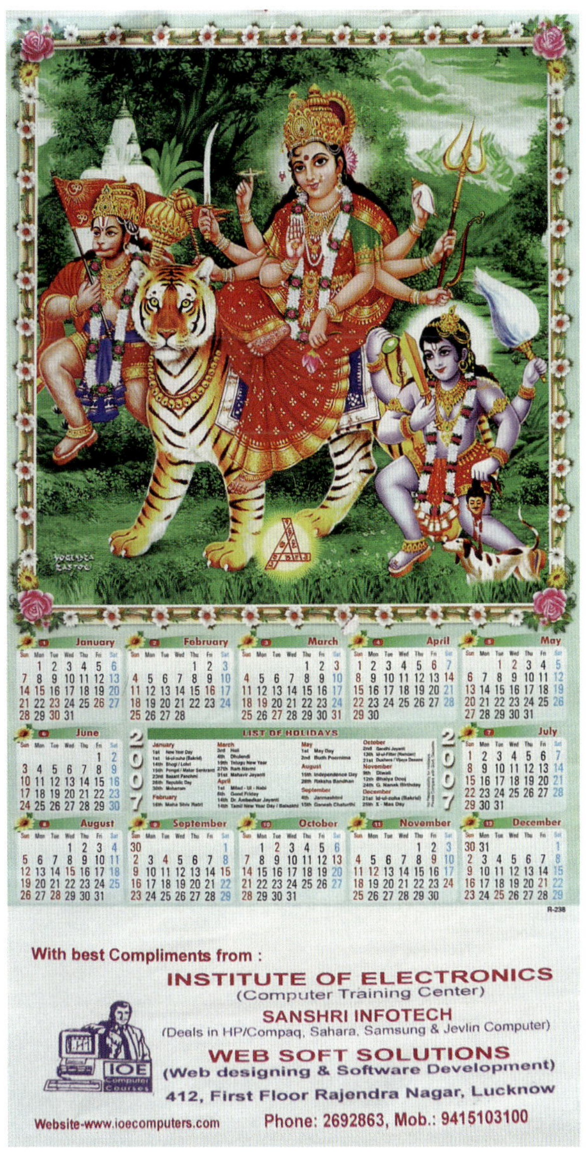

above, the trading communities, often Vaishnavas, who established themselves as indigenous capitalists in the decades leading up to India's independence in 1947. While there were local variations that inevitably catered to specific niche markets, the more centralized, pan-Indian mass culture industries were permeated by a visual idiom that constructed Indianness along specifically Hindu lines, even though these were directed towards the inclusion of minority communities by addressing Muslim, Christian, and "lower" caste themes.[7] This cultural hegemony was established not only through the involvement of Hindu trading communities in the publishing and pan-national distribution of prints, but also through the deployment of iconic imagery within a post-independence vernacular capitalist ethos, particularly through the adoption of calendars as an annual corporate gift – as a result of which this form came to be known on the subcontinent as "calendar art" or "bazaar art" (figs. 7–9).

7   See: Patricia Uberoi, "Feminine Identity and National Ethos in Calendar Art," in: idem, *Freedom and Destiny. Gender, Family, and Popular Culture in India*, Oxford University Press, New Delhi, New York, 2006, pp. 48–68.

Here, "bazaar" refers not just to the marketplace in general, but carries a more specific connotation in this context. The term "bazaar" was used by colonial administrators to describe the so-called "native" sector of the Indian economy, thereby demarcating as an arena of difference what was in fact an integral part of the colonial economy; indeed, the Indian Companies Act of 1882 refrained from exercising sovereignty over indigenous commercial firms by allowing them to be regulated by Hindu personal law as "Hindu Undivided Families."[8] This perpetuation of difference enabled rather than hindered colonial trade, allowing it to keep in place local structures of exploitation. It therefore resulted in the development of a parallel business ethos that did not follow the same rules as the European "market": a necessary but excluded *supplement* to the putatively universal history of capital.

The ethos of the bazaar's trading communities relied heavily on family, community, and personal networks for the circulation of credit and goods, keeping wealth within the family. Here, ritual performance was inseparable from the conduct of business because of the importance of social reputation and moral standing in an economy in which the circulation of credit depended on social relations rather than on being underwritten by formal legal institutions. Under such conditions, two things were critical to conducting business: a merchant's reputation in the community, and the ability to draw on his networks. Distributing calendars every year as corporate gift-cum-advertisements has been a way of lubricating business networks and annually reiterating social relations, with their religious or auspicious subject matter reinforcing the sacred and ethical nature of economic exchange: gods, lush landscapes, happy healthy babies, even modern cityscapes that signify wealth and progress. In this ethos, then, religion and commerce are deeply intertwined; perhaps the clearest symbol of this is the twinning of the words *shubh* [auspicious or sacred] and *labh* [profit] that appear on many calendars (fig. 9).

The religiosity in evidence here is not "spiritual" in the sense of being disconnected from material exchange and everyday life. But, as Charles Taylor has demonstrated at length, religion as we think of it today, in spiritual and otherworldly terms, is a specifically post-Enlightenment, specifically "North Atlantic" phenomenon.[9] Our "secular age" is characterized by the separation of church and state, and by the attendant retreat of the sacred from the public sphere into the "private" domain of the family – and also, I would argue, from the realm of aesthetics, the modern formulation of which is predicated on the supersession of the sacred by the aesthetic. The version of religion enduring in the public arena is culturalized, as it were: harnessed to the service of identity by providing a basis in "tradition." So which version of religion is in evidence in the bazaar prints? The mass production of these prints, their envisioning of a sacralized nation space, and their intimate relationship with commerce suggest that they are not fully consistent with a "secular" version of religion: for instance, while they do engender a certain domestication of religious practice, this is not accompanied by a systematic laicization of public space. At the same time, as their proliferation during the nationalist movement indicates, they are also harnessed to a thoroughly modern discourse of identity, as has emerged from the collapse of religion into "culture": modern Hindus like to insist that Hinduism is not a religion; it is a way of life.

Religiosity and Informality

I propose that the version of religiosity we see in Indian mass culture, at least up until the post-socialist economic reforms of the 1990s, has had its own peculiarly postcolonial trajectory, which stems from the supplementary position of the "bazaar" (the primary site for the production of vernacular visual culture) vis-à-vis the colonial market. As a result of this position, the vernacular culture industries – and the business ethos of which they are an index and a vehicle – have been pushed

8   See: Ritu Birla, "Capitalist Subjects in Transition," in: Dipesh Chakrabarty, Rochona Majumdar and Andrew Sartori (eds.), *From the Colonial to the Postcolonial. India and Pakistan in Transition*, Oxford University Press, New Delhi, 2007, n. p.

9   See: Charles Taylor, *A Secular Age*, Belknap Press of Harvard University Press, Cambridge, MA, 2007.

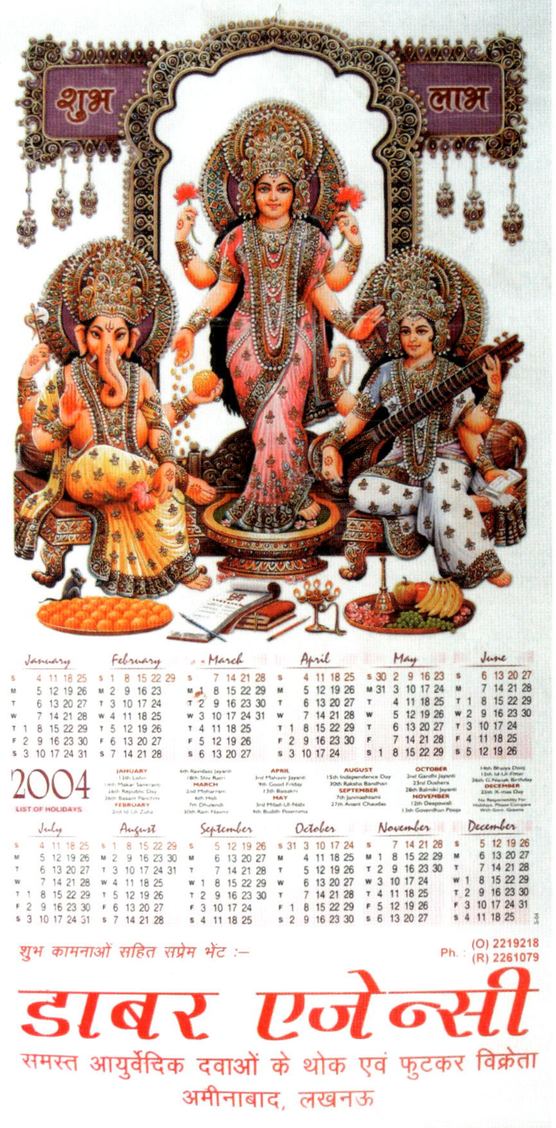

10   The inscription of "culture" as the external limit of the market through the colonial legal categorization of vernacular capitalists is described in: Birla, 2007.

into a domain of otherness in relation to the officially sanctioned public sphere, in ways that have been extraordinarily productive, but at the same time scandalous and illegitimate in terms of the political and aesthetic protocols of civil society. For by making a distinction between the market, as regulated by corporate law, and the "bazaar" as the "cultural" domain of the "Hindu Undivided Family" – a category that is familial, implicitly patriarchal, and explicitly religious –, colonial legal categories *structurally inscribed* the bazaar-as-culture as an arena of the informal and the private, where religion, culture, and commerce are inseparable.[10] After India achieved independence in 1947, this separation continued under the secular-modernist charter of the newly formed nation state and its elite (yet socialist) ideologues, with a number of implications for the kind of public, and the kind of religiosity, that has been addressed and inscribed by the cultural products of the bazaar.

11 Arvind Rajagopal, *Politics after Television. Religious Nationalism and the Reshaping of the Indian Public*, Cambridge University Press, Cambridge, UK; New York, 2001.
12 See: Partha Chatterjee, "Beyond the Nation? Or Within?" in: *Economic and Political Weekly*, January 4–11, 1997, pp. 30–34. Note that his use of "political society" differs from that of Antonio Gramsci, for whom it refers to dominant state institutions.
13 On this aspect of "porous legality" see: Lawrence Liang, "Porous Legalities and Avenues of Participation," in: *Sarai Reader 05: Bare Acts*, Sarai/CSDS, New Delhi, 2005, pp. 6–17.

First, even as a certain messianism and sacrality constituted the heart of Indian nationalism, there was little scope for this to register in the secular-modernist political and civic institutions of the independent nation – or indeed, in officially sanctioned and patronized cultural forms such as modernist art. Instead, religion was narrativized in cultural-identitarian terms rather than being recognized as an ongoing performative presence in public life (a good example of this is to be found in the writings of India's first prime minister Jawaharlal Nehru). Hence, while cultural forms such as calendar art flourished with the growth of indigenous capitalism, they came to be aligned with a vernacular constituency, as opposed to the secular-modernist, cosmopolitan, and English-educated elite, as well as to the left. This division formed the basis of what Arvind Rajagopal, writing in relation to the resurgence of Hindu nationalism in the late 1980s, has called a "split public."[11] It is also consistent with Partha Chatterjee's distinction between civil society and a wider "political society," an arena of difference distinct from liberal formulations of the polity, particularly relevant to the postcolonial context; Chatterjee makes this distinction in recognition of the continuing political claims of constituencies excluded from the state as well as civil society because of their social status, and/or their nonconformity with the norms of liberalism – perhaps chief among these being a secular worldview.[12]

However, as I pointed out earlier, even though this vernacular constituency was of secondary importance in relation to the state apparatus, it was still characterized by the hegemony of the Hindu, and more specifically Vaishnava merchant-caste trading communities of the bazaar, such that its cultural forms reinforced the marginalization or hegemonic accommodation of religious and other minorities. This anti-democratic, Hindu majoritarian tendency was able to flourish in the vernacular culture industries precisely because of the latter's marginalization by the sanctioned cultural forms of official state nationalism; this became abundantly clear as Hindu nationalist

political parties reemerged in the late 1980s, and immediately turned to the visual idioms of calendar art for use in their propaganda posters, processions, and videos.

What is more, as indigenous capitalism was subject to restrictions and sidelined by state enterprise under India's post-independence socialist model, resulting in a robust "parallel" or "black" economy, the vernacular culture industries emanating from this parallel business culture also tended to operate on an informal and/or semi-formal basis, at least up until the economic reforms of the 1990s. Thus, the calendar industry has depended on casual labor and informal distribution networks, while the Indian film industry, the largest in the world, has a notorious history of informal if not illegal sources of finance (including "Hindu Undivided Families" and crime syndicates): significantly, it was only granted official industry status in 1998. In other words, the pre-liberalization mass culture industries in India, in tandem with the "bazaar," have functioned under the legal and epistemological conditions of a putatively "private," "cultural" sphere excluded from the legitimate or formal "market." On the one hand, as we have seen, the existence of this parallel economic, cultural, and political sphere has provided a fertile ground for Hindu majoritarianism, but on the other hand, its informality or "porous legality" has also provided a means for wider economic participation and social mobility, particularly in the urban arena, as state controls over the economy were gradually eased.[13]

Often this participation has been achieved by the appearance onto the market of new technologies, enabling a reconfiguration of traditional occupations and social hierarchies: particularly media technologies such as audio cassettes, video, cable and satellite television, and of course digital media. In this connection, piracy and informal methods have played a key role in ensuring the successful introduction to the formal marketplace, as in the case of the ill-fated audio magnate Gulshan Kumar who, starting out as a roadside juice vendor, went on to make his fortune in the cassette industry via a combination of piracy and the exploitation of legal loopholes; now, ironically, Kumar's company, T-Series, perhaps the biggest player in the music and DVD industry, is strongly committed to safeguarding its own copyright.[14]

While Kumar swiftly and smoothly created a successful niche in audio and video, his foray into the film industry was literally fatal. Having built up a multimillion-dollar business in blank and prerecorded audiotapes, in 1990 Kumar entered film production. With the vast returns from music sales enabled by the boom in cassette tapes, the music in Hindi commercial films regained the dominance it had lost through the 1970s and 1980s when the action-film genre tended to be the foremost attraction. By the mid-1990s, the returns on the audio rights to a film were comparable to the exhibition rights in a major territory. In this scenario, audio producers became very powerful, particularly Kumar, who cornered about seventy percent of the market in film music rights. It was this power which was to seal Kumar's downfall. One morning in 1997, when coming out of a Shiva temple in Mumbai (Bombay), he was shot dead. This high-profile assassination brought to light the Mumbai film world's entanglements with an underworld that extended from Mumbai to Dubai, Hong Kong, and Southeast Asia. In part, this mafia has been financing films which have long relied on black money, but has also been involved in extortion from successful film industry personalities. Gulshan Kumar paid the ultimate price for not sharing his profits.

While the vernacular media have emerged from a domain of informality that merges with illegality, this domain, as I have argued, has also been a primary site for contemporary forms of religiosity – and here again, Gulshan Kumar, the devout Hindu, provides the preeminent example. Kumar's T-Series not only entered a preexisting film music market but also created an enormous new market for devotional tapes and DVDs, where its primacy continues well after Kumar's assassination. Indeed, his death seems to have imparted a special aura to the enterprise: photographs of Kumar, dressed in holy saffron and/or with a red prayer mark *(tilak)* on his forehead, figure on the covers of T-Series devotional tapes, CDs, and DVDs/VCDs, while footage of him at various pilgrimage sites is often featured in T-Series song depictions of Hindu devotional music. His devotion to Shiva is also spectacularly displayed through the building of gigantic cement statues of the deity at his recording studio at Noida, in Greater Delhi, and at Nageshwar, near Dwarka, an important Shiva pilgrimage site. Again, with these mega-statues we see how the vernacular culture industries prepare the ground for the emergence of yet another new religious form.

Neoliberal Devotions

In the trajectory I have traced from the medieval devotional movements, through anticolonial resistance, to contemporary urban piracy, the devotional appropriation of new media and visual technologies has been a site for various kinds of opposition: to priestly privilege, to colonial rule, and to the exclusionary legal and civic structures of the post-independence state and its officially sanctioned public sphere. In all such cases, however, these oppositional currents have also been subject to reterritorialization within new formations of power, harnessing them to institutional spaces and social hierarchy. In post-independence India this has resulted both in an elite-technocratic modern state and the rise of the merchant castes and a modern brand of majoritarian Hinduism. Particularly after the economic reforms of the 1990s, the compact between religiosity and technology is more in evidence than ever, as a reformulated hegemonic Hinduism is increasingly naturalized as part of the "Indian" identity in the global marketplace and at multicultural sites in the Indian diaspora. Greater attention is being paid to the national and regional vernaculars by a globalized formal corporate sector tapping into India's immense consumer potential, while at the same time the erstwhile vernacular constituencies are realizing that learning English represents their ticket to becoming part of the post-liberalization economy.

14 Ravi Sundaram makes this point about Gulshan Kumar in "Uncanny Networks. Pirate, Urban and New Globalisation," in: *Economic and Political Weekly*, January 3, 2004, pp. 64–71.

In this recent scenario, where vernacular capitalism interfaces with global capital and corporate protocols with the blessings of the post-socialist state, there has been yet another efflorescence of devotional image-making. Perhaps the most representative of these more recent forms of neoliberal religiosity is the vast temple complex of Akshardham in Delhi, built by the Swaminarayan sect, a global organization largely funded by diasporic or "non-resident" Indians (NRIs). This complex features a series of temples crafted using revived stone-carving techniques from various traditions around the country, an IMAX film, and walk-through animatronic displays about the sect's founder, made in collaboration with experts from Hollywood. A "boat ride" through "Indian civilization" worthy of Universal Studios, again featuring animatronic figures, presents a particular version of Indian history that emphasizes a classical Hindu "golden age" and skips over the Mughal period. The extent to which such representations are being naturalized as part of the "Indian" heritage is evidenced by the fact that on any given day, busloads of schoolchildren visit the site. This theme-park approach to religion is echoed in the proliferation of gigantic cement statues of deities (mostly Hindu, but also Buddhist) erected all over India since the 1990s, as the effects of India's economic reforms became palpable. Many of these statues are built with the dual purpose of reviving worship at a hitherto neglected temple (as in the case of Gulshan Kumar's Shiva statue at Nageshwara), and providing a hook for tourism. Thus, while there is no decline in the "cultic" aspects of religion, the neoliberal order ushers in an additional element of spectacularization, consistent with the visual modalities of consumerism: billboards, entertainment complexes, tourism, and the enormous shopping malls now thrusting up into the skylines of Indian urban centers. At the same time, at another level, mythological themes are being secularized for broader dissemination, as in the case of the push by Virgin Comics to follow up on the manga phenomenon by creating a futuristic version of the Ramayana epic entitled *Ramayan 3392 AD*, soon to be turned into an MMO by Sony Online Entertainment: an event keenly awaited by NRI (non-residential Indian) youth eager for online content which relates to their own "cultural heritage."

In these examples, again, spectacularization and exhibition value do not detract from the aura of the divine icon, but work towards a reauraticization based on new modalities of efficacy and engagement. I would like to conclude by suggesting that the developments as outlined in the above invite us to complicate the polar schema of cult and exhibition value, or auraticization and deauraticization, which attends narratives based on the assumption that modernity inevitably entails a movement towards secularism. The constantly changing forms of religious iconography and liturgy in India and their articulations with technological, economic, political, and social configurations demand instead a more nuanced and historicized approach to the ongoing transformations in practices that are too often unproductively lumped together under the rubric of the "religious," the "sacred," and/or the "spiritual." Each of these terms needs to be rethought and newly specified in light of the contemporaneity, and hence the ongoing mediation of the divine.

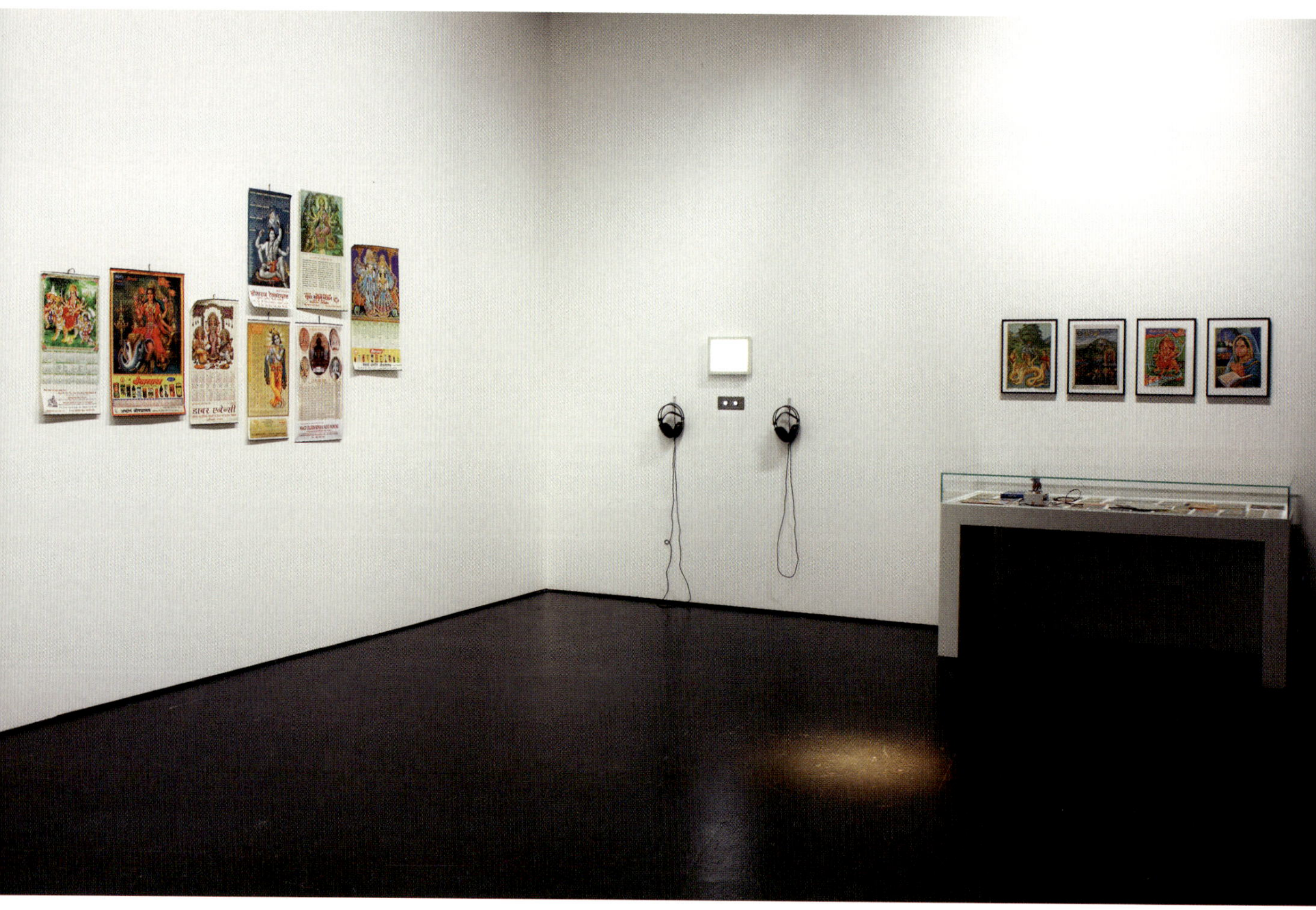

In India, religions reacted very quickly to new medial forms imported from the West in the last few decades. Mass production released the images from clerical control and enabled access to all areas of the audiovisual media and to the most diverse social contexts. Pasted up on room and house walls, on computer screens and car doors, hidden in purses or on medallions, printed on calendars and by means of various other advertising channels, the colorful flood of images now ensures that religious iconography characterizes the image of everyday India more than ever before. Consequently, the various incarnations of Hindu gods like Krishna or Saraswati can continue to exist as popular superstars alongside politicians and film stars in contemporary secularized media.

Kajri Jain
*1961 in Canberra, Australia,
lives and works in Toronto, Canada

Bazaar Religious Images,
assorted religious prints on paper,
postcards, stickers, calendars,
DVDs, 1 mantra box; 20 religious
prints: 11.5 × 17 cm, 13 postcards:
14.5 × 9.5 cm, 6 prints: 18 × 25 cm

*Continuum Between
Photography, Painting & Printing*
6 prints:
Yasoda Krishna, 35 × 25 cm
Baby Krishna, 36 × 24.5 cm
Shri Krishna, 35.5 × 25.5 cm
Yashoda Krishna, 25 × 34.5 cm
Temple, 18.5 × 25 cm
Temple, 18.5 × 15 cm

Mid-20th Century Offset Prints
5 prints:
Vishnu Bhajan, Shri Yamunaji,
Shree Ganesh Laxmi,
Shiva Ashirwad, Sita Pati Ram,
35.5 × 52 cm each

*Repetition & Difference:
Mass Reproduction & Iconography*
7 prints:
Shri Saraswati, 17.5 × 24.5 cm
Shri Saraswati, 13 × 18 cm
Shri Veerabhadra, 24 × 33.5 cm
Shri Veerabhadra, 25.5 × 36.5 cm
Veerabhadra, 24.5 × 37 cm
Ardhanarishvara: Shiva as Shiva
& Parvati, 24.5 × 34 cm
25 Darshan, 25.5 × 36.5 cm

*Early 21st Century Religious
Calendars from North India,*
2004–2008
8 calendars:
2007, 30 × 57.5 cm
2008, 29 × 57 cm
2006, 29 × 57.5 cm
2004, 29.5 × 57.5 cm
Super Service Station,
35 × 60 cm
2006 (Shri Baidyanath),
42 × 63 cm
2007 (Shri Baidyanath),
41 × 67 cm
Jain Poster, 35 × 60 cm

*Encounter of
Representational Techniques*
4 prints:
Krishna transposed
into European landscape,
25 × 36.5 cm
Shri Purna Giri Deviji, 22 × 32 cm
Shri Jotiba shrine, 25.5 × 35 cm
Dua Lady, 23.5 × 32 cm

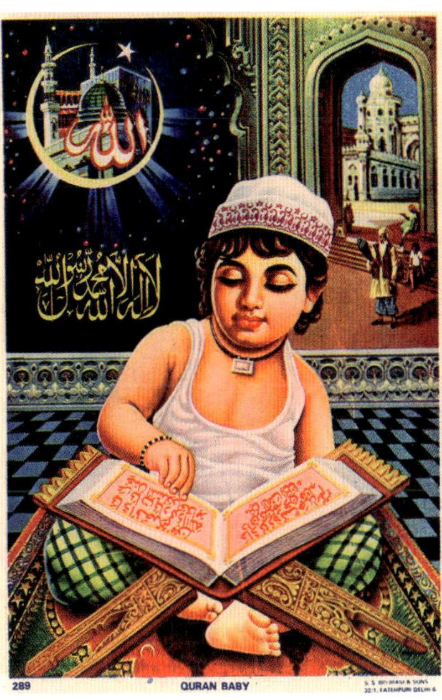

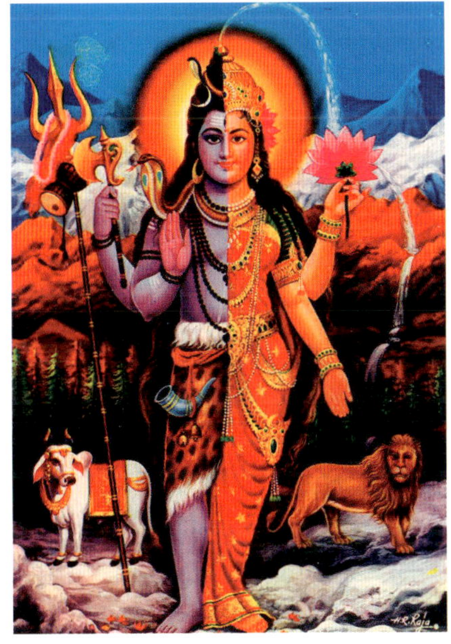

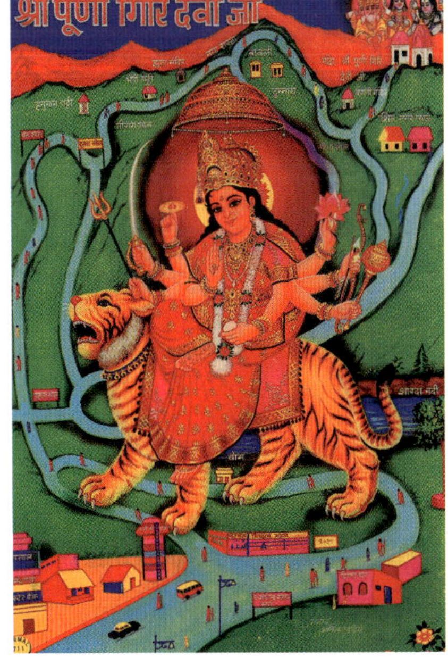

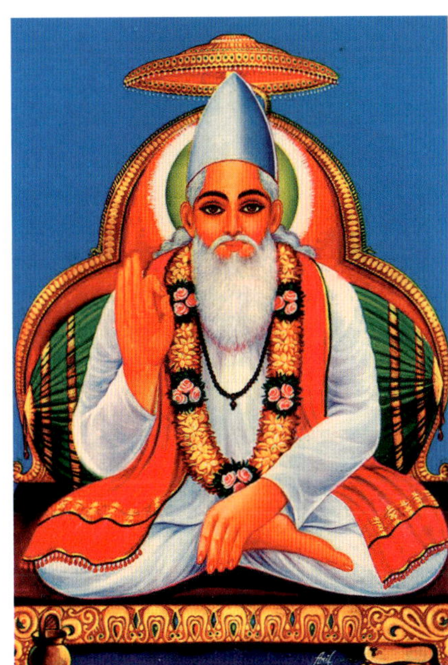

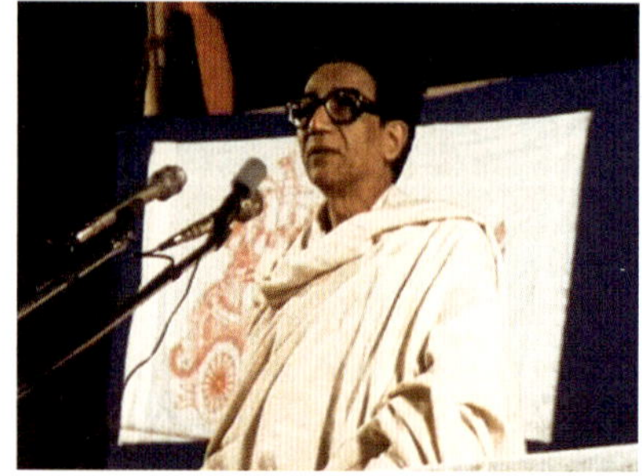
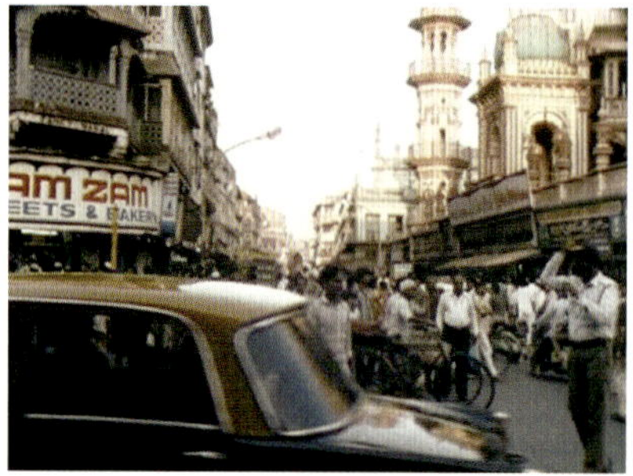
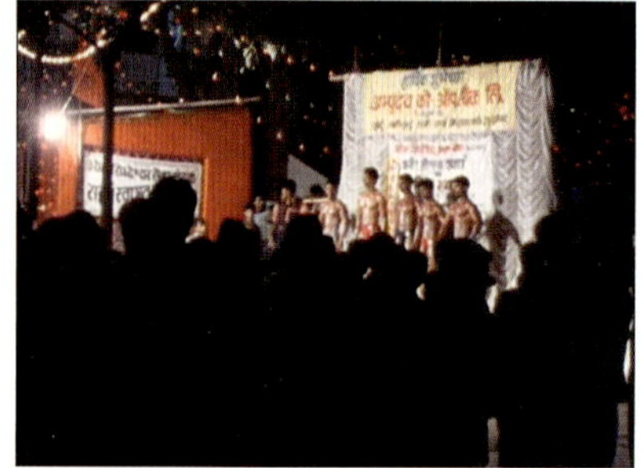
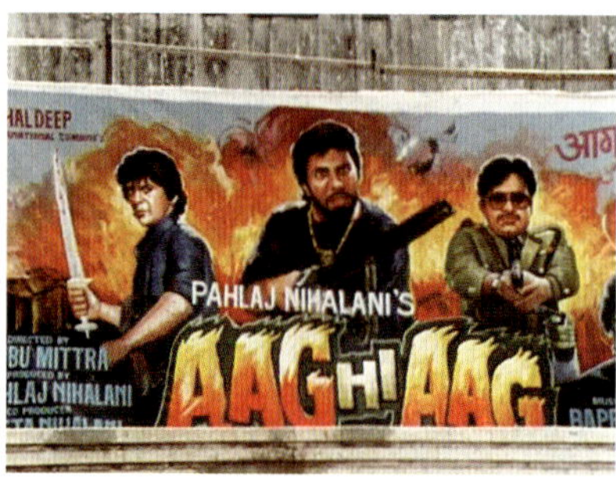

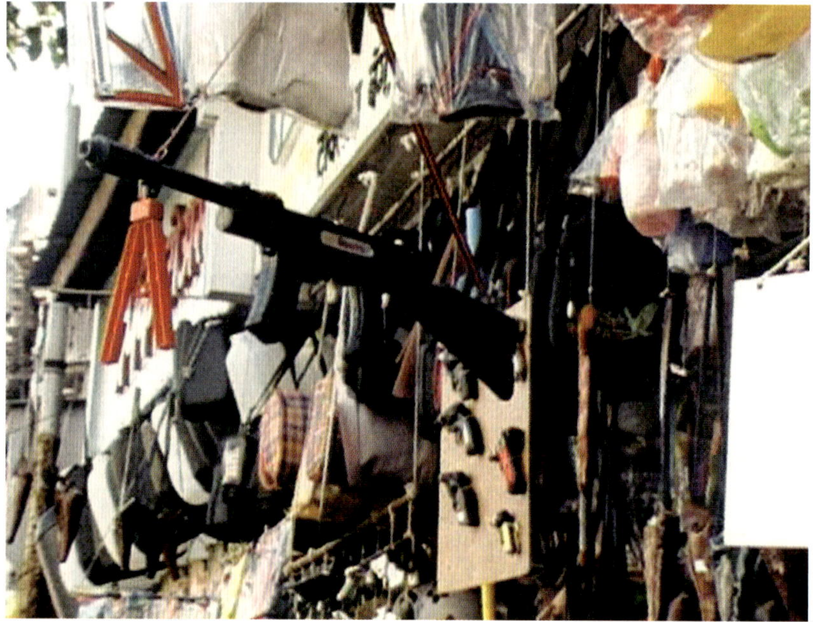

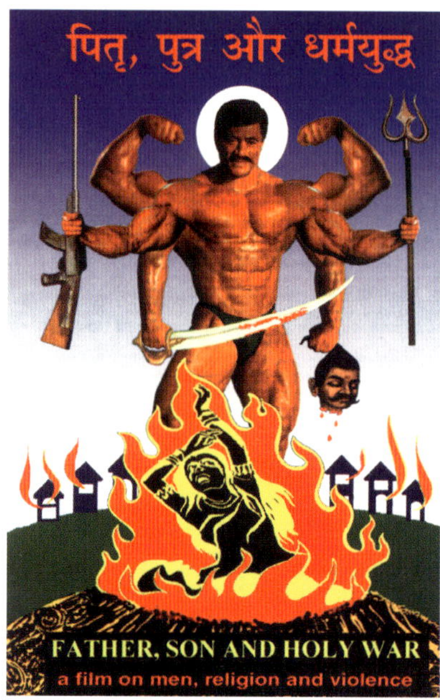

The two-part documentary film deals in its first part, *Trial by Fire*, with the traditional burning of widows *(Sati)* still practiced in India in 1994, as well as with the violence between Hindus and Muslims in Mumbai (Bombay). The second part, *Hero Pharmacy*, takes as its topic the fixation with masculinity in India, in which Patwardhan discerns one of the causes of sectarian violence against "the Other." The warrior tradition of Maratha and Rajput or action heroes like Arnold Schwarzenegger and "Macho Man" Randy Savage serve as foci for identification, whilst non-violence is considered within religious fanaticism as a sign of impotence. Scenes of mass gatherings, of despotic speakers, and fanatical listeners, images of excesses between Hindus and Muslims come together with interviews and statements to form a theory of religious violence.

Anand Patwardhan
*1950 in Mumbai,
formerly Bombay, India,
lives and works in Mumbai

Father, Son and Holy War (Part II),
1994, 16 mm film, digitized, color,
sound, 60 min, loop, stills from a
digital copy and poster

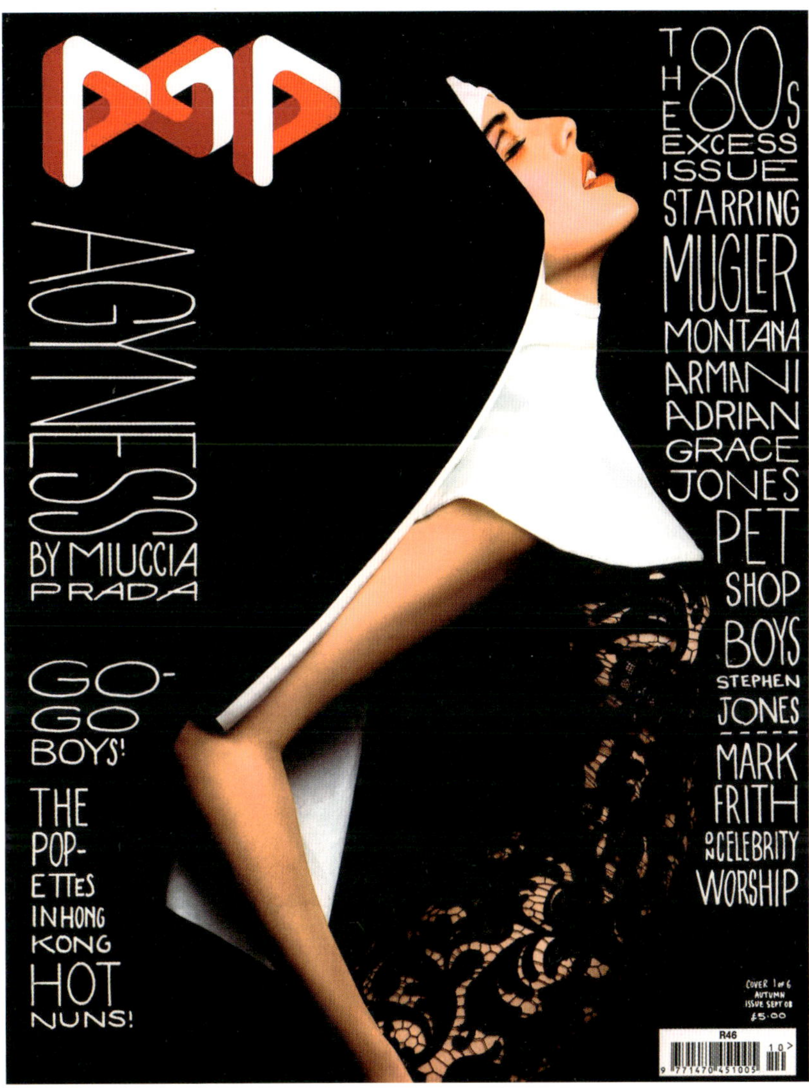

Miuccia Prada
*1949, Milan, Italy,
lives and works in Milan

True Faith, 2008,
6 covers for *POP Magazine*,
issue 19, September 2008

Katie Grand
Nun Head, 2008, photos for
POP Magazine, issue 19,
September 2008

Discussions on laicism, like the most recent one on the so-called German "Kopftuchurteil" [headscarf ruling] from 2003, show the potential for political conflict that can erupt for no other reason than wearing a particular item of clothing. Conversely, clothing has always expressed social affiliations and been a visible medium of philosophical convictions. Wearing the uniform vestments of an order, such as a nun's habit, does not express individuality, but emphasizes the communal adherence to that order; it is meant to signify a simple life of devotion to God. So the prescribed clothing was a costume devoid of color and decoration and made of humble material like cotton or linen. Miuccia Prada, a qualified political scientist and the head designer of her renowned Italian fashion house, went on to combine elegantly luxurious haute couture materials like fine lace and brocade with formal idioms drawn from religion. Her staging of six nuns for the cover of the British fashion magazine *POP* is both an avant-garde device and a symptom of the current trend towards fashionable piety. Similarly, the fashion photography of the British stylist Katie Grand follows the tradition of the blasphemous use of religious elements by pop stars like Madonna or Boy George.

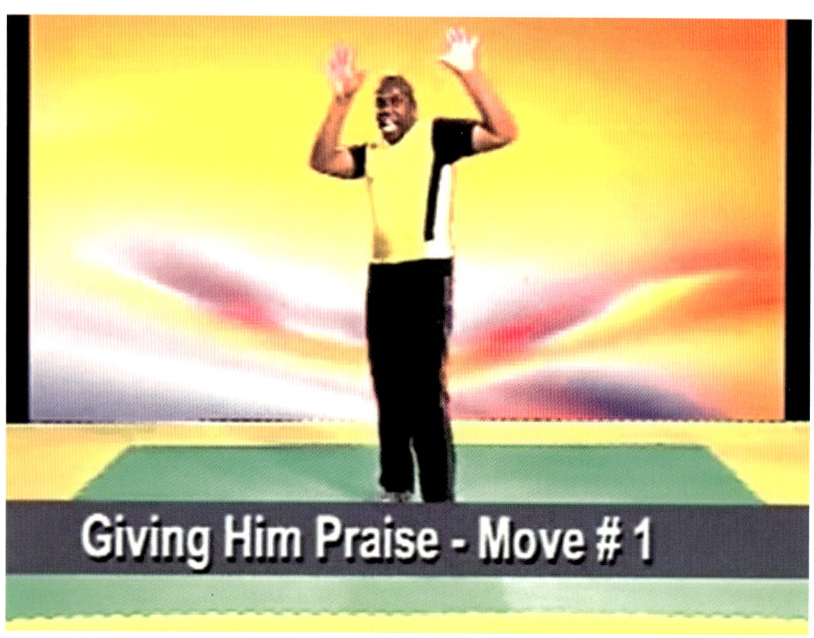

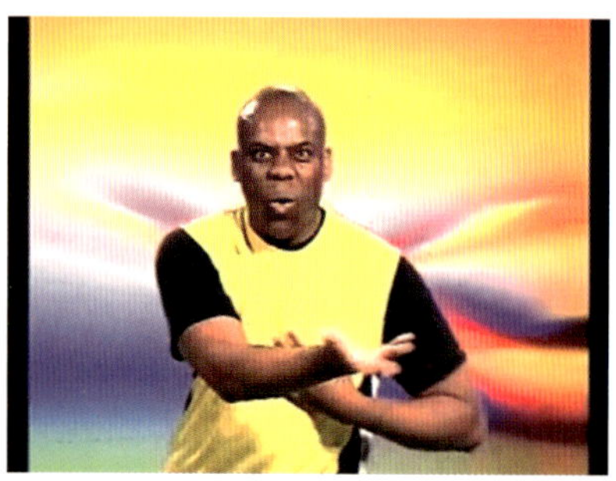
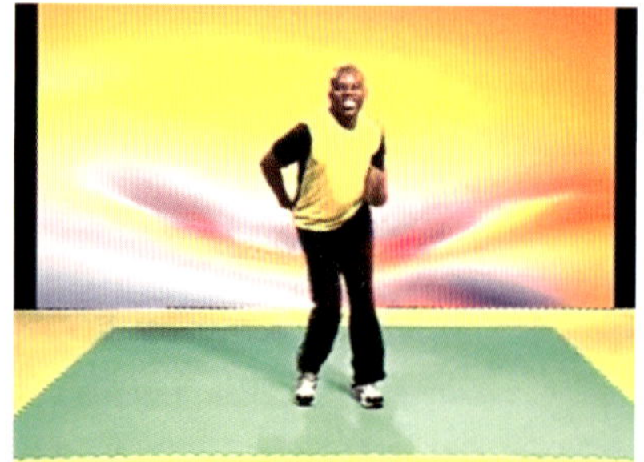

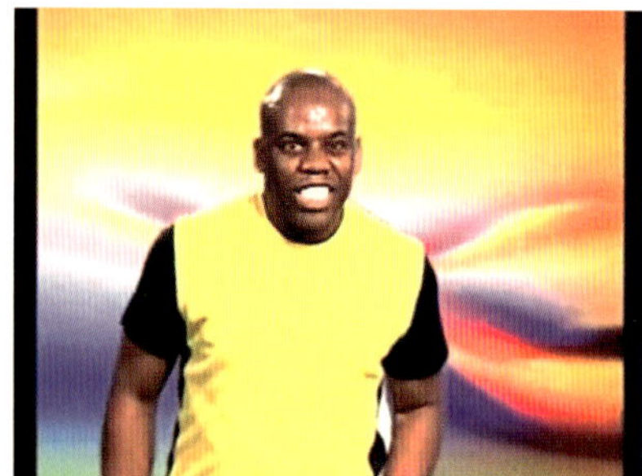
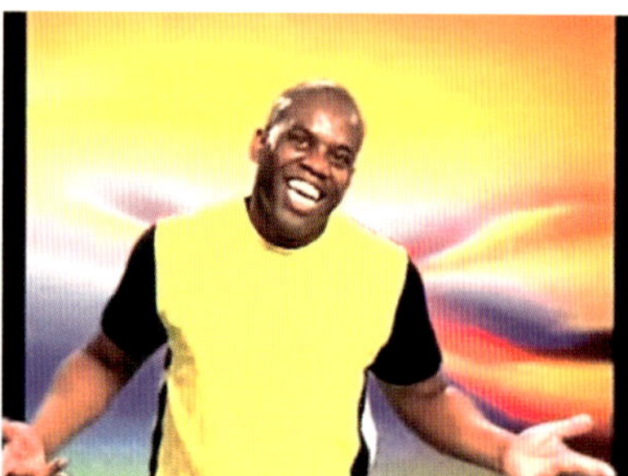

The American fitness coach and choreographer Paul Eugene is noted for his home aerobics courses distributed on DVD and broadcast on American breakfast television. Eugene thus finds himself part of the tense scenario of a hedonistic body cult elevating the body itself to a fetish worthy of worship while, at the same time, making it a temple to the human spirit. The intimate gymnastics exercise in front of the television set replaces morning prayer, the aerobics course church service. One no longer pays homage to the invisible. Instead, keeping one's own body in shape becomes praise to God's creation. As Eugene himself put it: "Praise You!"

**Gospel Aerobics
with Paul Eugene**
ca. 2005–2008, video, color,
sound, 19:30 min, 21:50 min,
32 min, 24:30 min, 24 min, loop,
stills from a digital copy

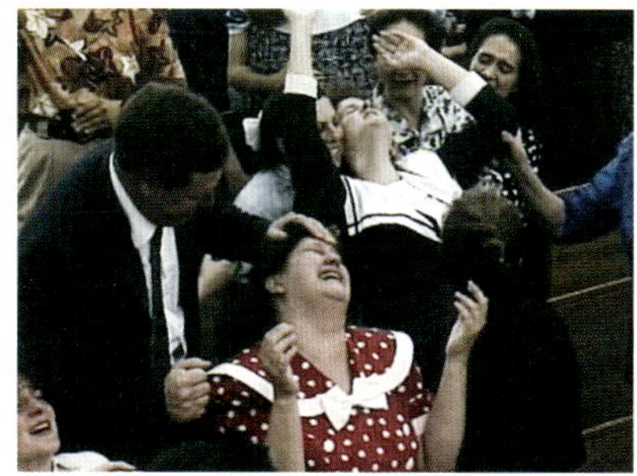 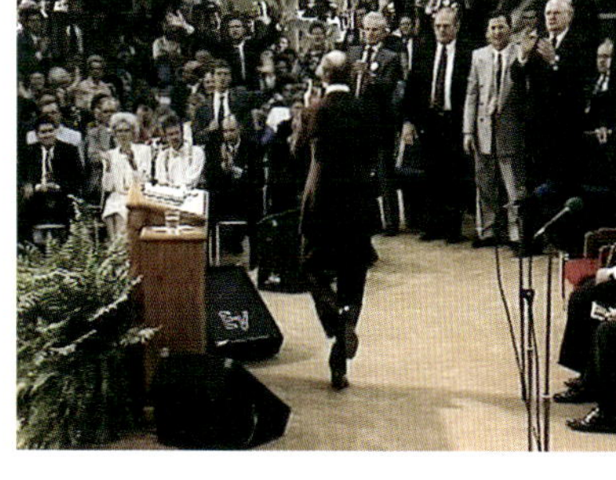

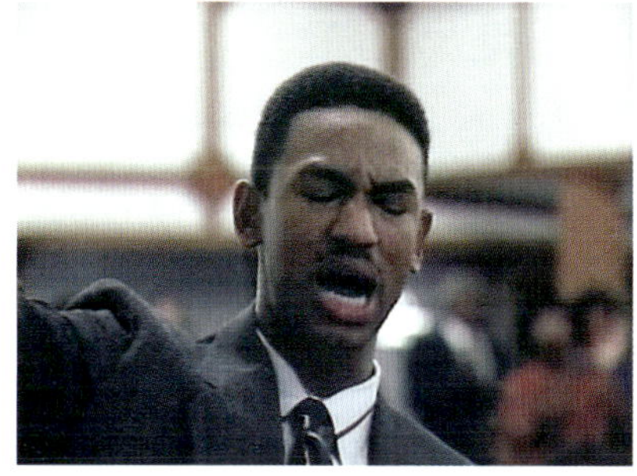 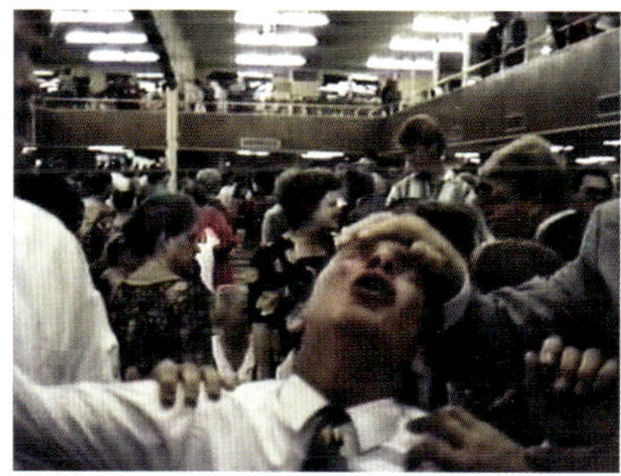

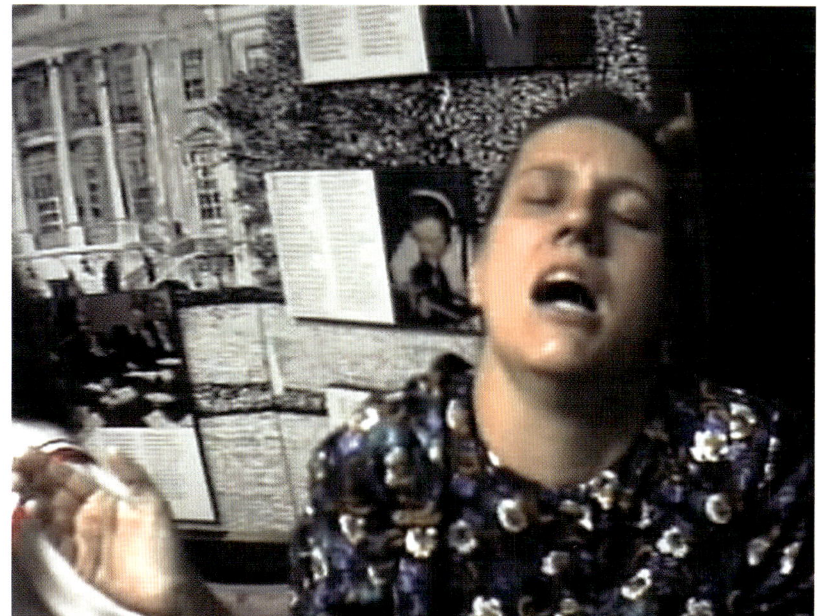

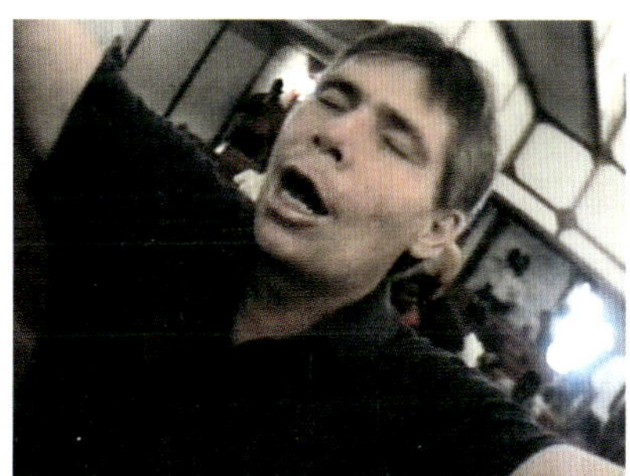 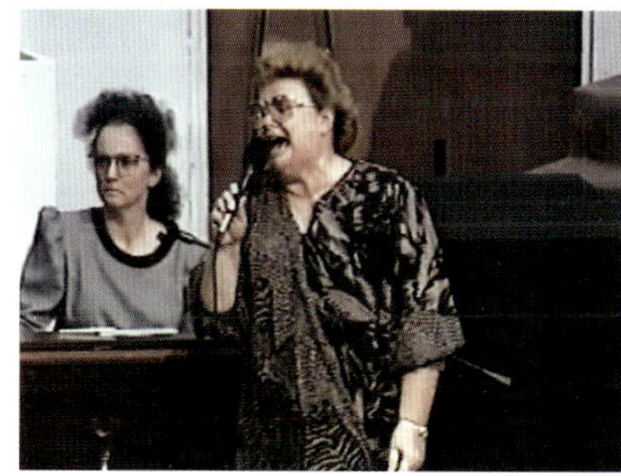

**Valie Export,
Ingrid and Oswald Wiener**
Valie Export, *1940 in Linz,
Austria, lives and works in
Cologne, Germany, and
Vienna, Austria
Ingrid Wiener, *1942 in Vienna,
Oswald Wiener, *1935 in
Vienna, live and work in Vienna

Das Unsagbare Sagen, 1992,
video, color, sound, 45 min,
extract of 12:50 min duration,
stills from a digital copy

Valie Export's numerous films,
videos, performances, and her
work as a curator bear out this
Austrian artist's genre-spanning
pursuits. In the early 1990s, she
collaborated with Oswald and
Ingrid Wiener in the documentary
Das Unsagbare Sagen [The Un-
speakable Speaking], placing at
its center forms of articulation far
removed from any linguistic structure or norms. The piece shows,
among others, aphatic speakers,
sound poets, and small children,
while the extract presented here
is devoted to the phenomenon
of glossolalia, or speaking in
tongues, that is, speaking without
intelligible meaning. This religious
practice was already mentioned
as a sign of belief in the New
Testament and is today practiced
mainly by Christian Pentecostal-
ists.

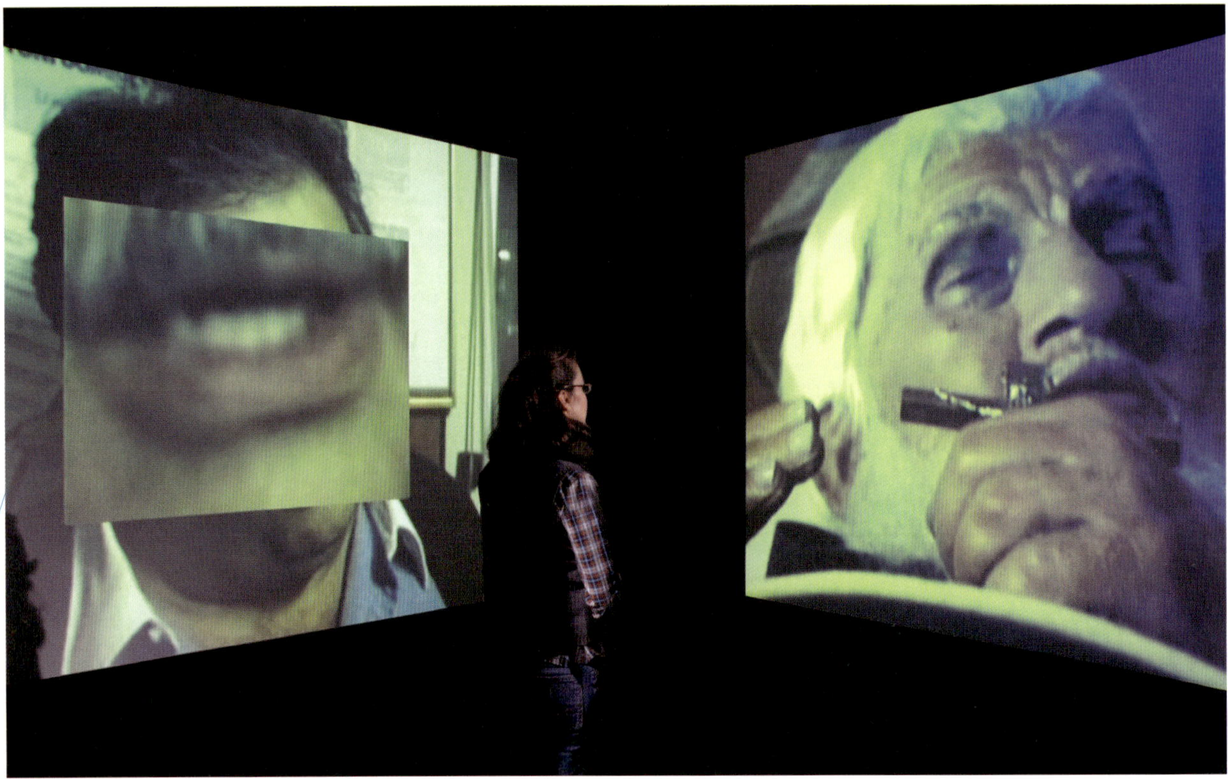

In their works, Dias & Riedweg often address perceptions of the private and the public. Their video installations oscillate the fine arts and performance art. The yearning after belief and religious observation is generally stronger than the suffering caused by a lack of information and material resources, and yet, the idea of God has always been something the individual needs, irrespective of their relationship to the state. The piece *Deus é boca (Gott ist Mund)* [God Is Mouth] deals with how this personal need is manipulated by state interests, and it creates a poetic visualization of the power of discourse: mouths that talk and their eager listeners, searching for something in which they can believe. What does a funk musician's mouth have in common with that of a frenetic preacher? And the mouth of a starved street vendor with that of a politician courting favors?

Dias & Riedweg
Maurício Dias,
*1964 in Rio de Janeiro, Brazil
Walter Riedweg,
*1955 in Lucerne, Switzerland,
live and work in Rio de Janeiro

Deus é boca (Gott ist Mund), 2002,
4-channel video installation,
color, sound, installation view
ZKM | Karlsruhe, 2009

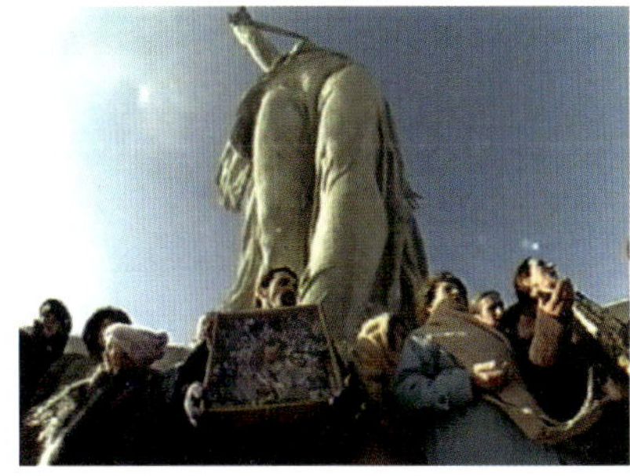
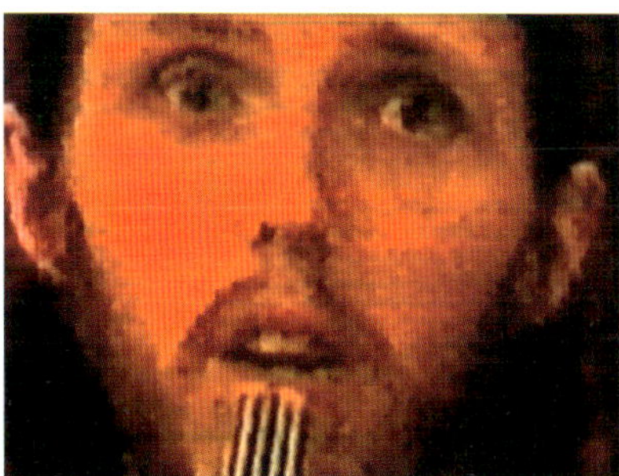
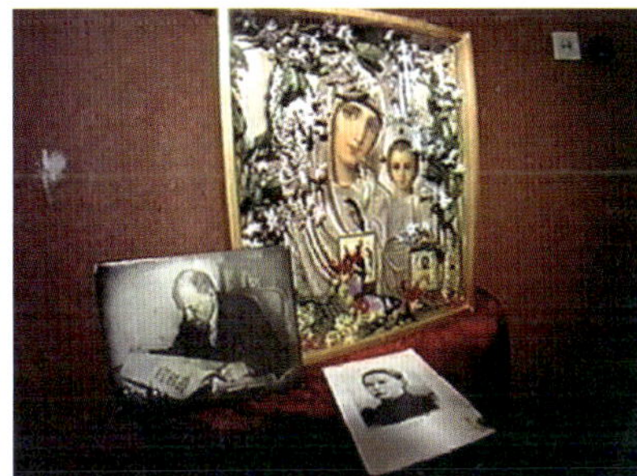
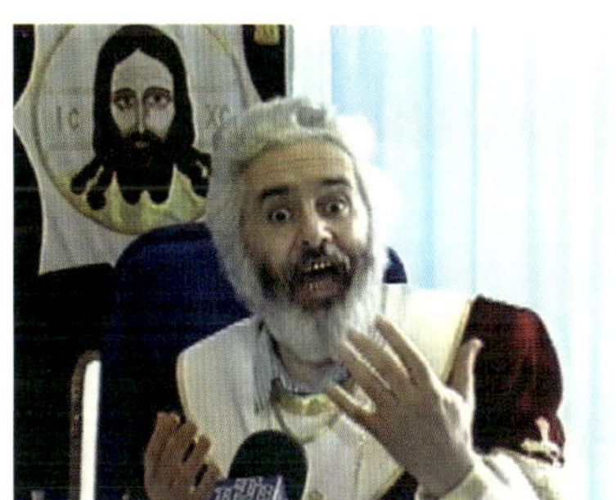

Vadim Zakharov
*1959 in Dushanbe, formerly
USSR, today Russia,
lives and works in Cologne,
Germany

*Der See der Vergessenheit /
Lake of Oblivion*, 2000,
video installation, color, sound,
30 min, loop, installation view
ZKM | Karlsruhe, 2009, and stills
from a digital copy

In his piece *Der See der Vergessenheit / Lake of Oblivion*, the artist
Vadim Zakharov, a member of the
circle of Moscow Conceptualists,
projects a video on sects and
modern "prophets." The translated text accompanying the video
can be listened to on headphones
in Latin, Old Greek, and in the
Gothic language. Zakharov ironically demonstrates in this work
how sects utilize oblivion as a
drug. In addition, by means of the
dead languages, he refers to an
omnipresent culture of forgetting.
While thematizing the conscious
manipulation of memory by religious groups, he also treats of the
abundance of information and
images in the media, which lead
to "waves of amnesia," to a constant deleting and replacing of
information.

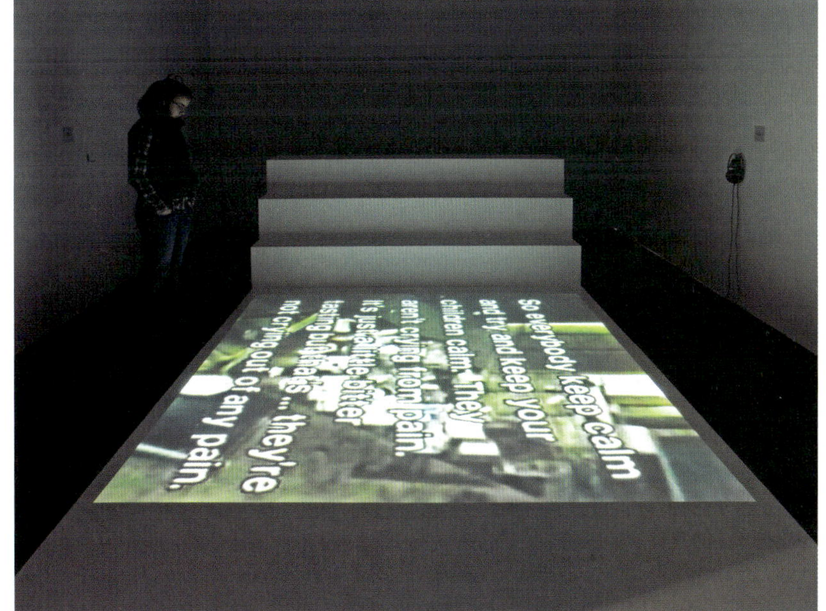

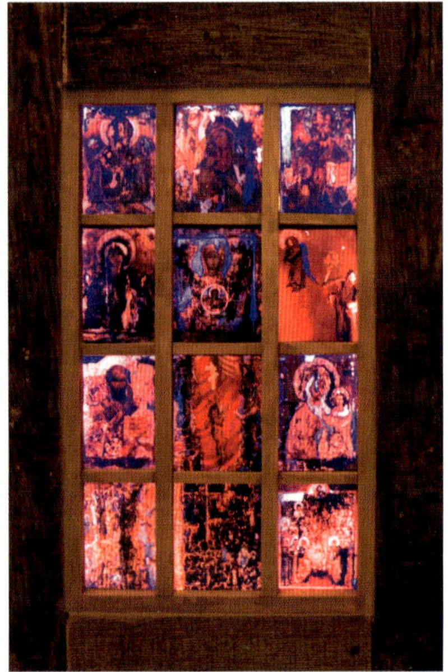
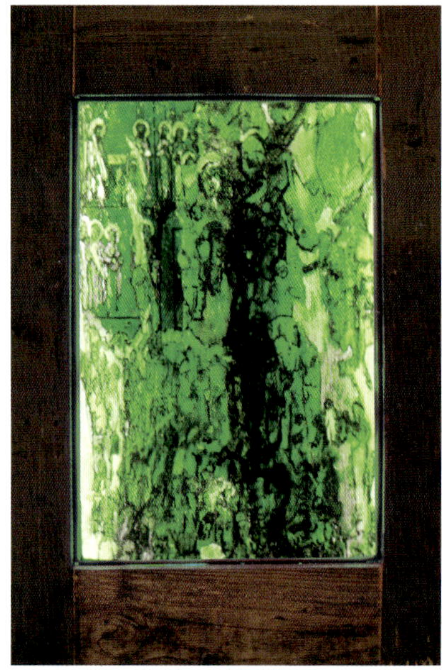
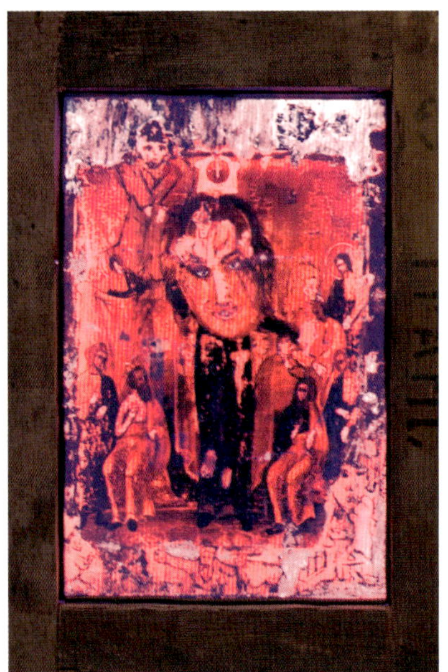
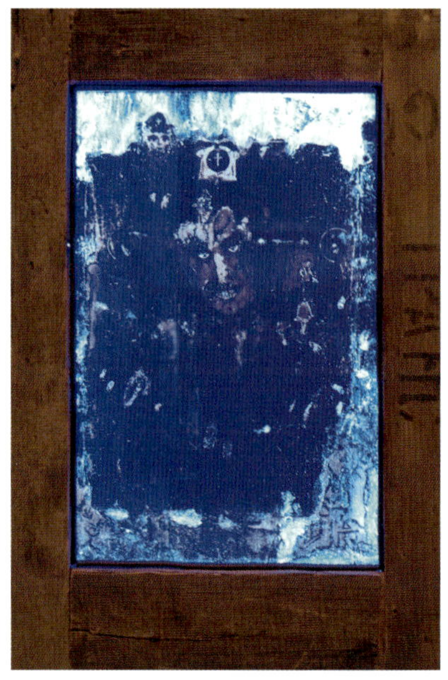

Hermes Zygott
*1964 in Saint Petersburg,
formerly Leningrad, USSR,
today Russia,
lives and works in Moscow, Russia

Sacred Reality #1, 2008
Orthodox XXI Century, 2008
Russian Monstrosities, 2008

Light boxes, wooden frame,
sound, 68 × 55 cm, 90 × 58 cm,
80 × 40 cm

The Russian poet and musician Hermes Zygott has subjected old, damaged Byzantine icons to loving reanimation. What Walter Benjamin described as "the loss of aura" here refers, above all, to the original artworks, which were previously elevated to cult objects but are now elbowed aside by the technical reproduction of images in modernity. As icons have always been defined by being worshipped, Hermes Zygott tries to restore the aura of these neglected models technically and fetch them back from oblivion into the focus of contemporary admiration. Installed on colorful light boxes, they now shine out, to the accompaniment of an electronic reinterpretation of Claudio Monteverdi's *Vespro della Beata Vergine*, in a new – electric – light.

Komar & Melamid
...We.Remember,...
..or.So.It.Seems..

Shortened and slightly revised version of the essay, first published in: Dore Ashton (ed.), *Monumental Propaganda,* instigated by Komar & Melamid, exhib. cat., ICI, New York, 1994, pp. 43–53. Translated from the Russian by Alex Halberstadt.

Soviet monuments loomed over our childhood, and as they disappear, we fear we may vanish with them. That is why we are trying to prolong their existence. We grew up in one of Moscow's oldest neighborhoods, one so small that everything was "just around the corner." As we later discovered, our grandparents took us for walks on the same boulevards and along the same route to Red Square. Wonders, heroes, and monuments surrounded us at every step. Every child knew that the Moscow Metro was one of the greatest wonders on earth, containing not only the world's most delicious ice cream, but many other attractions. There, as if in a dream, stairs moved magically up and down, and doors opened and closed by themselves. As incredible as it sounds, we really did live in a wonderland. Along with the entire nation, we floated up on the magical stairs toward an even more magical tomorrow. Our feet did not move – why should they? They had nowhere to run. Of course, the most amazing wonder of the world, the greatest miracle among all peoples and nations, was Lenin's immortal body. As soon as we passed Dolgorukiy and approached Red Square, we had to get in line. Soviet lines were famous throughout the world, and the line to see Lenin was the most famous of them all. Everything that belongs to the state soon creates a line, but the line in front of the Mausoleum was even longer than those in front of liquor stores during the years Mikhail Gorbachev waged war on the Green Serpent of alcoholism. The line started at the Alexander Garden, ran along the Kremlin wall, looped around the Memorial Obelisk for the Great Socialist Thinkers and Revolutionaries, and stretched all the way across Red Square. The obelisk was erected in honor of the three hundredth anniversary of the Romanov dynasty and, prior to the revolution, was crowned with a two-headed eagle. Lenin had the eagle removed and replaced the old inscriptions with the names of his favorite heroes. We remember that in the late 1960s, the Tomb of the Unknown Soldier replaced the obelisk which was moved to the distant Kremlin wall. Leonid Brezhnev apparently decided that it would be improper for strange, almost Jewish sounding names to obstruct the view of the Eternal Flame. The proximity to the Tomb of so many non-Russian names was considered incorrect; it was assumed that the names of unknown soldiers would sound more patriotic. But all of this happened much later. In our childhood, the obelisk stood in its old place, and we stood in line beside it, eating candy and reading the engraved names which only made the line seem longer. It seems we can remember them still: Marx, Engels, Liebknecht, Lassalle, Bebel, Campanella, Méliès, Winstley, T. More, Saint-Simon, Vallin, Fourier, Joris, Prudhomme, Bakunin, Chernyshevsky, Lavrov, Mikhailovsky, Plekhanov. And with these sweet, lovely names on our lips, we finally entered the Mausoleum. Illuminated like one of Caravaggio's subjects, the Founder of the New World slept in primordial darkness inside the stepped pyramid that bore the simple inscription, "LENIN." Red letters on black: It had always been this way, long before we were born, dating back to the seventh anniversary of the Great October Revolution.

Everything would have continued smoothly in the land of happy childhood if not for the unlikely events of spring 1953. The huge stone inscription on the Mausoleum changed. Now it consisted of two words: "LENIN STALIN." Nothing, not even a punctuation mark, separated the two men. They lay close together, draped in the flag as if in a red blanket. There was something at once familiar and unspeakably taboo about their closeness. After all, how many people in glass coffins populated your childhood, dear reader? It is not surprising that Lenin reminded us of Tchaikovsky's Sleeping Beauty and of the dead princess from Pushkin's fairy tale: "They laid the body of the young princess into a crystal coffin and carried her into the hollow mountain." The beloved leader was also reminiscent of Alexander Blok's Cleopatra: "She lies in a crystal coffin, neither dead nor alive." These passages could

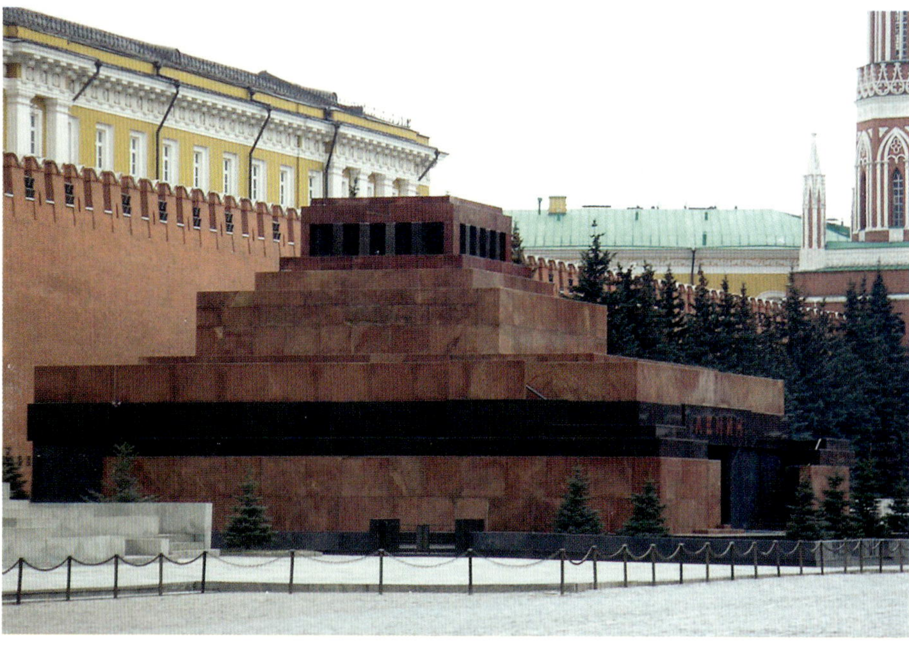

have been written about Lenin: Neither dead nor alive, resting in a crystal coffin inside a hollow mountain. And now with the addition of Stalin, the two sarcophagi resembled those displayed in the Gothic wing of the Pushkin Museum (which was named after the historian Tsvetaev before the Revolution). In that murky hall, a king lay in his glass coffin, with the queen on his left-hand side. A sudden curiosity and unexpected associations sent the mind reeling. On the pedestal of the most famous Soviet monument, for instance, a farm girl with a sickle stood on the left-hand side of a young worker bearing a hammer. A crazy question entered our minds: Was Stalin a woman? After all, he was also placed on Lenin's left. Then again, Lenin resembled a princess long before Stalin's arrival. In any case, the question remained: What if our leaders, who loved their people and therefore each other, were actually a man and a woman? Which was the "he"? Which was the "she"? How could we ascertain this? Only the leaders' faces and hands were visible through the glass. Perhaps that was all the coffins contained? If their brains were at the Institute of Marxism, then maybe their other organs were kept at even more secret institutions. What if they were castrated? Spinning around this unexpected question, our thoughts frenetically changed direction. What if our beloved leaders turned out to be sexless? In a way, the dead are sexless, as are statues. But maybe that was not true. Everyone knew the beautiful tales of Orpheus who loved the dead Eurydice, and of Pygmalion who married a statue. Despite knowing these myths, we could not imagine that depraved madmen were preserving these mummies, monuments, and portraits of our leaders for the same lascivious reasons. After death, Stalin and Lenin belonged to all humanity. Seeing the two heads inside the Mausoleum brought back the memory of the tiny hermaphrodites, which in turn gave birth to a new question: Which one was the Hermes and which the Aphrodite? The Greek gods were as familiar to us as the Soviet ones since, at school, we were taught to sketch their plaster heads in the academic style. So the issue of gender was unsettling. Both faces were brightly lit. Amazingly, Stalin was unshaven. His bearded cheeks reminded us of how the dead continue to grow hair. Nearby, Lenin's greenish cheeks seemed smooth as wax, flushed with a bright ruddiness that was painted on by some unspeakably privileged artist. These imperishable red and green cheeks reminded us of wax apples from still lifes we drew in art school. This simulacrum of immortality reminded us that *naturmort*, the Russian word for still life, borrowed from the French, literally means "dead nature." And while on the subject of apples, let us not forget Pushkin's Sleeping Beauty, poisoned by this very fruit. This mysterious two-headed androgyne was also evocative of the mother and father of all mothers and fathers – Adam and Eve. The symbols of original sin, the apple and the serpent, continually reappear in the crystal coffins of Russian poetry. The Russian Sleeping Beauty was poisoned by an apple and Cleopatra by a snake; Stalin's death was also attributed to poisoning. The cover of a magazine we found in a puddle of melting snow became forever etched in our memories: a large Kukryniksy illustration depicted a huge red hand that tore angelic masks from the faces of demonic Jewish doctors, the doctors who poisoned our great leader.

In 1953, the time of fairy tales had passed – now we found ourselves surrounded by real serpents and poisoned apples. It was hard to be a Jew in the land of mummies and pyramids. That year, many of our relatives lost their jobs. On the Metro escalator, complete strangers called us kikes. Many who had survived more difficult times, like the far away Albert Einstein and the great Russian composer Sergei Prokofiev who was not even a Jew died in the same year as Stalin. We were living in an increasingly complex world. Leaders and parents could no longer answer all our questions. Before, we were taught that we lived in paradise and that the West was hell, where every night the sun disappeared into a capitalist darkness. But after Stalin's death, birds of paradise with colorful plumage began to flock from the West: magazines, tourists, lighters, cigarettes, automobiles... And from Siberia, prisoners of the Gulag released by Nikita Khrushchev started to return home. As it turned out, hell was here in the East.

Later, when we began to study the history of Soviet art and the biography of Alexey Shchusev, the Mausoleum's architect, we discovered that the monumental change we witnessed in 1953 had occurred after the architect's death, and that it was one of the many changes the Mausoleum had undergone. In fact, the monument was altered many times during the architect's life. In his commissioned works, from the pre-revolutionary church in the Marfo-Mariinsky Convent to the KGB building and prison on Lubyanka, Shchusev demonstrated a truly professional flexibility. In one of his articles, he compared architecture with theater and admitted that, in accordance with the orders of the government, he frequently changed details of Lenin's Mausoleum. Starting in 1924, it was periodically closed to the public so that it could be rebuilt and its sole resident re-embalmed. These renovations always coincided with the major phases in Soviet history – the entire nation changed along with its leader's remains.

The first Mausoleum stood less than a year. Hurriedly constructed from wood, it resembled a pavilion of a county fair; in Blok's poem, Cleopatra's wax corpse was kept in just such a structure. The number of visitors who wanted to glimpse the newly deceased leader far exceeded that of any fair, and Red Square soon became deluged with pilgrims. The enormous line's resemblance to a snake again evoked associations of Lenin and Cleopatra. In the annals of Soviet art, this first Mausoleum is referred to as "temporary." The country was in the throes of the New Economic Policy which Lenin, before temporarily moving into his temporary monument, had called a "temporary setback." Everyone sought stability in those difficult years, and it seemed that the people's faith in the new regime depended on the literal preservation of Lenin's body. Unlike individual atheism which arises from skepticism, collective atheism is gullible and quick to believe. Therefore, the founder of the New World soon took the place vacated by God. The Patriarch's words were prophetic, and his body remained impervious to the passage of time. "Lenin lives forever," the nation sang; "Lenin is more alive than the living," we sang in school. Our holy relics, Lenin and the Mausoleum, together comprised the body/temple whose specter haunted Europe. While God slept in paradise, He promised us paradise on earth; that is why He remained here – if Lenin will not go to paradise, paradise will come to Lenin. Communism was promised to us, and the Mausoleum was the symbol of our covenant; the immortal leader who slept within was our hostage.

The second Mausoleum was also made of wood but decorated in the Art Deco style. It survived an entire five years and served as both a burial place and a tribune. On high holidays, statesmen could now make speeches and wave from atop the monument. Below, the working people strolling through Red Square could wave back and smile. Both parties were spectators and participants in this performance which was part military parade, part carnival. Gradually, along with the government, the Mausoleum itself began to resemble theater. The protagonist's crystal coffin was commissioned by the constructivist Konstantin Melnikov.

In 1929, officially named the Year of the Great Change, the wooden attraction was dismantled and replaced by a third, granite Mausoleum. This time Shchusev succeeded in creating an unexpected synthesis of Russian avant-garde and Soviet kitsch. A new period in Stalinist architecture was beginning which, in parody of the well-known terms, we like to call "post-avant-garde" or "proto-postmodernism." This era went down in history as the "period of liquidation of the landowning class and the creation of collective farms." In 1933, the coffin was rebuilt. The glass lid was made non-reflective. The next year, Sergei Kirov's murder stunned the nation and marked the beginning of Stalin's purges and the construction of underground tunnels between the Mausoleum and the Moscow Metro which were completed in the year of the Great Terror.

The Mausoleum was not only the spiritual center of Red Square and Moscow, but of the entire world. From then on, rising from the planet's fiery core and passing through the center of Lenin's body, the earth's axis did not simply reach toward the sun. It passed through Stalin's shiny, squeaky boots and rose higher, separating the left and right halves of his moustache; only then did it resume its journey to the sun. Not the real sun, mind you, but the sun at the center of the golden Soviet seal that rested on the generalissimo's white cap. There, within the seal's wreath of golden wheat, the axis stopped at the intersection of the hammer and sickle, becoming forever bound to the tiny earth illuminated by the red light of a single five-pointed star that twinkled above. Nothing was higher. The whole world was contained in the center of that famous white cap. No other country included the entire planet in its emblem. However, as we later discovered, the state of New York does. We are destined, it seems, to live out our lives in a place that considers itself the center of the universe.

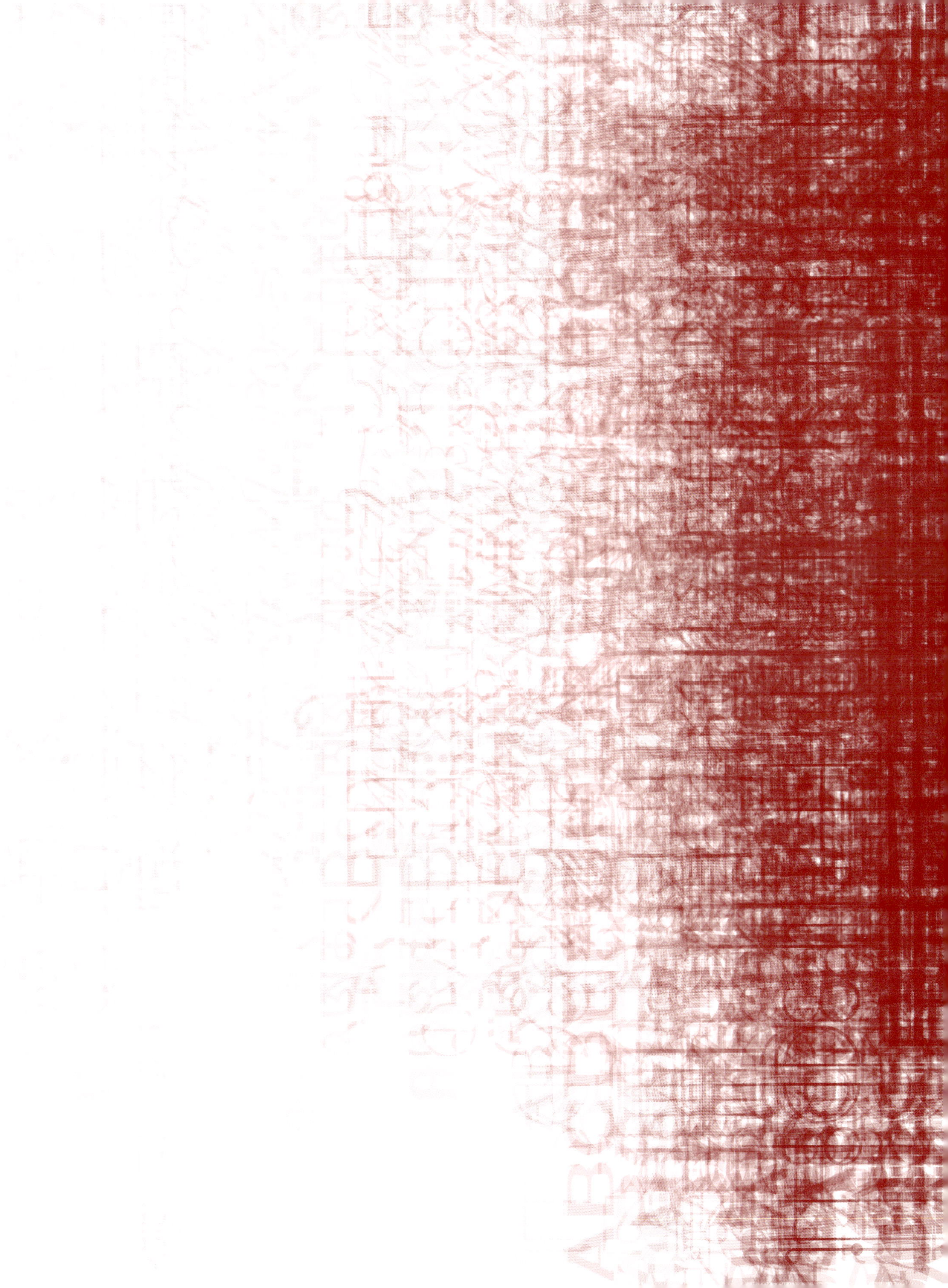

Natalia Schmidt

.On.Gregor.Schneider's.
......*Cube*.Project.....

"The most interesting characteristic of the cube is that it is relatively uninteresting. Compared to any other three-dimensional form, the cube lacks any aggressive force, implies no motion, and is least emotive. Therefore it is the best form to use as a basic unit for any more elaborate function, the grammatical device from which the work may proceed. Because it is standard and universally recognized, no intention is required of the viewer. It is immediately understood that the cube represents the cube, a geometric figure that is uncontestably itself. The use of the cube obviates the necessity of inventing another form and reserves its use for invention."

Sol LeWitt, "The Cube," 1966, in: Alicia Legg (ed.), *Sol LeWitt*, exhib. cat., Museum of Modern Art, New York, 1978, p. 172. Originally published in: "The Cube," in: *Art in America*, July–August 1966.

"At the Venice Biennale in the summer of 2005, the Piazza San Marco was to have been the site of an architectural colloquy between the Campanile, the Basilica, the Palazzo Ducale, the arcades, and a large black cube. [...] Measuring about thirty-nine by forty-six feet and sitting on a low pedestal, the cube was to be placed at the back of the trapezoid-shaped Piazza, slightly off-kilter, on the axis between the Basilica and the Campanile. The structure would have consisted of a free-standing scaffolding clad on all sides with a curtain of heavy black fabric. The association with the Kaaba, the holiest site in Islam, would have been as intentional and unmistakable as the radical contrast between the temporary construction and the walled shrine."

Parkett, 76, May 2006, pp. 6–9.

"'We find it a great shame; after all, we're dealing with a grandiose work that would have become an icon of sorts for this year's exhibition,' said Alessandra Santerini, Biennale spokesperson."

dpa, June 2005

"Until now, a consensus seems to have reigned in the West that the freedom of even highly provocative art is an expression of liberal societies. Yet, with the invigorated self-awareness of the Catholic Church, this consensus appears to be crumbling. The word is that other religions have maintained the perception that also art is not allowed to do everything. The decision by the most important art festival in the world to retreat from possible critique by Islamists offers new nourishment to this debate."

Die Welt, June 15, 2005

"Thinking through the Venetian decision logically would mean barring all art that can be thought of as even remotely connected with a religious system; indeed, to defeat it already before it emerges.

The history of aesthetic provocation in Europe during the past two hundred years would thereby have to be rewritten: as a single melange of Judeo-Christian sensibilities rather than as a fruitful quarrel over symbols and signs."

die tageszeitung, June 15, 2005

"The information that provocative art has treated Christian symbols in ironic and profane ways is also a play with fire. In contrast to pious Christians who, as a rule, do not reply violently to offense, diligent Muslims have increasingly turned to weapons; they have murdered extensively in Madrid and attempted to blow up the Strasbourg Christmas market, including the Cathedral. For that reason, it is not a sign of cowardice, but rather of a particular sense of responsibility when the Venetians refuse to host the jet-setting art elite and offer themselves and their city as a target to the terrorists."

Frankfurter Allgemeine Zeitung, June 16, 2005

"The fact that we have a worldwide system of electronic visualization, which is also employed in Islamic countries on a daily basis, is due to the willingness by Europeans since antiquity to develop a system of visual communication and art within the context of their Christian religion that was to constitute the basis of the free media world: That which began as pious depiction of the saints later became a sphere for the unfurling of artistic individuality and also blasphemy. [...] It is important to remember in this context when faithful Moslems complain or threaten to make a violent complaint, that the European art and media industries have annexed holy Islamic sanctuaries in exactly the same way as the artist Gregor Schneider sought to do with a replica of the Kaaba in Venice (where, by the way, the Saint Mark's Basilica plays with Islamic architectural details)."

Die Welt, June 17, 2005

"The debates raging in the conflict over the Muhammad caricatures have made clear that the political effects of indiscriminate or intentional provocation directed at the one or the other side place a lasting burden on the conciliation of cultures and religions. [...] The Italian government and Venetian officials had feared a denigration of Islam and its consequences – including problems with terrorism."

www.medienfabrik-b.de, last visited: June 23, 2009

"All prior considerations of this type and the preventive offsetting of a discursive risk are, in truth, alien to art. Art is beholden to the ruthless will of its visible realizations. Only its genuine presence, and this also applies to Conceptual art – the concept is a reality because it ratifies feasibility – provides information about what we are dealing with. All other considerations are extra-artistic, for example, political, sociological, or psychological."

The above quote was taken from the unpublished catalogue text by Eugen Blume, curator of
the Hamburger Bahnhof, who unsuccessfully campaigned for the realization of the Cube.

"With Cube Berlin 2006 we are now dealing with a monumental black cube, a classical case of product redeclaration [...] What evil demons commanded Schneider to realize the black box at any price, as if from a gift from a disliked aunt that has to be put somewhere, anywhere? Miniaturized, projected, depoliticized, transferred from the public realm into the museum, the cube would simply be complacent arts and crafts: another black square in front of the wall."

Frankfurter Allgemeine Zeitung, December 8, 2005

"The reluctance on the part of Berlin, on the contrary, appears far less understandable. Schneider is not the only one to wonder if fear of terrorism has influenced artistic freedom."

die tageszeitung, December 8, 2005

"General Director Peter-Klaus Schuster [General Director of the National Museums in Berlin and Director of the Neue Nationalgalerie in Berlin until the end of October 2008] has now informed him [Gregor Schneider] that St. Mark's Square, with its colonnades, is the only place suitable for presentation."

Der Tagesspiegel, December 8, 2005

"That which evoked 'political concern,' two rejections making major waves in the media, and a discussion about the freedom of art last year seems to have currently yielded to Hanseatic placidity. [...] The Hamburger Kunsthalle has now expressed interest."

Hamburger Abendblatt, March 8, 2006

"Muslims are perplexed – since when have the feelings of Muslims been considered ahead of time? Already back then, the Central Council of Muslims in Germany expressed their regrets about the prohibition, which they felt to be 'non-beneficial to the dialogue between Muslims and Christians.'"

www.islam.de/4873.php, March 9, 2006, last visited: November 26, 2008

"'The artwork is not meant as provocation, but rather, the opposite: A temporary monument of tolerance,' claimed new Kunsthalle Director [Kunsthalle Hamburg] Hubertus Gaßner."

Mittelbayerische Zeitung, March 10, 2006

"In the context of the Malevich exhibition, however, the Cube becomes historically infused and hubris. It magnifies the cult image of Suprematism once again, thereby equating belief in art and belief in God – which for many might seem like ridiculing religion. Naturally, art is allowed to do that, too. Only, perhaps a 'monument of tolerance' might look a bit different […] [Schneider] aims for postmodern apathy, he takes away meaning from the form, makes it arbitrary. And this arbitrariness is something that one can definitely condemn, in the Orient as well as in the Occident."

Die Zeit, March 16, 2006

"Art begins where violence ends."

Ahmet Yazici in: *Hamburger Abendblatt*, June 10, 2006

"I never said monument – but that is, once again, typical of the media, to make something sappy out of it. I said a sign of tolerance; that is more abstract, less emotionally charged. I never intended to admonish anyone. On the contrary, I think it's horrible when art admonishes; if it's good it doesn't do that."

Hubertus Gaßner in an interview with the author on June 27, 2006

"Part of the conflict of cultures is that there are extremely diverse views about the dignity of art or objects considered holy. We are inclined to celebrate the fact that this respect has disappeared in the Occident as one of the fruits of the Enlightenment. But that doesn't mean that we have a lease on a world scale. There are more than a billion people throughout the world for whom this object remains a highly unique secret whose answer is known by belief alone."

Der Tagesspiegel, March 7, 2007

"Muslim representatives continually emphasize that they have no objections to the Cube, as they did in early February at a panel discussion with the artist at the Kunsthalle. Ahmet Yazici, representative of the Alliance of Islamic Communities in Northern Germany, even said that Muslims could possibly feel 'truly understood and not merely flattered.' 'I have never heard Muslims say that they think the Cube is a bad thing.' Perhaps a lot of Muslims would even visit the exhibition, as quasi-preparation for pilgrimage to Mecca."

Focus, March 19, 2007

"The beholder, however, does not at all set off the anticipated explosive political effect. In the context of the Ungers Bau [Ungers building] and mainly through the context of the exhibition, the association steps clearly back behind the cool abstractness of the form."

Frankfurter Rundschau, March 23, 2007

"'Malevich himself wanted to build exactly this cube – for Lenin's grave, actually,' said Gaßner, the curator."

International Herald Tribune, April 16, 2007

"With his ideas [Gregor] Schneider […] has become a scandal artist of late. Already in 2005, when he wanted to erect his 'Black Cube' in the dimensions of the Kaaba from Mecca on St. Mark's Square in Venice, there were discussions that led to the banning of the work. In 2007, he showed it at the Hamburger Kunsthalle without protests or terror threats. The Cube was no more than an artwork. But ever since the announcement of his latest project [exhibiting a dying or recently deceased person] (which is in fact an old project planned back in 1996), the populace has been seething […]"

Die Welt online
www.welt.de/kultur/article1932938/Morddrohungen_inklusive.html,
April 24, 2008, last visited: November 30, 2010

The selected quotations offer insight into the ambivalent debate, ongoing since 2005, about Gregor Schneider's *Cube* project. As soon as the artwork was excluded from the 2005 Venice Biennale at the last minute, countless international newspaper articles and press releases dealing with this artwork appeared. The Italian press, however, failed to publish a single article about the work's exclusion from the Biennale.

Art is meant to be the *translation* of liberty. Nonetheless, for most people it is difficult to accept or even tolerate the fact that there are things in the world that defy definition. Except a very few areas – among them art and death – almost anything can be determined. Thus, behind the apparent boundlessness of artistic freedom, suspicions often arise as to the abuse of legally defined freedom.[1]

When a cube-shaped Apple Store was built in New York on 5th Avenue in 2006 – named "Apple Mecca" and was thus meant as a Kaaba quote (Kaaba: in Arabic cube) – the press and public barely took any notice. During construction, the store was initially covered in black and was later unveiled at the opening. The luminous company logo – a bitten apple – hangs isolated inside the glass construction. This staging could have just as easily been interpreted as a discrediting play on Islam as "the fall of mankind" (particularly since the interior of the Kaaba is entirely empty). But since art was not at issue, no offense was taken – apparently, commercial freedom knows no bounds.

What, then, does it mean to raise the question of the "freedom of art," or rather, to limit, doubt, and *translate* it, when it is itself difficult to define?

In contrast to the reaction to the Apple Store, the majority of the press was overly sensitive in reacting to the proposed *Cube*, whereby the basic tenor was to accuse the project of speculative provocation without taking into account the context in which it was created.

Gregor Schneider has always worked with spaces. In this connection, duplications, repetitions, and isolation of spaces play a central role and thus pose the question of the *de-finition* of space and identity. This issue is also at the heart of the *Cube* project: the work was already conceived in 2004 for repeated, temporary presentation at different public sites and meant to be modified according to each context.

"Originally, what interested him [Schneider] about the Kaaba was that it is the primal image of a house, and yet in the midst of hundreds of thousands of people encompasses an entirely unknown and isolated space."[2] In addition, this volume permits references to Judeo-Christian culture and also the art of Western modernity both in terms of form and meaning. To put it quite generally, the nature of a space, other than geometric-architecturally defined space, is, per se, generally questionable and questioning and thereby also always a question of Being (*Sein*), both in its

1   See: Klaus Staeck, "Kunst und Öffentlichkeit," in: Hans-Otto Mühleisen (ed.), *Grenzen politischer Kunst*, Schnell + Steiner, Munich, Zurich, p. 77.
2   No author, *Magazin für Kunst, Architektur, Design*, no. 11, March 2007, p. 3.

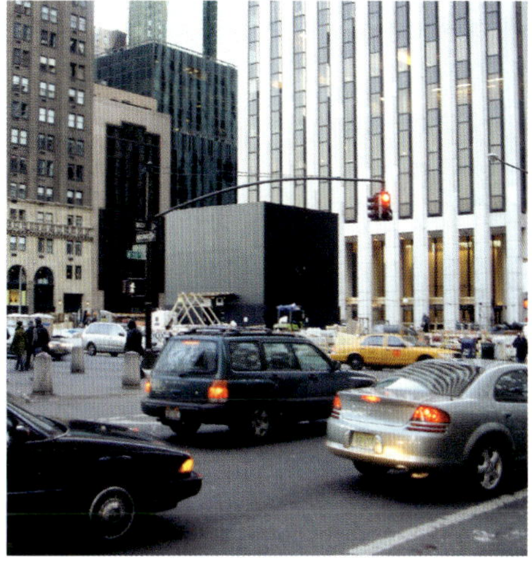
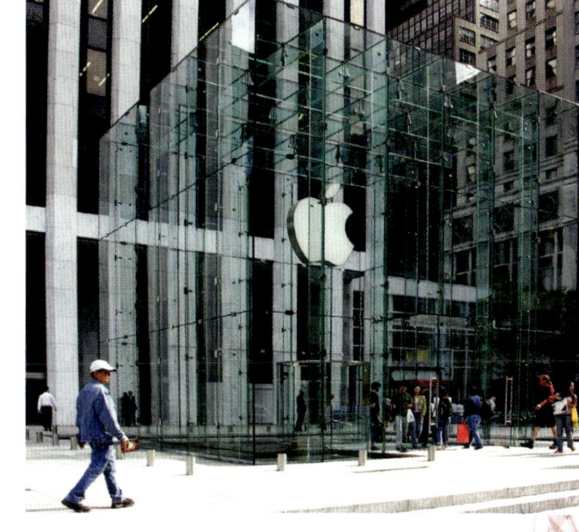

3 See: Jacques Derrida, *Aporien. Sterben – auf die "Grenzen der Wahrheit" gefaßt sein*, Fink, Munich, 1998, pp. 14ff.
4 See: Martin Buber, *I and Thou*, Charles Scribner's Sons, New York, 1958.
5 Quote from the unpublished catalogue text on *Cube Berlin 2006* by Eugen Blume.
6 See: Walter Benjamin, "Über Sprache überhaupt und über die Sprache des Menschen (1916/17)," in: idem, *Aura und Reflexion. Schriften zur Ästhetik und Kunstphilosophie*, Hartmut Böhme (ed.), Suhrkamp, Frankfurt am Main, 2007, pp. 95–110.

character (in terms of a definition of borders, etc.) as well as of who, where, how, and what is found inside and outside of it. Accordingly, truth would be a certain reference to the "space" it terminates or determines. Hence, freedom would be the *trans*-posing of this truth within these border(s).[3] Above all, the *Cube*, understood as a space of "thou," commensurate with Martin Buber's definition of the term in his book *I and Thou*[4], could have initiated a dialogue on the concept of "in-between" inherent to his "dialogical principle", which in turn would have resulted from the complexity of the similarity between the *Cube* and the Kaaba. Thus, it could have at least opened a discursive field between Islam and the West as well as in the field of contemporary art – especially in the context of an event such as the Venice Biennal. Instead, the proposal – in Venice in 2005 and in Berlin in 2006, as well as in any of the other sites at which the *Cube*'s installation was prevented – set off an unprecedented media debate that transformed the "in-between" to a discrepancy between original intentions, preventive rejection, and public perception.

One year later, a realization of the *Cube* in front of the Hamburger Bahnhof in Berlin and at other sites of the city, such as inside the Neue Nationalgalerie, was prevented just as it was in the Venetian context, since this context was negatively charged psychologically and politically and dominated the

unencumbered assertion of this sculpture in a place clearly defined as being one of art. This inscribed narrative was, and has since remained, inseparable from the object: "In the digital simulation, the black facade of the sculpture cuts a huge black square in the faux-castle facade of early capitalist industrial architecture: A daunting enlargement of that quintessential icon of modernity, which, by way of a radical reduction, claimed a metaphysical dimension of art beyond all confessions. Having long since become a metaphor of free, self-affirmative form due to its free, open structure, it exposes itself to the risk of not being perceived as art. This provocation is also the popular, shared property of art calendars and coffee table books. What would now cause someone to interpret Gregor Schneider's sculpture in the same way as it was in St. Mark's Square in Venice? Would it be naive to assume that from now on the issue centers on a work that allows for all associations, also that of being an abstract sculpture, originally resulting from work with the Kaaba, but departing from the latter in the genesis of its realization as a much too narrow reference?"[5]

Thus, the question of the media aspect itself arises, both in terms of the site at which this idea is communicated, and what is disclosed by "the immediacy of all intellectual communication,"[6] in this case, the journalistic debate.

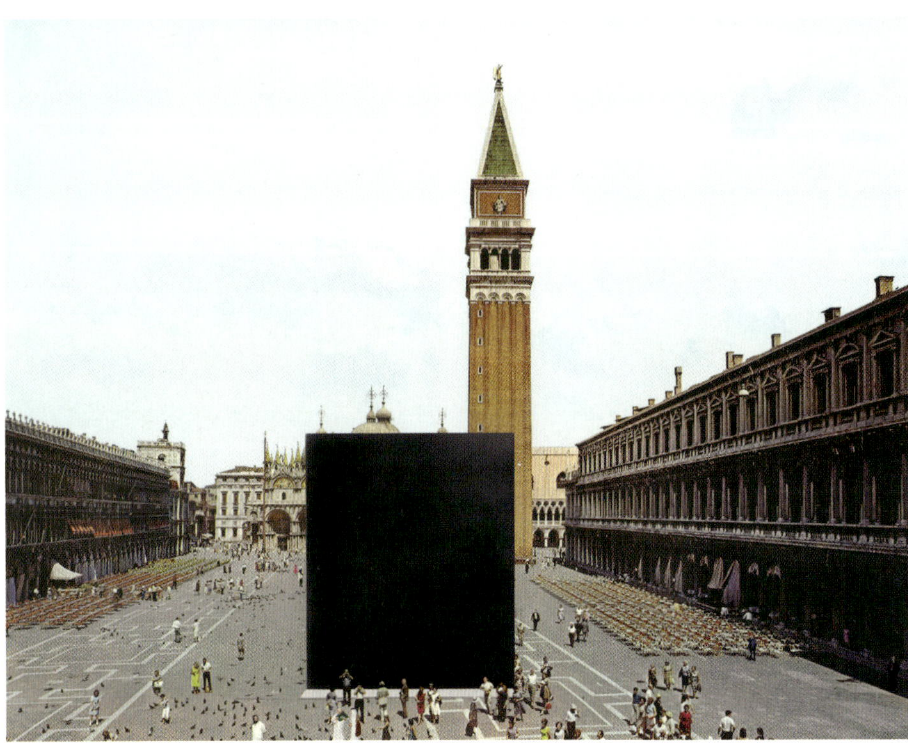

< *Cube Venice*, 2005, visualization for the intended presentation at the St. Mark's Square in Venice on the occasion of the Venice Biennal

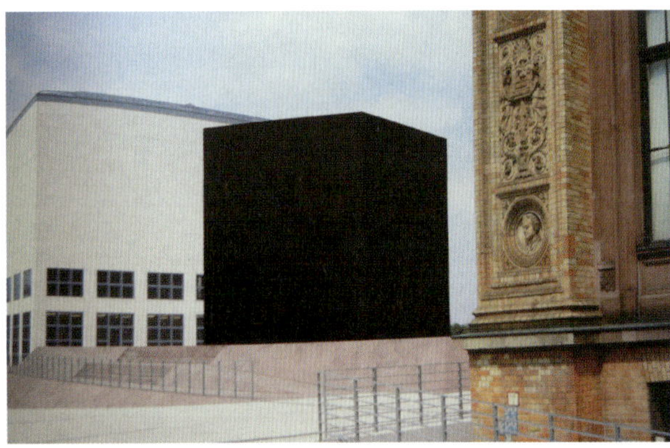

v *Cube Hamburg*, 2006, realized on the occasion of the exhibition *Das schwarze Quadrat. Hommage an Malewitsch*, Hamburger Kunsthalle, 2007, visualization of the *Cube* in front of Hamburger Kunsthalle facing the Galerie der Gegenwart

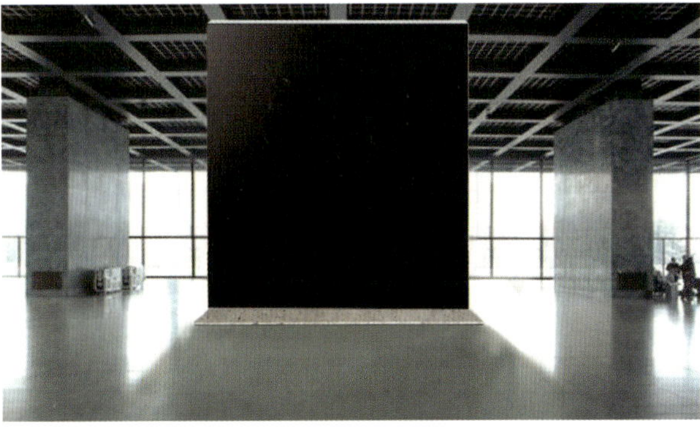

v v *Cube Berlin*, 2006, visualization for the intended presentation at Neue Nationalgalerie, Berlin

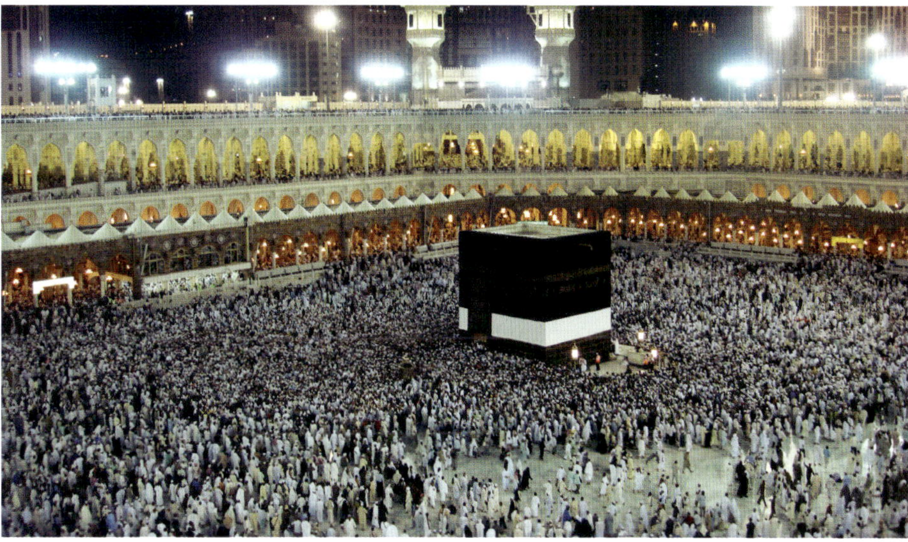

7 Silvia Naef contradicts the picture mainly constructed of fundamental Muslims in the media of "a basically iconoclastic Islam" in her book *Bilder und Bilderverbot im Islam*. She concludes that there is no general prohibition of images in Islam, mainly in the secular space. Silvia Naef, *Bilder und Bilderverbot im Islam. Vom Koran bis zum Karikaturenstreit*, Beck, Munich, 2007, p. 7.

8 For both the realization in Venice as well as in Berlin, Schneider suggested alternatives, less exposed sites and variants of the sculpture (Venice: smaller cube on a float, Berlin: Cube in the Nationalgalerie).

9 Under the Berlusconi government, Gregor Schneider was d enied even a presentation of his ideas in the catalogue in the context of the Biennal 2005, after they were not realized. The curators were powerless« against political censorship.

10 Gregor Schneider on 3sat, "Kulturzeit," October 26, 2006, available online at: http://de.youtube.com/watch?v=IClcwn5rmvM, June 24, 2009.

11 Quote from the unpublished catalogue text on *Cube Berlin 2006* by Eugen Blume.

12 The *Cube* was realized in the context of the exhibition *Das schwarze Quadrat. Hommage an Malewitsch*, Hamburger Kunsthalle, 2007.

It is a rather remarkable fact that this debate about an unrealized artwork went on for two years, even before the work was allowed to assert itself aesthetically, and that it was subjected to a different discursive potential other than its own: Not that artworks causing furor is anything new, especially when sighted by today's religiously charged political realm, or when they take up a position in public space. The exposed realization of the *Cube* on St. Mark's Square in Venice was also central to triggering a discussion in the media, as was its intention – the concept was laid out for that. Yet, what is explosive about the *Cube* is that it provoked a debate without having been realized. What this debate revealed, above all, were the reigning misconceptions about the Islamic prohibition of images relating to the replication of what is, after all, Islam's central sacred site. That very false "image"[7] could have been revised to a certain degree through a realization,[8] or at least a differentiated discussion of the *Cube*. Instead, the project – whether due to ignorance or political calculation – was politically instrumentalized[9] and abused, fostering prejudices and thereby erecting a frontline between cultures, in a war that – not only since 2001 – has mainly been fought via symbolic acts, although in their original "roots, desires, wishes,"[10] and fears they are actually quite similar.

"To speculatively recall a Kaaba, which most people never saw in its original form, only resulted from a journalistic idea of an artwork. It is simply the newspaper that wafted wind of the building from Venice here beforehand, something which had little if anything to do with its reality. And even if it is admissible, and it is admissible, to know of Schneider's confrontation with the Kaaba, that does not alter the integrity of his work. In this line, it remains a sign of respect; a form developed out of deep veneration for a significant sacred building and its mysteries which, with its great abstraction, should one want to become involved in the political aspect of this possible reception, struggles for nothing other than freedom."[11]

Until the realization of the *Cube* in 2007 in Hamburg,[12] where the museum carried out the necessary mediation to the press and the Muslim community in advance, there was very little interest in the Islamic perspective on the project as a whole. Instead, false assumptions and claims with regard to the prohibition of replicating the Kaaba were maintained, thereby stirring up fears. The press reports only rarely mentioned Gregor Schneider's assistant, a faithful Moslem, who developed the idea together with the artist, or Nadeem Elyas, the former Chairman of the Central Council of Muslims in Germany,

13 See: Silvia Naef, 2007, p. 17, pp. 131–137.

14 Ralf Elger (ed.), *Kleines Islam-Lexikon. Geschichte, Alltag, Kultur*, Beck, Munich, 2008, p. 163.

15 "'It is not forbidden to depict the Kaaba, there are depictions enough,' as former Chairman of the Central Council of Moslems, Nadeem Elyas, emphasized already in 2005." No author, "Umstrittener Kubus errichtet," in: *Hamburger Abendblatt*, March 19, 2007.

16 Quote from the unpublished catalogue text on *Cube Berlin 2006* by Eugen Blume.

17 Ibid.

18 See: Rita Bischof, "Der Raum, die Malerei und der Tod. Skizze zu einer Geschichtsphilosophie der Moderne in der bildenden Kunst," in: Hans Matthäus Bachmayer, Otto van de Loo and Florian Rötzer (eds.), *Bildwelten – Denkbilder*, Boer, Munich, 1986.

19 Georges Didi-Huberman, *Ce que nous voyons, ce qui nous regarde*, Editions de Minuit, Paris, 1992.

20 The Kaaba was already a cult site in pre-Islamic times. It is said that Adam, the first of the prophets, built the Kaaba. After the destruction of the Kaaba, Abraham is meant to have rebuilt it together with his son Ismael – likewise in pre-Islamic times. References to all three monotheistic religions in which Abraham played a central role are thereby possible. Formally, references to non-Islamic architectural formal languages were also possible. See: Elger (ed.), 2008, p. 163. See: Friedhelm Mennekes, "The Ka'aba and St. Peter's Square: Perspectives of Sacred Space," in: Gregeor Schneider (ed.), *Cubes: Art in the Age of Global Terrorism*, Charta, Milan, 2006, pp. 51–63.

21 John Stuart Mill, *On Liberty*, 1860, available online at: www.constitution.org/jsm/liberty.htm, June 24, 2009.

22 In several press articles the debates and the discussions about the non-realized *Cube* were interpreted as the actual artwork.

although possible risks were discussed with him in advance. In the Islamic world it is not forbidden to reproduce or replicate the Kaaba, since it has its genius loci in Mecca and Islam knows no idolatry, it is therefore not a revered object. The "prohibition of images" in Islam aims primarily at figurative depictions and their cult worship, whereby key in the prohibition of an image is mainly the moral context that an image represents or in which it appears.[13] According to Islam, any possible architectural similarities or references of the *Cube* at St. Mark's Square to the Kaaba in Haram as-Sharif would not have caused a negative shift in meaning or present a slur since the Kaaba is unique in being "the first house of God on Earth"[14] and since in its function – it prescribes the direction of prayers – as well as its construction, the Kaaba differs from the temporary construction of the *Cube*.[15] For these reasons alone, a "profanation on Christian soil" through a purely visually similar sculpture as was feared in several newspaper articles, would not even be possible.

"It is entirely senseless to assume that Gregor Schneider could possibly produce a close relationship to the Kaaba such that it would quasi hijack the Muslims and attempt to desecrate them on Western soil. His sculpture is nothing more – and art history alone decides on its quality – than a contemporary artwork by a Western artist. The beholder is at the mercy of a concrete energy field, which results simply from the power of the constructed design and its arrangement in the surrounding space."[16]

Numerous photos of the Kaaba circulate on the Internet – professional and amateur ones (many of them with a mobile phone) taken for the most part during a pilgrim's hajj. Ranging from the religious-ecstatic, the reverent, tourist, and simply inquisitive through to commercial "views" of the Kaaba – some with descriptive commentaries in English and put on "international" websites by Muslims (not only on Arabic or Islamic ones) –, these circulating images turn the Kaaba into a *secularized* body, which means it becomes public and therefore "accessible as 'material' in a total cultural context."[17] Even the sacred, mystified interior of the Kaaba, accessible to a privileged class only, is no longer a secret: due to the Internet's powers of distribution, it is visible to all – even though entrance to the mosque is permitted exclusively to Muslims.

The criticism, in part erroneous, primarily established a weakness which could actually be a target for terrorist attacks insofar as it made an admission of this threat legible as self-censure: In this way, the *Cube* and the Kaaba were stylized as a phantom of Islamic threat.

Decisive is the fact that the *Cube* presents a political, argumentatively charged volume through the media debates that preceded it, which means that it can never be an impartial sculpture again. Instead, it becomes a mirror image of an inner social reality that no longer seems to know an exterior. It becomes an eye that sees itself when looking,[18] but cannot intervene; disclosing the "losing gaze," as Georges Didi-Huberman refers to it in his book *Ce que nous voyons, ce qui nous regarde* [What We See, What Looks at Us][19] – the inability to recognize something familiar – a quote such as that "non-aggressive" cube proclaimed by Sol LeWitt, which speaks of a time when art could still appeal to a "might be," to a different perspective of reality as the offered or actual one, and demand a discourse. And it also shows the inability to find in the "foreign" something that is actually not so foreign to us.[20]

In his essay *On Liberty* (1859), John Stuart Mill analyzes freedom of public opinion and discussion: "The fact […] is, that not only the grounds of the opinion are forgotten in the absence of discussion, but too often the meaning of the opinion itself."[21] Accordingly, the press and mass media are, based on their nature, not discursive sites. Thus, the discussion about the *Cube* is not the artwork,[22] as it has been denied the site in which discourse might once have been possible.

The idea behind the White Cube was this aporetic site harboring within that particular narrative which cannot be put in words, since it constantly reformulates itself and

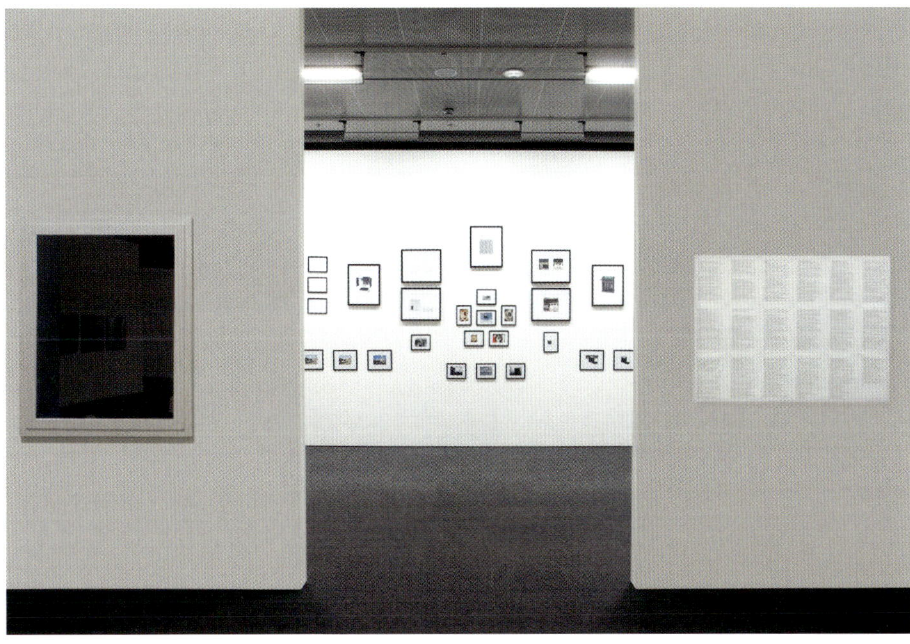

23 Neither in Venice nor in Berlin were alternatives accepted that would have depicted the work in a changed size, color, or site. A black cube draped in white and a cube built inside the museum were rejected. "I would have built the *Cube* in the way that is currently possible as this form would document our situation." Gregor Schneider, 3sat, "Kulturzeit," March 3, 2006.

24 Meant are the political and the cultural policy level.

25 *Cur:* why, wherefore, in: *Latin Dictionary*, available online at: www.math.ubc.ca/~cass/frivs/latin/latin-dict-full.html#C, June 24, 2009.

26 *Cura:* management, administration, care, concern, charge, in: *Latin Dictionary*, available online at: www.math.ubc.ca/~cass/frivs/latin/latin-dict-full.html#C, June 24, 2009.

27 "Curare: Etymology: Portuguese & Spanish *curare*, from Carib *kurari* "[…] any of certain complex arrow poisons of South American Indians that have a paralytic action." In: *Merriam-Webster unabridged*, available online at: http://unabridged.merriam-webster.com/cgi-bin/unabridged?va=curare&x=0&y=0, January 20, 2009.

the space. As an intellectual reference point, as a *discursive zone*, it was constitutive as a condition precisely for Conceptual art, such as that of the 1960s and 1970s, although this art to some extent departed from the institution in order to carry out the very discourse required by Conceptual art.

Yet, in the case of the "Black Cube," it seems that the condition as a condition has changed. The fact that the *Cube* could not be discussed, not even in the museums, which claim to be the "keepers" of the contemporary,[23] ends in a divergent concept of the curatorial. It appears that several levels which contradict one another are blending here, such that the "borders" seem to become or to be permeable.

By definition, the task of curatorial positions is to preserve certain truths and values, such as liberty. Such truths and values are difficult to define and can be translated differently according to the context. One might believe that in terms of the preservation of curatorial interests, the most emotional level is the "irrational," religious one, which might possibly feel undercut in its freedom if its "feelings" are not respected. But it is precisely this level that proves to be the least emotional

in the entire debate. Instead, the political decisions appeared to be the most emotionally disturbed ones. How else can one explain the overlapping of the other two curatorial levels,[24] which on the one hand attempted to defend a/their territory, and on the other occupied their territory? How is it that this occupying "care" [*Sorge*] blocked a field of differentiated opinion, while at the same time, through curatorial negligence, endured the design and mobilization of false ideas?

The discussions surrounding the *Cube* exposed the "non-ideological field" of art as porous in that a real occupation of political guardianship became blatant, so that it was no longer possible to pose the question of the "*Cur*"[25] – the why and wherefore – when it is relevant, "now." Hence, this project has above all become a touchstone of "curatorial freedom." Precisely by virtue of the question of artistic freedom, which turns against all legal stipulations and dogma, this project identifies above all society's inhibition. The idea of the *curare* (having concern, caring for)[26] of the highest values thus moves rather into the phonetic vicinity of the *Curare*, an arrow poison existentially paralyzing for body and language: "Those who are hit, fall." [27]

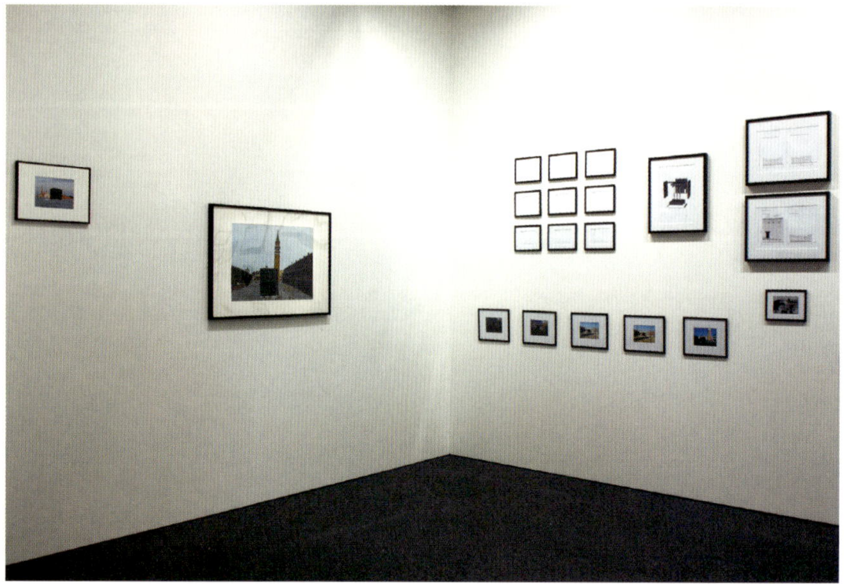

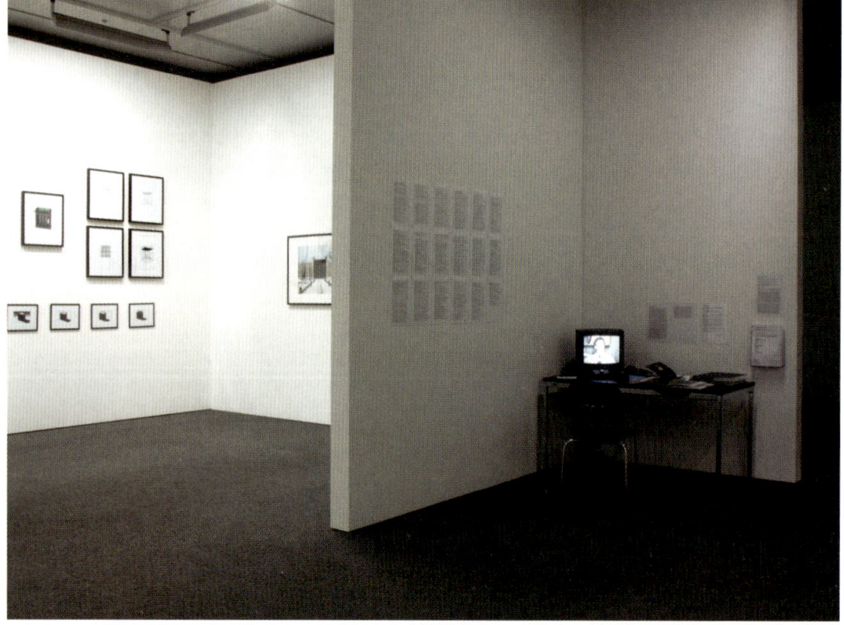

Gregor Schneider has always worked with spaces. He became known above all through his labyrinthine-hermetic *Haus u r*, which has been in permanent adaptation since 1985. Engaging with space stands in the center of Schneider's *Cube* project. Originally, he was interested in the way the Kaaba (in Arabic: cube), the central sanctuary of Islam, represents the prototype of a house and yet encloses a completely isolated space amidst hundreds of thousands of people. Moreover, it refers to all three monotheistic religions, as well as Western modernity. In 2005, the *Cube Venice* was supposed to be shown in the context of the Venice Biennale. Yet, due to political censorship – even though there is no ban of picturing the Kaaba in Islam – the work was not exhibited. Instead, it circulated in the media as a phantom of the Islamist threat. It was not until 2007 that the *Cube* could be realized in Hamburg and demonstrate its peaceful potential for dialogue.

Cube Documentation
2005–2008

Gregor Schneider,
*1969 in Rheydt, Germany,
lives and works in Rheydt

Natalia Schmidt (curatorial
concept), *1981 in Munich, lives
and works in Berlin and Karlsruhe

Selected documentary materials
(photographs, drawings, video)

Michèle & Mischa Kuball
Black Cube / Apple NYC, 2006,
3 photographs

Klaus Biesenbach
Cube, 59th Street, New York, 2006,
1 photograph

Natalia Schmidt, Boris Burghardt,
and David Howoldt
Cube Collage, 2006, video, color,
sound, 23 min, loop, installation
views ZKM | Karlsruhe, 2009

Further research material
(photographs, press articles,
video), essays from Jimena
Blázquez Abascal, Eugen Blume,
Yaşar Erdoğan, Angela Vettese,
and others

IRWIN
founded in 1983
Dušan Mandić, *1954
Miran Mohar, *1958
Andrej Savski, *1961
Roman Uranjek, *1961
Borut Vogelnik, *1959

Corpse of Art, 2003–2004,
mixed-media installation, wood,
textile, wax, hair, vase, flowers,
installation view ZKM | Karlsruhe,
2009

The Slovenian artists' collective
IRWIN has frequently reflected
the symbolism and the aesthetics
of East and West European avant-
gardes. Their installation *Corpse
of Art* copies the circumstances
of the laying out of Kazimir
Malevich's corpse in his Leningrad
flat in May 1935 by displaying it in
the Suprematist coffin designed
by his student, Nikolai Suetin,
according to Malevich's own
concept. IRWIN shows the *Black
Square* alone above the coffin –
and leaves out the two realistic
images from Malevich's work,
which flanked the Suprematist
icon in the original arrangement.
In this way, IRWIN simultaneously
radicalizes and undermines
Malevich's totalitarian claim to
mould not only his whole life but
also his own death. As a symbol
of the failure of Malevich's utopias
of Suprematism, IRWIN has erected a memorial to them, making
Malevich's displayed corpse into
the medium of his universal ideas
beyond his own death.

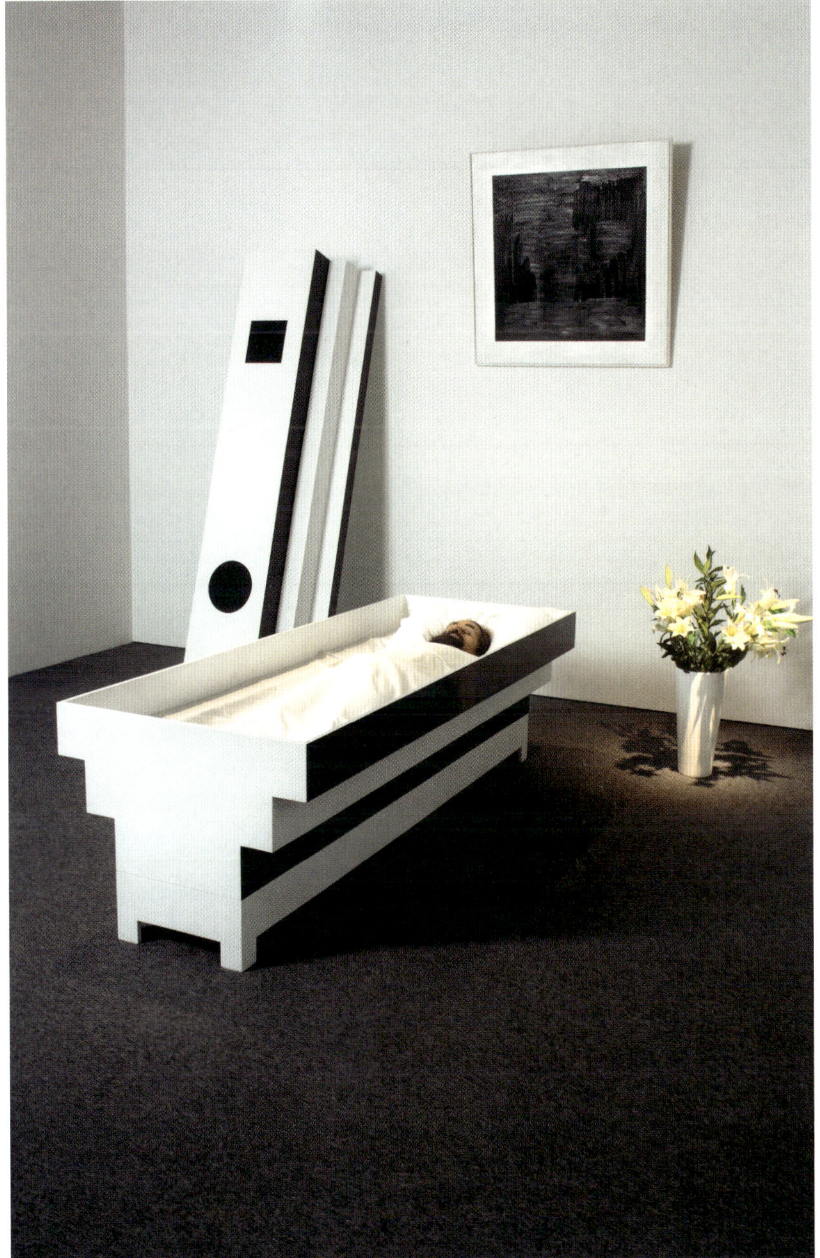

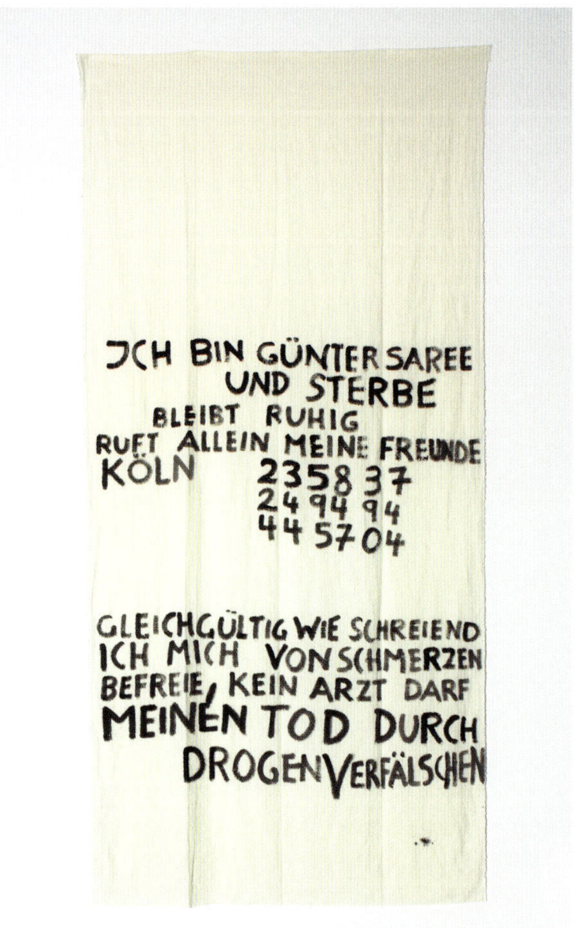

The works of the artist Günter Saree are heavily influenced by performance and Conceptual art; characterized by linguistic structures and immateriality, they were often executed in public spaces. Within the context of one of his later works, the *Projekt zur Verkürzung der bewussten Lebenszeit* [Project for Shortening the Conscious Time of Life], conceived for the documenta 5 in 1972, it was intended that visitors are able to undergo a brief narcosis with the help of an anesthetist. Forms they had to fill in beforehand informed them about the usual mortality rate (1:6000) of such a narcosis and contained questions regarding their preferences as to a funeral, should the need arise. A certificate subsequently presented to them was supposed to attest to the gap in their consciousness. However, the event was prevented through intervention by the Hessian Medical Association. If, in this happening, Saree introduced the taboo subject of death into the context of art rather casually, he took a far more extreme step in the following year. Meanwhile, incurably ill with cancer himself, he now made his own dying and death into a subject of his work for public consideration. Up until just before his death in May 1973, he went to exhibition openings – mostly equipped with a tape recorder – where he involved the people present in conversations on death and how they imagined it. As artifacts, various audio documents, as well as photographs and signed X-ray images of his cancer-stricken body testify to the way he himself dealt with his sickness. To make certain that he would be able to experience his death as he wished and "genuinely," from March 1973 onwards he carried with him a shroud he had designed, intending to put it on, even if he should collapse: "I AM GÜNTER SAREE AND I AM DYING. REMAIN CALM. CALL ONLY MY FRIENDS. COLOGNE 235837/249494/ 445704. REGARDLESS OF HOW MUCH I MAY SCREAM TO RELIEVE MY PAIN, NO DOCTOR MAY FALSIFY MY DEATH WITH ANY DRUGS." In his final actions, Saree variously challenged the taboo surrounding dying and death. They testify to the desperation of a man terminally ill and to his wish not to depart unnoticed. Thus, they also anticipate today's discussions on determining our own dying. Above all, Saree treated the issue of how art treats death with arguable consistency (and not just representationally), irrevocably erasing the boundaries between dying and performance, between life and art, and so already anticipated the debate on Gregor Schneider's room for a dying person.

Günter Saree
*1940 in Cheb,
today Czech Republic,
†1973 in Cologne, Germany

Sterbetuch, 1973,
(reconstruction 2008),
installation view
ZKM | Karlsruhe, 2009

Documentation material,
1972–1973

Schlingensief

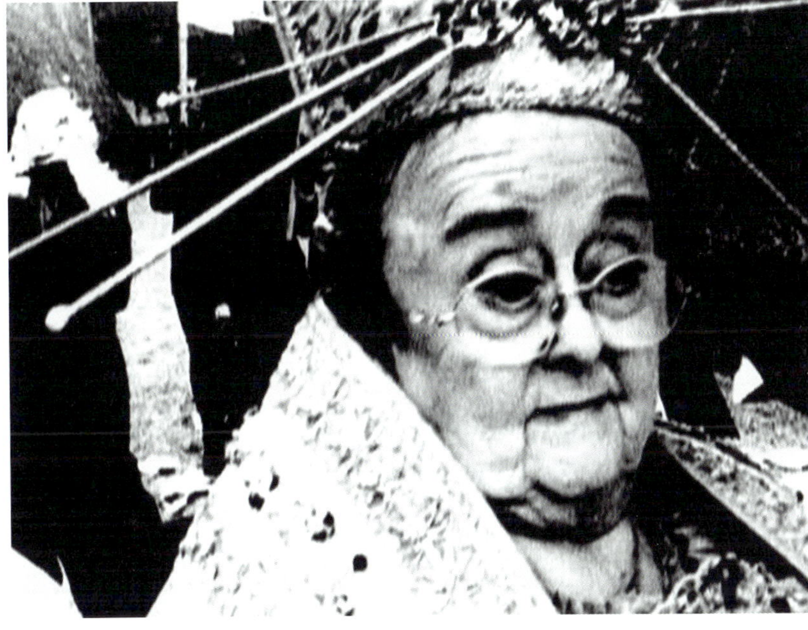

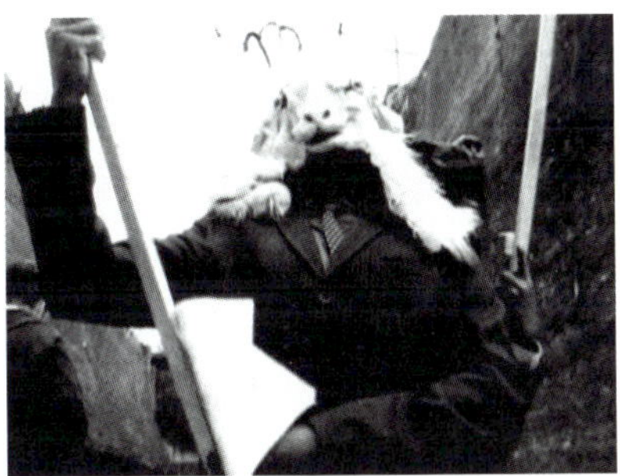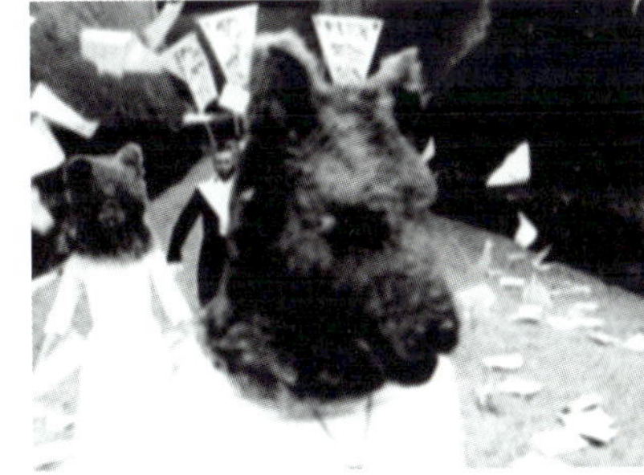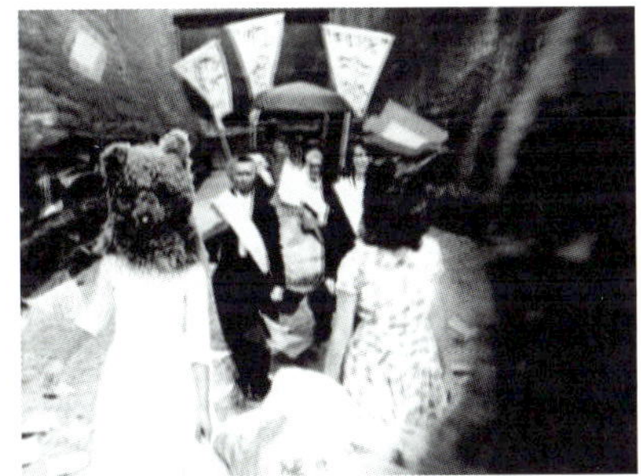

Christoph Schlingensief
*1960 in Oberhausen, Germany,
† 2010 in Berlin

Drei Sonnen / Prozession, 2008,
16 mm film, digitized, b/w,
sound, 4 min, loop, stills from
a digital copy

Prophecy, transience, and religiosity are the basic themes at the core of the work *Der König wohnt in Mir* [The King Lives in Me] by the performance artist and director Christoph Schlingensief. On a stage of rough boards, he interweaved the filmic and photographic impressions of a journey to Nepal with the everyday course of a (Western-socialized) sick person's sufferings and led the observer through a sequence of rooms furnished with medical stage props. Beginning in the waiting room, we pass through the consulting room, an operating theater, and a recovery room as far as the place of leave-taking. Alongside photographs, each of the rooms receives one of the six external video fireplaces, which show pictures of monks, sacrificial ceremonies of a brickworks, and a hospice in India. Schlingensief staged himself in them as a distanced traveler – which he did not remain for long, however only a short time after his return, he was diagnosed with a life-threatening illness. In a sense of foreboding, the previously created progression already ended in a Beuys room (or also: a diagnostic room), which relates to the latter's installation *Zeige deine Wunde* [Show Your Wound] from the 1970s: this also took as its theme illness and transience and is simultaneously an avowal and appeal, as according to Joseph Beuys, we "have to manifest the illness, we want to cure." The video installation is further supplemented by a film piece produced as part of the Duisburg RuhrTriennale 2008: *Drei Sonnen / Prozession* [Three Suns / Procession] forms that part of the play *Eine Kirche der Angst vor dem Fremden in mir* [A Church of Fear of the Strange Inside of Me], which centers on Schlingensief's personal experience with illness. He made use of the powerfully contrasting black-and-white pictures from the procession of a Catholic mass, to which were added some passages drawn from the text he recorded on cassette during the initial acute phases of his illness. The work, thus produced, bears testimony to the intimate, oppressive nature of Schlingensief's offensive and public confrontation with his own illness and the fear of death.

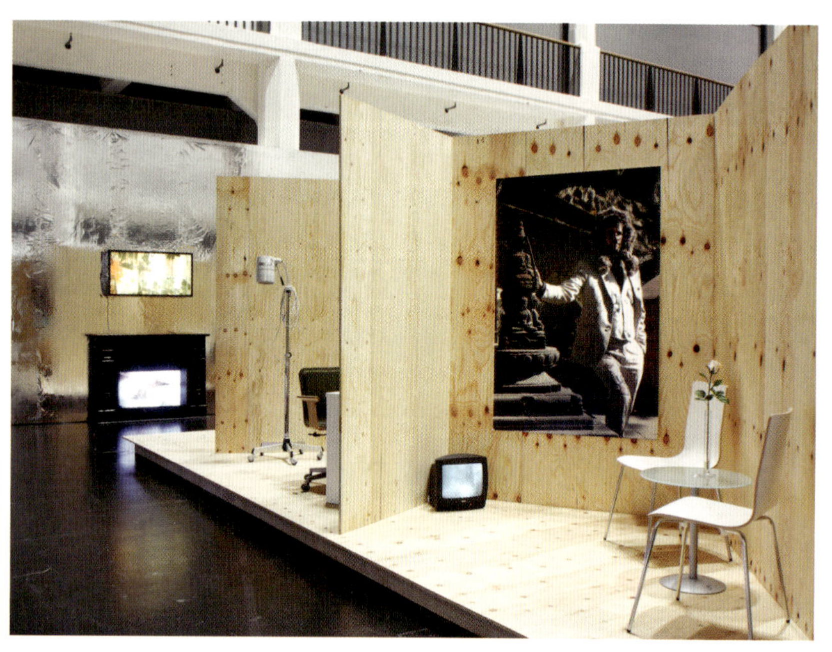

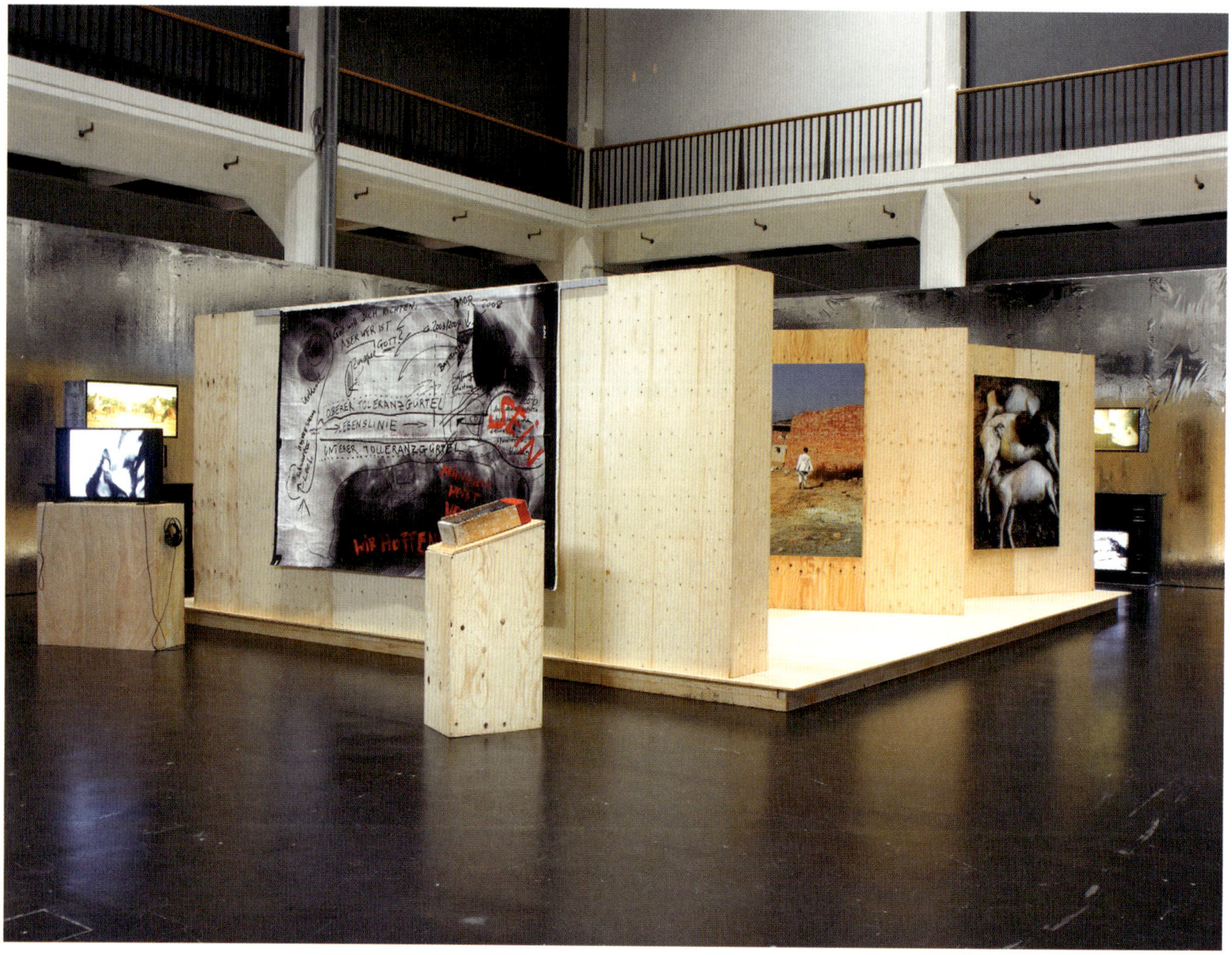

Gott will dich richten.
ABER WER IST GOTT?
OBERER TOLERANZGÜRTEL
LEBENSLINIE →
UNTERER TOLERANZGÜRTEL
SEIN
WIR HOFFEN

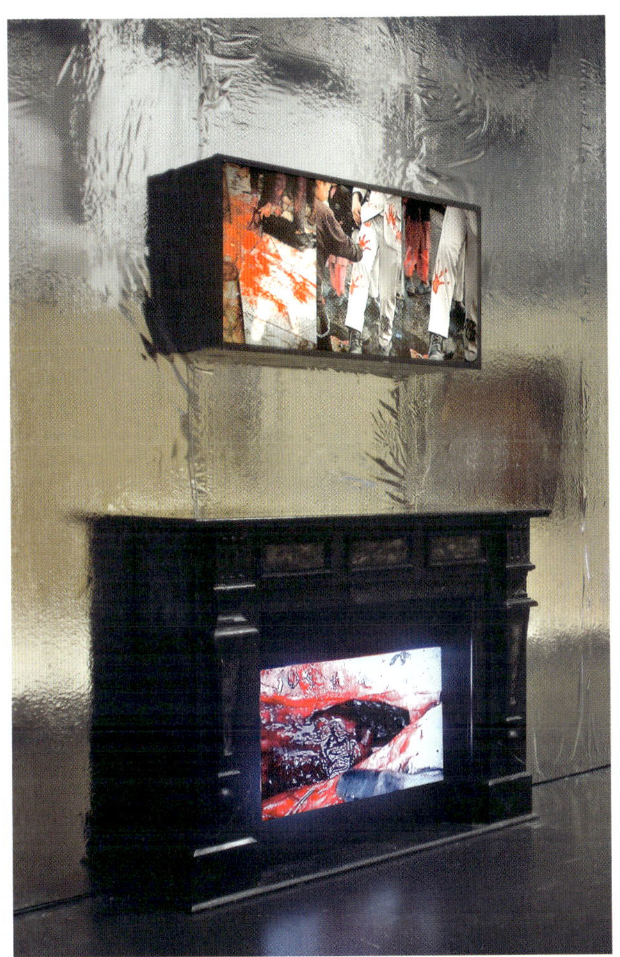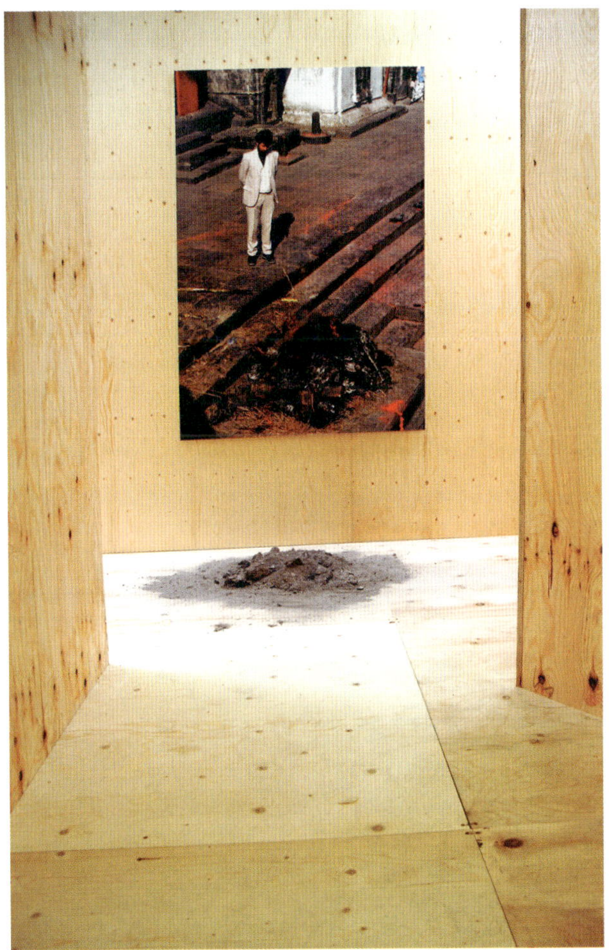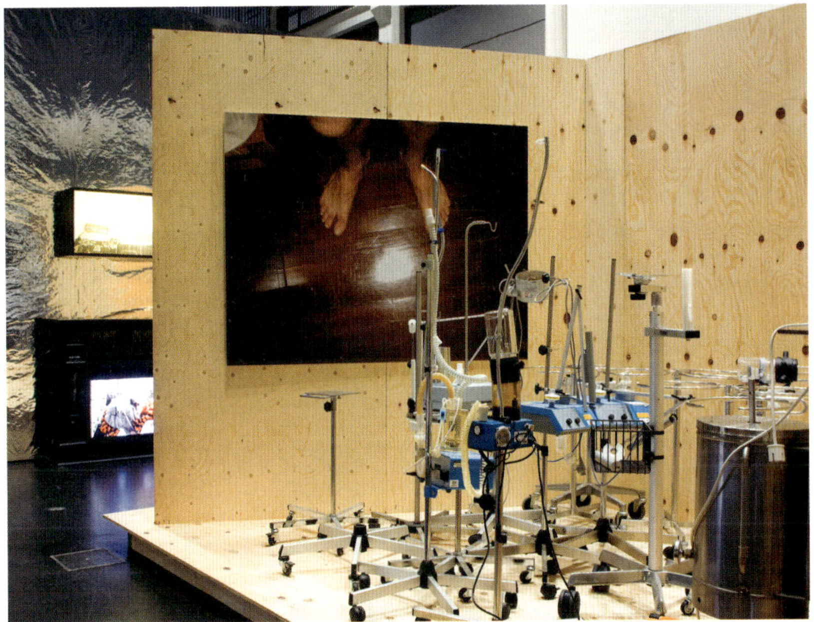

Christoph Schlingensief

Der König wohnt in Mir, 2008,
mixed-media installation,
dimensions variable,
installation views ZKM | Karlsruhe,
2009

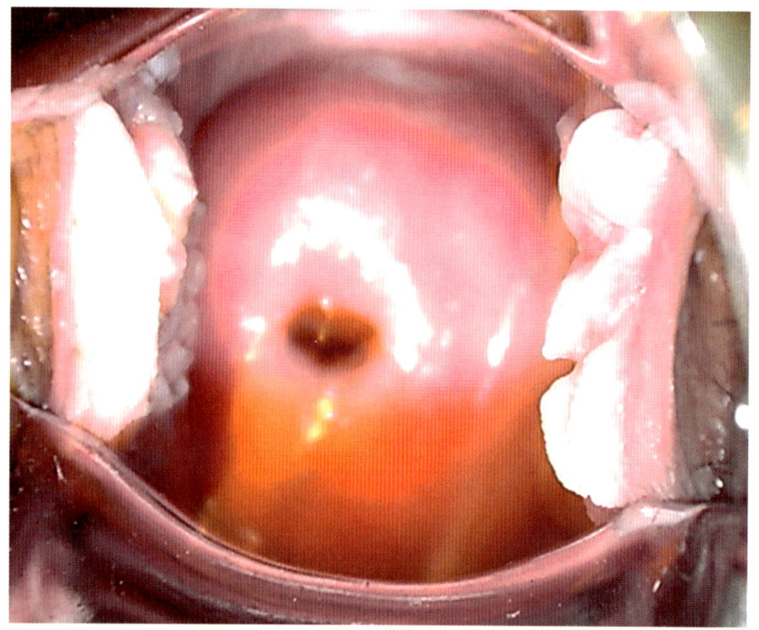

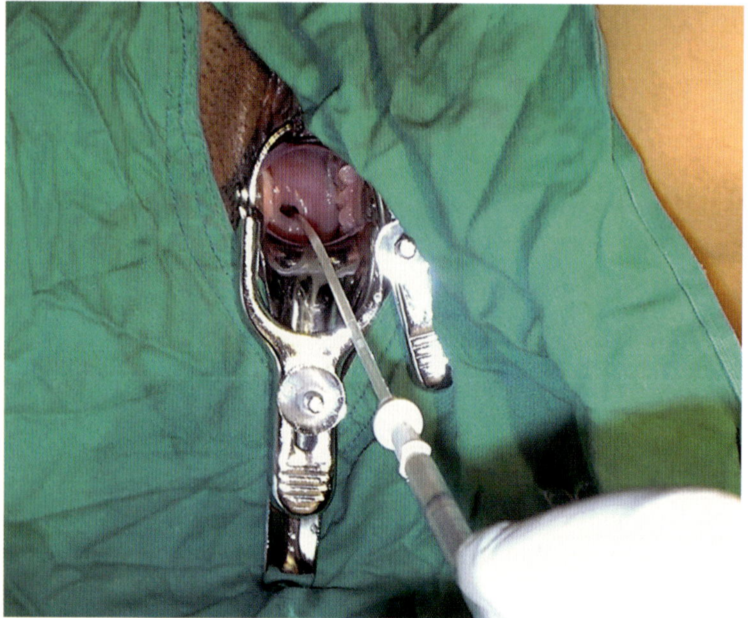

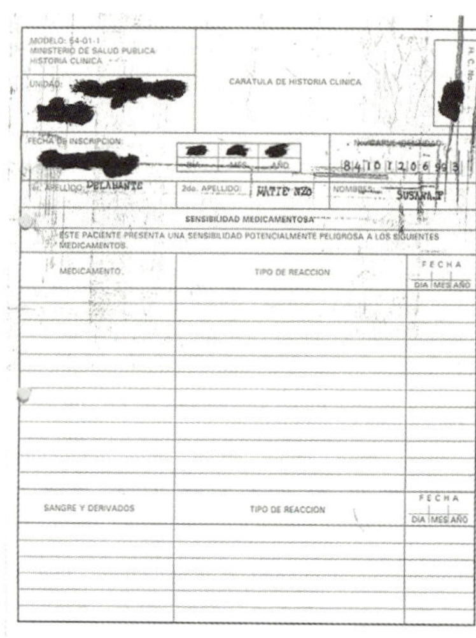

**Susana Pilar
Delahante Matienzo**
*1984 in Havana, Cuba,
lives and works in Havana

*El Escandalo de lo Real /
The Scandal of the Real*,
2006–2007,
heterologous artificial insemination, 2 photographs, inkjet print,
2 copies of medical documents

In a self-experiment, the artist had herself inseminated with a dead man's semen. Seventy-two hours after death had occurred, the semen was still fertile, as was confirmed by the medical report on her pregnancy. Today's biotechnology makes possible the artificial manipulation and the designing of every single moment in life – from insemination until the moment of death – and casts doubt on the nature of life as a given and natural destiny. Susana Pilar Delahante Matienzo's experiment demonstrates once more that where life begins, where it ends, and where the boundaries run between art, technology, and nature, is no clear-cut matter

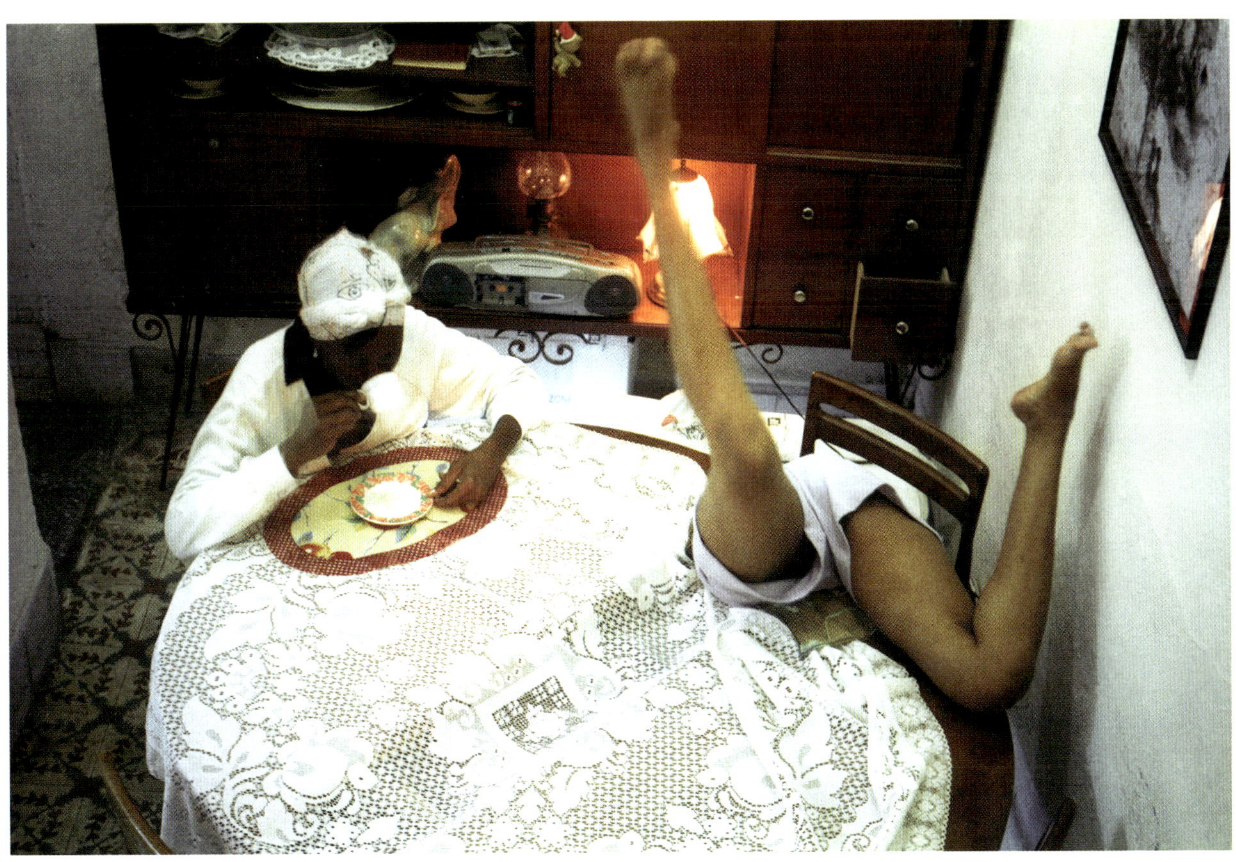

**Susana Pilar
Delahante Matienzo**

*Anexión oculta /
Hidden Annexation*, 2008,
6 photographs, inkjet print,
70 × 100 cm each

The inseparable unity of life and death is the central theme in Susana Pilar Delahante Matienzo's artistic oeuvre. If life is regarded, at the same time, as a slow process of dying, then whether something appears dead or alive becomes a question of viewpoint. In what she stages in her series of photographs *Anexión oculta / Hidden Annexation*, the artist symbolizes this connection and demonstrates in absurd situations how a constant presence of death can look and be arranged in harmony with everyday life.

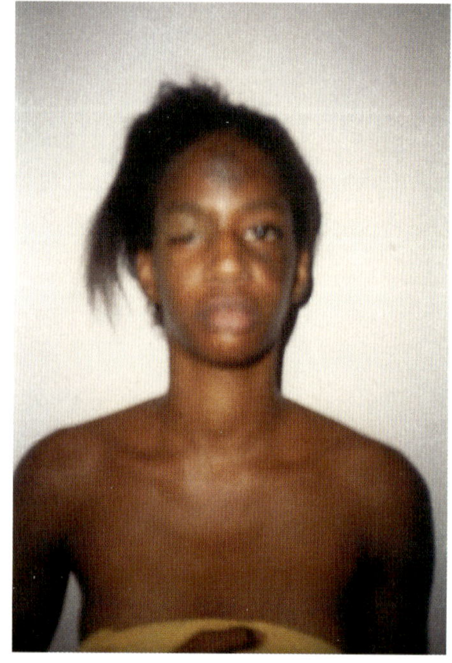 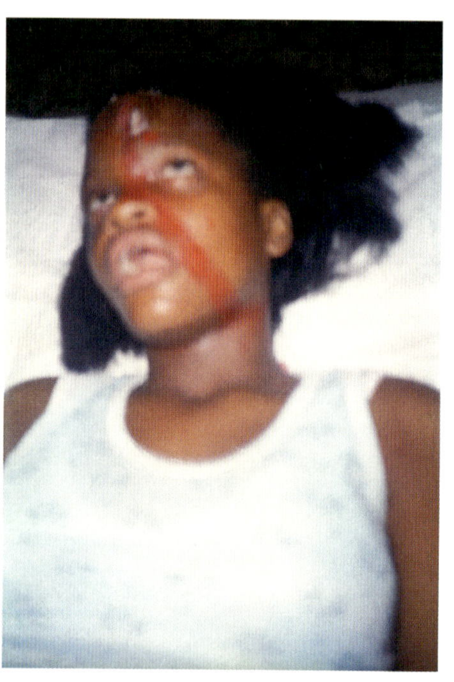

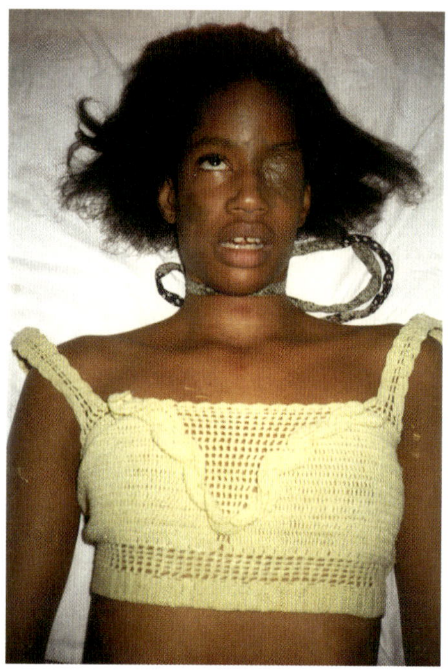 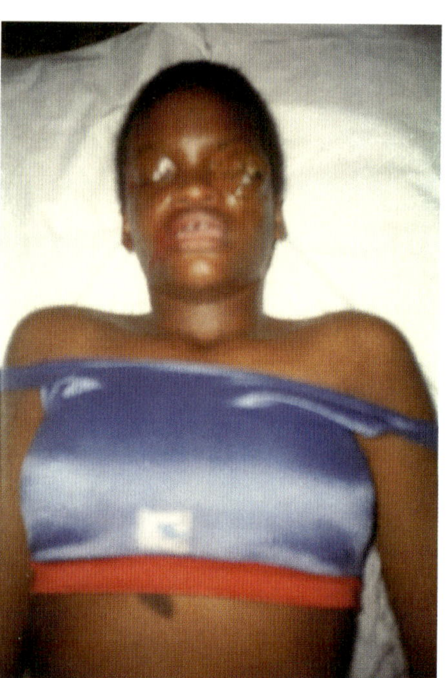

Susana Pilar Delahante Matienzo's elaborately staged productions featuring herself as a corpse form part of a long tradition of artists' self-portraits, which, above all, served as a memento reaching beyond death and attempting to keep the artist's memory as vivid as possible. By contrast, in her photographs Delahante Matienzo immortalizes a materialistic truth by simultaneously addressing the objectifying gaze of the photographic camera and the moment of death as the production of an image as well as of a corpse. With the works in this series, the artist also refers to the suffering of female victims of violent crime, in whose honor she seeks to leave a memorial.

**Susana Pilar
Delahante Matienzo**

Sin título / Untitled, 2002,
4 photographs, inkjet print

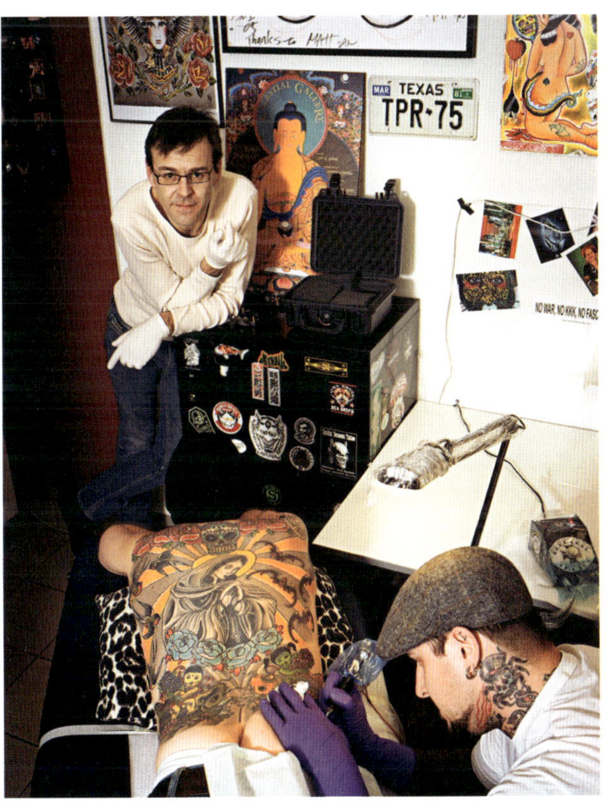

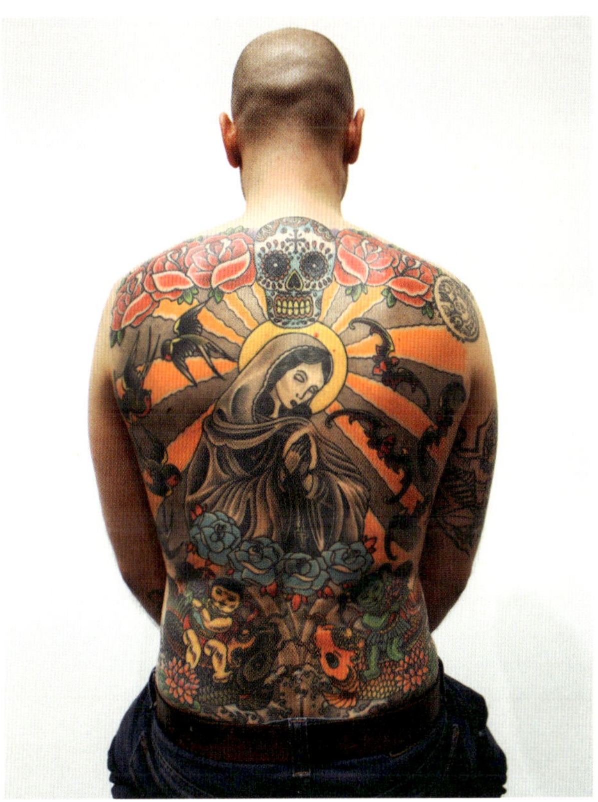

Wim Delvoye
*1965 in Wervik, Belgium,
lives and works in Ghent, Belgium,
London, and New York

TIM, 2006–2008,
tattoo

The Belgian conceptual artist Wim Delvoye has made a name for himself through his unconventional way of approaching his projects, which testify to his wit and irony, as well as, quite often, to a certain sarcasm. His work *TIM* is ethically as well as legally controversial. Tim Steiner, who lives in Zurich, had a motif designed by Delvoye tattooed on his skin which plays on, in addition to the Virgin Mary – with a death's head floating above her –, elements from Asian mythology as well as from cartoon culture. This work was then put up for sale. According to the contractual agreement, the buyer of this live piece of art not only acquires the right to publicly exhibit the skin painting, they may also have it at their disposal after Tim Steiner's death.

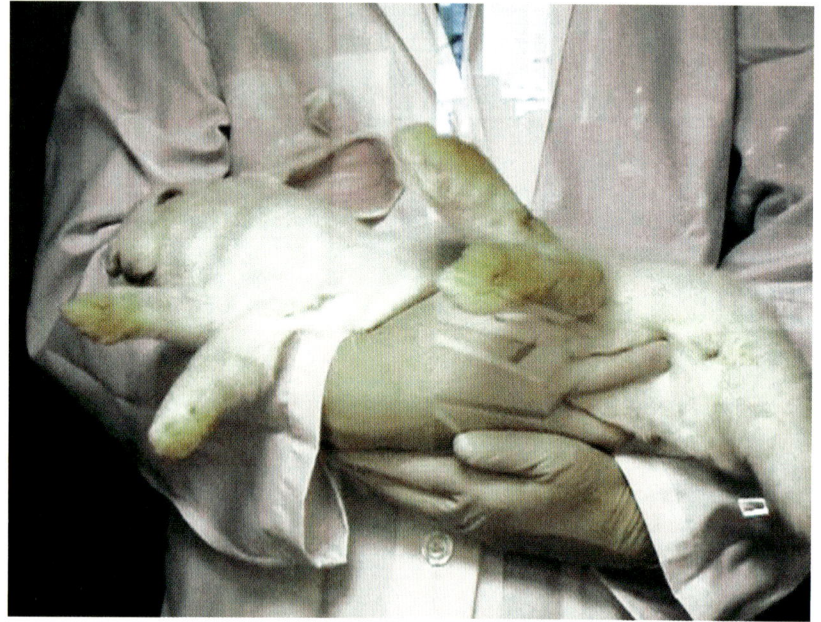

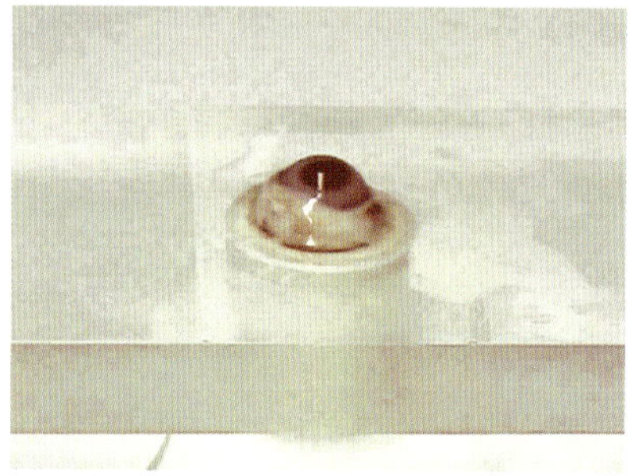
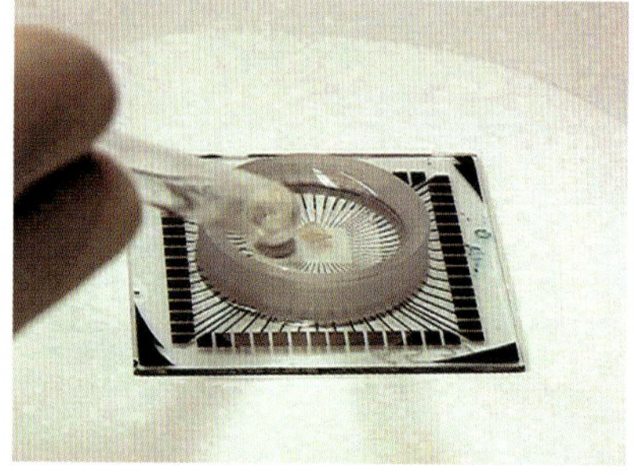
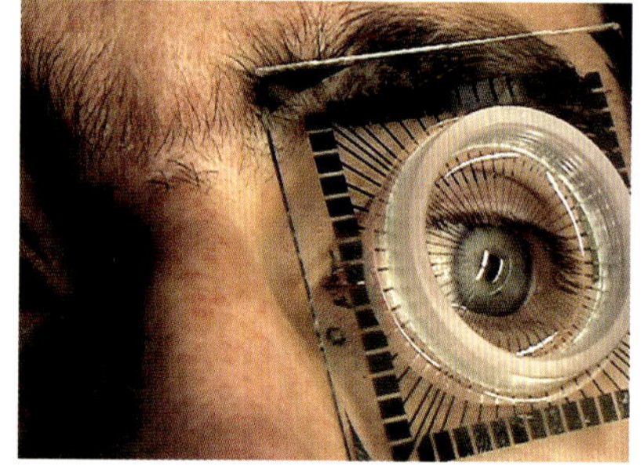

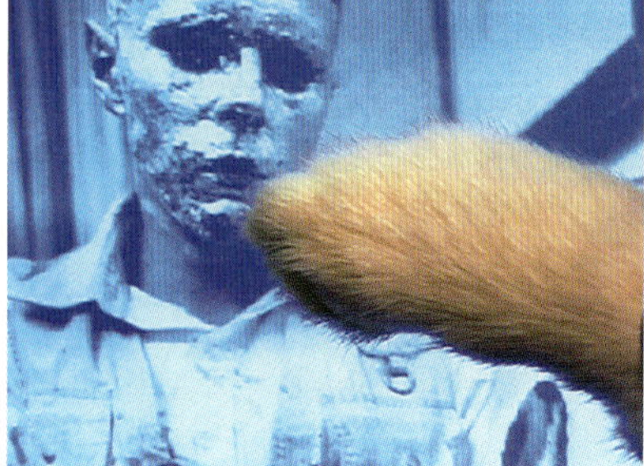
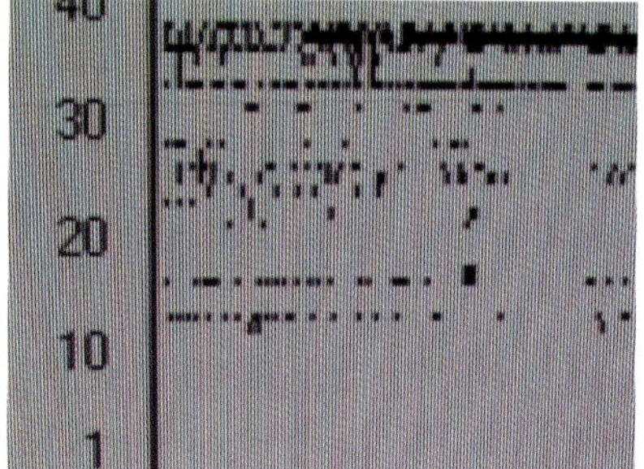

In her video work *Wie der tote Hase dem toten Beuys den Menschen erklärt* [How the Dead Hare Explains Human Beings to the Dead Beuys], Dorcas Müller refers to the action *Wie man dem toten Hasen die Bilder erklärt* [How You Explain Pictures to a Dead Hare] (1965) by Joseph Beuys. With a dead hare on his arm, he went through a Düsseldorf gallery from object to object, in order to explain these to the hare, and so makes it into a medium of understanding pictures and of intellectual catharsis. Dorcas Müller's video installation shows the animal as the object of performative-scientific experimental design. Whilst the dead hare in the laboratory is shown a picture of Beuys, a neurochip registers the optical data received on the animal's retina and transforms them into a bar code. The hare's eye reacting reflexively becomes a nexus between life and death.
Note: No animals were harmed for the making of this video.

Dorcas Müller
*1973 in Reutlingen, Germany, lives and works in Karlsruhe

Wie der tote Hase dem toten Beuys den Menschen erklärt, 2004, 3-channel video installation, color, sound, 4:30 min, loop, stills from a digital copy

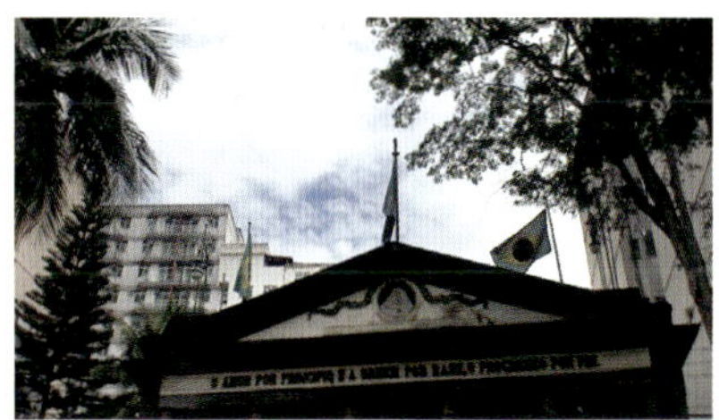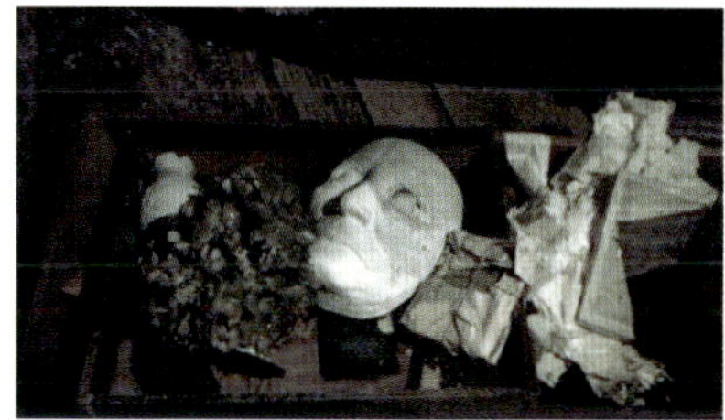

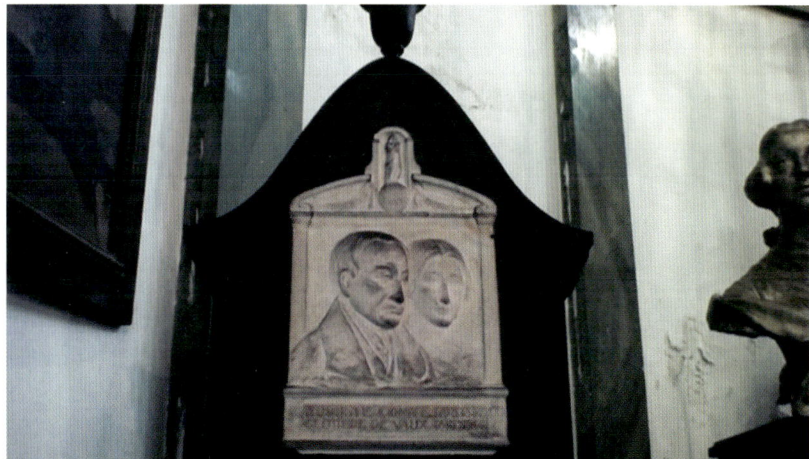

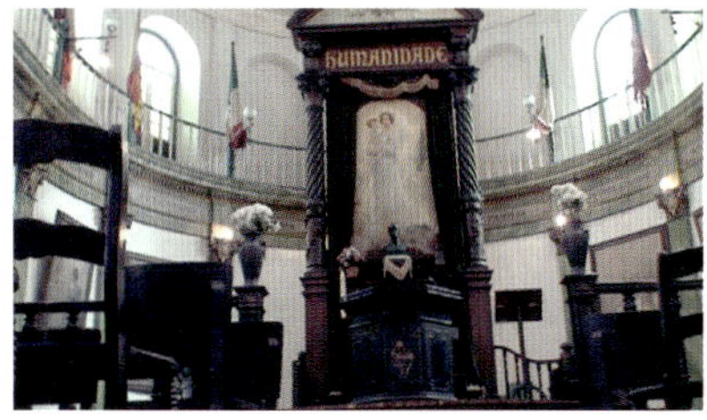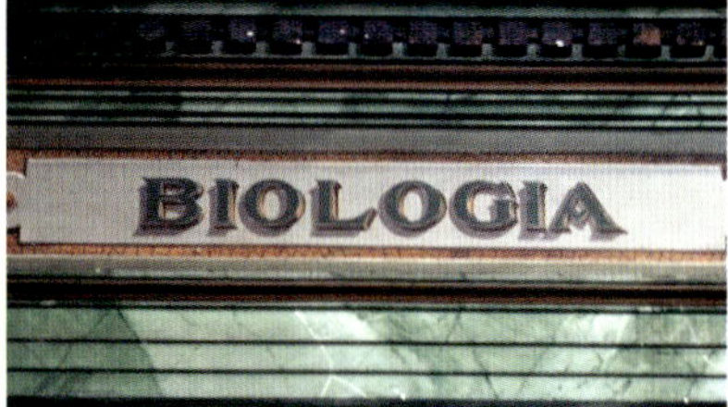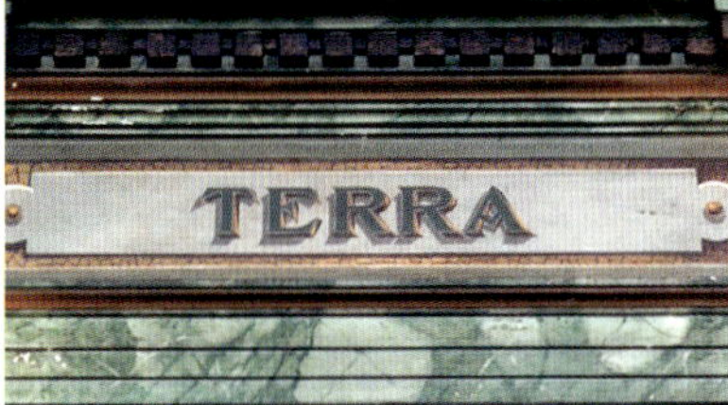

Florian Meyer
*1976, Berlin,
lives and works in Karlsruhe

Igreja Positivista, 2008,
video, color, sound, 16:30 min,
loop, stills from a digital copy

Auguste Comte (1798–1857) was a French mathematician and philosopher. The positivist philosophy he founded was marked by a quasi-religious faith in scientific discovery and progress. Comte's motto "Love as principle, order as foundation, progress as goal" still exists in a shortened form – "Order and Progress" – on the Brazilian flag today. The video work *Igreja Positivista* [Positivist Church] documents the interior of a temple of the positivist church in Rio de Janeiro, which was founded on Comte's teachings. In it, the abandoned church building comes across like a mausoleum for the project of an "atheistic Catholicism," whose core consists of love, compassion, and respect for human achievements, as well as Comte's admiration for women as the ethical and moral models for family and society.

Korpys/Löffler
Andree Korpys
*1966 in Bremen, Germany,
lives and works in Berlin
Markus Löffler
*1963 in Bremen,
lives and works in Bremen

Für ein Leben nach dem Tod, 2006,
video, color, sound, 72:30 min,
loop, still from a digital copy

*Für ein Leben nach dem Tod
(Generalaudienz Audienzhalle
15. Dez. 2004, Generalaudienz
Petersdom 24. Nov. 2004,
Petrusskulptur Petersdom
12. Okt. 2004)*, 2006,
C-prints, 100 × 68 cm each

The video installation *Für ein Leben nach dem Tod* [For a Life After Death] accompanies the two artists, accredited as journalists, through the Vatican for a period of one year. In combination with some of their drawings, a portrait of the last months in the life of Pope John Paul II took shape in a diary-like form. The selected scenes, on the one hand, document the staging of rituals in the Catholic faith while, on the other, the artists point to the church's implicit economy and politics relating to the media, for which the Pope himself acts as the most important politician and media star in the Vatican. However, between these scenes, there are also sequences with flocks of birds in flight, which, in Christian iconography, have symbolized souls ascending into eternity since time immemorial.

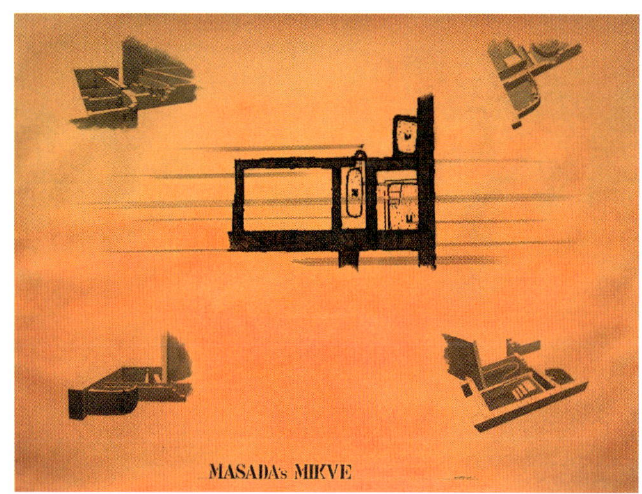

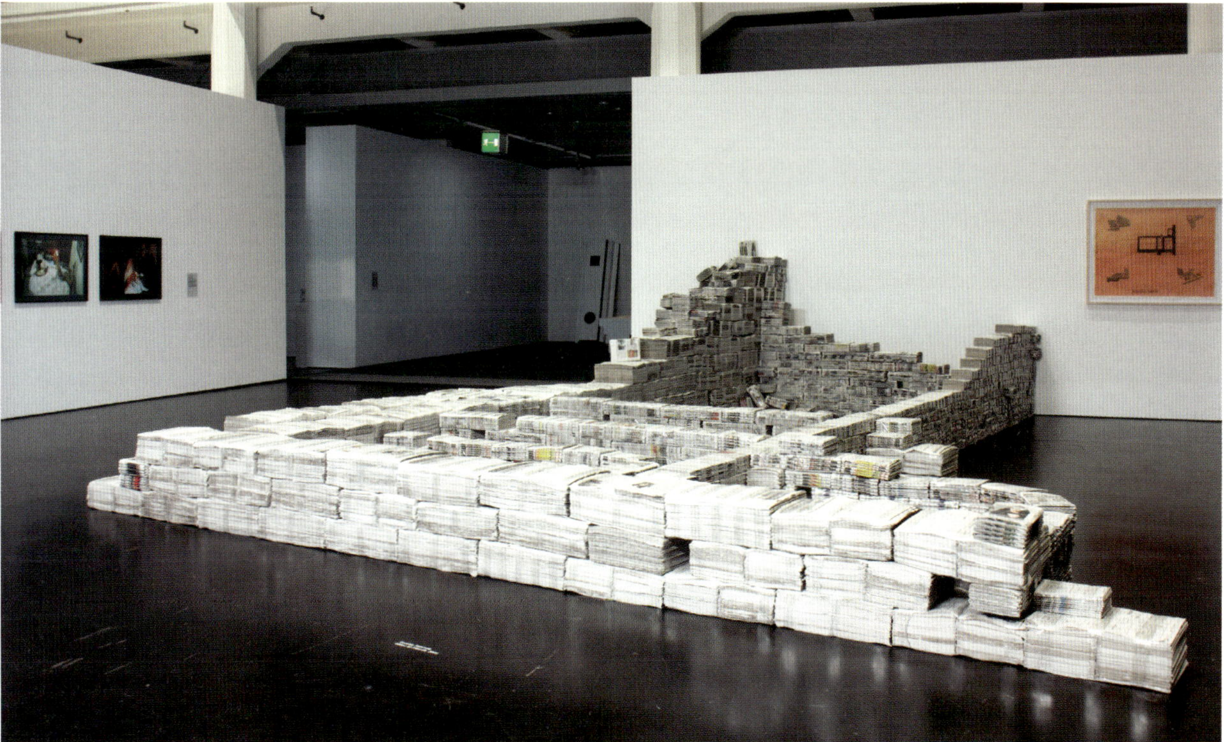

Osvaldo Romberg
*1938 in Buenos Aires, Argentina,
lives and works in New York
and Philadelphia, USA

Mikve at Masada, 2008,
mixed-media installation,
stacked newspapers, installation
view ZKM | Karlsruhe, 2009

Masada's Mikve, 2008,
drawing, watercolor, 96 × 126 cm

Mikwe denotes both a Jewish ritual of bathing and a bathhouse. *Masada* is the name of a Jewish fortress on the eponymous mountain in Israel overlooking the Dead Sea. It was built about 40 B.C. by King Herod and until today plays a great role in the history and mythology of Zionist ideology. In his installation, Osvaldo Romberg relocates the foundation walls of the original royal bathhouse by reconstructing them with layers of newspapers. In doing so, he points to the ephemerality of the news, which dominates our everyday life, and at the same time demonstrates how, as a collection of wastepaper, it forms the walls of the archive enclosing the cultural space of humanity and transporting it through time.

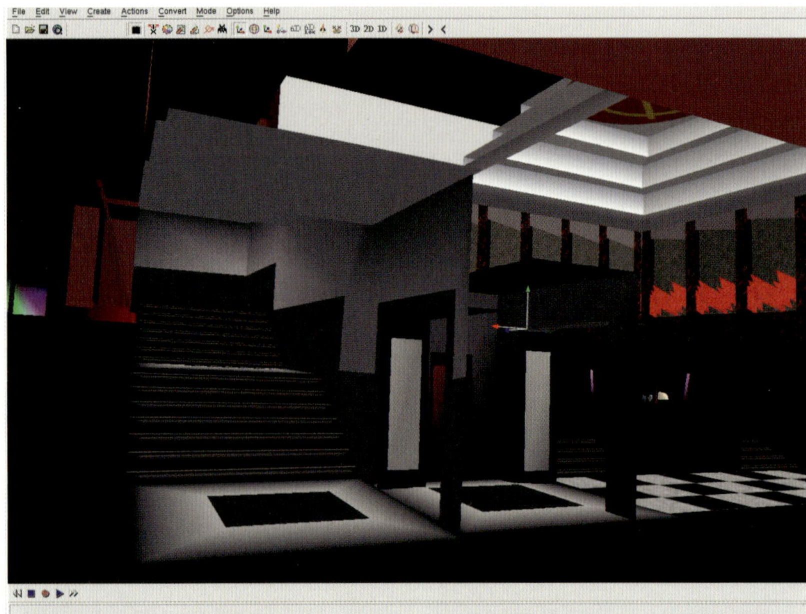

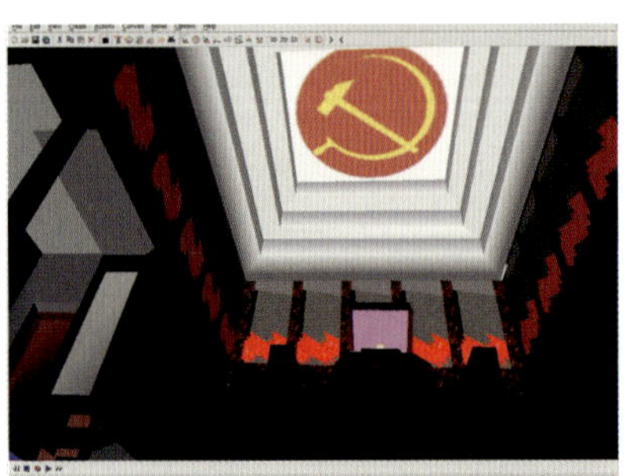

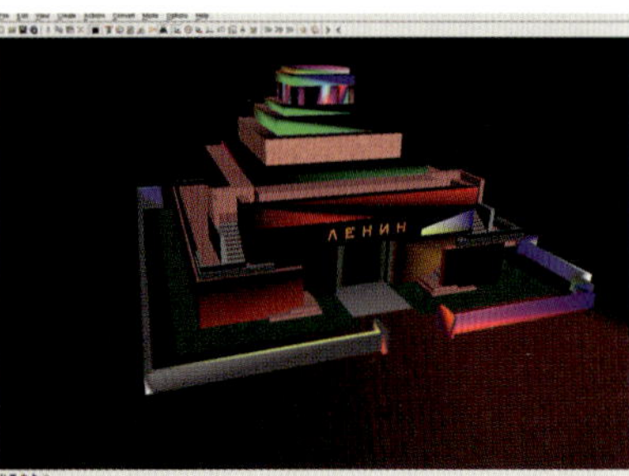

**Lenin Mausoleum
Documentation**

Maxim Kononenko, *1971
Alexey Naumenkov, *1966
Natalia Struchkova, *1969
Timur Yudin, *1968
all live and work in Moscow

Virtual Mawsolej W. I. Lenina,
1998/2008, 3-D computer model
VRML/ParallelGraphics, screenshots

Alexey V. Shchusev
Lenin-Mausoleum, 1924/2008,
5 historical photographs,
inkjet print, 30 × 40 cm each

Geneviève Zondervan
Lenine (Portrait of Lenin), 1953,
oil on canvas, 27 × 22 cm

Installation view ZKM | Karlsruhe,
2009

When Stalin suggested preserving Lenin's corpse in sempiternally, Trotsky is said to have replied: "If I have understood Comrade Stalin correctly, he is suggesting we replace the relics of St. Sergius of Radonesh and St. Seraphim of Sarov with the relics of Vladimir Ilyich." After Lenin's death on January 20, 1924, his widow, Nadezhda Krupskaya, tried in vain to prevent a cult forming around Lenin. The Lenin Mausoleum on Red Square in Moscow, at first provisionally designed out of wood and later of granite by the architect Alexey V. Shchusev, became a center for cultic pilgrimage. Today, the embalmed corpse of Lenin still lies there displayed on its bier.

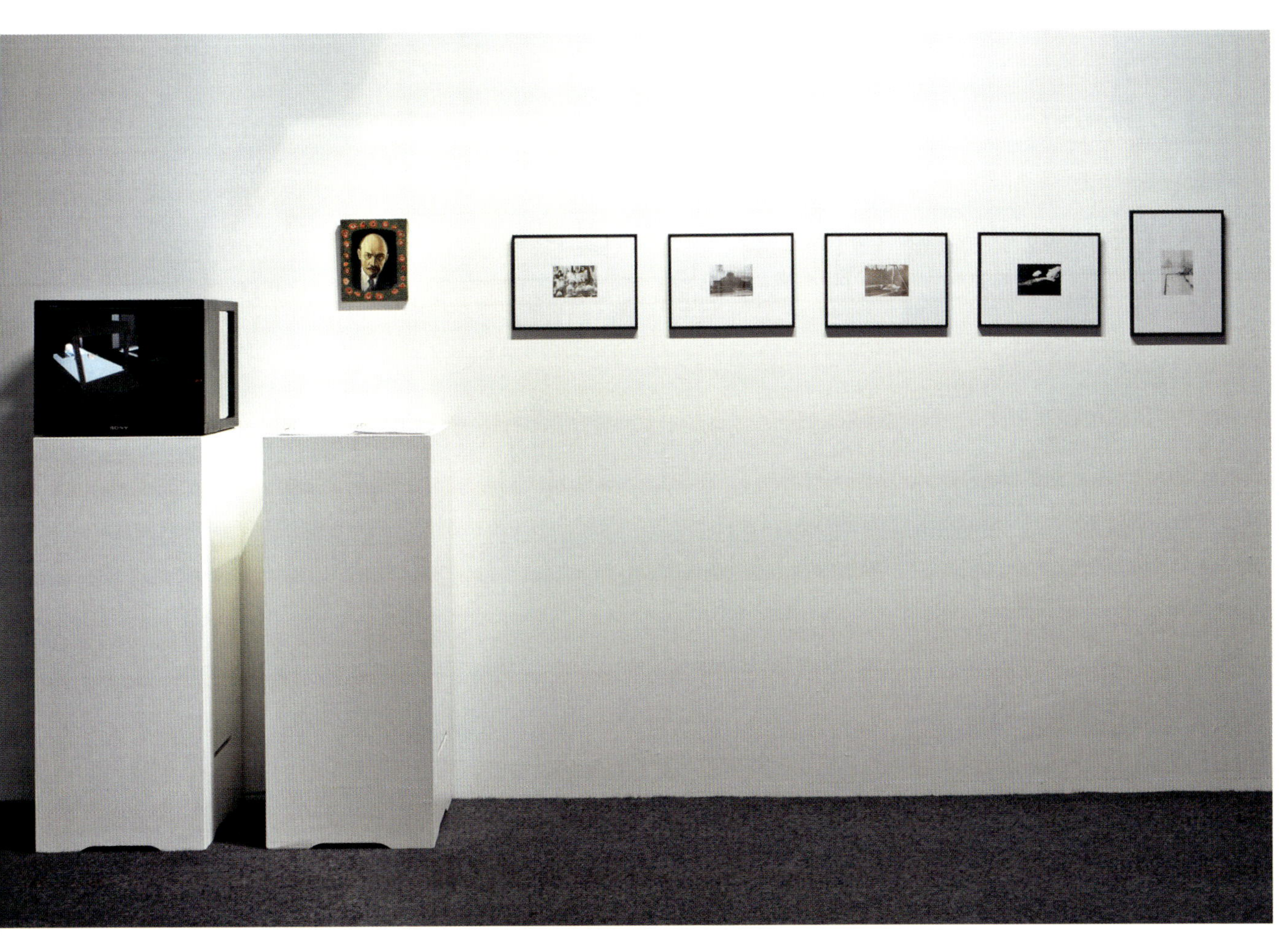

Henry Zemel

.When.the.Time.Comes.

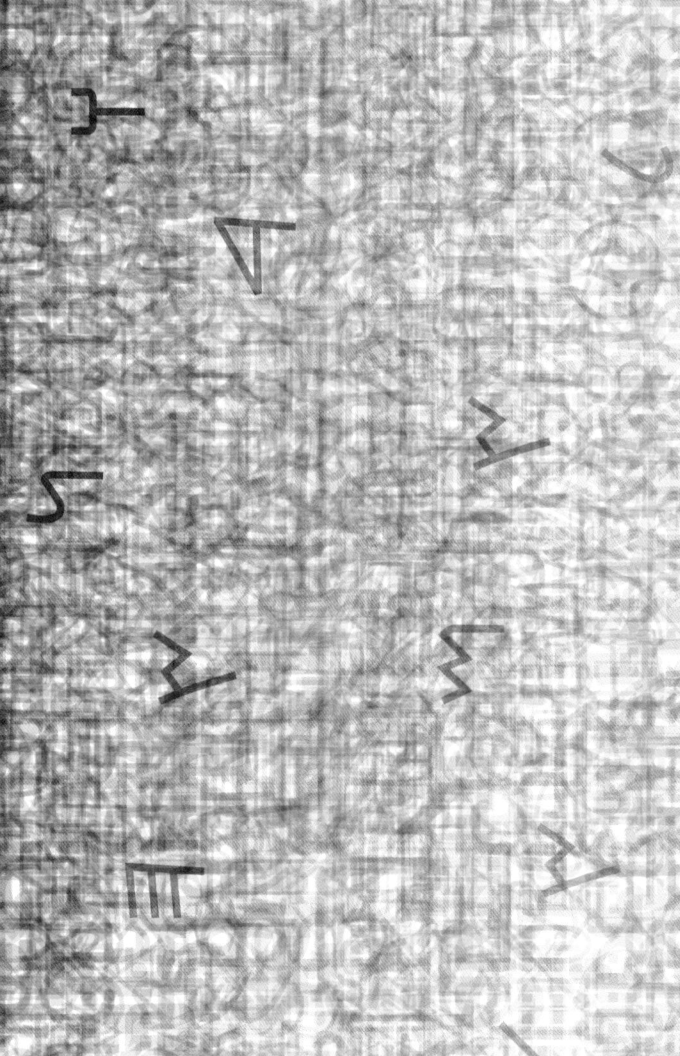

Chart of History and Ante-History

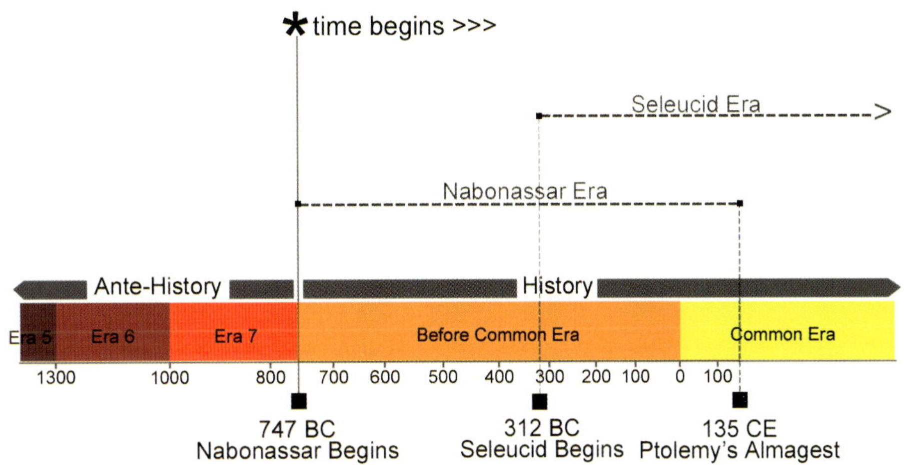

An Unfinished Revolution

Five centuries ago, Nicolaus Copernicus set the stage for the development of modern science. He challenged the age-old notion that the earth was immobile at the center of the cosmos. Few scholars were able to master the complex mathematics of his tome *On the Revolutions of the Heavenly Spheres*, first published in the year 1543. The effort hardly seemed worthwhile. The question as to whether the sun revolved around the earth or the earth around the sun did not bear on the planting of fields or harvesting of grain. Moreover, Copernicus' model did not furnish more accurate results than the earth-centered theory worked out fifteen centuries earlier.

The first printing of *On the Revolutions* had a run of about 400 copies followed soon after by a second printing of 500 copies. About half these volumes are extant today, often copiously annotated in the handwriting of the 16th century's leading scholars. Despite mixed reviews, the book got modern science rolling. It called into question the foundations of received wisdom and thus put astronomical theories "in play."

Copernicus sought to blunt the radical character of his thesis by citing its ancient roots. The introduction to the book refers to philosophers who thought the earth moved. The channels whereby their contrarian ideas persisted are obscure. Romans and Greeks generally wrote on perishable material, and the survival of a text required that fresh copies be made as the old ones disintegrated. However, the heliocentric model persevered, which suggests contrarian ideas remain resilient to historical obliteration.

Authorized ideas endure – be they valid or not. The failings of the Copernican model lay in the author's acceptance of a longstanding belief about the celestial order. Aristotle had claimed the ancients gave the "upper place" to the immortal gods, and accordingly he reasoned their environs were indestructible and timeless.

Copernicus, a Christian prelate, did not worship the planet-gods of the Greek pantheon. Nevertheless, he did grant the celestial bodies of the upper place a measure of divinity. He framed the goal of his endeavor thus:

"Our problem is to demonstrate, in the case of the five planets as in the case of the sun and moon, all their apparent irregularities as produced by means of regular and circular motions (for these are proper to the nature of divine things which are strangers to disparities and disorders)."

> **> >>** From quarry to palace to museum the bull will go…

An animation of a Man/Bull sculpture transported to King Sennacherib's palace at Nineveh and then in modern times to the British Museum.

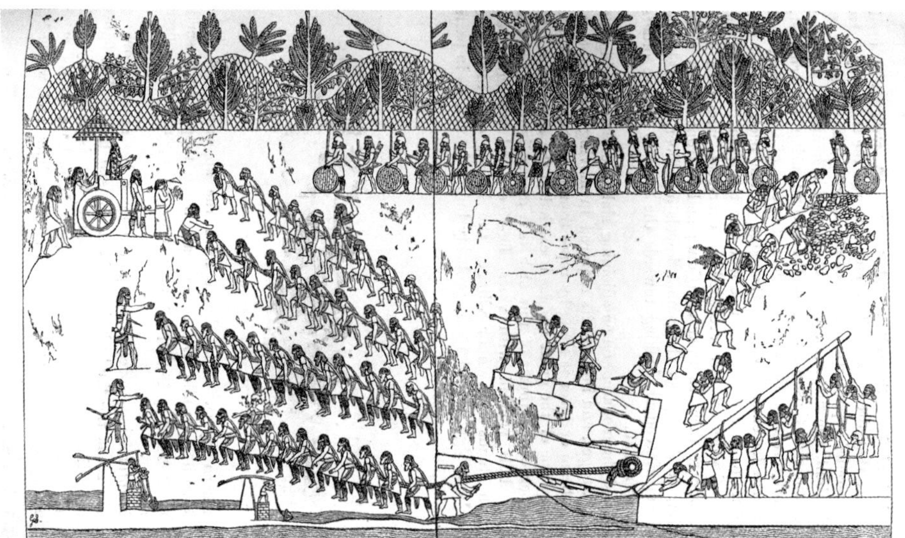

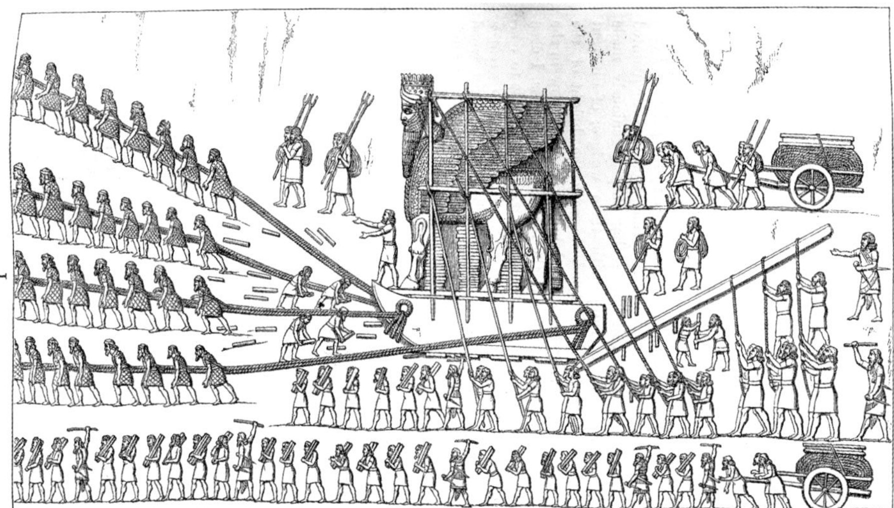

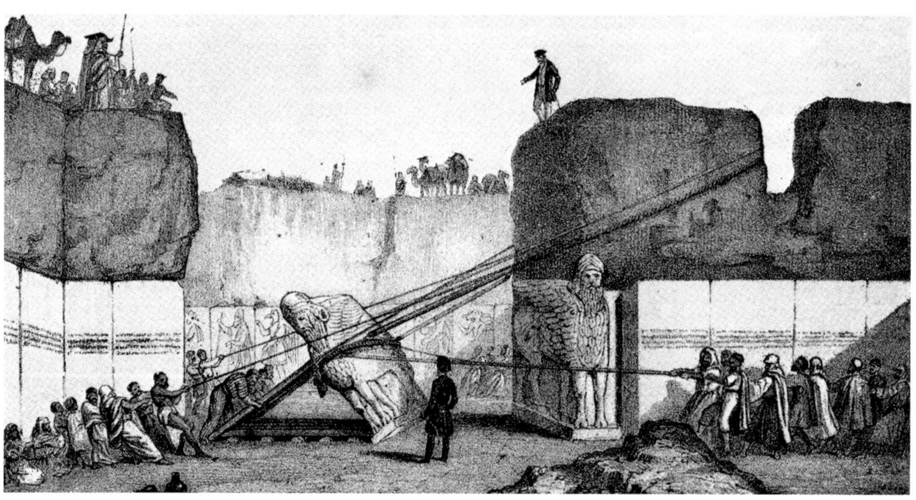

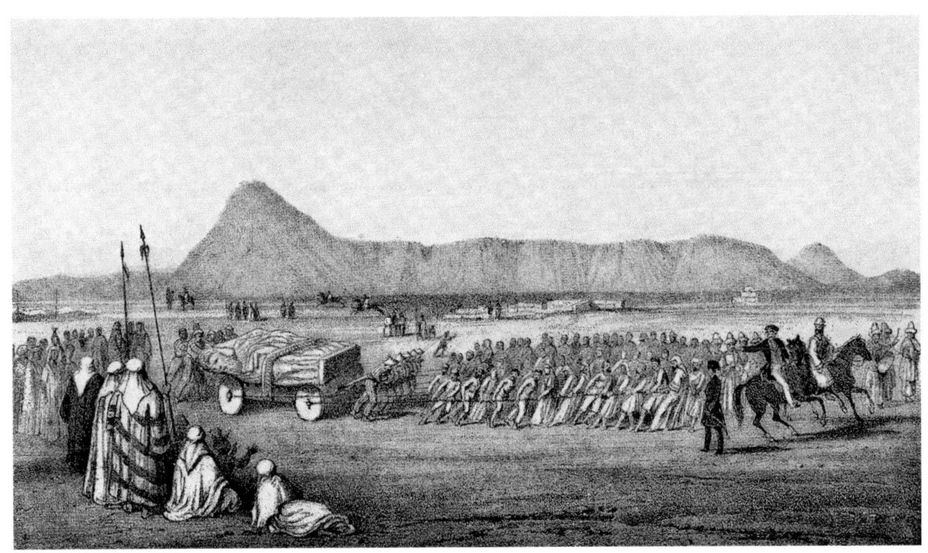

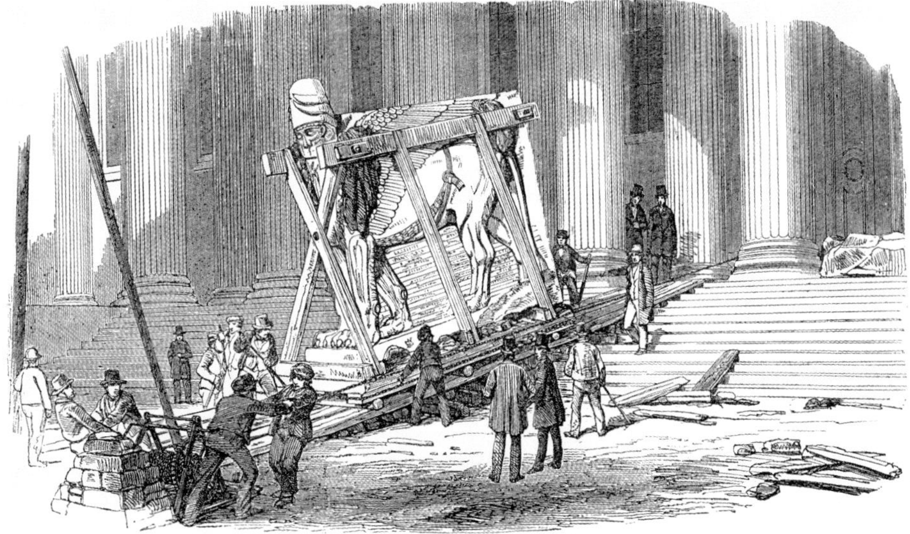

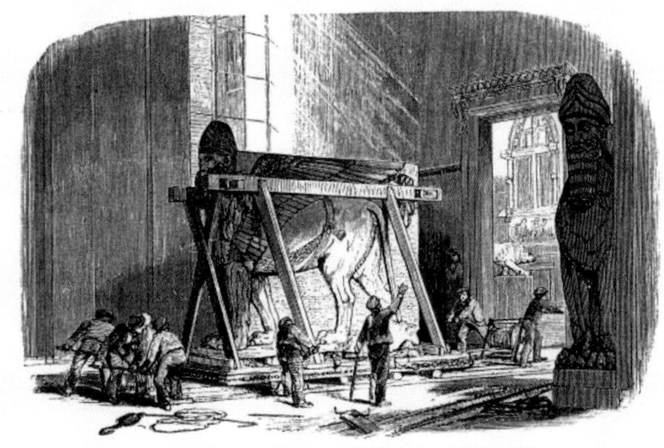

Moving one of the Lions from Nineveh, in the British Museum.—Feb. 12th, 1852.

The proper nature of the divine things above has a shrouded history. The rationale for their divine nature was obscure even to Aristotle. The philosopher generally developed his line of reasoning logically, but in this instance, his conception of the things above rested solely on the authority of "ancient and truly traditional theories." Further, he maintained that the ancients believed the heavens "contained in itself the infinity of time." The ancients certainly accepted the divinity of celestial bodies, but they conceived time differently than Aristotle.

In the Beginning

Both science and religion agree there was a beginning. Science says the beginning happened about sixteen billion years ago, whereas religion favors a date more like six thousand years ago.

Conceivably there was no beginning, and time went round and round as depicted in the film *Groundhog Day* (1993). Each morning the protagonist Phil (Bill Murray) awakens to the sound of an alarm clock, whereupon the events of the day unfold precisely as they did the previous day. It is Groundhog Day every day, same dialogue, same happenings. Everyone, other than Phil, is oblivious to the replay of the day. The film revolves around Phil's hilarious handling of his Sisyphus-like predicament.

The film's premise would most likely appeal to the Aymara-speaking people of South America. They seem to conflate past and future: when referring to the past, the Aymara sweep their hands and arms forward, gesturing back over their shoulder when indicating the future. Their basic word for *back* or *behind* relates to *future*. An Aymara seeing *Groundhog Day* might say the gringos finally got it right.

The inclination to look back in order to see the future has an odd appeal. Wall Street traders scour spreadsheets of old data seeking the secrets of the business cycle; the science of geology posits an oft-repeated cycle of mountains eroding away and then rising again. And generally, what goes around comes around. The notion of a regular replay of events is rooted in ordinary experience. Night follows day, the seasons arrive in due course, and the stars trace a repetitive pattern.

Ancient people – really ancient, before the empires of Rome, Greece, and Persia – considered the planets and other celestial apparitions as embodiments of gods. These beliefs characterized the *Astral Age*, a period when the core tenet was *as above, so below, and as below, so above*. For believers, it followed that the sequence of happenings in the mundane world was cyclical, since the gods in the celestial realm disappeared and reappeared over and over again.

To foretell the future, seers studied past cycles. Science in the Astral Age entailed working out the duration of a cycle and the sequence of happenings within that cycle. The cycles supposedly recurred endlessly, except for perturbations in the *true* god-ordained order. The responsibility of accounting for any disparity between belief and experience fell to a priestly class.

The Astral Age does not have a history, at least not in the usual sense. The period does not have a chronology. Astral Age scribes kept records of events within a cycle, but they had no reason to order the cycles. Among the ancient Maya, the past-is-future notion underlay the 52-year calendar known as the Calendar Round. The Calendar Round format specified particular days within a 52-year cycle, but it did not continue the tally of days from one Calendar Round cycle to the next.

Another distinctive cycle, this one originating in Western Asia, was the jubilee period of 49 (or 50) years. In the Jubilee Year, the Old Testament records that debts were forgiven, slaves were freed, and land was returned to the original owner. The ancient custom restored the state of affairs existing at the start of the Jubilee, in the belief that conditions over the next 50 years would evolve as in previous jubilee periods.

The Astral Age notion of *cyclical* time morphed into *linear* time at a specific juncture in recorded history. The transformation was revolutionary. It involved a complete overhaul of humanity's standing in the cosmos.

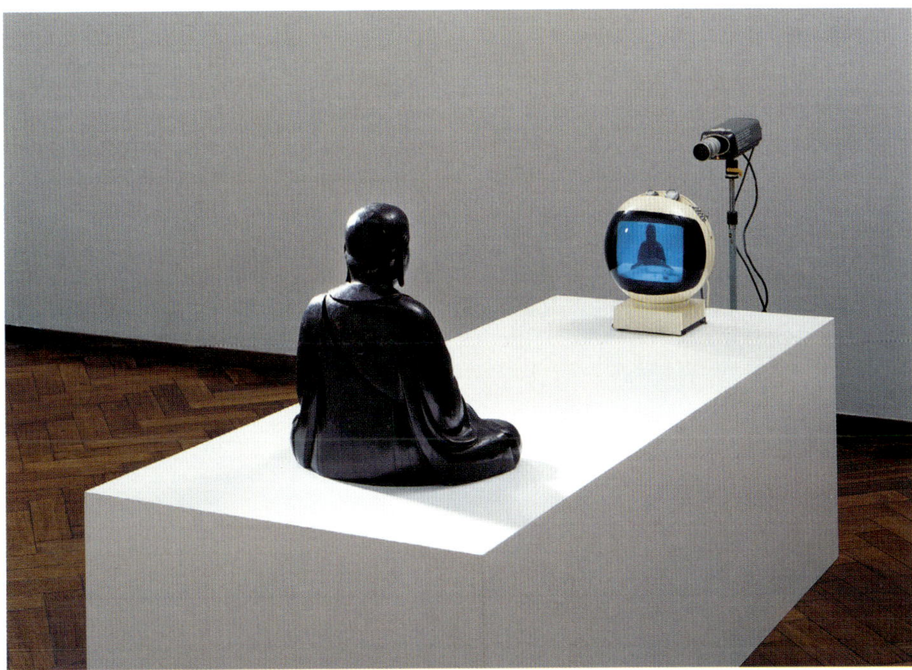

The conversion did not happen concurrently in all cultures, and many elements of the old thinking persisted even as new models of the cosmos developed. Much of the history of how the change came about remains obscure, but the recent influx of ancient texts has expanded greatly what is known about the transformational period.

Adventurers and scholars during the past two hundred years have turned up immense caches of ancient artifacts. Boatloads of relics from the civilizations of Western Asia journeyed to European and American ports. A haul in the heyday of nineteenth century exploration might have tallied some 25,000 objects. Over a million artifacts with cuneiform inscriptions have landed in museums and private collections around the world.

The new documentation indicated that the generally accepted history of the ancient Near East was fundamentally flawed. But instead of discarding traditional views, historians found ways to fit the nonconforming data into the preexisting picture. The chronology historians accept today is basically the same as had been elaborated early in the nineteenth century. And the timeline acknowledged by nineteenth century historians did not differ substantially from the model proposed by their seventeenth century predecessors, who in turn relied on the work of yet earlier historians.

The exemplary studies made by historians in the past are indispensible to an understanding of antiquity, but recently uncovered primary material surely assumes precedence where it clashes with, contradicts, or modifies accepted accounts. The fresh data are available in books and journals, and excerpts have trickled onto the Internet. A valid reading of the history recorded by early civilizations now appears doable. The following pages constitute a first draft.

Nabonassar 747

A browse through Aristotle's *On the Heavens* is great fun for fans of detective yarns. In a climactic scene, Aristotle rounds up the usual suspects – philosophers – and analyzes their theories about the motion of celestial bodies. He eliminates one theory after another until a single logical thesis remains – his own. The denouement spelled out in Aristotle's investigation of the heavens

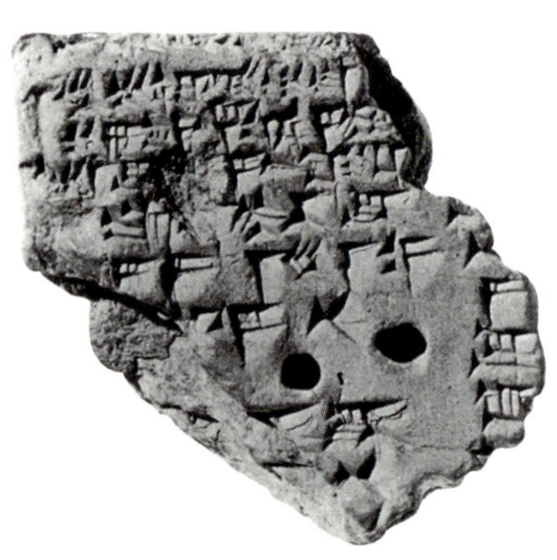

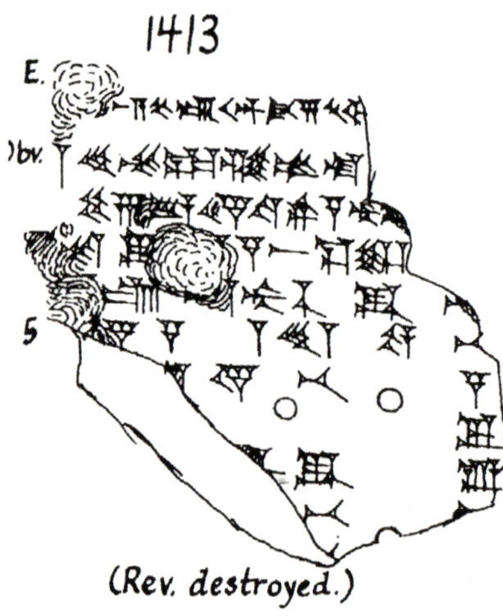

0. At the command of Bel and Beltija may it go well.
1. 1,40. Accession year [of …]
2. Month XII, (after) 5 month, the 14th, morning watch, … […]
3. 2,10. Year 1. Month VI, [the 1]5th (?), onset (?). It began in the north […]
4. […] the south wind blew. It set eclipsed. Month VI was in[tercalary.]
5. [Month XI, the 1]4th, onset (?). 1,40° remained to clearing.
6. [Year 2. Month] V, the 14th, it made a total (eclipse).
7. [Month XI] omitted.
8. [Year 3. Month V, omitt]ed. Month VI was intercalary.
9. […] … […]

stationed the earth at the center of the cosmos for the next two thousand years.

Aristotle reasoned that the circle is primary, the circle being the most perfect form, and so the heavens must move in a circle. Following Aristotle, a mathematical description of the circular orbits of planets and stars became the Holy Grail sought by Hellenistic astronomers. The quest proved exceedingly difficult, because a proper description required fitting together a great deal of information. The skywatchers of the preceding Assyrian, Babylonian, and Persian empires had made detailed astronomical observations that the mathematical description had to assimilate.

The problem remained unresolved for 500 years. Early in the second century C.E., Claudius Ptolemy devised a circular orbit theory that satisfied the accumulated data. He fixed the earth at the center of the cosmos and had the planets and stars move in a complex lattice of circular *epicycles*. Ptolemy's astronomical composition usually goes by its Arabic title, *Almagest* [The Greatest]. It put forward a comprehensive theory of astronomical trajectories that pinpointed the location of stars and planets on any given date, past and future.

Ptolemy writes he had in his possession records of astronomical observations going back to the time of King Nabonassar of Babylon. He incorporated the data into the *Nabonassar Era*, a time-reckoning scheme that began in 747 B.C., the first year of Nabonassar's reign. Which means, the year Nabonassar 1 is 747 B.C.

In addition to Ptolemy's testimony, a Babylonian account of astronomical events in Nabonassar's reign has survived. The cuneiform inscription describes four lunar eclipses in sufficient enough detail for modern astronomers to date the earliest of the eclipses to Nabonassar 1.

Other early dates, astronomically confirmed, come from Chinese records. The multivolume *Chinese Classics* includes a table of more than thirty solar eclipses over the period 720 B.C. to 495 B.C.

Skywatchers in the East and West launched modern observational astronomy in the eighth century B.C. when they began to include an ongoing count of days in their data. The continuous day count indicates that the skywatchers had discarded the notion of circular time. The new concept matured over a lengthy period, but for the sake of convenience the start of *linear time* may be set at 747 B.C. Henceforth, societies could date events along a timeline that stretched endlessly into the future and no less endlessly back into the past.

Lunacy

With the end of the Astral Age, the moon emerged as one of the chief deities in

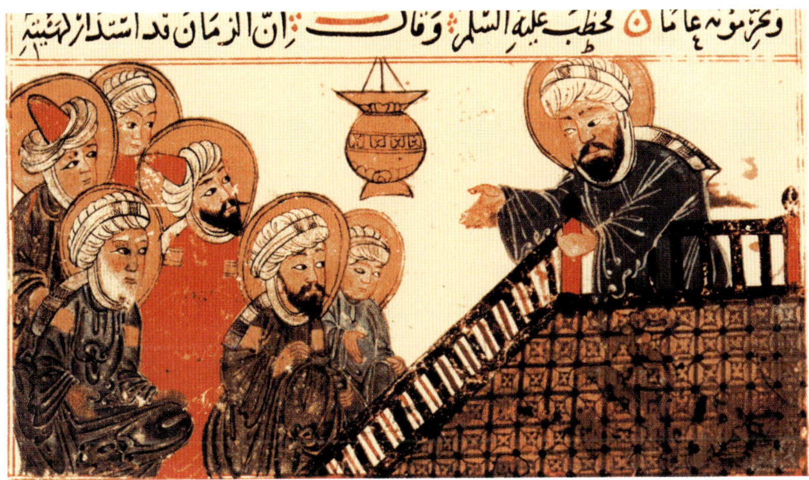

Mesopotamia. Numerous observations of the moon are recorded in the astronomical data accumulated by Assyrian Kings. Sky-watchers sending reports to the king took a 30-day month as good news, while a 29-day *hollow* month signaled unlucky days ahead. They frequently noted the day of the full moon, as lunar eclipses only occur at full moon. The astronomical texts state, "one god was seen with another"; an apt description of the full orb of the moon rising at dusk in the East while the setting sun was still visible in the West. (At dawn the situation reverses, the moon disappears in the West opposite the sun coming up in the East.)

Complex lunisolar calendars based on the sun and moon supplanted the solar calendars of the Astral Age. The older calendars had relatively simple schemes. On any specific date, the night sky displayed the same stellar configuration irrespective of the year (except for a one-day shift in leap years). Hence, skywatchers could partition the sky and link each section to a span of calendar dates.

The new lunisolar calendars had no fixed connection to the stars. The year of twelve lunar months had about 354 days, which shifted calendar dates eleven days a year relative to the stars and sun. The extra month added to keep the lunisolar calendar in step with the solar cycle moved the dates back 30 days.

The introduction of lunisolar calendars marked the end of the cyclical notion of time. Lunar-based astronomy envisioned the upper place of the immortal gods in a novel way that challenged and eventually overturned the established order. The ensuing astronomical developments were eminently successful. They enabled astronomers to predict the dates and descriptions of lunar eclipses and the possible dates of solar eclipses. Subsequent civilizations, from China to Rome, used lunar calendars, which have remained popular to this day.

Scientific progress in Western Asia after 747 B.C. burgeoned, much as it did after the revolution Copernicus initiated. His heliocentric astronomy made possible the advances of Johannes Kepler, Galileo Galilei, and Isaac Newton. Likewise, the lunar-based astronomy that began in 747 B.C. opened the ancient world to scientific inquiry. The complexities of the lunar phases engendered a sophisticated mathematics and physics that could not have existed in the Astral Age.

Time Marches On

Numerous faiths and philosophies emerged after 747 B.C. Within a few centuries, an assortment of novel belief systems had supplanted Astral Age religion. The new creeds typically featured an individual or school – Confucius and Lao-Tzu in China, the Latter Prophets in Judah, Buddha in India,

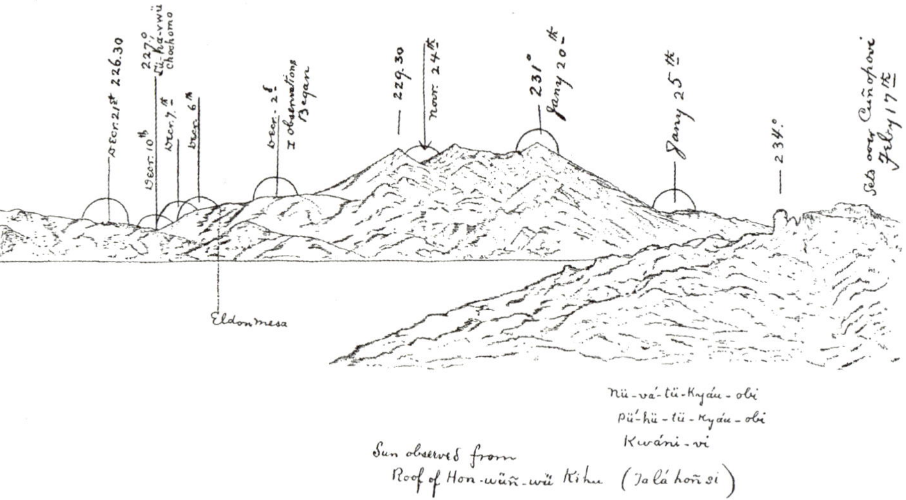

Zoroaster in Iran, and the Milesian philosophers in Greece. These transformative figures established enduring worldviews.

Additionally, a new form of fortune telling pegged to a person's date of birth acquired a following. In the Astral Age, the connection above to below affected all mundane happenings, but the new *natal astrology* charted a person's entire life path from the celestial configuration at the person's birth.

The influence of Astral Age concepts had waned by the late fourth century B.C. when Alexander III of Macedon marched his armies over Western Asia from India to Egypt. He conquered Mesopotamia and ascended to the Babylonian throne in Year Alexander 1. Subsequent years had the names Alexander 2, Alexander 3, and so forth. The custom of using a king's reign to name calendar years had been in place in Babylon since the seventh century B.C. It allowed for a continuous count of years, but only when accompanied by a complete list of kings and the number of years each king reigned.

After Alexander died his empire fragmented, and a military notable, Seleucus, emerged as the ruler of the eastern territory centered in Mesopotamia. The first calendar to exploit fully the notion of linear time came about under King Seleucus and his successors. Rather than name the first year of a reign <king name> 1, Seleucid kings numbered their calendar years from the accession of Seleucus I, and hence the calendar kept an ongoing count of years.

The Seleucid Era (S.E.) calendar was an accurate lunisolar calendar. Beginning in S.E. 1 – 312 B.C. –, the calendar extended an endless timeline into the future. A Nostradamus-like oracle could name the exact date when his prophecy would come true 500 years in the future. More to the point, astronomers had a convenient means of dating their predicted observations. They also employed the S.E. calendar to organize astronomical and historical data recorded in old calendars.

Calendar Wars

Astral Age consciousness did not sink into oblivion peacefully. The entrenched worldview defended its stance politically and intellectually against the new faiths and philosophies. In some ways, the ancient conflict paralleled the current brawl between intelligent design and science, which partisan rhetoric has boiled down to a question of time – six thousand years or sixteen billion?

In recent decades, scrolls found in caves near the Dead Sea provide a window on the passions aroused when ancient traditions clash with modernizing trends. One community portrayed in the scrolls remained faithful to Astral Age customs, while the rival camp embraced contemporary practices. Both factions were monotheistic, but they held radically different views of the cosmos they believed God had ordained.

The texts of the *Dead Sea Scrolls* include sections from nearly all the canonical books of the Old Testament. In addition, the preserved texts contain lengthy tracts from the pseudepigraphical *Book of Enoch* and *Book of Jubilees*. These books are canonical in the Ethiopian Orthodox Church, but heretofore Western historians had considered them of doubtful authenticity. They tell of customs unheard of among Jews.

Close to the caves where the Scrolls were found, archaeologists excavated the village of Qumran. Commentators offered several theses linking the site to the Scrolls. Possibly, a colony of scribes engaged in copying texts produced the Scrolls and hid them in caves. The scribal settlement might be a proto-Christian Essene community, since the texts reputedly allude to historical events from 150 B.C. to 50 C.E. Despite these unresolved issues, the Scrolls substantiate that a considerable population adhered to a heterodox form of Judaism.

The *People of the Scrolls* upheld Astral Age traditions. They regulated the life of the community around a solar calendar that preserved a fixed connection between the celestial and mundane realms. The calendar had a year of 364 days, plus nameless days added to fill out a solar year.

The texts of *Enoch* and *Jubilees* express revulsion for the community of Jews that had forsaken the 364-day calendar. Normative Judaism used a lunisolar calendar. Their religious observances were not coordinated with the stars. The People of the Scrolls fervently believed the implementation of the lunisolar calendar destroyed the cosmic harmony ordained by God.

Seven

The formation of a canonical text goes through four phases. First, the existing manuscripts are assembled. They include passages that will be designated as normative, but no manuscript incorporates the entire canonical version. The next stage involves deciding on appropriate passages. The selection process may be skewed, possibly creative, though the approved version must conform to the traditions underpinning the text. In the third stage, the canonizers determine which reading of each word and paragraph reflects the approved tradition. The final stage requires the elimination of all nonconforming manuscripts. A text cannot become canonical until the production of new manuscripts or books with variant readings ceases. The course of standardization is complete only when copies that differ from the official norm are destroyed.

The making of a canonical text generally takes centuries. An exception to the slow-moving process occurred in the fifty years following the invention of movable type. From Gutenberg's beginnings in 1450 to the end of the century, printing establishments published 28,000 titles and circulated millions of copies. These volumes may be the primary source of numerous canonical texts, since printers frequently discarded the old and often deteriorating manuscripts that formed the basis of a published book.

The fabrication of approved texts was common throughout history, though specific instances may be difficult to pin down. Berosus, a third-century-B.C.-Babylonian historian and astronomer, reportedly wrote that King Nabonassar (of the Nabonassar Era) eradicated the records of his predecessors. Berosus' own writings have not survived, but his account, if true, indicates the elimination of the Astral Age canon began straight away with the onset of historical times.

The final period of the Astral Age was *Era 7*, an epoch that featured a seven-day week and a 364-day calendar year. In Babylon, King Nabonassar's alleged cleansing was effective, seeing as few consequential remnants of Era 7 have surfaced. Elsewhere in Mesopotamia, the number *seven* appears as a common salutation in Assyrian correspondence: "To the king, my lord, my god, my sun… Seven times seven I fall down at the feet of my lord." Additionally, the 364-day calendar shows up

> **v** >> Panels from the *Mayan Dresden Codex* depicting the 364-day calendar (#31a,b,c & #32a) with explanatory annotations

The 364-day calendar appears prominently in the codices. The Mayan treatment of the calendar was mathematically elegant. Their scheme merged the 364-day year with a 260-day *primary cycle* to generate a composite cycle with a period of exactly 5 years: $5 \times 364 = 7 \times 260 = 1{,}820$ days.

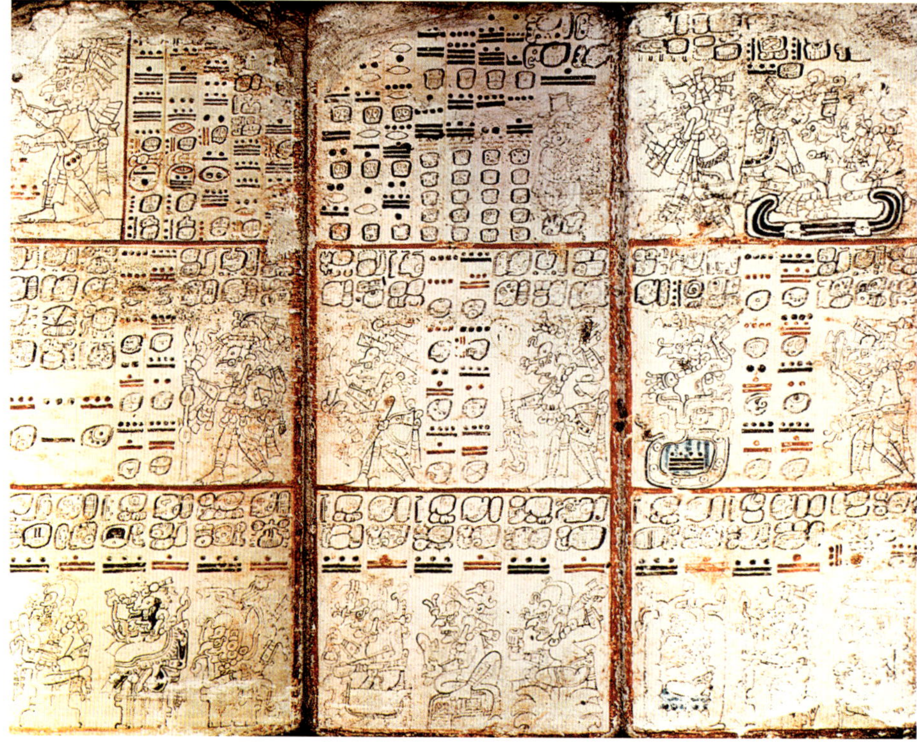

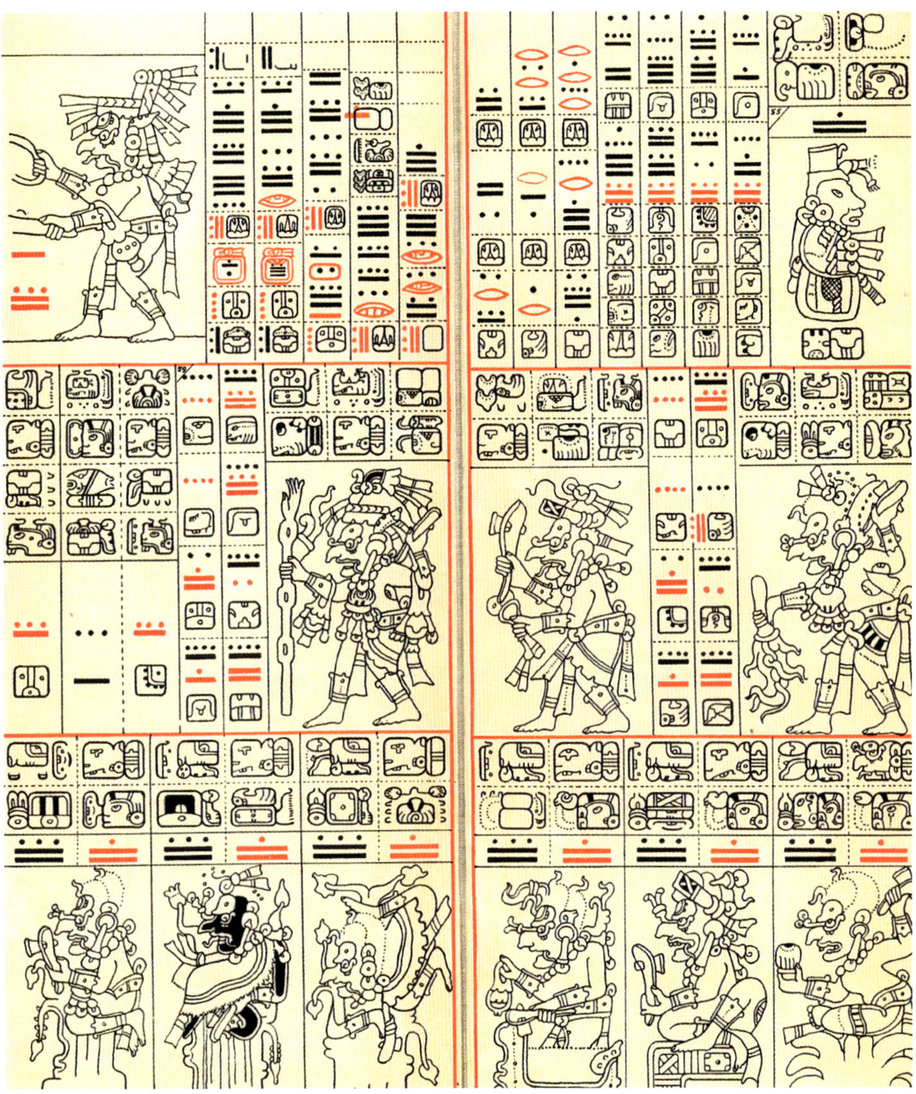

in an Assyrian astronomical record as a set of 26 asterisms in a sky of 364 units.

The 364-day calendar appears prominently in the books of *Enoch* and *Jubilees*. These texts come from a time before the canonization of the Bible and the elimination of variant writings. In contrast, the standardized texts of the Old Testament contain no overt mention of a 364-day calendar or any calendar at all. However, since canonical versions are constrained to follow the traditions behind the texts, it should not be overly difficult to discern a 364-day calendar implicit in the standard Bible.

The Old Testament cites seventeen dates. They are found in the *Pentateuch* and *Joshua*. Intriguingly, the dates specify only the month and the day of the month, but not the year. For example: The Flood began "in the second month, on the seventeenth day of the month" (*Genesis* VII, 17).

The Israelites arrived at the Wilderness of Sin "on the fifteen day of the second month" after departing out of the land of Egypt (*Exodus* XVI, 1).

They left Sinai in the second year, "in the second month, on the twentieth day of the month" (*Numbers* X, 11).

Moses spoke to the Israelites "in the fortieth year, in the eleventh month, on the first day of the month" (*Deuteronomy* I, 8).

The people came out of the river Jordan "on the tenth day of the first month" (*Joshua* IV, 19).

The year appears irrelevant to the dating of the events. The process of creating a canon would not countenance a sizable number of pointless dates. Actually, the dates are of no consequence in a lunisolar calendar, but reading them as dates in a 364-day calendar results in a sensible interpretation.

An outstanding feature of the 364-day calendar of exactly 52 weeks is the link between a date and the corresponding day of the week. A date consisting of a month and the day of the month specifies one of the seven days of the week. The year is superfluous.

According to rabbinic tradition, the calendar count of days began on the fourth day of creation, Wednesday, when God made the sun, moon, and stars and "let them be for signs, and for seasons, and for days and years." Consequently, if Wednesday marks the beginning of the year – every year – then a translation of the seventeen Bible dates into the 364-day calendar leads to a remarkable conclusion. None of the dates falls on the Sabbath! Hence, the activities described as taking place on the seventeen dates – traveling, building, and declaiming – did not violate the Sabbath day of rest.

In addition to the dates mentioned in the *Pentateuch* and *Joshua*, the *Book of Jubilees* records an additional dozen dates from the era of the Patriarchs. Again, the dates of travel and work do not fall on the Sabbath. These dates did not survive the analysis of the canonizers and they are not included in standard Bibles. It appears the People of the Scrolls regarded the 364-day calendar of Era 7 as the temporal framework of the whole *Pentateuch*, whereas the canonical version restricted the calendar's scope.

All seventeen calendar dates noted in the standard Bible, except for one Sunday date, fall on Wednesday (French *mercredi* = Mercury day = Nabu day) or Friday (French *vendredi* = Venus day = Ishtar day). The influence of the planet gods Nabu and Ishtar during the Astral Age was not limited to Judaism. These planet gods were central to the customs and belief systems throughout Western Asia. Nabu occupied the seventh level in the celestial pantheon and Ishtar the sixth.

Eras and Numbers

Assyrian Kings Lists, *Egyptian Pharaohs Lists*, *genealogies* catalogued in the Old Testament, and similar lists of early leaders were compiled after 747 B.C. These documents reflect the first efforts to put Astral Age cycles in order. They include valid information, but their timelines misrepresent the character of the period prior to 747 B.C. Consequently, the chronology underlying the modern treatment of the Astral Age is unreliable. A fruitful approach, at least initially, would be to set aside linear historical interpretations and view ancient happenings from an *ante-historical* perspective. (The neologism *ante-history* distinguishes Astral Age accounts from happenings that occurred post-747-B.C.)

An outstanding characteristic of ante-history was the emphasis placed on number. In this regard, ancient researchers resemble their modern counterparts, except for one telling factor. Modern science prizes the most precise value of measurable observations, i.e. the more places after the decimal point the better, whereas Astral Age thinkers sought the *truth* of the cosmos in terms of simple integers.

The numbers associated with Era 7 derive from seven and its multiples. The division of the 364-day year into 7×52, 14×26, and 28×13 sections shows up in preserved records worldwide, although not uniformly. The week of seven days does not appear prominently in Chinese or Mayan documents, but both civilizations took note of the 28 stations of the moon.

The era before Era 7 highlighted the number *six*. *Era 6* featured a week of six days and a calendar year of 360 days partitioned every which way. Mesopotamians divided the year into twelve months of thirty days, the Mayans split it into eighteen intervals of twenty days, and the Egyptians segmented their calendar

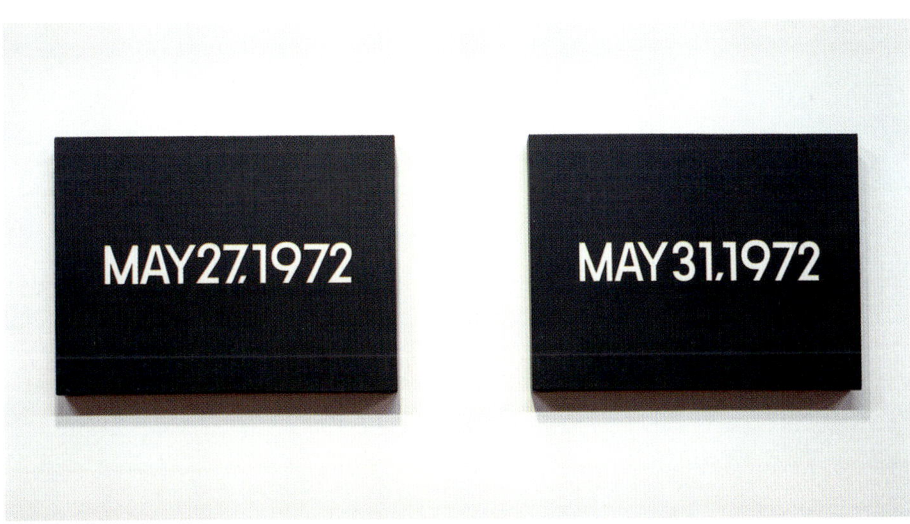

into thirty-six decans of ten days. Assyrians broke up the day into six double hours of light and six double hours of night.

The numbers associated with Era 6 and Era 7 are evocative, but they fall short of positively characterizing each era. The weight of evidence based on numerology is limited due to the recycling of noteworthy numbers. Iconography likewise has a comparable weakness, inasmuch as iconic forms often survive from one era to the next. Hence, a historically prominent number or icon may have several interpretations, and linking it firmly to a specific era is problematic.

The linear timeline that early commentators imposed on the Astral Age has passed through many hands since 747 B.C. Nonetheless, the existence of Era 6 and of Era 7 is secure, even if their chronology is rough. As a first approximation, Era 7 corresponds to the Assyrian Kings List from the tenth to the eighth century B.C., contemporaneous with the Western Zhou in China and the period of Kings in Israel.

The kings that appear in the Assyrian Kings List from the fourteenth to the tenth century B.C. are questionable, though the duration of several centuries seems reasonable. This period is Era 6, which corresponds to the Shang Dynasty of China and the interval from Moses to King David in the Old Testament.

Prior to Era 6, there exists substantial evidence of an Era 5 based on a five-day week. A calendar year of 350 days is attested, but without a clear connection to the five-day week. The information applicable to *Era 5* is sparse and difficult to sort out unambiguously.

A Quarter Day

In early historical times, new faiths and philosophies based on extraordinary figures emerged in China, Judea, India, Iran, and Greece (see chapter: "Time Marches On"). The list accounts for all well-documented ancient civilizations except Egypt. That land also had a religious innovator – Pharaoh Akhenaton – but conventional chronology situates his reign long before historical times. He supposedly ruled in the fourteenth century B.C. as a pharaoh of the Eighteenth Dynasty. However, Egyptian chronology is not secure. A shift of the Eighteenth Dynasty to the eighth century B.C. would transpose Akhenaton's reign to the end of the Astral Age, at the beginning of history. He belongs to the company of Buddha, Confucius, Zoroaster, and other creators of worldviews.

The conventional chronology of Egypt rests on a foundation of *Sothic dating* theory and the *Pharaohs List* of Manetho, an Egyptian priest who lived in the third century B.C. His writings have not survived. Several renditions of the Pharaohs List turned up in the work of later historians, but the versions are inconsistent. Manetho remains an important

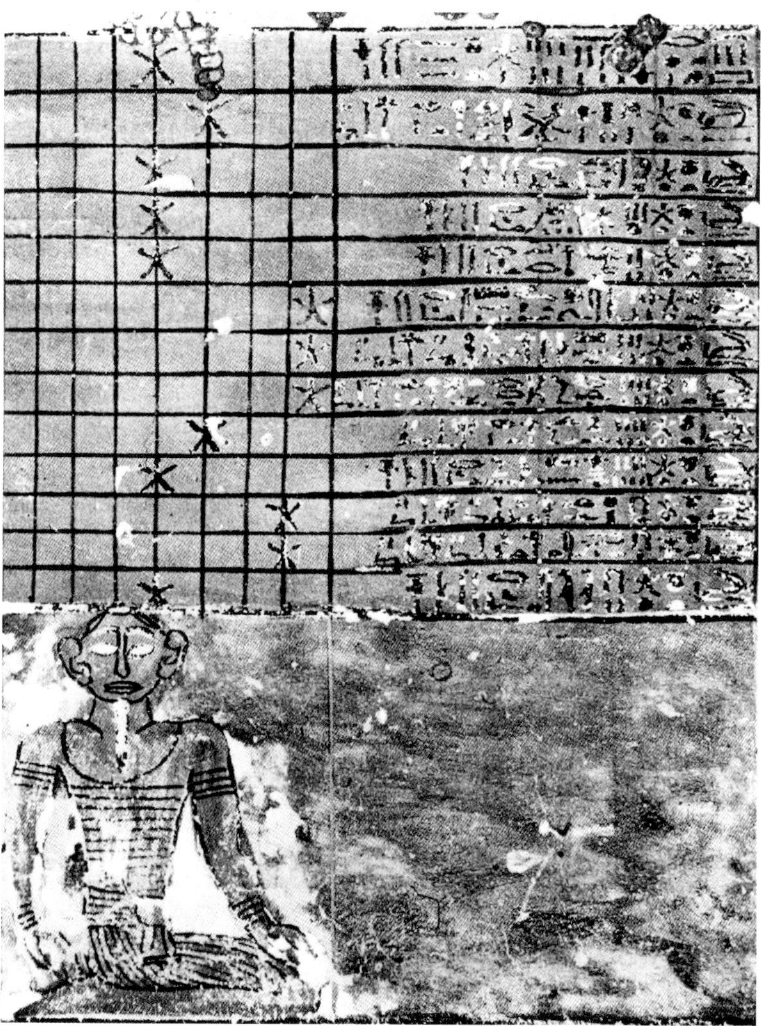

figure in the history of Egyptology, but confidence in the validity of his list has paled.

As for Sothic dating, the theory remains influential. It plays into the portrayal of Egypt as an everlasting land of desert sands, a steady Nile, and eternal pyramids. Long ago, the Roman rulers of Egypt touted the antiquity and the conservative nature of Egyptian society. They maintained Egyptian sages were the most ancient bearers of wisdom. Not to be outdone, their Christian adversaries pointed out that the patriarch Abraham preceded the Egyptian sages, and that in this case Judeo-Christian knowledge was more ancient and more valid.

Sothic dating theory presumes the Egyptians utilized a single civil calendar for more than three millennia. It had twelve named months of thirty days plus five days tacked on at the end of the year. This 365-day scheme acquired the name *Wandering Year Calendar*, because it lacked the quarter day needed to keep in step with the sun. Every four years, the astronomical event marking the start of the year fell one day later in the calendar.

The Wandering Year Calendar supposedly ticked off 365 days year after year, without a hiccup, never varying throughout Egypt's purported long history. Of course, there is no ante-historical evidence supporting a single unvarying calendar. Standard Egyptian chronology lists more than twenty dynasties in the two millennia of Egyptian ante-history, which

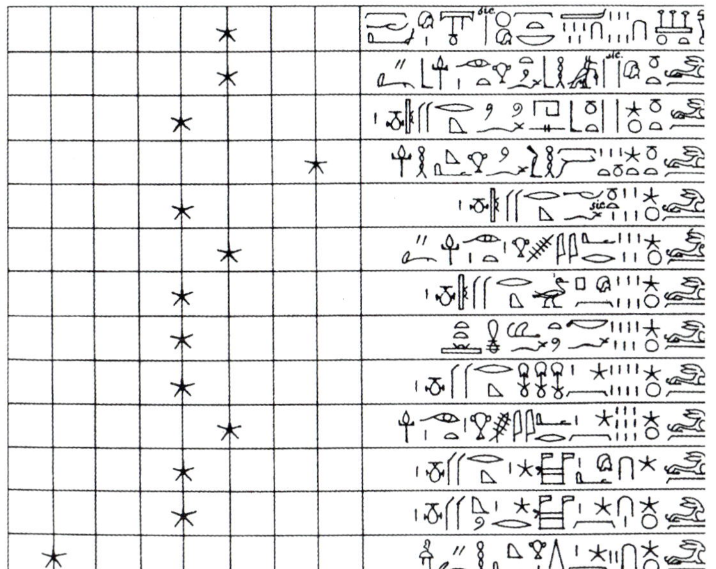

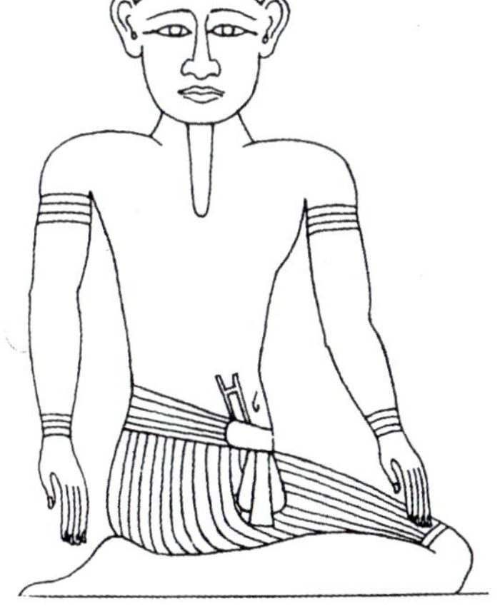

belies the fabled stability of its society or calendar. China had fewer dynastic swings over
the past 2,000 years, but its actual records register fifty major calendar changes and a hundred minor ones. If Egypt's calendar ever had a
365-day cycle during the Astral Age, it did not
endure unperturbed over long periods.

The details of the early Egyptian calendar
are a long-standing mystery. The deliberations
generally focus on a quarter day. Did the traditional calendar have 365 days or 365 and a
quarter days? While under Persian suzerainty
(ca. 525 B.C. to 330 B.C.), Egyptian documents were dated several ways – in a Wandering Year calendar, a Persian lunisolar calendar,
or double dated in both calendars. However,

data on the native Egyptian calendar before
and after the Persian period are spotty.

The information from Greek and Roman
times is contradictory. Censorinus, a Roman
author of the third century C.E., states Egypt
always had a 365-day calendar. His view is balanced by earlier chroniclers. Diodorus Siculus
portrays the Egyptians of Thebes as adding five
and a quarter days to their year of 360 days,
thus filling out the cycle of the year. And Pliny
and Strabo tell of the calendar secrets revealed
to Eudoxus by the temple priests of Heliopolis.
The renowned Greek astronomer had learned
that the traditional calendar had a four-year
intercalation cycle. This intercalated calendar must have been a well-kept secret, as the

information so impressed the Greeks that it remained noteworthy centuries later.

The calendar debate resurfaced in the early seventeenth century C.E. The philologist Joseph Scaliger, heralded as the father of modern chronology, argued that the traditional Egyptian calendar had 365 and a quarter days. His eminent adversary, Dionysius Petavius, held to the established position that the calendar year forever had 365 days. The stance of Petavius prevailed. The unperturbed Wandering Year Calendar and Sothic dating theory are standard fare in current Egyptology.

Early Egyptian calendars, like all Astral Age calendars, had to match the cycle of the sun and the stars. Regardless of whether the *true* calendar had 360, 364, or 365 days, the addition of ex-calendar or nameless days kept these ideal calendars in step with the solar year.

An equinox was the astronomical event commonly used in antiquity to monitor the length of the solar year. As the sun rose in Egypt due East on equinox morning, a much anticipated spectacle occurred. The eastern face of the Great Pyramid of Giza and other pyramids oriented to the cardinal directions lit up while the other sides remained in shadow. It is tempting to imagine priests and dignitaries assembled on the Giza plateau to bear witness as the first rays of the rising sun illuminated the immense monument.

Lopping off a quarter day from the traditional solar calendar set the start of the year wandering. The equinox no longer marked the beginning of the calendar year. In effect, the Wandering Year Calendar eliminated the pyramid's central role in Egyptian rites. This epochal calendar revision may have been imposed by a foreign power, likely the Persians, who reduced Egypt to a mere satrap of the empire.

Sumer and Akkad

The decipherment of cuneiform writing began centuries ago when European travelers returning from Western Asia brought home tales of strange markings incised on crumbling monuments. By the early nineteenth century, investigators had managed to decipher Old Persian, an Iranian language. This cuneiform script was a relatively simple mix of alphabetic and syllabic signs. The translations of Old Persian paved the way for the difficult task of sorting out the forms of the Akkadian script prevalent in Assyria and Babylonia.

A major breakthrough in deciphering Akkadian was the discovery that the script was both syllabic and logographic. A single sign could represent a word or, alternatively, a set of signs might represent the word's syllables. The syllables were further divisible into simpler syllables, and hence the syllabic rendering of a word was not unique. That was not all. Investigators discovered a sign generally had multiple values. A single sign could signify several words (multivalent) as well as several syllables (polyphony). Translators read the cuneiform sign ⬦ as *umu* [day], *pisu* [white], *shamash* [Sun-God]; and syllabically as ud, ut, u, tu, tam, bir, pir, lah, lih, hish, and *his*. Plus certain syllables had quite a few representative signs (homophones).

Despite the daunting multiplicity of readings, investigators spelled out the words of common inscriptions and established that the language of the texts was Semitic. The question then arose: Why would Assyrians and Babylonians have concocted and retained an exceedingly complicated writing system? The favored explanation envisioned the Akkadian script as an adaptation of a pre-existing writing system that was not Semitic. Thus was born the notion of the Sumerians, a non-Semitic people who wrote and spoke a non-Semitic language.

The origins of the Sumerians remained obscure. Several nineteenth and early twentieth century investigators saw an Aryan connection, while others categorically denied their existence. The skeptics argued that the script underlying Akkadian was an early Semitic writing system, maybe a code of some sort. In effect, they purged Akkadian of the Sumerian script, which disposed of the spoken Sumerian language and thus the actuality of a Sumerian people.

The standard theory accepted today was framed in the nineteenth century. It credited Sumerians with the invention of writing, and the Akkadians afterward built their writing system *on top of* Sumerian. The Akkadian script supposedly mingles Sumerian and Akkadian signs. A scribe could choose to write an Akkadian word using Sumerian signs, Akkadian signs, or a combination of both. For example, if French writing were constructed *on top of* English as in Akkadian/Sumerian, then a single French sign could represent the French word *ciel*, sky. And in syllables, *ci-el* could take the form *sea* plus *ell*, represented by an English sign for *sea* and a French sign for *elle*.

As the scope of cuneiform studies widened in the twentieth century, investigators found many Western Asian languages apparently had Sumerian embedded in their writing system. The discovery was vexing, as it seemed hardly possible that Sumerian could be the basis of written Western Asian languages as diverse as Eblaite, Urartian, Hittite, Elamite, Akkadian, etc. Possibly, investigators proposed, Western Asian scribes wrote in one language to be read in another. The alleged practice was common enough to have acquired a definition. Alloglottography describes the use of one writable language for the purpose of writing another language, or writing a text in a language different from the language in which it is intended to be read.

A more reasoned interpretation would recognize that the original writing system underlying Akkadian was not Sumerian, but a fully logographic script written and read by people speaking diverse languages. The script was neither Semitic nor non-Semitic. It was designed for a multi-lingual environs. The script eventually developed as a shared means of communication throughout Western Asia, just as the mainly logographic writing of modern China brings together a widely dispersed population that does not have a common speech.

In retrospect, the hypothesis of an indigenous Sumerian people inhabiting Sumer arose from a European craving for roots. Northern Europeans of the nineteenth century considered themselves to be the pinnacle of creation or, in secular circles, the apex of evolution. It seemed only fitting that their forebears had invented writing. On this basis investigators fleshed out a comprehensive Sumerian his-tory – where the Sumerians originated, what they looked like, the wars they fought, and the eventual demise of their civilization. In the 1920s, an historian could write, "Three generations ago the existence of Sumerians was unknown to the scientific world; today their history can be written and their art illustrated more fully than that of many ancient peoples."

In subsequent decades, the conventional picture of Sumerian civilization faded. The Sumerian physiognomy was the first attribute annulled. Early on, investigators working in southern Mesopotamia had discovered distinctive images of a people, often depicted as bald. They were considered native to the region and hence Sumerian. The discovery of similar images far north forced a revision of Sumerian racial characteristics.

Other findings necessitated a reformulation of Mesopotamian history. Initial studies had made warfare between the Sumerian and Semite races the central issue around which the historical narrative developed, but a reassessment of the data showed an affinity existed between the so-called races. There is a story, for example, of a Sumerian queen who gave her son a Semitic name; he then gave his son a Sumerian name, and the son later went on to employ a vizier with a Semitic name. This interchange of Sumerian and Semitic names within the same family indicates racial differences were of little importance. The weight of evidence led investigators to reinterpret the alleged warfare between Sumerians and Semites as a regional conflict rather than as a competition between the races.

By the 1960s, Sumerians had lost all their distinctive attributes except one. A philologist wrote, "The appellation 'Sumerian' should be taken as meaning 'Sumerian-speaking people' and nothing else." That is, Sumerian customs, gods, looks, artifacts, and so forth were indistinguishable from neighboring people whose native tongue was Semitic or another regional language. Prevailing opinion nowadays acknowledges that the only indisputable evidence of a Sumerian-speaking people is their script. The existence of this script is the *sine qua non* of the received version of Mesopotamian history.

In addition to Sumerians, the fabricated timeline of ante-history includes several other fictive peoples. Supposedly the Amorites were foreigners who infiltrated Mesopotamia from the West. They ruled over Babylon and conquered wide swathes of Western Asia. King Hammurabi, the famed law-giver of Hammurabi's Laws, was an Amorite. Nevertheless, the Amorites are more ethereal than the Sumerians. They exist in name only – literally. The foreign Amorites, so the story goes, immediately adopted the writing and customs of the Mesopotamian society they conquered, and therefore left no Amorite language texts or characteristic artifacts.

Amorite origins are obscure, though *Amorite* appears in the Old Testament *('emuri)*, Egyptian *(Amar)*, Akkadian *(Amuru)*, and other West Asian texts. Their so-called Sumerian name is *MAR.TU*, synonymous with *West*. The Amorites have a remarkably rich history for a people who did not leave any physical evidence of their existence. Investigators have identified thousands of Amorite names in the written documents of major Western Asian cities. The doings of these philologically conjured Amorites dominate the history of the Old Babylonian period.

The empires that populate the received version of early Mesopotamian history are illusory. However, actual civilizations did exist during the period. Their records have survived, and so has a great deal of valid writing about the early period. If the scripts were deciphered and the texts properly translated, a novel insight into societal origins would emerge.

We Still Look Up to Heaven

The geocentric versus heliocentric depictions of the solar system presented ancient skywatchers with disagreeable alternatives. If the stars and planets circled a stationary earth, they had to move at an incredibly fast speed. They ostensibly completed a full

The book is written in a universal logographic script based on common icons. Regardless of cultural background, one should be able to understand the text. A font library computer program accompanies the book. The user can type English or Chinese sentences, and the computer will instantaneously translate them into the language of icons. The font library serves as a dictionary that will have practical applications in the future.

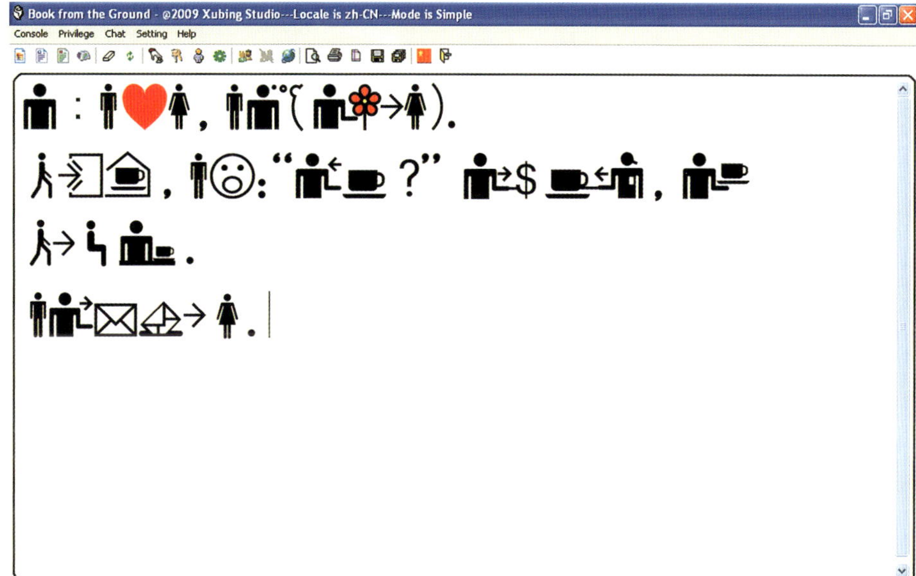

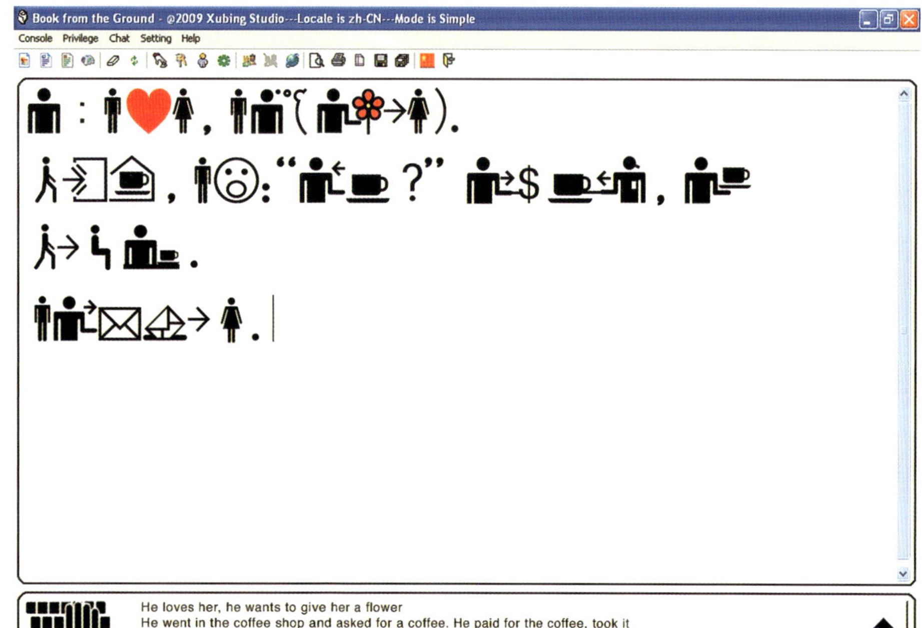

circuit of the sky in one day, every day. Only gods could accomplish such a feat.

The heliocentric thesis was equally unappealing. The earth is really big and gives no palpable indication of movement. Furthermore, if the earth revolved around the sun in the course of a year, then the observed configuration of the stars would have to change – unless the stars were incredibly far away. The two theories had their advocates. Aristotle opted for a secure geocentric cosmos and Copernicus set the earth moving, but both accepted the Astral Age notion that the celestial realm was divine.

Mesopotamian sages of the ante-historical period contended with a different dilemma. They reasonably expected the planet-gods would inhabit an ordered stable realm. Yet, they saw the cycle of the moon was irregular, alternating unpredictably between 29 and 30 days; the sun and stars required slightly more than 365 days to fill out the year; and the periods of Mercury, Venus, and Mars varied considerably from one cycle to the next. Obviously, something was amiss in the conduct of the gods.

The sages had a ready explanation for the gods' erratic ways. The central tenet of the creed *as above, so below* included the rider *as below, so above*. This implied that inappropriate societal behavior had a counterpart in the celestial realm. The discordant activities of the gods were a reflection of communal disarray. Hence, the effort to regulate society on the part of judges, priests, architects, astronomers, and state officials had the all-encompassing goal of furthering an ideal cosmic order. (Contrariwise, if a society perceived the planet-gods as fundamentally anarchic, the conviction *as above, so below* encouraged disruptive social behavior.)

The ideal cosmos envisioned by the Mesopotamian sages rested on a simple premise. All phenomena should be describable in terms of whole numbers. The cycle of daylight and night is measured as one day and therefore the sages reasoned all celestial periods must happen over an integer number of days. The task of determining the uncorrupted design of the celestial realm

fell to astronomers. They worked out the *true* pattern of the cosmos based on a set of idealized cycles and conjunctions of the planet-gods. This model served as a template for the world below, including temple architecture, ritual practices, law codes, and army formations. The common structure *above* and *below* engendered a sense of cosmic harmony.

Ironically, the ancient sages might have seen in Newton's concept of the solar system a vindication of their theology. According to the apocryphal story, a falling apple triggered Newton's theory. He realized that the *gravity* drawing the apple to the earth was a *force* acting to draw together all bodies, including the earth and the planets. Newton's Universal Law of Gravitation integrated *above* and *below* in a way the ancients never imagined, but in keeping with their fundamental belief *as above, so below*.

An epic movie recounting the sweep of world history might conceivably feature a scene of an imaginary meeting between Newton and a Mesopotamian sage in period costumes strolling through an apple orchard. The sequence would have Newton recount his efforts to work out the chronology of nations. His extensive studies took in the writings of Greek and Roman authors, the Bible, and many commentators. He tells the sage that an edited version of his findings was published in 1728, one year after his death. Newton complains the book failed to render his ideas adequately. But then, he admits ruefully, his proposed chronology was not compelling.

The sage appears shocked. He asks, "What about our literature? You certainly must know our history in great detail. We inscribed it on clay to make sure the knowledge of our civilization would endure. Do you know nothing of these writings?"

Newton is perplexed. He does not know of any Mesopotamian inscriptions on clay.

The sage consoles Newton. When your people come to explore our land, they will discover our literature, and thus learn what we experienced and deemed important to record.

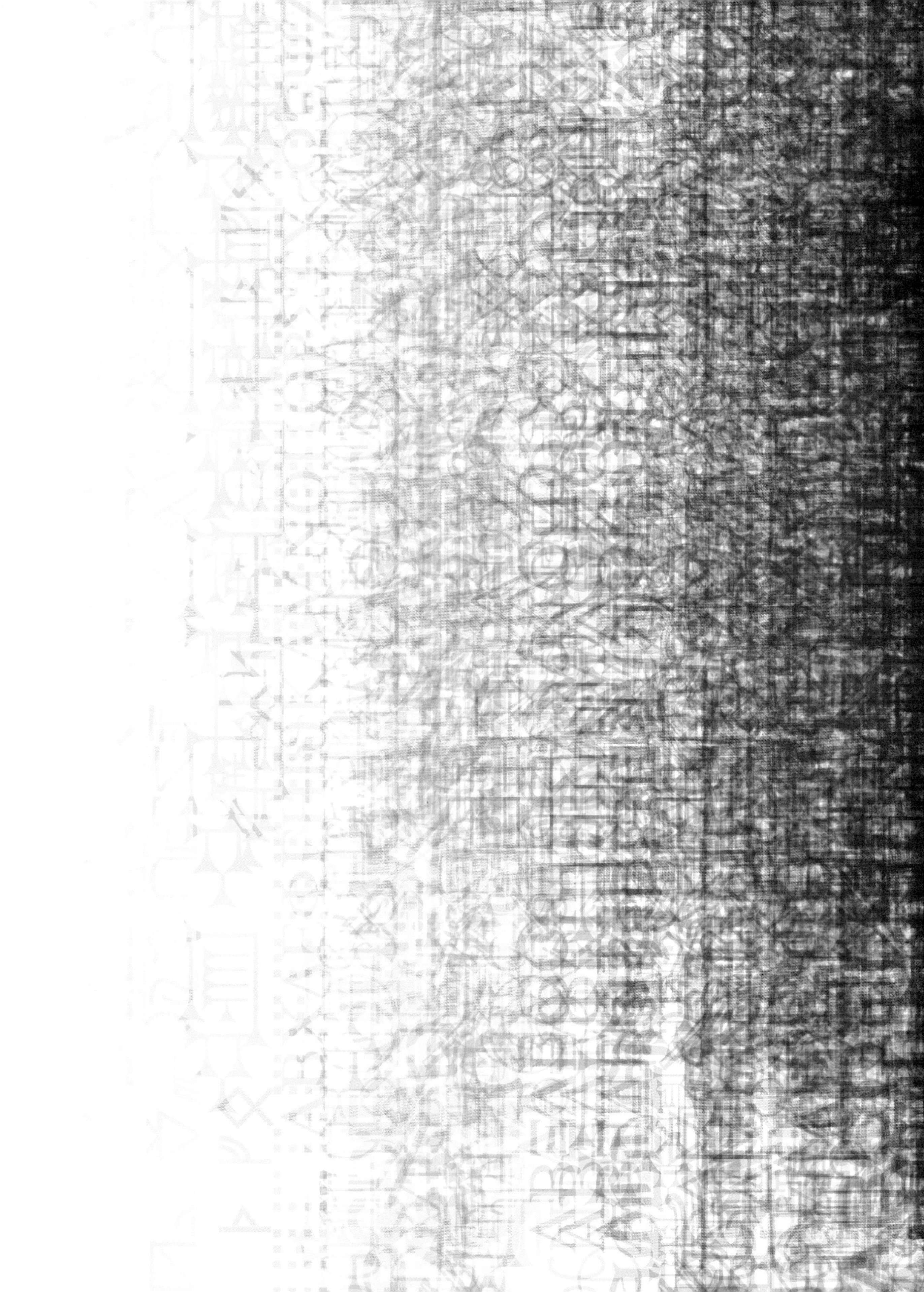

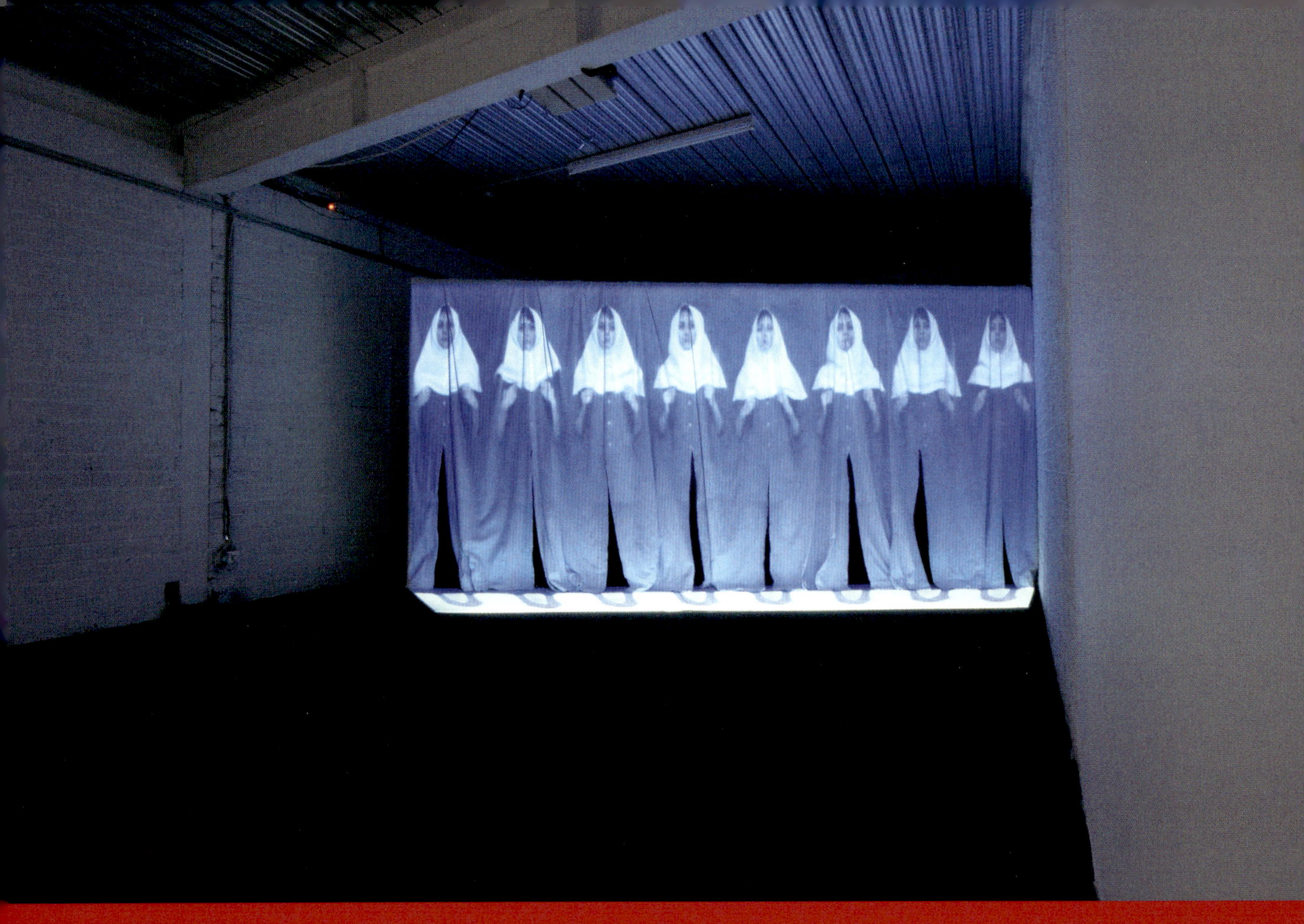

Right page top

Left
**Susana Pilar
Delahante Matienzo**
*Anexión oculta /
Hidden Annexation*, 2008,
6 photographs, inkjet print

Center
Günther Saree
Sterbetuch, 1973,
reconstruction 2008

Right
Rabih Mroué,
*On Three Posters. Reflections
on a video-performance*, 2006,
video, color, sound, 18 min

Right page bottom

Korpys/Löffler
Für ein Leben nach dem Tod, 2006,
video, color, sound, 72:30 min

Installation views
The Model, Sligo, Ireland, 2009

Above
Barbad Golshiri
ᴍᴧᴍɪ , 2008, video installation,
color, sound, mixed media,
dimensions and runtime variable

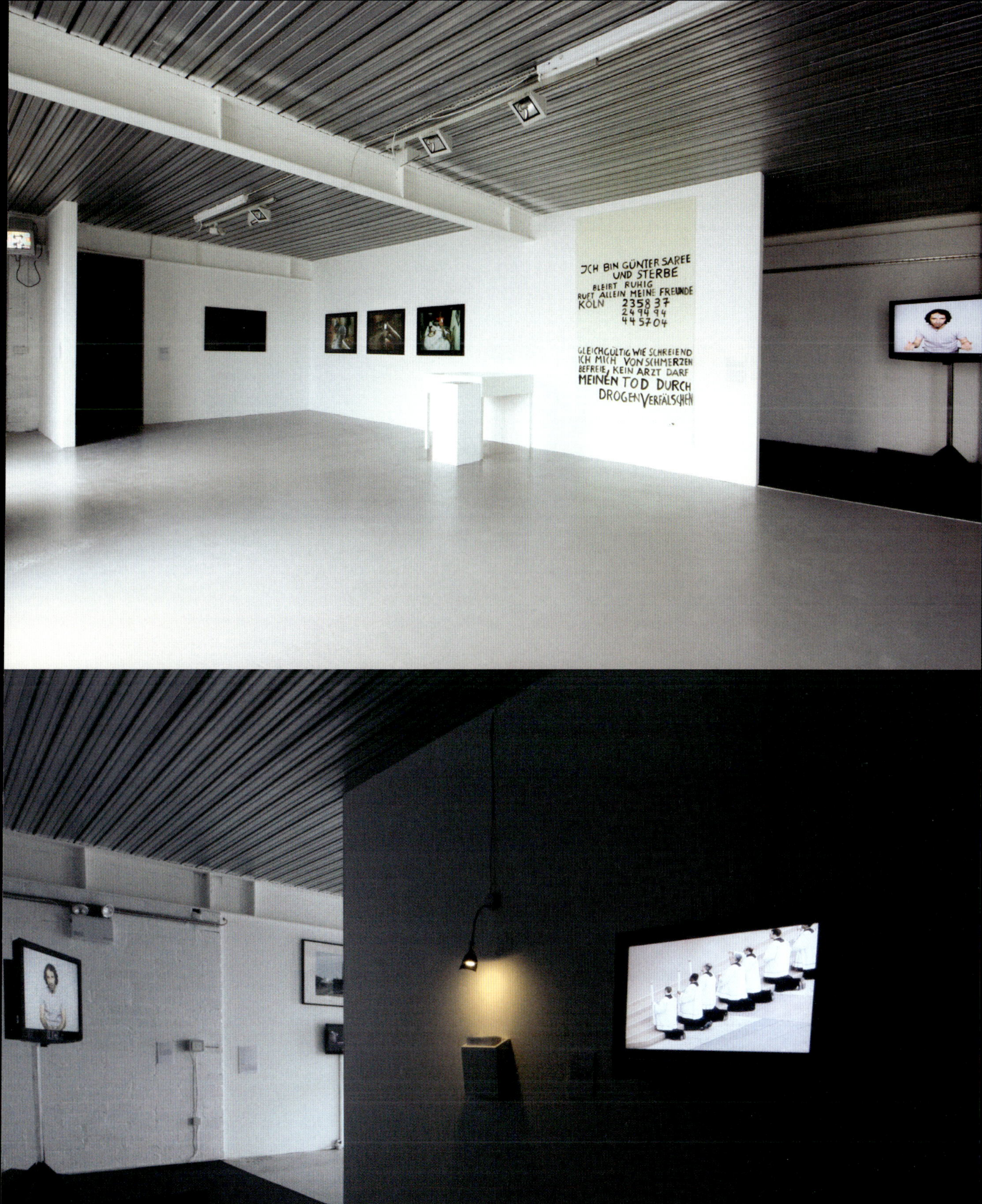
ICH BIN GÜNTER SAREE
UND STERBE
BLEIBT RUHIG
RUFT ALLEIN MEINE FREUNDE
KÖLN   235837
             249494
             445704

GLEICHGÜLTIG WIE SCHREIEND
ICH MICH VON SCHMERZEN
BEFREIE, KEIN ARZT DARF
MEINEN TOD DURCH
DROGEN VERFÄLSCHEN

Right page top

Sang-Kyoon Noh
Twin Jesus Christs, 2001,
sequins on polyester resin and
fiberglass, 267 × 265 × 78 cm each

Right page bottom

Nira Pereg
Sabbath 2008, 2008, 1-channel
video projection, color, sound,
7 min

This page

In the front
Boris Groys
Religion as Medium, 2006,
video lecture, color, sound,
25 min

In the back
**Lenin Mausoleum
Documentation**
1998/2008

Installation views
The Model, Sligo, Ireland, 2009

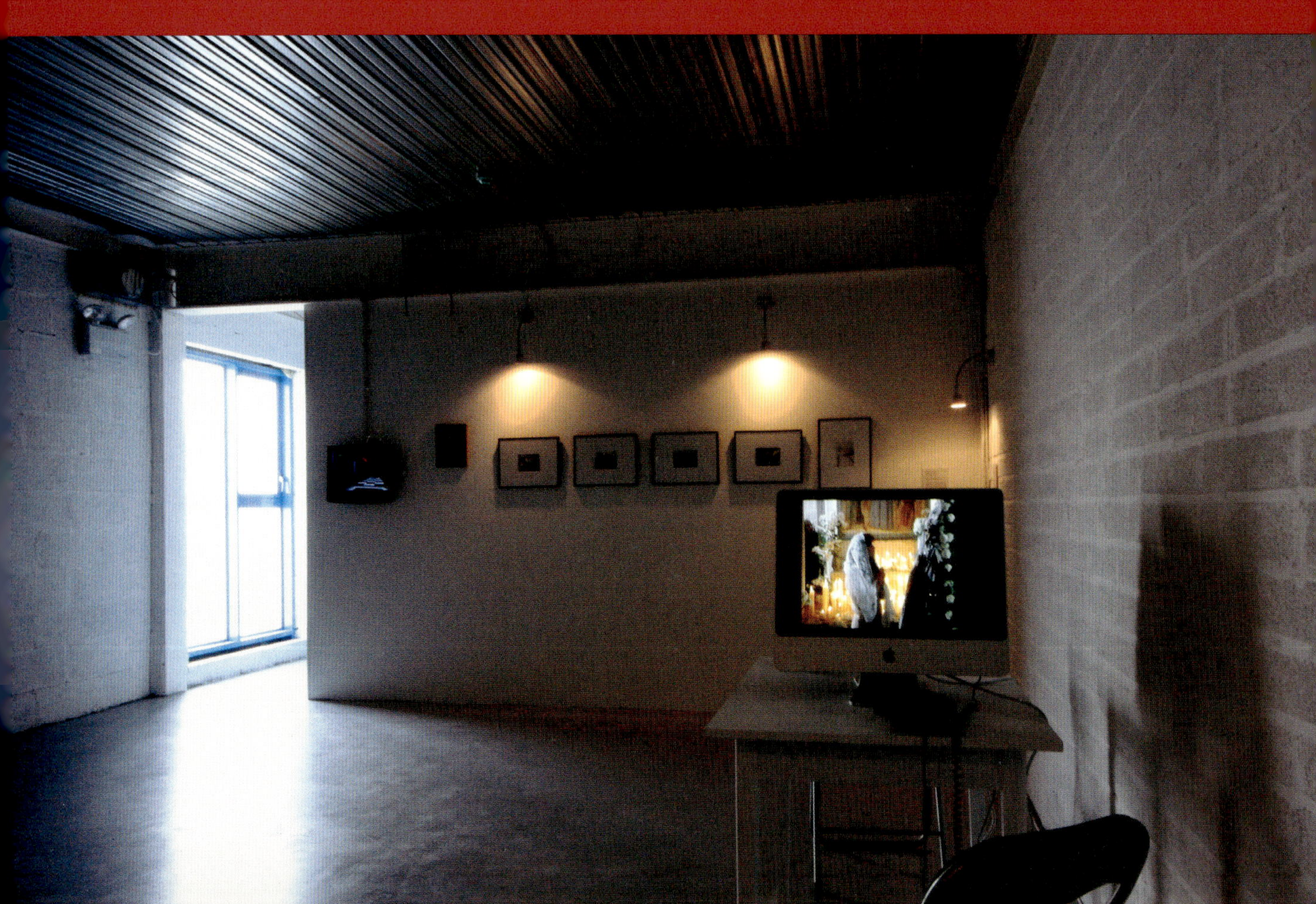

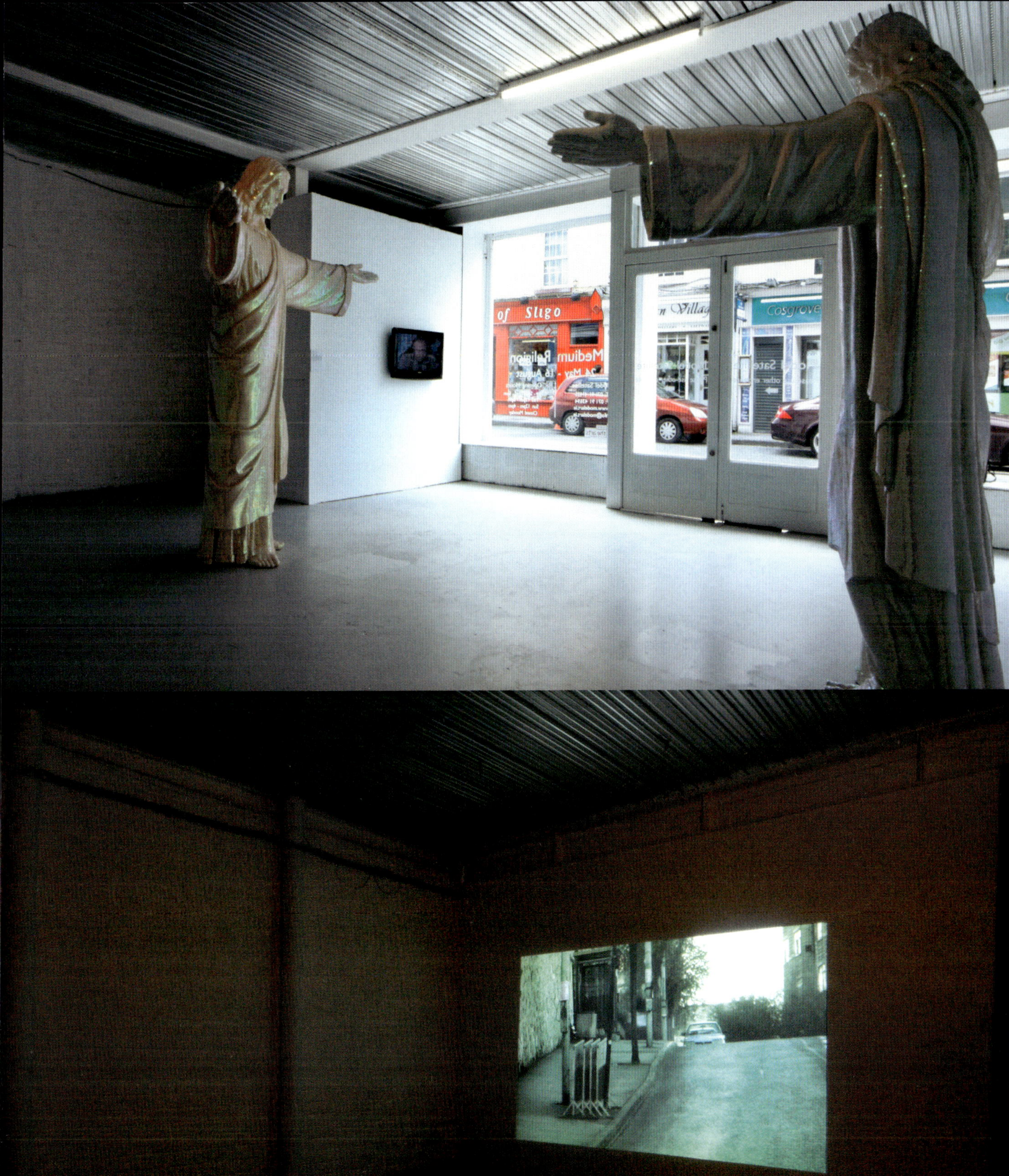

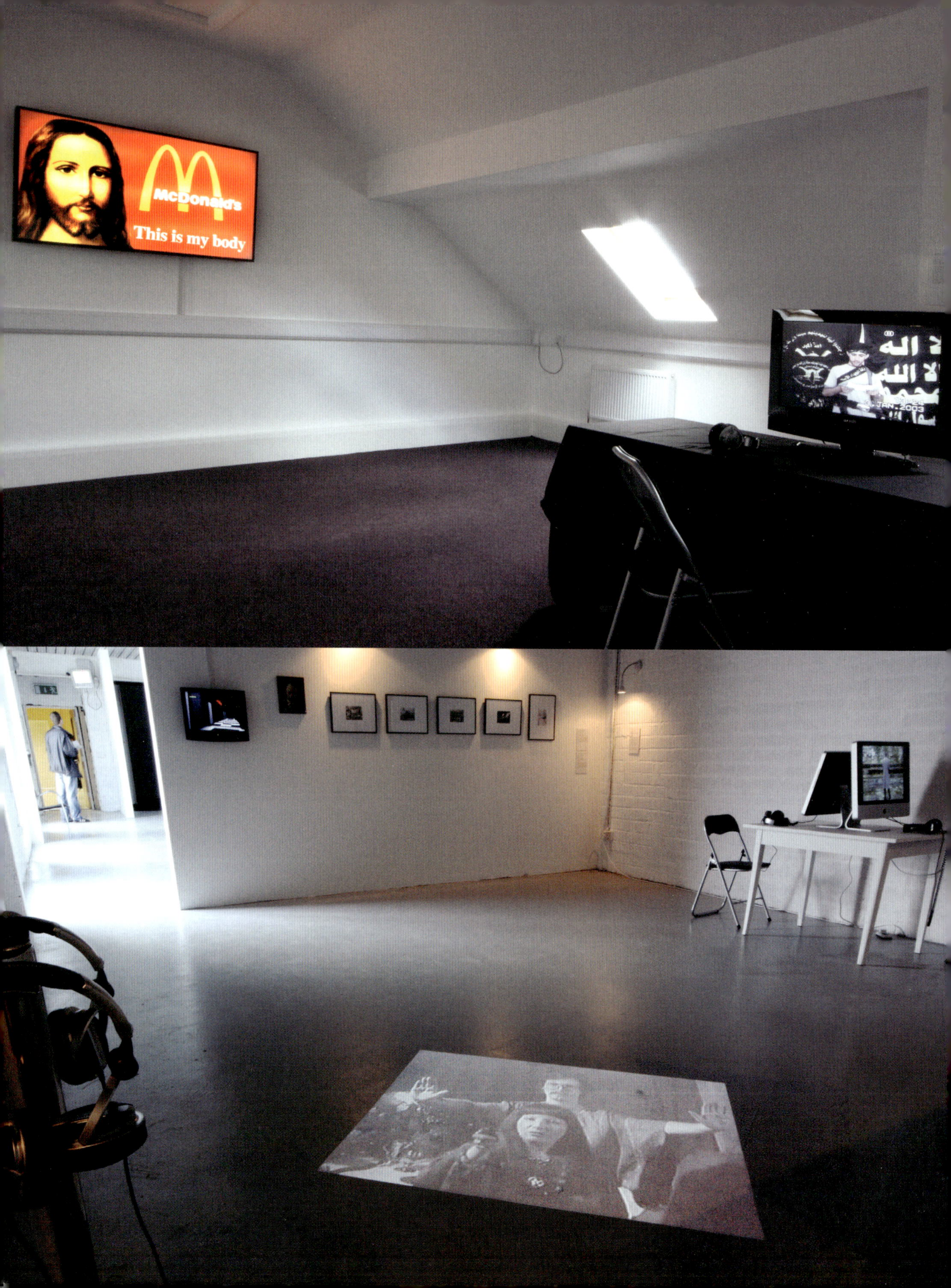
McDonald's
This is my body

Left page top

Left
Alexander Kosolapov
This is my body, 2002,
light boxes, 82 x 150 cm each

Right
Rabih Mroué
*On Three Posters. Reflections
on a video-performance,* 2006,
video, color, sound, 18 min

Left page bottom

In the front
Vadim Zakharov
*Der See der Vergessenheit /
Lake of Oblivion*, 2000,
video installation, color, sound,
30 min

In the back
Boris Groys
Religion as Medium, 2006
and **Lenin Mausoleum
Documentation**
1998/2008

This page

Top right
Gregor Schneider
Cube Venice, 2005,
photograph

Bottom right
**Natalia Schmidt
Boris Burghardt
David Howoldt**
Cube Collage, 2006,
video, color, sound, 23 min

Left
Rabih Mroué
*On Three Posters. Reflections on a
video-performance*, 2006, video,
color, sound, 18 min

Installation views
The Model, Sligo, Ireland, 2009

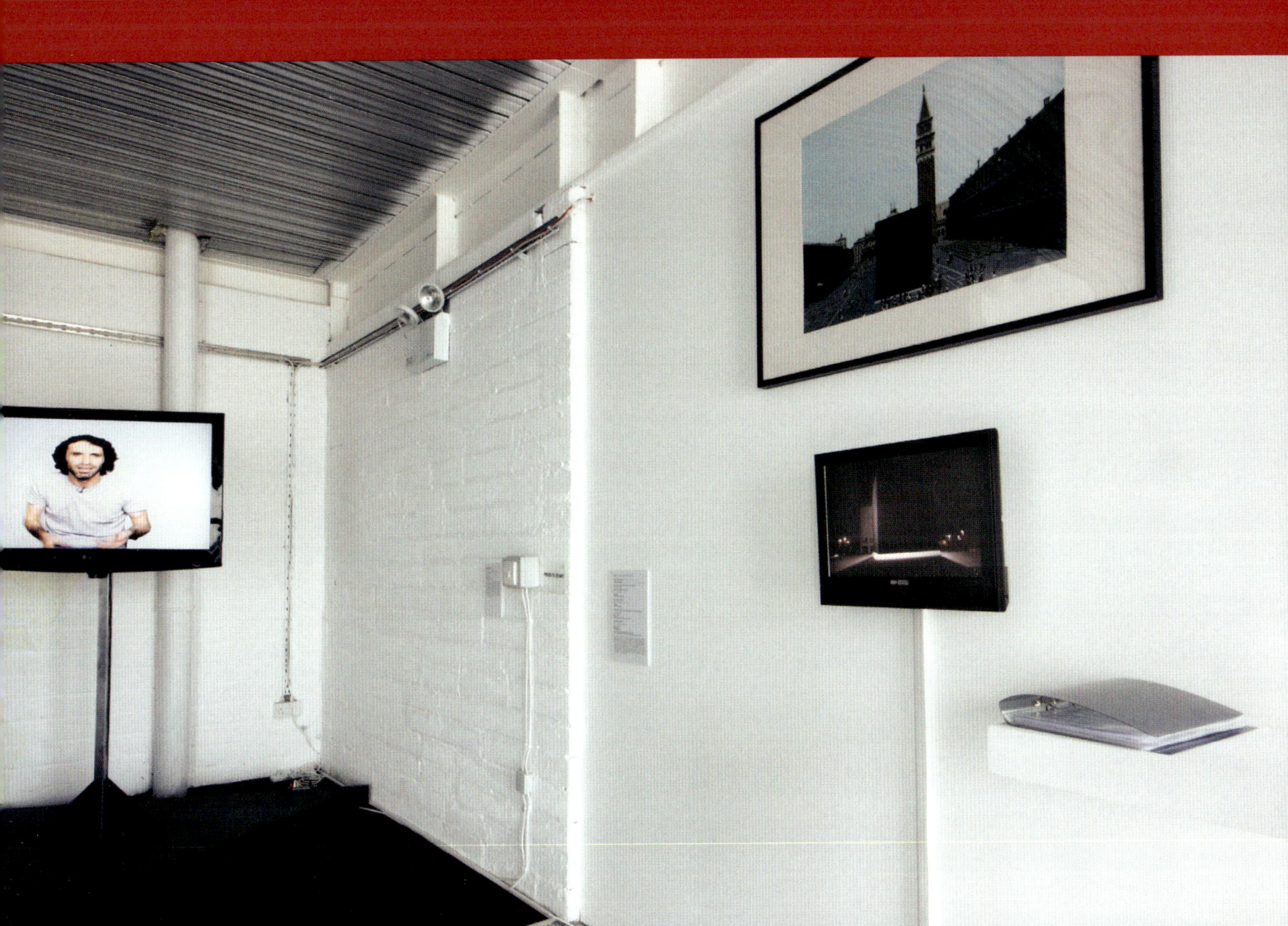

Artists in the Exhibition

■ **Adel Abdessemed**
God is Design, 2005
Video animation made from
3,050 drawings (b/w, sound)
4:44 min, loop
Courtesy the artist and
David Zwirner, New York;
Christine König Galerie,
Vienna

■ **Oreet Ashery**
Dancing with Men, 2003
Video (color, sound)
3 min, loop
Courtesy Oreet Ashery

Oh Jerusalem, 2005
Video (b/w, silent)
4 min, loop
Courtesy Oreet Ashery

*Self Portrait as Marcus Fisher
1–5*, 2000
5 photographs (inkjet print,
original: Polaroid)
101.5 × 80 cm each
Photographer: Manuel Vason
Courtesy Oreet Ashery

■ **Maja Bajevic**
Double Bubble, 2001
Video (color, sound)
3:36 min, loop
Courtesy Galerie Peter
Kilchmann, Zurich;
Galerie Michel Rein, Paris

■ **Peter Bogers**
The Secret of the Most High,
2003
Video installation (color, sound)
10 min, loop
Courtesy Netherlands Media
Art Institute, Amsterdam
With the kind support of the
Royal Netherlands Embassy,
Berlin. **Koninkrijk
der Nederlanden**

■ **Christoph Büchel**
كفاحي [My Struggle], 2006
1,000 copies of *Mein Kampf*
(Arabic translation),
tarp, cashier box, chair,
pallets, boxes
Courtesy the artist and
Hauser & Wirth Zürich London

*Tomorrow's Pioneers
(Farfour)*, 2007
Video (color, sound)
10:59 min, loop
Courtesy the artist and
Hauser & Wirth Zürich London

■ **Paul Chan**
1st ~~Light~~, 2005
Digital video projection
(color, silent)
14 min, loop
Courtesy of Greene Naftali,
New York

■ **Susana Pilar
Delahante Matienzo**
*Anexión oculta /
Hidden Annexation*, 2008
6 photographs (inkjet print)
70 × 100 cm each
Courtesy Susana Pilar
Delahante Matienzo
Produced in cooperation
with ZKM | Center for
Art and Media Karlsruhe

*El escandalo de lo Real /
The Scandal of the Real*,
2006–2007
Heterologous artificial
insemination, 2 photographs
(inkjet print), 2 copies of
medical documents
Courtesy Susana Pilar
Delahante Matienzo
Produced in cooperation
with ZKM | Center for Art
and Media Karlsruhe

Sin titulo / Untitled, 2002
4 photographs (inkjet print)
Courtesy Susana Pilar
Delahante Matienzo
Produced in cooperation with
ZKM | Center for Art and Media
Karlsruhe

■ **Wim Delvoye**
TIM, 2006–2008
Tattoo, Courtesy Sammlung
Reinking, Hamburg

■ **Dias & Riedweg**
Deus é boca (Gott ist Mund),
2002
4-channel video installation
(color, sound)
© Dias & Riedweg, 2002
Courtesy of Galeria Vermelho,
São Paulo and Galeria
Filomena Soares, Lisbon

■ **Valie Export,
Ingrid and Oswald Wiener**
Das Unsagbare Sagen, 1992
Video (color, sound)
45 min, extract of 12:50 min
Script: Oswald Wiener
Direction and design:
Valie Export, Ingrid and
Oswald Wiener
Camera: Valie Export and
Ingrid Wiener
Sound: Oswald Wiener
Editor: Heinrich Mis
Production: P.R.E.TV on behalf
of ORF/"Kunststücke"

■ **Omer Fast**
CNN Concatenated, 2002
Video (color, sound)
18 min, loop
Courtesy gb agency, Paris

A Tank Translated, 2002
4-channel video installation
(color, sound)
German subtitles
Courtesy gb agency, Paris

■ **Barbad Golshiri**
mʌmi , 2008
Video installation
(color, sound, mixed media)
Dimensions and runtime
variable
From 'Odyssey-i project'
Courtesy Barbad Golshiri
Produced in cooperation with
ZKM | Center for Art and Media
Karlsruhe

■ **Boris Groys**
Religion as Medium, 2006
Video lecture (color, sound)
25 min, loop
Courtesy Boris Groys
Produced in cooperation with
ZKM | Center for Art and Media
Karlsruhe, 2006,
commissioned by
Schirn Kunsthalle Frankfurt

Unsterbliche Körper, 2007
Video lecture (color, sound)
29 min, loop
Courtesy Boris Groys
Produced in cooperation with
ZKM | Center for Art and Media
Karlsruhe, 2007, and
in cooperation with
Associazione Culturale il
Vento del Cinema Roma

■ **Huang Yong Ping**
*Loups et chèvres regardent la
vidéo de Aïd-el-Kebir*, 2006
Mixed-media installation
(mounted animals, carpets,
video)
Dimensions variable
Courtesy Huang Yong Ping

■ **IRWIN**
Corpse of Art, 2003–2004
Mixed-media installation
(wood, textile, wax, hair, vase,
flowers)
Dimensions variable
Courtesy Galerija Gregor
Podnar, Berlin/Ljubljana

■ **Romuald Karmakar**
Hamburger Lektionen, 2006
Digital projection (color, sound)
133 min, loop
Courtesy farbfilm verleih GmbH

■ **Vitaly Komar**
Mandala # 1 (from the *Three-Day Weekend* project), 2005
Tempera and oil on canvas
122 × 122 cm
Courtesy Vitaly Komar and
Ronald Feldman Fine Arts,
New York

Forbidden Fruit No 2
(from the *Three-Day Weekend*
project), 2004–2005
Collage
100 × 75 cm

*The Horizon at the End of the
Tunnel* (from the *Three-Day
Weekend* project), 2004–2005
Collage
100 × 75 cm

Flashbacks (from the *Three-Day
Weekend* project), 2004–2005
Collage
100 × 75 cm

All: Courtesy Vitaly Komar and
Galerie Sandmann, Berlin

■ **Beryl Korot and Steve Reich**
The Cave, 1993
5-channel video installation
(color, sound)
Courtesy Beryl Korot (video)
and Steve Reich (music)

■ **Korpys/Löffler**
Für ein Leben nach dem Tod,
2006
Video (color, sound)
72:30 min, loop
Courtesy Meyer Riegger,
Karlsruhe

*Für ein Leben nach dem Tod
(Generalaudienz Audienzhalle
15. Dez. 2004, Generalaudienz
Petersdom 24. Nov. 2004,*

*Petrusskulptur Petersdom
12. Okt. 2004)*, 2006
3 C-prints
68 × 100 cm each
Courtesy Meyer Riegger,
Karlsruhe

■ **Alexander Kosolapov**
This is my body, 2002
This is my blood, 2002
Light boxes
82 × 150 cm each
Courtesy Guelman Gallery

■ **Florian Meyer**
Igreja Positivista, 2008
Video (color, sound)
16:30 min, loop
Music: Olga Neuwirth,
HOOLOOMOOLOO
Klangforum Wien, Kairos
0012242KAI
© by G. Ricordi & Co.
Munich, Sy. 3342
Courtesy Florian Meyer

■ **Rabih Mroué**
*On Three Posters. Reflections on
a video-performance*, 2006
(Rabih Mroué / Elias Khoury:
Three Posters, Ayloul Festival,
Beirut 2000)
Video (color, sound)
18 min
Courtesy of Sfeir-Semler
Gallery

■ **Dorcas Müller**
*Wie der tote Hase dem toten
Beuys den Menschen erklärt*,
2004
3-channel video installation
(color, sound)
4:30 min, loop
Courtesy Dorcas Müller
Thanks to Günther Zeck and
Thomas Knoefel

■ **Sang-Kyoon Noh**
Twin Jesus Christs, 2001
Sequins on polyester resin
and fiberglass
267 × 265 × 78 cm each
Courtesy Sang-Kyoon Noh

For the Worshipers, 2008
Sequins on polyester resin
and fiberglass
Dimensions variable
(head: 84.5 × 69 × 46.5 cm,
hand 1: 75 × 44 × 51 cm,
hand 2: 77 × 40 × 46 cm
Courtesy Sang-Kyoon Noh

■ **Nira Pereg**
Sabbath 2008, 2008
1-channel video projection
(color, sound)
7 min, loop
Courtesy Nira Pereg
Produced in cooperation with
ZKM | Center for Art and Media
Karlsruhe

*Location 8 – Ramot Polin /
Polish Hills*, 2008
14 photographs (C-prints)
60 × 80 cm each
Courtesy Nira Pereg

Kept Alive, 2008
12 photographs (C-prints)
70 × 100 cm each
Courtesy Nira Pereg

■ **robotlab**
bios [bible], 2007
Robot installation
Dimensions variable
Courtesy robotlab
Produced in Cooperation with
ZKM | Center for Art and Media
Karlsruhe
With the kind support of KUKA,
Wintopo, Papier Union, Lamy,
Armstrong, Cordier

■ **Osvaldo Romberg**
Mikve at Masada, 2008
Mixed-media installation
(stacked newspapers)
Courtesy Galerie Heike Curtze
Wien | Berlin
Produced in cooperation with
ZKM | Center for Art and Media
Karlsruhe

Masada's Mikve, 2008
Drawing, watercolor
96 × 126 cm
Courtesy ZKM | Center for Art
and Media Karlsruhe

■ **Anri Sala**
Uomoduomo, 2000
Video (b/w, no sound)
1:41 min, loop
Courtesy Sammlung Goetz

■ **Günter Saree**
Documentation material
1972–1973
Courtesy Prof. Reiner Speck,
Cologne and Erhard Klein,
Bad Münstereifel
Photo © Franz Fischer, Bonn

Sterbetuch, 1973
(reconstruction, 2008)
Joachim Hirling, ZKM | Center
for Art and Media Karlsruhe,
2008

■ **Konrad Balder Schäuffelen**
Abwurfstange, 1990
Deer antler, gold
80 × 40 × 40 cm
Courtesy Konrad Balder
Schäuffelen, Munich

■ **Christoph Schlingensief**
Der König wohnt in Mir, 2008
Mixed-media installation
Dimensions variable
(space: 6.6 × 7.3 m, chimneys
112 × 150 × 40 cm each)
Photographs: Aino Laberenz
and Christoph Schlingensief
Videos: Christoph
Schlingensief
Editing: Lilli Kuschel,
Stefan Schmied, and
Christoph Schlingensief
Courtesy of Christoph
Schlingensief & Kunstraum
Innsbruck, 2008

Drei Sonnen / Prozession, 2008
16 mm film, digitized
(b/w, sound)
4 min, loop
Film: Christoph Schlingensief
Editing: Heta Multanen and
Christoph Schlingensief
Courtesy Christoph
Schlingensief

■ **Michael Schuster**
Golgatha, 2008
Oak crosses with
aluminum spray cans
(3 multiples from the edition
No More Nails, 2005,
edition: 56 copies + 5 A. P.)
56 × 25 × 8 cm each
Courtesy Artelier
Contemporary, Graz

■ **Wael Shawky**
The Cave, 2006
Video (color, sound)
12:45 min, loop
Courtesy Wael Shawky

Al Aqsa Park, 2006
Computer animation
(b/w, sound)
30 min, loop
Courtesy Wael Shawky

- **Jalal Toufic**
  *The Sleep of Reason. This Blood
  Spilled in My Veins*, 2002
  Video (color, sound)
  32 min, loop
  Courtesy Jalal Toufic

- **Vadim Zakharov**
  *Der See der Vergessenheit /
  Lake of Oblivion*, 2000
  Video installation (color, sound)
  30 min, loop
  Courtesy Vadim Zakharov

- **Hermes Zygott**
  Sacred Reality #1, 2008
  Orthodox XXI Century, 2008
  Russian Monstrosities, 2008
  Light boxes, wooden frame,
  sound, 68 × 55 cm, 90 × 58 cm,
  80 × 40 cm

Music: reinterpretation of
Claudio Monteverdi's *Vespro
della Beata Vergine* (1610),
Guns P. Holman and
Hermes Zygott, 2008
Courtesy RNA Foundation

Documentary Installations in the Exhibition

- **Video messages by Osama
  Bin Laden (Usāma ibn
  Muhammad ibn Awad
  ibn Lādin)**
  2001, 2004
  Video (color, sound)
  5 min, loop
  5:40 min, loop
  http://de.youtube.com/watch?
  v=ADhfC6KjcJQ (May 8, 2009)

- **Gospel Aerobics
  with Paul Eugene**
  ca. 2005–2008
  Video (color, sound)
  19:30 min, 21:50 min, 32 min,
  24:30 min, 24 min, loop
  www.pauleugene.com
  (Dezember 2, 2010)

- *God's Generals*, 2008
  Documentary video material,
  found footage (color, sound)
  15 min, loop
  Produced by ZKM | Center for
  Art and Media Karlsruhe, 2008

- *Jerry B. Jenkins & Tim LaHaye:
  Left Behind. Eternal Forces*,
  2006
  Computer game, video collage,
  and 12 novels
  Video collage: produced by
  ZKM | Center for Art and Media
  Karlsruhe, 2008

- **Kajri Jain**
  Bazaar Religious Images
  Assorted religious prints on
  paper, postcards, stickers,
  calendars, DVDs, 1 mantra box
  Courtesy Kajri Jain
  Further credits see this volume,
  p. 157

- **Debate on
  Cologne Mosque project**
  Documentary material (archi-
  tectural designs, photographs,
  graphics, texts)
  Courtesy Architekturbüro
  Paul Böhm, DITIB / Türkisch-
  Islamische Union der Anstalt
  für Religion e.V., and
  Bürgerbewegung Pro Köln e.V.

- **Lenin Mausoleum
  Documentation**

  **Maxim Kononenko,
  Natalia Struchkova,
  Alexey Naumenkov,
  Timur Yudin**
  Virtual Mawsolej W. I. Lenina,
  1998/2008
  3-D computer model,
  VRML/ParallelGraphics
  Courtesy Maxim Kononenko,
  Natalia Struchkova, Alexey
  Naumenkov, Timur Yudin

  Alexey V. Shchusev
  Lenin-Mausoleum, 1924/2008
  5 historical photographs
  (inkjet print)
  30 × 40 cm each

  Geneviève Zondervan
  Lenine (Portrait of Lenin), 1953
  (Exhibited in *De Marx à Staline*,
  Paris 1953)
  Oil on canvas
  27 × 22 cm
  Courtesy Sarah Wilson

- **Anand Patwardhan**
  Father, *Son and Holy War
  (Part II)*, 1994
  16 mm film, digitized
  (color, sound)
  60 min, loop
  Courtesy Anand Patwardhan

- **Miuccia Prada**
  True Faith, 2008
  Concept, styling, and casting:
  Miuccia Prada
  Photographs: Sebastian Faena
  Sittings editor: Katie Grand
  POP Magazine, issue 19 /
  September 2008, 6 covers,
  pp. 201–209

  Katie Grand
  Nun Head, 2008
  Photographs: Sebastian Faena
  Fashion editor: Katie Grand
  POP Magazine, issue 19,
  September 2008, pp. 210–239

- **Dorna Safaian**
  *After being interpreted by a
  machine (the blind; the dead;
  realism)*, 2008
  Video installation (color, sound)
  Runtime variable, loop
  Editing: Kevin Mateew
  Courtesy Dorna Safaian
  Produced in cooperation with
  ZKM | Center for Art and Media
  Karlsruhe

- **Gregor Schneider**
  Cube Documentation,
  2005–2008
  Selected documentary
  materials (photographs,
  drawings, press articles,
  essays, video, audio)
  Courtesy Gregor Schneider
  Curatorial concept:
  Natalia Schmidt

  Michèle & Mischa Kuball
  Black Cube/apple NYC, 2006
  3 photographs (inkjet print)
  14 × 11 cm each
  © Photo: Michèle Kuball /
  Archive Mischa Kuball,
  Düsseldorf 2006

  **Natalia Schmidt,
  Boris Burghardt,
  and David Howoldt**
  Cube Collage, 2006
  Video (color, sound)
  23 min, loop
  Courtesy Natalia Schmidt,
  Boris Burghardt, David
  Howoldt

- **Internal Scientology videos**
  Tom Cruise Scientology
  [Medal of Valor], 2008
  Tom Cruise Scientology Video
  [monologue], 2004
  Video (color, sound)
  0:53 min and 9:35 min, loop
  www.youtube.com/watch?
  v=dh2uS-Om_Bs
  (November 29, 2010)
  www.youtube.com/watch?
  v=UFBZ_uAbxSO
  (November 29, 2010)

- **Joshua Simon**
  Shahids, 2003–2008
  Video collage (color, sound)
  20 min, loop
  Editor: Oded Bajayo
  Courtesy Joshua Simon

- **UC Berkeley
  Journalism Project**
  God, *Sex & Family*
  Website
  A UC Berkeley Journalism
  Project funded by the
  Carnegie-Knight
  Initiative
  http://newsinitiative.org/ucb/
  (November 29, 2010)

  Faces of Faith, 2008
  Second Life panel discussion
  Recorded 3-D animation
  (color, sound)
  76 min, loop
  A UC Berkeley Journalism
  Project funded by the
  Carnegie-Knight
  Initiative
  http://archive.treet.tv/
  faces_faith
  (November 29, 2010)

Hent de Vries Dutch philosopher, received his doctorate in philosophy at the University of Leiden in 1989 and held the Chair of Metaphysics and Its History at the Department of Philosophy at the University of Amsterdam from 1993 to 2002. Hent de Vries is director of the Humanities Center at the Johns Hopkins University, Baltimore, USA. Since 2003, he is professor in the Humanities Center and the Department of Philosophy at Johns Hopkins University. He is the editor/author of *Religion and Violence: Philosophical Perspectives from Kant to Derrida* (2001), *Religion and Media. Cultural Memory in the Present* (2001), and *Religion: Beyond a Concept* (2008).

Boris Groys born 1947 in East Berlin, is a philosopher, essayist, art critic, media theorist, and an internationally acclaimed expert on late-Soviet postmodern art and literature, as well as on the Russian avant-garde. He studied philosophy and mathematics at the University of Leningrad and received his Ph.D. in 1992. Since 1994 he is professor of arts, philosophy, and media theory/studies at the Karlsruhe University of Arts and Design and since 2005 Global Distinguished Professor of Russian and Slavic Studies at the Faculty of Arts and Science, New York University. In 2006/2007 he received a Senior Scholarship by the Courtauld Institute of Art, London. His writing engages the wildly disparate traditions of French post-structuralism and modern Russian philosophy; see, for example: *Unter Verdacht. Eine Phänomenologie der Medien Media* (2000)and *Ilya Kabakov. The Man Who Flew into Space from his Apartment* (2006) and *Art Power* (2008).

Kajri Jain born 1961 in Canberra, Australia, works as assistant professor at the Centre for Visual and Media Culture at the University of Toronto Mississauga. In her research she is focusing on South Asian visual culture, cinema, and art. In 2007, she published *Gods in the Bazaar: The Economies of Indian Calendar Art*.

Vitaly Komar born 1943, and
Alexander Melamid born 1945, are a team of Russian-born American Conceptual artists. In 1967, they graduated from the Stroganov School of Art and Design. They are the founders of the Sots art movement, which is the Soviet equivalent of the Western Pop art movement. Since 1976, their works have been exhibited internationally. Being dissidents of the Soviet Union, they became U.S. citizens in 1978. Their last collaborative work took place in 2003.

Rabih Mroué born 1967 in Beirut, Lebanon, is an actor, director, and playwright. He studied theater at the University of Beirut. In 1990 he began to create his own plays, performances, and videos. His mostly critical works are concerned with the political and economical context of Lebanon and the Near East.

Dorna Safaian born 1984 in Tehran, Iran, studied art science, media theory, philosophy, aesthetics, and media art at the Karlsruhe University of Arts and Design. She received her M.A. in 2008 (supervisor Prof. Boris Groys) and held a research fellowship by ZKM | Center for Art and Media Karlsruhe. Dorna Safaian currently lives and works in Berlin.

Natalia Schmidt born 1981 in Munich, studied art science, media theory, philosophy, and media art at the Karlsruhe University of Arts and Design, as well as cultural studies in Berlin. In her research she is currently focusing on the concept of the curatorial. Natalia Schmidt lives and works in Berlin and Karlsruhe.

Joshua Simon born 1979 in Tel Aviv-Jaffa, Israel, lives and works in Tel Aviv-Jaffa. He is curator of several exhibitions, focusing mostly on political or social topics, and also works as director of short films and writer for magazines. In 2007 Simon curated the first Israeli Biennial, the Herzliya Biennial of Contemporary Art, presenting more than seventy artists. Simon is co-editor of *Maayan*, a poetry and art magazine, and editor of *Maarvon*, the only Israeli cinema magazine.

Peter Sloterdijk is professor of philosophy and theory of media at the Academy of Fine Arts Vienna and at the Karlsruhe University of Arts and Design, where he was elected dean in 2001. In 1983, his work *Critique of Cynical Reason* became the best-selling book of German philosophy in the twentieth century. In 2005 he inaugurated the Emmanuel Lévinas Chair at the Académie Européenne in Strasbourg and received the Sigmund Freud Award for Scientific Prose. In 2006 he was honored with the distinction "Commandeur de l'Ordre des Arts et des Lettres" by the Republic of France. He also received the Lessing Prize for Criticism (2008) and the BDA Architectural Criticism Award (2009). His most recent publications include *Gottes Eifer. Vom Kampf der drei Monotheismen* (2007) and *Du mußt dein Leben ändern. Über Anthropotechnik* (2009).

Henry Zemel is head of the Caeno Foundation, New York, which supports historical and physical research pertaining to the chronology of events, epochs, and civilizations. He hosted the symposium "What Was Old Is New Again" at ZKM | Center for Art and Media Karlsruhe in 2008.

Peter Weibel born in Odessa in 1944, studied literature, medicine, logic, philosophy, and film in Paris and Vienna. Besides his various activities as artist and curator, his publications about art and media theory have earned him international renown. Since 1984 he is professor at the University of Applied Arts Vienna. After heading the digital arts laboratory at the Media Department of New York State University at Buffalo from 1984 to 1989, he founded the Institute of New Media at the Städelschule in Frankfurt am Main in 1989. Between 1986 and 1995, he was in charge of the Ars Electronica in Linz as artistic director. In 1993 he became chief curator at the Neue Galerie Graz, Austria. Since 1999 Peter Weibel is Chairman and CEO of the ZKM | Center for Art and Media Karlsruhe. Besides many other prizes and decorations, he was awarded an honorary doctorate by the University of Art and Design Helsinki in 2007. In 2008 he was awarded the French distinction "Officier dans l'Ordre des Arts et des Lettres," and in 2010 the Austrian Cross of Honour for Science and Art I. Class.

Slavoj Žižek born 1949 in Ljubljana, Slovenia, is a philosopher, psychoanalyst, and cultural theorist. Žižek has been a visiting professor at, among others, the University of Chicago, Columbia University, London Consortium, Princeton University, The New School, the University of Minnesota, the University of California, Irvine, and the University of Michigan. He is currently professor at the European Graduate School, as well as international director of The Birkbeck Institute for the Humanities at Birkbeck, University of London, and president of the Society for Theoretical Psychoanalysis, Ljubljana. Žižek has published over fifty books (translated into twenty languages) on topics ranging from philosophy and Freudian and Lacanian psychoanalysis to theology, film, opera, and politics, including *Lacan in Hollywood* (2000) and *The Fragile Absolute: Or Why Is the Christian Legacy Worth Fighting For?* (2000). His latest publications include *Violence: Big Ideas/Small Books* (2008), *First As Tragedy, Then As Farce* (2009), and *The Monstrosity of Christ: Paradox or Dialectic?* (2009, with John Milbank).

. . . . The . Exhibition . . . .

ZKM | Center for Art and Media Karlsruhe, Germany, November 23, 2008 – April 19, 2009

Director and CEO
Peter Weibel

Curators
Boris Groys, Peter Weibel

Project management
and scientific assistance
Anne Däuper, Antonia Marten

Assistance
Sebastian Bollmann

Curatorial assistance
to Boris Groys
Nicole Sudhoff

Film research
Dagmar Riedl-Somma

Head of museum and
exhibition technical services
Martin Häberle

Technical project management
Matthias Ossmann

Technical management
Ronny Haas (architecture),
Rainer Gabler (art handling),
Werner Hutzenlaub (media
technology), Dirk Heesakker
(IT technology)

Technical staff
Mirco Frass, Christian
Nainggolan, Gisbert Laaber,
Akiro Hellgardt, Bertold
Dieterich, Helge Grey, Claudius
Böhm, Heiko Hoos, Hubert
Krauth, Jean-Michel Dejasmin,
Jörg Baier, Julia Beister,
Klaus Hebenstreit, Lutz Fezer,
Manfred Schmieder, Manfred
Stürmlinger, Marco Preitschopf,
Martin Boukhalfa, Michael
Feldbausch, Niels Burchert,
Peter Gather, Raphael Dobler,
Silke Fehsenfeld, Susanne
Pawelzyk, Tanja Goetzmann,
Volker Becker, Heike Aumüller,
Esther Stephan, Max Kosoric,
Martin Brandt, Joachim Hirling

Office of museum technical
services
Anna Reiss, Alexandra Kempf

Registrar
Marianne Meister,
Cathrin Langanke

Conservators
Hanna Barbara Hölling,
Antoaneta Ferres

Video documentation
Christina Zartmann, Moritz
Büchner, Judith Wunschik

Sound recording
Johannes Seibt

Exhibition graphics
Boris Dworschak

Public relations
Friederike C. Walter,
Evelyne Astner

Marketing
Barbara Schierl

Museum communication
Janine Burger, Banu Beyer,
Carolin Knebel, Henrike Plegge,
Marianne Spencer

Library
Petra Zimmermann, Christiane
Minter, Regina Strasser,
Ulrike Barwanietz

Media library
Claudia Gehrig, Hartmut Jörg,
Andreas Brehmer

Event management
Viola Gaiser, Monika Weimer,
Hartmut Bruckner, Hans Gass,
Mona Taller, Manuel Weber,
Dominik Willisch

Building services engineering
Peter Futterer, Peter Kuhn,
Klaus Wirth, Martin Braun,
Klaus Gerstner, Jörg Hartmann,
Hartmut Kampe, Peter Kiefer,
Thomas Schaeidt, Karl Stumm,
Karl Valentin

IT support
Joachim Schütze,
Volker Sommerfeld

Website
Silke Altvater, Heike Borowski,
Manfred Hauffen

The Model, Sligo, Ireland, May 24 – August 16, 2009

Director/Curator
Séamus Kealy

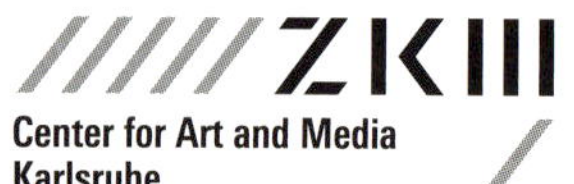

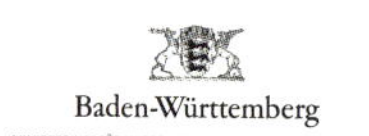

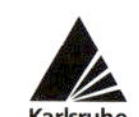

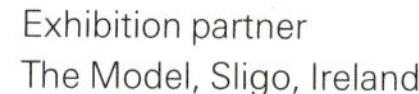

Editors
 Boris Groys, Peter Weibel

ZKM | Publications
 Jens Lutz, Miriam Stürner,
 Katharina Holas

Assistance
 Natalie Kraus, Nicole Sudhoff

Copy editing
 Justin Morris

Translations
 Jeremy Gaines, Justin Morris,
 Stan Jones & Anja Welle, Lisa
 Rosenblatt, Steven Lindberg

Authors of artists' texts
 Evelyne Astner, Heike
 Borowski, Sebastian Bollmann,
 Anne Däuper, Bianca Girbinger,
 Antonia Marten, Isabel Meixner,
 Nicole Sudhoff

Design
 Holger Jost in cooperation with
 Neues Sortiment, Karlsruhe,
 Germany

Lithography
 COMYK Roland Merz,
 Karlsruhe, Germany

Printed and bound by
 Kraft Druck GmbH, Ettlingen,
 Germany

Paper
 LuxoSamtoffset, 150 g/m²

This book was set in
 Univers (Linotype),
 Times (Linotype),
 and OCR B

Published by
 Verlag der Buchhandlung
 Walther König, Köln
 Ehrenstr. 4
 50672 Cologne, Germany
 Tel. +49 (0) 221 205 96 53
 Fax +49 (0) 221 205 96 60
 verlag@buchhandlung-
 walther-koenig.de

Distribution

Switzerland
 Buch 2000 c/o AVA
 Verlagsauslieferungen AG
 Centralweg 16
 CH-8910 Affoltern a. A.
 Tel. +41 (0) 44 762 42 00
 Fax +41 (0) 44 762 42 10
 a.koll@ava.ch

UK & Eire
 Cornerhouse Publications
 70 Oxford Street
 GB-Manchester M1 5NH
 Tel. +44 (0) 161 200 15 03
 Fax +44 (0) 161 200 15 04
 publications@cornerhouse.org

Outside Europe
 D.A.P.
 Distributed Art Publishers, Inc.
 155 6th Avenue, 2nd Floor
 New York, NY 10013
 Tel. +1 212 627 1999
 Fax +1 212 627 9484
 www.artbook.com

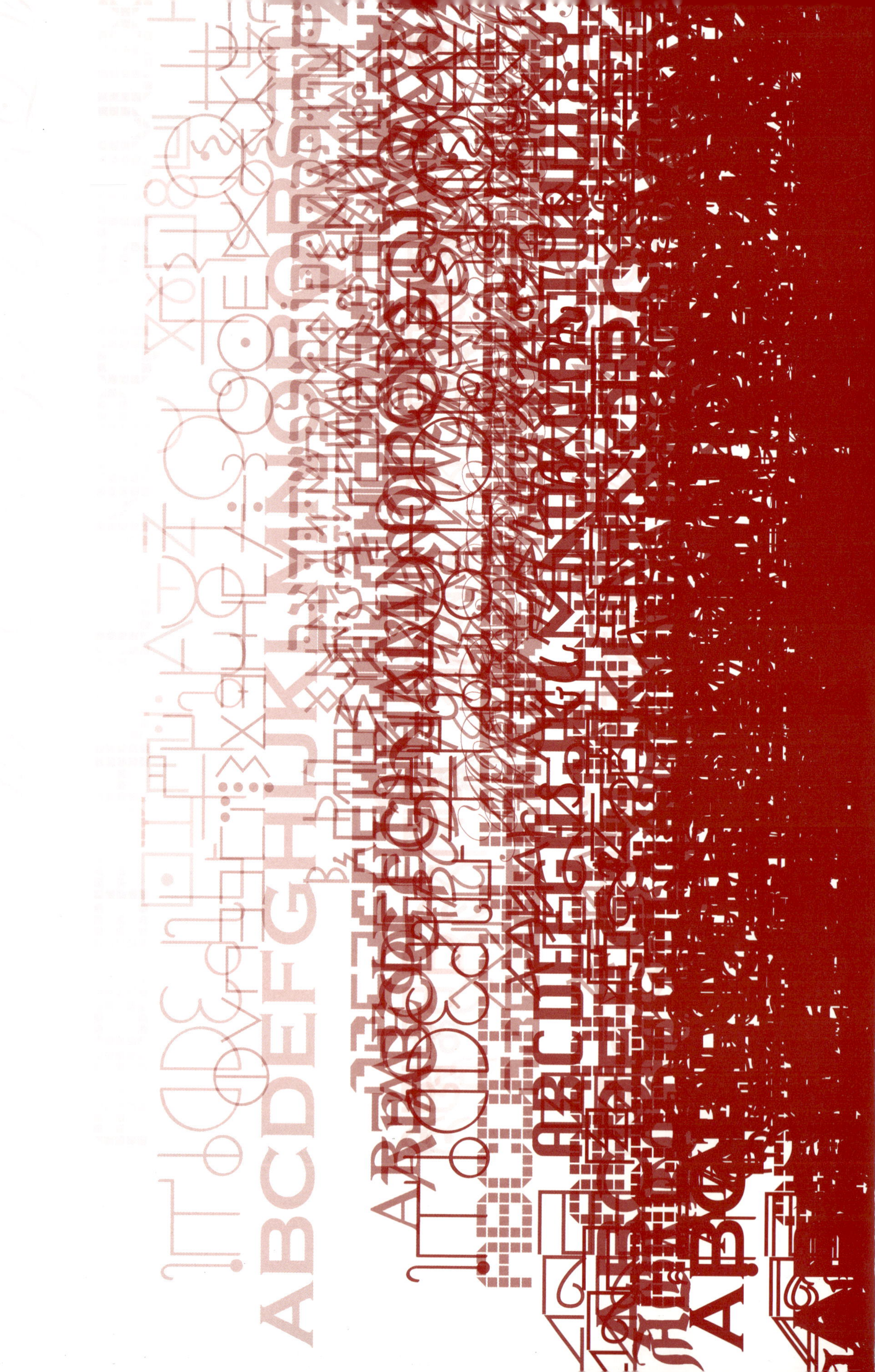